The Night the War Was Lost

Charles L. Dufour

University of Nebraska Press
Lincoln and London

First Bison Book printing: 1994
Most recent printing indicated by the last digit below:
10   9   8   7   6   5   4   3   2   1

Library of Congress Cataloging-in-Publication Data
Dufour, Charles L.
The night the war was lost / by Charles L. Dufour.
p.   cm.
Includes bibliographical references and index.
ISBN 0-8032-6599-9
1. New Orleans (La.)—History—Capture, 1862.   I. Title.
E472.88.D84   1995
973.7′31—dc20
93-47281
CIP

Reprinted by arrangement with the Civil War Round Table
of New Orleans, Inc.

∞

☆ ☆ ☆ ☆ ☆

The Night the War Was Lost

☆ ☆ ☆ ☆ ☆

Preface to Revised Edition

Thirty years after the publication of *The Night the War Was Lost,* the author is still haunted by the concluding sentence of the preface:

> These acknowledgements in no way shift the responsibility from the author for whatever errors remain in the book. These, he prays, have been reduced to a minimum.

This new, limited edition of *The Night the War Was Lost* provides the author with the opportunity to beat his breast publicly for the mistreatment of three names.

The author knew full well that the Confederate diarist, Mary Boykin Chesnut had no "t" in the middle of her name. But he put one in on his own and none of the proof-readers, including himself, "cracked the chestnut." This error appears on pages 362, 381, and 413.

Then there was Edwin Stanton, Lincoln's Secretary of War. The author would like to believe that a typographical error called him Edward instead of Edwin, but the truth, as revealed by the original manuscript, demands another "mea culpa" by the author. This error appears on pages 135, 158, and 425.

The third error involved the middle initial of my scholarly friend Bill Rooney who is cited in both the bibliograhy and notes a William H. Rooney, when in fact he is William E. Rooney. This error appears on pages 366 and 370.

The author is happy to make these revisions and, finally after three decades, get the albatross of error off his chest.

But the author stands by his judgments that were set forth in the book in 1960:

He still believes that the fall of New Orleans to Farragut in April, 1862 precluded British and/or French recognition of the Confederacy. And European recognition was an absolute necessity for the South to have won its independence.

He still believes responsibility for the fall of New Orleans lies with Jefferson Davis and Secretary of Navy Stephen R. Mallory for their incredible unawareness of the threat to the South's greatest city.

He still believes that President Davis treated General Mansfield Lovell after the fall of New Orleans with vindictive injustice.

If there is anything an author enjoys, it is to have another author agree with him. This is particularly true in the controversial arena of history. So it is with great appreciation that the author thanks Daniel E. Sutherland for the support of his theories concerning the fall of New Orleans in "Mansfield Lovell's Quest for Justice: Another Look at the Fall of New Orleans." *Louisiana History,* Vol. XXIV, No. 3 (1983), 233-259. He wrote:

> Not until 1960 and publication of Charles Dufour's *The Night the War Was Lost* did anyone write what Lovell would have considered an accurate account of the fall of New Orleans. Dufour clears Lovell entirely and concludes that Jefferson Davis was "unjust" in his treatment of the general. Davis's attempts to cover

up evidence, distort facts and obstruct an official investigation, says Dufour, resulted from "the consciousness that the responsibility for the fall of New Orleans rested squarely at the door of the President of the Confederacy and his Cabinet"....Dufour is right. If anything, his conclusions are not strong enough.... [Davis] and his administration actively and deliberately tried to burden Lovell permanently with responsibility for the Confederate loss of New Orleans. p. 234.

The Night the War was Lost had two printings at the time of the Civil War Centennial, but it has been out of print for many years. The author thanks the Civil War Round Table of New Orleans and the Memorial Hall Foundation for undertaking this republication and is especially pleased that the net proceeds from this volume will go to the Confederate Museum of the Louisiana Historical Association.

Charles L. Dufour
July 4, 1990

☆ ☆ ☆ ☆ ☆

Contents

	PREFACE	9
1	*Louisiana Leaves the Union*	15
2	*New Orleans Girds for War*	25
3	*The Guns of Sumter*	33
4	*Apathy Mans the Ramparts*	45
5	*The Blockade Begins to Pinch*	59
6	*Alias the "Turtle"*	71
7	*Enter General Lovell*	87
8	*The Tifts Build a Warship*	99
9	*New Orleans Awaits Invasion*	111
10	*The Ambitious Lieutenant Porter*	125
11	*A Plan—But Whose?*	135
12	*Outfitting the Fleet*	149
13	*New Orleans Becomes Jittery*	163
14	*Farragut Enters the River*	187
15	*If There Had Been Radio*	207

Contents

16   The "Bummers" Open Up   219

17   The Hour of Decision   241

18   Farragut Runs the Gantlet   265

19   Panic in the Streets   287

20   "By the Power of Brutal Force"   299

21   The End of Confederate New Orleans   317

22   Aftermath   331

     SOURCES AND BIBLIOGRAPHY   355

     NOTES   369

     INDEX   411

Preface

THERE IS A GROWING OPINION AMONG CIVIL WAR STUDENTS THAT THE war was won in the West. The Virginia campaigns had the glamour, but the decisions that mattered were won on the lines of the western waters—the Tennessee, Cumberland, and Mississippi rivers.

Long before the Confederacy was crushed militarily, it was defeated economically. By the time battle fatigue and attrition and overwhelming opposition finally brought the defeat of southern armies, the Confederate home front had already collapsed.

The economic defeat of the South was achieved by the Union Navy, which blockaded or captured many of the important Confederate ports during the first year of the conflict. Moreover, by its operations on the inland waters of the South, the Union Navy not only shared in but in many instances made possible Federal successes on land.

Accordingly, today many Civil War scholars contend that Mr. Lincoln's admirals, not his generals, broke the backbone of the Confederacy. The present author holds with the views that the Civil War was won in the West and that it was won by the Federal Navy, not the Federal Army.

This book is an attempt to pinpoint both the place and the time in the West where the Union Navy won the crucial decision which, three years in advance, pointed the way to Appomattox. It was on the Mississippi River, below New Orleans, in the pre-dawn hours of April 24, 1862, when Flag Officer David G. Farragut with fourteen vessels ran past Forts Jackson and St. Philip to put the South's great city at his mercy.

Until recent years, the naval operations of the Civil War were more or less neglected. Chief to remedy this neglect were two historians of the United States Naval Academy, Charles Lee Lewis and Richard S. West, Jr. Professor Lewis' two-volume biography of David Glasgow Farragut is a classic, and Professor West's biographies of Gideon Welles and David Dixon Porter, together with his many articles in the *United States Naval Institute Proceedings*, have thrown the important light of modern scholarship on the inner workings of the United States Navy during the Civil War.

The author wishes to acknowledge his debt to the works of Messrs. Lewis and West, which served as beacons as he attempted to chart a true course through thousands of pages of documents, both published and unpublished, concerning the fall of New Orleans.

The author would be remiss, too, were he not to acknowledge his debt to the Library of Congress and to the National Archives, whose vast resources for research are matched only by the co-operation which they extend to researchers.

Equally co-operative in the matter of making photostatic copies of manuscripts were the Huntington Library at San Marino, California, the New York Public Library.

The author is under heavy obligation to many persons, libraries, and historical groups for assistance in his research, but especially to the following:

Roger Baudier of New Orleans; Vergil Bedsole, director of the Department of Archives and Manuscripts at Louisiana State University, and his staff, Marcelle Schertz, Virginia M. Ott, and Elsa B. Meier; Bertha L. Bard, reference librarian, Cooper Union Library, New York; Howson W. Cole, curator of manuscripts, Virginia Historical Society, Richmond; Amelie Cornay of New Orleans; Richard Colquette of Houston; Thomas E. Crowder of the Emory University library; Richard Foster of New Orleans; Mrs. Connie Griffith, Tulane University Archives; Robert Greenwood, Howard-Tilton Library, Tulane University; Thomas R. Hay of Locust Valley, New York; James J. Heslin, assistant director and librarian, New York Historical Society; Robert H. Land, Library of Congress; E. B. "Pete" Long of Chicago; Edwin Leland of New Orleans; Betty Maihles, reference department, Howard-Tilton Library, Tulane University; Professor Grady McWhinney, University of California; Miss Bessie Pool of New Orleans; Mrs. Mildred Parham of New Orleans; John R. Peacock of High Point, North Carolina; Mattie Russell, curator of manuscripts, Duke University Library; Ray Samuel of New Orleans; Frank B. Sarles, Jr., of Richmond; Dr. Garland Taylor, former director of libraries at Tulane University; Mrs. Carolyn A. Wallace, Southern Historical Collection, University of North Carolina; Lee Wallace of Arlington, Virginia; Ezra Warner of La Jolla, California; Mrs. Dorothy Whittemore, reference department, Howard-Tilton Library, Tulane University.

John Hall Jacobs, librarian of the New Orleans Public Library, and his staff gave generously of their time, especially the Louisiana Department under Margaret Ruckert. No one can write about New Orleans in any way without placing himself under obligations to Miss Ruckert. To her, too, goes gratitude for a meticulously prepared index.

Kenneth T. Urquhart, director of Memorial Hall of the Louisiana Historical Association, New Orleans, rendered invaluable assistance in making important source material readily available.

To Leonard V. Huber of New Orleans go double thanks—for generously making available from his magnificent print collection material for illustrations, and reading the proofs with a vigilant eye.

Also meriting thanks on two counts are my *States-Item* colleagues, Crozet Duplantier, Dan Galouye, and Russ Kintzley, who read both the manuscript and the proofs, making valuable corrections and suggestions in both readings.

Grateful acknowledgment is also made to another colleague,

Hermann B. Deutsch, and to Rene LeGardeur, Donald Schultz, and William B. Wisdom, all of New Orleans, for their painstaking reading of the proofs and their readily accepted marginal comments.

To Polly LeBeuf go special thanks for "living" with the manuscript as long as the author. She typed it in every stage of its development and not only read the proofs advantageously but read them twice.

These acknowledgments in no way shift the responsibility from the author for whatever errors remain in the book. These, he prays, have been reduced to a minimum.

Charles L. Dufour

The Night the War Was Lost

1

Louisiana Leaves the Union

WHEN THE PEOPLE OF LOUISIANA WENT TO THE POLLS ON NOVEMBER 6, 1860, they were unanimous on one thing: they did not want Abraham Lincoln as President.

Louisiana, despite its strong commercial ties with the Union, went for the secession candidate, John C. Breckinridge, whose plurality over runner-up John Bell was 2477 votes. The popular balloting went: Breckinridge, 22,681; Bell, 20,204; Stephen A. Douglas, 7625. Mr. Lincoln was completely shut out.[1]

The national election of Lincoln evoked a great variety of strong opinions, from ultraconservative to ultrarabid. One was expressed by the New Orleans *Crescent*: "The day of compromise is gone . . . As well attempt to bring to life an Egyptian mummy, thousands of years dead, as to restore the Union upon its former foundations. The soul of the Union is dead, and now let's bury the body."

The uninhibited John Maginnis, editor of the *True Delta* and the most vociferous anti-secessionist in New Orleans, spoke for a large segment of the Irish, and his bold comments after Lincoln's election demonstrate that there was a strong Union sentiment in New Orleans: "Lincoln cannot, however disposed himself, . . . do aught against the rights of any section of the Union . . . Why then, under such circumstances, should Louisiana countenance designs against the Union . . . ?"[2]

Despite Louisiana's self-interest, despite the many anti-secessionists and anti-secession newspapers in the state at the time of Lincoln's election, public opinion began to shift. The highly conservative New Orleans *Bee*, which during the secession crisis reminded its readers that it had been "uniformly attached to the Union," advanced gradually into the ranks of the secessionists:

November 8: "What we should do may in our opinion, be summed up in a single word: Wait. It will be time to fight Lincoln with gunpowder and the sword when we find either that constitutional resistance fails, or that he and his party are bent on our humiliation and destruction. We are for the Union so long as it is possible to preserve it. We are willing to go with Louisiana, but every good citizen is bound to use his best efforts to make Louisiana herself go right."

December 14: "We are doomed if we proclaim not our political independence."

December 17: "At this period it is entirely safe to declare that there exists no Union party in Louisiana, and that New Orleans, formerly the most conservative portion of the State, is now the hotbed of Secession."

January 28: "We rejoice that Louisiana has acted as best becomes her renown for gallantry, courage and determination. She has done her duty, and now leaves the consequences to God."

The pressure began to tell even on individuals. John Purcell, a Unionist residing in New Orleans, wrote in his diary for January 29: "I am myself drifting into secession ideas."

British consul William A. Mure reported to Lord John Russell, Foreign Secretary, on December 13, 1860, that on his return to New Orleans from leave he "was not prepared to find the feeling in favour of Secession so strong or general as it is in this City and State."[3]

A large measure of the credit for solidifying New Orleans opinion for secession belonged to the pulpit eloquence of Dr. Benjamin M. Palmer, Presbyterian divine, whose Thanksgiving Day sermon breathed hell-fire and damnation to abolitionists. Dr. Palmer was the most popular minister in New Orleans, and when he preached he commanded the attention not only of his flock but of the newspapers as well. Regularly the journals reported his words or editorialized upon them.

The First Presbyterian Church, on Lafayette Square, was packed when Dr. Palmer entered the pulpit. He held his audience spellbound for two hours as he defended slavery and called upon the people of the South to "reclaim the powers they have delegated."

He asserted that the foes of the black race were those who "intermeddled on their behalf," that "every attribute of their character fits them for dependence and servitude . . . Freedom would be their doom." He proclaimed the South the defender of "the cause of God and religion" and characterized the abolition spirit as "undeniably atheistic."

Southerners had four cardinal points of duty during this crisis, thundered Dr. Palmer, "to ourselves, to our slaves, to the world, and to Almighty God." He emphasized the "solemnity of our present trust, to preserve and transmit our existing system of domestic servitude, with the right, unchallenged by men, to go and root itself wherever Providence and nature may carry it. This trust we will discharge in the face of the worst possible peril."

The militant clergyman pointed the path the South must take and called upon the people in their respective states to summon "men who bring the wisdom, experience and firmness of age to . . . take all the necessary steps looking to separate and independent existence; and initiate measures for framing a new and homogeneous confederacy."

He sent his audience out of the church imbued with the thought that "the position of the South is at this moment sublime. If she will arise in her majesty, and speak now as with the voice of one, she will roll back for all time the curse that is upon her. If she succumbs now, she transmits that curse as an heirloom to posterity. . . ."

An eyewitness, years later, recalled the profound impression of Dr. Palmer's sermon on his listeners:

It confirmed and strengthened those who were in doubt; it gave directness and energy to public sentiment—so that perhaps no other public utterance during that trying period of anxiety and hesitancy did so much to bring New Orleans city and the entire state of Louisiana squarely and fully to the side of secession and the Confederacy ... After the benediction, in solemn silence, no man speaking to his neighbor, the great congregation of serious and thoughtful men and women dispersed; but afterwards the drums beat and the bugles sounded; for New Orleans was shouting for secession.[4]

The tide of disunion in Louisiana rolled on stronger each day. Before the legislature met on December 10, in answer to Governor Thomas O. Moore's call for a special session, there was no doubt that it would authorize a convention to consider Louisiana's future relations to the Union. The legislature set the election of delegates to the convention for January 7, 1861, but, conveniently ignoring the state constitution, refused to submit the question of a convention to a popular referendum. Thus, as one historian put it, the Louisiana legislature took "the first illegal and revolutionary step towards secession."[5]

Two sets of convention candidates waged a vigorous campaign for three weeks.[6] One group was for immediate, separate, and unconditional secession. The other group represented many shades of opinion but was in general agreement that Louisiana should not act unilaterally, but only in concert with the other southern states. These self-styled Co-operationists included in their number some out-and-out Union men, but their position became an academic one shortly after the convention electioneering began, for on December 20, South Carolina led the parade of southern states out of the Union. And by election day in Louisiana, the machinery was in motion to remove from the Union Mississippi, Alabama, and Florida, all of whom joined South Carolina by January 11.

The popular vote for delegates was close: Secessionists 20,448; Co-operationists, 17,296. The result in New Orleans was also close, so close, in fact, that a swing of 191 votes would have given the city to the Co-operationists in the popular vote. The city totals were: Secessionists, 4358; Co-operationists, 3978. The convention was scheduled to meet in Baton Rouge on January 23, and the conservative *Picayune* reluctantly admitted: "Louisiana will be with the seceding states as fast as the forms of making the enactment by ordinance can be got through at the Convention on the 23rd."[7]

On January 8, the anniversary of the Battle of New Orleans was celebrated with the usual enthusiasm, but more exciting events than patriotic street demonstrations were brewing to put Louisiana, through its governor, in open rebellion against the United States before Union ties were declared severed by the convention.

It perhaps did not occur to Governor Moore that he was treading in the footsteps of the despised fanatical abolitionist John Brown when he ordered out the Louisiana militia to seize the Federal arsenal in Baton Rouge, Forts Jackson and St. Philip, which guarded the Mississippi River approaches to New Orleans, Fort Pike at the eastern entrance to Lake Pontchartrain, and the barracks below the city.

Governor Moore seized the property, he later explained, "to prevent a collision between Federal troops and the people of the State." He feared, he said, that the fortresses, "capable of being used for the subjugation of the country," might be employed "to annul the declared will of the people." He acted, he said, after receiving information "which did not leave me in doubt as to my public duty."

This information came on January 10 from Louisiana's senators, Judah P. Benjamin and John Slidell, who jointly telegraphed from Washington to Daniel W. Adams of the Military Board in New Orleans: "Secret attempts continue to be made to garrison Southern ports. We think there is special reason to fear surprise from Gulf squadron." The same day, Slidell telegraphed Governor Moore in Baton Rouge: "The danger is not from St. Louis, but from sea."[8]

So Governor Moore instructed Major Paul E. Théard to "hold the forts, and defend them against any and all attacks to the last." The "capture" of Fort St. Philip and Fort Jackson, seventy-five miles below New Orleans, assumed the nature of an *opéra bouffe*. Major

19

Théard, with a force of seventeen officers, four musicians, and one hundred fifty-one men, descended the river on the steamer *Yankee* on January 10, and at 8 P.M. called upon Henry Dart, keeper of Fort St. Philip, to surrender. Inasmuch as Mr. Dart's military resources consisted of himself and a dozen negro slaves, he wasn't inclined to put up a defense. A newspaper account of the seizure said that Mr. Dart, on being called on to surrender, replied to Major Théard that "he had no objection in the world." Leaving a detachment at Fort St. Philip, Major Théard crossed the river to Fort Jackson, where Sergeant H. Smith turned over the keys under protest and then did his best "to make the men feel as comfortable as possible."[9]

The seizure of Fort Pike, which guarded one of the two entrances to Lake Pontchartrain, the back door to New Orleans, was also a jolly outing. But not so the seizure of the arsenal at Baton Rouge, commanded by a one-armed veteran of the Mexican War, Brevet Major Joseph A. Haskins, whose force consisted of about sixty artillerymen and twenty men of the Ordnance Corps under Lieutenant J. W. Todd. Haskins, a brave and determined man, prepared to defend against attack as soon as he learned that Colonel Braxton Bragg of Governor Moore's staff had assembled seven companies of militia on North Boulevard, barely a quarter of a mile from the arsenal.

Governor Moore sent Colonel Braxton Bragg and Colonel J. W. Taylor to Haskins with a written demand to surrender. "The safety of the State of Louisiana demands that I take possession of all government property within her limits," wrote Governor Moore. "You are, therefore, summoned hereby, to deliver up the barracks, arsenal, and public property now under your command. With the large force at my disposal this demand will be enforced. Any attempt at defense on your part will be a rash sacrifice of life."

Major Haskins' natural fighting instincts were aroused by the governor's note, particularly as he had artillery, which the militia did not. He replied that he would be damned if he would surrender. "I've lost one arm in the defense of my flag and I will lose the other, or even my life if necessary, before I surrender to that lot of ragamuffins on the Boulevard," he exclaimed.

The militia, aroused by Major Haskins' contemptuous comment, wanted to move at once. However, discretion tempered their impetuous valor when it was learned that two cannons, with cannoneers standing by ready for action, were mounted at each of the two entrances to the government post.

Governor Moore attempted to negotiate with Major Haskins, but the old warrior stubbornly refused to surrender an artillery post to a force of infantry. It would take artillery and a larger force to compel him to yield the arsenal. So Governor Moore sent to New Orleans for the Washington Artillery to create a force to which Major Haskins could honorably surrender.

When the Baton Rouge militia heard of the governor's plan they felt this was a reflection upon their courage, and their resentment against Governor Moore soon created problems of discipline. In vain were orders issued; useless were arguments and persuasions. One company, the Creole Guards, marched to the State House, stacked their arms, and disbanded, their officers tossing away their commissions.

Another company, the Baton Rouge Pelicans, to fife and drum marched from the camp to their armory on a route that led close to the arsenal, thereby almost precipitating the first land fighting of the Civil War. As the Pelicans approached closer and closer the determined cannoneers at the entrance of the arsenal prepared to resist an attack. Their cannons were loaded almost to the muzzle with grapeshot, and they waited with lighted matches ready to be applied to the touchholes of the cannon. However, the Pelicans wheeled at the next street and continued to their armory. Had they marched any farther in the direction of the arsenal, the intrepid Haskins, having no way of knowing their intentions, would surely have greeted them with a volley of grape.

The companies which had remained in camp were dismissed with orders to report back the following morning, because the New Orleans reinforcements had been delayed by fog on the river. Upon the arrival of the Washington Artillery and the other New Orleans troops, Major Haskins capitulated, signing an agreement with Governor Moore on January 11.

Major Haskins marched his forces out of the arsenal to the tune of "The Girl I Left Behind Me" and deliberately paraded through most of the town on his way to the steamboat landing. Their ruffled feathers smoothed, the Baton Rouge militia took possession of the arsenal, while the New Orleans troops steamed down the river for home. The casualties reported by the Washington Artillery were slight: "Sergeant Buck Miller fell down a cellar when performing a 'backward dress,' and two privates, who were overcome by the excitement, were brought in under arrest."[10]

Thus was settled bloodlessly the first martial incident, and Louisiana was definitely committed to secession.

On the same day that the Baton Rouge arsenal surrendered, a detachment of infantry under Captain Charles M. Bradford took possession of the Marine Hospital and informed Collector of Customs Frank M. Hatch, titular superintendent of the hospital, that 216 invalids and convalescent patients had to be moved out to make way for the state troops being mustered into service.

The seizure of the hospital unleashed a bitter attack on Governor Moore from the Secretary of the Treasury, John Dix, who called it "revolting to the civilization of the age." The northern press picked up the theme. The New York *Herald* was shocked at "the discreditable conduct on the part of the State authorities," while the New York *Times* considered it the "most unfeeling outrage which has yet been perpetrated by the Disunionists," and many other eastern papers characterized the seizure as "outrageous." Months later, Secretary of War Simon Cameron wrote President Lincoln: "The violent seizure of the U.S. Marine Hospital at New Orleans was only wanting to complete the catalogue of crime."

Actually, the incident of the Marine Hospital was accompanied by none of the "inhumanity" attributed to Louisiana authorities by Washington and the northern press. The sick were not immediately displaced, and eventually were transferred to the Charity Hospital in the city.[11]

On January 23 the convention assembled in Baton Rouge and it wasted no time. After electing a former governor, Alexandre Mouton, as president, it drafted at once an ordinance of secession. It was printed and made the special order of the day of January 25.

The Co-operationists tried to divert the majority from their determined course by proposing substitute ordinances, but to no avail.

On January 26, when the ordinance of secession was called up, the Co-operationist delegates asked for a recess. They knew the game was up; they knew that when the vote was called only a handful of them would stand against taking Louisiana out of the Union. They decided to ask the convention to let them explain their position. Twenty minutes later, with all the delegates back in their seats, the calling of the roll began. Not many minutes later, Louisiana had voted itself out of the Union, the vote in favor of secession being 112 to 17.[12]

After the secretary of the convention had tabulated the vote, the rules were suspended to permit President Mouton to leave the chair and cast his vote, which he did in favor of the ordinance, making the official vote 113 to 17. Returning to the chair, President Mouton proclaimed: "In the virtue of the vote just announced, I now decree the connection between the State of Louisiana and the Federal Union dissolved; and that she is a free, sovereign and independent Power."

Governor Moore entered the chamber at this moment, preceded by the state flag. There was a prayer by the Reverend Linfield, the flag was blessed by Father Hubert, and with the signing of the ordinance of secession, Louisiana, all ties with other states of the Union broken, took its place among the family of nations. The significance of this called for another piece of immediate legislation concerning the free navigation of the Mississippi River "by all friendly States bordering thereon . . . and the right of egress and ingress of the mouths of the Mississippi by all friendly States and Powers . . ."

When the telegraph brought the news of the passage of the ordinance of secession to New Orleans, a "perfect furore of enthusiasm" gripped the city. Suddenly, all at once, the bells of the fire-alarm telegraph rang furiously all over the town and guns began booming at the foot of Canal Street. People rushed into the streets to congratulate one another on Louisiana's independence, and from windows of private homes and business offices the Pelican flag of Louisiana appeared.[13]

With the lights and the flags and the rockets and the booming guns, and the noise and animation in the streets, New Orleans let off the steam that had built up to the bursting point since Lincoln's election. "Everyone seemed to breathe more freely," observed the *Crescent*. "Everyone's heart beat with a more rapid and pleasurable pulsation, and the determination was everywhere evinced to defend the sovereignty of Louisiana, come what might . . ." The *Picayune* expressed the same relief: "The deed has been done. 'We breathe deeper and freer' for it. The Union is dead; and with it all the hopes and all the fears which divided and agitated our people."[14]

2

New Orleans Girds for War

THE WINTER SEASON IN NEW ORLEANS WAS ALWAYS A GAY AND EXCIT-
ing one, and there was hope that the winter of 1860–61 would be
one of the gayest of them all. The crops had been excellent, and
with cotton and sugar commanding good prices, money was abundant and the city was packed with free-spending visitors.

Each year, after the yellow-fever season, when the first cool
weather signaled the retreat of Bronze John to his pest-laden
swamps, wealthy planters from all over the South arrived at New
Orleans.

Here, also, came rich visitors from the North to substitute the
temperate winter climate of New Orleans for the discomforts of
home and to attend the opera and the theater and to join in the
merriment of Mardi Gras in the pleasure-loving metropolis of the
South. The salons and drawing rooms of the St. Charles and St.
Louis hotels, ablaze with light and filled with music and revelry,
were the scenes of brilliant balls and gala soirées, crowded with
bejeweled and exquisitely gowned beauties of the South.

New Orleans, by the very nature of its French founding and
Spanish rule, was not a typically southern city. Its cosmopolitanism,
however, had never before been so pronounced as it was in the

census year of 1860. Its total population of 168,675 contained 64,621 foreign-born, from more than thirty different countries, and nearly four out of ten foreigners were Irish.[1]

Ships from the Seven Seas tied up at the wharves, and the Levee was strewn with incredible piles of varied merchandise, vying for space with innumerable hogsheads of sugar and bales of cotton, and kegs, boxes, and crates of apples, bacon, beans, beef, and butter; corn, cottonseed, cheese, flour, glassware, and hemp; lead and leather; molasses, oats, onions, and oil; pickles, pig iron, potatoes, and pork; rice, rope, and rosin; soap and shingles; tobacco and twine; and wool, wheat, and whisky.[2] The chief export of New Orleans was cotton, which in the Crescent City was truly king. In 1860, almost sixty per cent of the port receipts of $185,211,254 were in cotton worth $109,389,228.[3]

New Orleans' commercial prosperity on the eve of secession was reflected not only in its river and ocean trade but in its strong banking facilities. In March 1860, the report of the United States Secretary of the Treasury showed that New Orleans had thirteen banks with a total capital of $24,496,866, with deposits of $19,777,812 and specie in the vaults amounting to $12,115,431.[4] Commerce was booming when Abraham Lincoln was elected President of the United States on November 6, 1860.

Almost immediately, a reaction set in in New Orleans. Money suddenly became hard to come by. One businessman wrote an up-state planter: "Times are tight in this place and I hear no one expressing hopes of any change for the better. You cannot give your cotton away for freight . . ."[5] The unsettled political conditions led to unsettled business conditions. Military preparations to seize the forts and other Federal properties had thrown New Orleans into a state of excitement. Volunteers organized and drilled on the Levee, in public parks, squares, streets, and even "in the marts of commerce the drum-beats and the blare of trumpets drowned the busy hum of trade." Uniforms became commonplace on every corner.[6]

Unlike the gay, carefree winters of the past, such was the state of affairs in the city when the convention, having accepted the Common Council's invitation to continue its sessions in New Orleans, reassembled on January 29 in the Lyceum Hall of City Hall. The atmosphere around the City Hall was charged with excitement. The galleries and other available space were crowded. Men moved hurriedly about and all was commotion and animation until Dr. Benjamin Palmer, ever ready to pray in the cause of secession, walked the few feet from his church to the City Hall and gave the deliberations his blessing.[7]

The first order of business was the election of delegates to represent Louisiana at the convention of southern states called to meet in Montgomery on February 4. Judah P. Benjamin and John Slidell, who had represented the state in Washington, distantly trailed John Perkins of Madison Parish and Alexandre De Clouet of St. Martin Parish, who were elected from the state at large.

Then came the voting for the delegates of the four districts. The first district balloting resulted in a victory for Charles M. Conrad over the historian Charles Gayarré, 84 to 36. In the second district, Duncan F. Kenner was an easy winner over three other nominees, one of whom was Zachary Taylor's son, Richard Taylor, soon to win renown as a Confederate general officer. Unopposed, Edward Sparrow was named to represent the third district, whereas Henry Marshall of De Soto Parish edged B. L. Hodge of Caddo Parish, 62 to 54.

Attempts were made to issue instructions to the delegates to Montgomery, but they were beaten down after several hours of debate. Then these "most eminent citizens of Louisiana, men of high character, and deeply interested in the prosperity of the State" hurried off to Alabama, to help create the Confederate States of America.[8]

The convention returned to its business. It authorized the seizure of the United States Mint, with $389,000, and the Custom House, with $122,000. And so, by the end of January 1861, all United States property in Louisiana had been seized. Forts Macomb and Livingston had meanwhile been occupied.

On February 2, Richard Taylor of St. Charles Parish presented an ordinance establishing a regular military force for Louisiana. Taylor, as chairman of the Military and Naval Affairs Committee, reported to the convention that Louisiana was "utterly defenseless" and that Fort Jackson was in great need of "important repairs . . . immediately." His ordinance provided for one regiment of artillery, with eight companies of officers, noncommissioned officers, and 86 privates, and one regiment of infantry, with eight companies of officers, noncommissioned officers, and 90 privates. This entire force of between 1700 and 1800 men would be commanded by a major general. All the officers would be appointed by Governor Moore. There was little debate on Mr. Taylor's military ordinance and it soon passed.[9]

Louisiana, with six delegates at Montgomery, had a diplomatic corps. Adoption of Taylor's ordinance gave Louisiana a standing army. Louisiana now needed a flag. So the convention turned next to creating a banner for the independent commonwealth of Louisiana. A committee was picked; it deliberated a week and reported back with a new flag for Louisiana.

On February 12, shortly before 11 A.M., the convention moved in a body to Lafayette Square, across St. Charles Street from the City Hall. To a twenty-one-gun salute by the Washington Artillery, Louisiana's new flag was run up the flagpole atop City Hall. A great cheer rose from the large crowd as the new flag of thirteen blue, white, and red stripes with a yellow star in a red field whipped in the breeze for the first time. This ceremony over, the convention delegates trooped back into the City Hall and promptly voted an adjournment until March 4, to await developments in Montgomery.[10]

Meanwhile, Governor Moore had picked his military high command for the newly created Louisiana Army. He named his military aide, Colonel Braxton Bragg, major general. Bragg, late of the Third Artillery, had come out of the Mexican War with honors but in 1854 had resigned from the Army in a huff with Secretary of War Jefferson Davis and had settled as a planter on Bayou Lafourche, about fifty miles west of New Orleans. Governor Moore appointed Major George Deas, late of the Fifth Infantry, as adjutant general, and Lieutenant Colonel A. C. Myers, late of the Fourth Infantry, as quartermaster general. He picked the popular Louisiana Creole, Major P. G. T. Beauregard, as colonel of engineers in command of the artillery regiment. The appointments were cheered and the comment of the *Picayune* was typical: "These are the elite of the army of the late United States. No four men in the whole rank and file of that gallant service have higher standing for skill, courage and conduct in their noble profession."

However, the assignment was not popular with Major Beauregard. Just back from West Point, Beauregard had served a scant week as Superintendent of the Military Academy, departing when his native state seceded from the Union. Although Braxton Bragg outranked Beauregard in the old Army, the latter felt, with some justification, that, because he was a Louisianian and had been engineering officer in charge of the defenses of Louisiana from 1850 to 1860, the top military command in the state belonged rightfully to him.

Accordingly, Beauregard was disinclined to play second fiddle to Bragg, and politely refused Governor Moore's appointment.[11] The governor then named former Governor P. O. Hébert, a West Point graduate, to the post. Beauregard, in a gesture of conspicuous humility, enlisted as a private in the Orleans Guards, composed of Creole blue bloods.[12] But he began to pull strings in Montgomery for a brigadier general's commission in the Confederate Army, an assignment which was soon forthcoming.

Before Beauregard left New Orleans he made recommendations to the Military Board urging it to "look to our most vulnerable point, the Mississippi River." He stated that, in the present condition of Forts Jackson and St. Philip, "any steamer could pass them in broad daylight," and on a dark night, the forts, even in a proper state of defense, could not prevent the passage of steamers without the assistance of "a properly constructed raft, or strong wire-rope across the river" to delay vessels for half an hour under the cross fire of the forts. He emphasized that construction of a floating boom at the forts was the first thing to be done, and he suggested that John Roy, his former assistant architect at the Custom House, would be of great assistance in its construction. The river, Beauregard told the authorities, was the most important of the several avenues of approach to New Orleans.

He further urged that Forts Jackson and St. Philip be armed with the heaviest guns obtainable, and recommended that the largest pieces on the land fronts of the forts be moved to the river fronts and that the heavy guns of other Louisiana fortifications be temporarily installed in the two river forts.

Roy called on Colonel Hébert, who at first showed interest in the pontoon boom and told Roy to inquire about for available lumber. But when Roy reported back the next day, Colonel Hébert "did not seem to pay any attention to what I reported any more than he had forgotten [remembered] what he sent me after." The importance of the boom seemed to have soon passed out of everyone's mind, for that very day Colonel Hébert instructed John Roy to prepare to make gun carriages at the Custom House.[18]

New Orleans was filled with an air of expectancy during these days before Louisiana formally joined the Confederate States of America. People were uncertain as to what the future held, but there were few who thought that secession necessarily meant war. Most of them, with logically marshaled arguments, proved the impossibility of war.

The exciting times were not without some fears, and a self-appointed group of "Minute Men" came into existence to track down spies in New Orleans. These inquisitors, men of breeding and social position, claimed that "the public emergency was so great as to justify them in examining all strangers who excited suspicion." Soon the newspapers took up the campaign, and frequent became the arrests of persons who were charged with being abolitionists or suspected of being spies, or of having been heard to utter "incendiary language."[14]

When the Louisiana convention reconvened in New Orleans on March 4, the chief business at hand was the consideration of the Confederate Constitution adopted at the Montgomery convention and sent to the various states for ratification. On March 15, a resolution providing for the submission of the permanent constitution of the Confederate States to the people of Louisiana was introduced, with considerable popular support for the idea.

But when the ordinance came to a vote on March 16, it was overwhelmingly rejected, 88 to 12. For one reason or another, twenty-nine members of the convention did not bother to attend the session. Sharp criticism by both the *Picayune* and the *True Delta* of the convention's action is solid evidence that there was considerable feeling in New Orleans that the rights of the people had been trampled upon. The *Picayune* said:

"The Convention decided . . . by an overwhelming majority, that they will not submit the constitution to the people. It was a fearful responsibility they have assumed, and one which carried with it the obligation to see that the State receives no harm from the compact they are about to adopt, for they have disarmed her of the right to see to it for herself."[15]

Another futile attempt to have the constitution referred to the people was made on March 21, when Joseph A. Rozier offered a substitute for an ordinance providing for immediate ratification. Rozier's measure asked for the calling of a state convention to take the sense of the people on the adoption or rejection of the constitution. He declared that "the whole secession movement and the action of this convention were characterized by a total disregard of the voice of the people." To the charges that he had not signed the ordinance of secession, Rozier admitted that he had not, but he was willing to stand by it "as it declared Louisiana a free and sovereign State." He said that those who signed the ordinance of secession had now deserted it; they were transferring their allegiance to South Carolina, Georgia, Alabama, and the others, all foreign states. Rozier said he wanted Louisiana to remain separate and alone until the future dictated the proper course the state should take. Lengthy debate followed, but by a 94–10 vote Rozier's ordinance was tabled. Moments later, the convention ratified the Confederate Constitution by a 107–7 vote.

On March 25, the convention transferred the forts, arsenals, Mint, Custom House, and lighthouses Louisiana had seized, to the Confederate government, and the next day the convention adjourned. Louisiana, which for sixty days had been an independent state, was now a full-fledged member of the Confederate States of America.[16]

3

The Guns of Sumter

THE GUNS THAT STARTED BOOMING IN CHARLESTON HARBOR AT 4:30 A.M. on April 12 had their echo in New Orleans that afternoon. For days the city had been in excitement over possible action at what the newspapers called the two "seats of war"—Charleston and Pensacola. For days people had speculated as to whether the Union forces in Fort Sumter and Fort Pickens would make some kind of demonstration. Would General Beauregard, who commanded at Charleston, or Braxton Bragg, now a Confederate brigadier general in command at Pensacola, fire the first shot? Everybody agreed that some sort of action was inevitable; still many, following the advice of the *Picayune*, felt "it is idle to indulge in speculation."

But New Orleans continued to speculate. It felt something was up when Major Gaston Coppens and his Louisiana Zouaves hurried off for Pensacola on April 5 to join Bragg's force on the mainland, across the bay from Fort Pickens, on the western tip of Santa Rosa Island. Each morning, subscribers to the papers eagerly turned to the telegraphic reports, expecting to read sensational news from Pensacola or Charleston. In the afternoons, crowds gathered around the bulletin boards in front of the newspaper offices with the same expectation. "But, thank God, those who like the smell of gunpowder have been disappointed," exclaimed the *Picayune*, "and we sincerely hope they will not have a better chance for a long time to come."[1]

On April 10, another New Orleans unit, the Orleans Cadets, under Captain Charles D. Dreux, left for Pensacola. Its departure, to the fond farewells of families and sweethearts, served to heighten the tension and excitement in New Orleans. The telegraphic news in the papers of April 11 reported that a Confederate attack on Fort Sumter was imminent, and people crowded around the bulletin boards in even greater numbers than before for the latest word from Beauregard. The exhausting suspense continued the next morning, when readers of the *Picayune* read dispatches from Charleston saying the attack on Sumter was expected hourly. At last, on the afternoon of April 12, the stirring news came: Beauregard had fired on Sumter!

Immediately the word spread and thousands descended upon the newspapers, jamming the offices as they clamored for papers. The *Picayune* reported its busiest day since the Mexican War. It was "literally besieged, and it was impossible for anyone who had any other business than to procure a paper to get within speaking distance." All over town people in all walks of life had only one topic of discussion.[2]

Upon receipt of the news of Fort Sumter, Governor Moore issued the call for all volunteer troops of Louisiana to assemble with arms and equipment at the earliest moment at their armories. In New Orleans, the citizen soldiers hastened to respond, and the sound of drum and fife and marching men soon filled the streets of the city at all hours of the day, and even at night. New companies, of course, were forming almost daily, picturesque units such as the Tiger Rifles, commanded by a man who called himself Alex White, who had been to the penitentiary for killing a man in a steamboat altercation; companies such as the Perrit Guards, the gamblers' company, admission to which required that "one must be able to cut, shuffle, and deal on the point of a bayonet"; companies such as the old Dominion Guards, whose captain was the famed filibuster

Roberdeau Wheat, who had served as a general in Mexico with Juan Alvarez, in Nicaragua with William Walker, and in Italy with Garibaldi. Promoted shortly to a major, Rob Wheat would take under his wing the obstreperous Tiger Rifles and several other companies to form a madcap battalion which would soon win fame in Virginia under the name of Louisiana Tigers.[3]

One of the showiest companies seen on the streets of New Orleans was a cavalry unit named Wilson's Rangers, organized by another group of gamblers. Followers of this ancient way of life have always abounded in New Orleans, and this particular group was not insensible to patriotic appeals, especially as military service lent itself admirably to the practice of their profession. George Devol, famed Mississippi River gambler, was a member of Wilson's Rangers, and in later years he recalled the whimsical manner in which the cavalrymen prepared for the coming of the Yankees. He wrote:

> We armed and equipped ourselves, and the ladies said we were the finest looking set of men in the army. If fine uniforms and good horses had anything to do with it we were a fine body. When we were ordered out to drill (which was every day), we would mount our fine horses, gallop out back of the city, and the first order we would receive from our commanding officer would be: "Dismount! Hitch horses! March! Hunt shade! Begin playing!" There was not a company of cavalry in the Southern army that obeyed more promptly than we did . . . We would remain in the shade until the cool of the evening, when the orders would be given: "Cease playing! . . . Prepare to mount! . . . March!" When we would get back into the city, the people would come out, cheer, wave handkerchiefs, and present us with bouquets; for we had been out drilling in the hot sun, preparing ourselves to protect their homes from the Northern invaders.[4]

New Orleans was rapidly taking on the appearance of an armed camp. Tailors worked day and night to complete colorful uniforms for Turcos, Zouaves, Chasseurs, and dozens of others. Seamstresses kept their sewing machines humming as they turned out company colors for the various units, and young and old were seized with military ardor and patriotism.

A Union woman, living with southern relatives in New Orleans, recorded in her diary that "the children play only with toy cannons and soldiers; the oldest inhabitant goes by every day with his rifle to practice; the public squares are full of companies drilling, and are now the fashionable resorts." She noted that the women were being urged to learn how to shoot so that when the men were off to battle, they would be able to protect themselves. "Every evening after dinner," she wrote, "we adjourn to the back lot and fire at a target with pistols."

But the women busied themselves in other ways, rolling bandages, preparing cartridge bags out of red flannel, making uniforms and shirts and underclothing for the volunteers. Even little girls found activity in these martial preparations. They were kept busy trotting around their neighborhoods with subscription lists for various companies, some seeking a flag, others equipment, and still others uniforms.[5]

The excitement of the times brought business of all kinds to an end in New Orleans. "Our city looks like a camp," wrote one brokerage house to an upstate client. "Business of all kinds at a stand and the whole community preparing with alacrity for the struggle for independence." Another firm explained that business was suspended because "our City is in a state of extra excitement," while a third brokerage house confessed to a planter, "We are much in want of money."[6]

Rumors, all generally wild, filled the city, some provoking false fears and others arousing false hopes. There was much concern on April 15, immediately after the surrender of Fort Sumter, over the report that several Federal ships of war had made their appearance at the mouth of the Mississippi. New Orleans was utterly unprepared for such an eventuality, and, indeed, had Federal vessels made the attempt, they could have easily steamed up the river to New Orleans. The realization of this in some circles in New Orleans increased the uneasiness provoked by the rumor. Colonel P. O. Hébert, who succeeded Bragg in command of the Military District of Louisiana, issued an order to close Southwest Pass, one of the two usable entrances into the Mississippi River.[7]

Meanwhile there was considerable activity on the river, where seagoing steamers, tied to the wharves, loomed as very attractive objects to Governor Moore and his advisers. One of the biggest, fastest, and best vessels in the port was the *Bienville*, owned in New York and commanded by Captain James D. Bulloch. A former United States naval officer, Bulloch was one of a number of lieutenants who had been detailed by the government to go into the mail steamer service some years before the war to acquire experience on steam vessels. Having obtained a lucrative command, Captain Bulloch resigned his naval commission and remained in private shipping. He was a native of Georgia, and there never was any doubt as to where his sympathies reposed should the secession crisis bring on war. Accordingly, the day after the firing on Fort Sumter, April 13, and the day before the scheduled sailing of the *Bienville* for New York, Captain Bulloch wrote to Judah P. Benjamin in Montgomery offering his services to the Confederacy, explaining, however, that he first had to take the *Bienville* back to New York and return it to its owners.

Having posted his letter, Captain Bulloch returned to the *Bienville* to hasten preparations for sailing on the morning of April 14. Later on the thirteenth, two members of the Louisiana Military Board, accompanied by the ship's agent in New Orleans, came to the *Bienville* and told Captain Bulloch that the ship was needed for the Confederate naval service and asked him to name a price, which Governor Moore would readily meet.

"I replied that I had no authority to sell the ship," Bulloch related in his memoirs, "and therefore could not fix a price, nor could I make any arrangements for transferring her to the Confederate States."

This did not satisfy Captain Bulloch's visitors from the Military Board, and they told him that if he didn't accept the proposition offered, it would probably be necessary to take the ship by force. They left, promising to inform Bulloch at a later hour of Governor Moore's decision.

"The Governor . . . and the members of the Board of War knew precisely my position," wrote Bulloch, "and the proposal for the purchase of the ship was made in a very friendly way." But he was determined neither to sell the *Bienville* nor to give her up without resistance. "It was inexpressibly painful to contemplate the possibility that I might be forced into collision with the Government I was willing and had just offered to serve," he wrote.

Knowing full well he could not fight, Captain Bulloch was prepared to make a run for it, if any attempt were made to seize the *Bienville*. He had the mooring line shifted so that it could be slipped from on board and he ordered the engineer to get up steam. Aided by a four- or five-knot current in the Mississippi, he had no fear of not getting away, nor did he expect to be stopped by the forts. Fortunately, at 10 P.M. word came from Governor Moore that his offer to purchase the *Bienville* was still open, but if Captain Bulloch still rejected it nothing would be done to prevent the *Bienville*'s sailing the next morning. Governor Moore had referred the matter to the Confederate authorities in Montgomery and President Davis had wired back: "Do not detain *Bienville*; we do not wish to interfere in any way with private property." The next day the *Bienville* sailed on schedule. After Bulloch turned the vessel over to its owners in New York, he joined the Confederate service.[8]

Some of the New Orleans companies were not too meticulous as to how they enlisted their troops. Nor was there any squeamishness on the part of the agents to whom a bonus of two dollars was paid for every recruit brought in. The bonus system led to nothing less than "inducing" men to volunteer by knocking them down, trussing them up, and carrying them off to the company rendezvous.

Mure, the British consul, was kept busy securing the release of Englishmen, Irishmen, and Scotsmen who had "volunteered" in this manner without being able to get any word to their families as to their whereabouts.

Early offenders were Captain Roberdeau Wheat's Old Dominion Guards and Captain Alex White's Tiger Rifles. Mure complained to Governor Moore on April 27, 1861:

"I have just been informed that several bodies of armed men

supposed to belong to Military Companies, in the course of being organized, are going about the city in small squads, who seize British subjects, and carry them off by force to their Rendezvous. One of these cases is that of a man named David Condon, who was attacked on the Levee, between 9 and 10 o'clock today, knocked down, and carried to the Rendezvous on Front Levee and Common St. I am informed that he was subsequently seen by his friends, taken off in a Furniture Cart, guarded by four men with muskets. . . ."

Other instances piled up rapidly, and Mure was in almost constant communication with Governor Moore for several days. He reported the facts to Lord John Russell at the Foreign Office on May 3, 1861:

> Some of the Military Companies sent armed parties through the city and carried off by force men indiscriminately to the Camp or temporary barracks threatening them with violence unless they enlisted. As soon as I learned that British subjects were treated in this outrageous manner, I addressed a Communication to the Governor calling upon him to release those men who had been kidnapped, and take the necessary steps to put an end to their illegal acts. The Governor at once disclaimed them, and said that "they met with his unqualified condemnation." He issued an order for the discharge of those British subjects "illegally mustered into the service." A great many similar cases have since occurred but as about 30 British Subjects have now been discharged I hope that these outrages will not be repeated.

But they were. The British consul, writing to the *Picayune*, reported that "one woman alleges that her husband was seized on his way to procure medical help for their child, and it was three days before she discovered the rendezvous where he was confined, and when she saw him he was tied with cords and so disfigured by bruises that she scarcely recognized him . . . There have been about 60 cases of impressed British subjects reported at my office."[9]

As troops poured into the city the citizens of New Orleans, young and old, turned out in large numbers to encourage the marching men. When the steamboats landed with troops from the interior, crowds were always on hand at the Levee, no longer piled high with produce but crowded with piles of boxes of muskets and ammunition, gun carriages, and other articles of war. And as the young volunteers stepped down the gangplanks, formed their ranks, and marched out Canal Street to Camp Walker, newly established on the Metairie Race Course, the cheers of the people mingled with the martial cadences of fife and drum, "the never ceasing beat of which is heard, morning, noon and night."

Within a couple of weeks Camp Walker proved unsuitable, and it was decided to establish a new camp in the piny woods across Lake Pontchartrain, at Tangipahoa, on the Jackson Railroad eighty miles above New Orleans. The ground was high and shaded with lofty pines, and excellent water was at hand. On May 12 a detachment was sent to lay out the camp. By May 15 practically all the troops had been moved to Camp Moore, so named in honor of the governor.[10]

During the military activity which had begun with secession and had stepped up steadily after the firing on Fort Sumter, there were many arrests made—usually at the instance of self-appointed vigilantes—of persons deemed enemies of the South. Dr. Metcalf, a dentist, was arrested for holding "opinions considered as insulting to the community," but was released when the attorney general ruled that the opinions were not treason. An indiscreet teacher was fired by the school board "for indulging in presence of her scholars in expressions of anti-Southern sentiments." An Ohioan who had lived for some time in Louisiana was seized as a dangerous and suspicious character and sent to the workhouse "for quiet meditation." Samuel Murdock, an old man who had resided in New Orleans since 1852, was haled before a judge "for being an abolitionist and a person of dangerous and unfriendly proclivities towards the South." Fortunately for the old man, the judge knew him "as one who had worked for the cause of humanity," and released him after a severe reprimand for "giving too much latitude to his tongue, without meaning any harm." Sheldon Guthrie, longtime citizen of New Orleans, was brought before Mayor Monroe "on a charge of being a well known heretic and professor of the faith of the apostles of free-niggerism." When Mr. Guthrie "made no concealment of his abolition proclivities," Mayor Monroe invited him to leave the city by June 15. James Hill was picked up for using "incendiary language against the South," and John White was arrested on an aggravation of the same charge because he expressed himself before Negroes. "These men will soon find out that, in the present state of things, it is not safe, to indulge in this unamiable habit," warned the *Picayune*.[11]

In addition to the routine activity into which New Orleans had settled there was an increasing amount of news which stirred the interest of most citizens. Books for subscription to stock in a propeller steamer to be fitted out as a privateer were opened, and $50,000 of the proposed $100,000 was subscribed the first day. The *Picayune* pointed to the success of the privateers *Calhoun*, *Ivy*, and *Music*, which had brought in a number of northern prizes, among them a ship with 800 tons of ice, a product which New Orleans needed badly. "This great success," said the paper, "will give vast encouragement to many capitalists and others, to embark in this lucrative enterprise . . ."[12]

On May 17, British consul Mure informed the New Orleans newspapers that he had received word that the rumored blockade would be effective on or about May 25. Neutral vessels at New Orleans would be allowed fifteen days to leave port after the blockade was established.

On May 21 came the news of North Carolina's secession, and the southern Confederacy was now complete. Three days later, on May 24, word reached New Orleans that Federal troops had invaded Virginia.

But the news with the greatest consequence to New Orleans came on May 27, when it was reported that at 2 p.m. on the previous day the United States man-of-war *Brooklyn* had dropped anchor off Pass a Loutre, the eastern entrance into the Mississippi River. The *Brooklyn* immediately dispatched a boat to Fort Jackson to inform the commander, Major Johnson K. Duncan, that the blockade would take effect from that moment. The blockaders lost little time in putting the pinch on New Orleans, for on May 30 the *Brooklyn* seized the bark *H. E. Spearing* with a $120,000 cargo of coffee from Brazil, and the next day another blockader, the *Powhatan*, apprehended the *Mary Clinton* with a cargo of rice, peas, and other products. "The blockade at the mouth of the River has been commenced by the War Steamer Brooklyn!" entered T. K. Wharton in his diary. "We must take her." But this all-important idea doesn't seem to have occurred to those in authority in New Orleans, at least not with any degree of urgency, for some time to come.[18]

The same day the news reached New Orleans that Federal blockaders had seized vessels at the mouth of the river, Major General David E. Twiggs arrived to command the Confederate forces in the newly established Department No. 1, which included southern Alabama and Mississippi and all of Louisiana, presenting an exposed coast from Florida to the Texas border. Twiggs, unwilling in March to accept a brigadier general's commission tendered him by President Davis, was appointed major general on May 22, and ordered to New Orleans, at the behest of Attorney General Judah P. Benjamin and the Louisiana delegation in the Confederate Congress. Upon receipt of his orders at Pascagoula, Mississippi, the old general hurried to New Orleans, where he assumed command on May 31, "looking in fine health."

A native of Georgia, Twiggs was born in 1790. At the age of twenty-two, he was commissioned captain in the Eighth Infantry early in 1812, and he fought gallantly in the second war with England. He had attained the rank of colonel in the Second Dragoons when the Mexican War broke out but was promoted to brigadier general. He served with great distinction in Mexico, particularly in the storming of Monterrey, where his exploits won the brevet of major general and the presentation of a sword by a resolution of Congress.

At the time of Lincoln's election, Twiggs was one of four general officers on the United States Army roster, the other three being Winfield Scott, John E. Wool, and William S. Harney. Twiggs was in command of the Department of Texas when secession came. Twiggs' sympathies were all with the South in the crisis, and he soon induced himself to surrender the military forces, stores, and arms under his command to the state of Texas and offer his services to the Confederacy. The old general was no doubt as gallant as all the New Orleans papers said he was, and certainly his records in the War of 1812 and the Mexican War justified the praise heaped upon his snowy locks. But at seventy-one, with the infirmities and incapacity of age pressing upon him, General Twiggs was hardly the man to defend the most important city in the Confederacy.[14]

The people of New Orleans, quite naturally, would have preferred to have General Beauregard in command. Not only was Beauregard a native son, but for more than ten years before the war he had been in charge of army engineering projects in Louisiana and he knew the Mississippi River and other navigable approaches to the Crescent City. Next to Beauregard, the people would have welcomed General Braxton Bragg, who was also familiar with the New Orleans area, but to a much lesser degree than the "Hero of Sumter." Beauregard and Bragg had each entertained the hope of receiving the New Orleans command. But Beauregard was in Virginia, importantly engaged in guarding the approaches to Richmond at Manassas Junction, while Bragg, still eager for the New Orleans assignment, was defending Pensacola. Seventy-one-year-old David E. Twiggs, with more than a half a century of service in the United States Army, was the only general officer that the Confederate government could provide at the time—and the time was late, exceedingly late.[15]

4

☆ ☆ ☆ ☆ ☆

Apathy Mans the Ramparts

IT IS INCREDIBLE HOW CASUAL THE CONFEDERACY WAS ABOUT THE defense of its greatest city, New Orleans. Louisiana had seceded on January 26, 1861, and early in February the Confederate States of America came into being. But it wasn't until more than two months later that the Confederate government got around to sending Major M. L. Smith, a West Point graduate and an engineering officer, to New Orleans.[1]

When the city learned in April that a Federal fleet had gone to sea from New York, considerable anxiety developed, as everyone knew New Orleans was in no way prepared for an invasion. Governor Moore reported the city's agitation in a telegram to Secretary of War Walker on April 10, adding: "The forts can be passed. We are disorganized, and have no general officer to command and direct. I doubt the policy of draining this place of troops to be sent to Pensacola." The next day the governor reported his dissatisfaction to Attorney General Benjamin, who immediately telegraphed back that New Orleans' fears "are without cause." He assured Moore that "the fleet is not destined for your city" and pointed out that "delay in sending the troops to Pensacola may cause serious disaster."[2]

Benjamin, as early as April 9, had promised that an "officer of high rank" would soon be dispatched to New Orleans. Yet it was not until the last day of May, fully seven weeks later, that General Twiggs arrived in New Orleans to take command of Department No. 1. The general, old and enfeebled as he was, quickly realized that Department No. 1 was in a near-defenseless state. On June 10 he reported to Secretary of War Walker that "this department is very badly off for men and ammunition"; on June 18 he reiterated that "ammunition is very scarce"; and still another week later he was reporting that "we are very much in want of ammunition." He said that he had sent out to buy up all the powder in New Orleans and that he now had on hand 400 kegs.[3]

The reason for the shortage of troops was soon known to General Twiggs. In April several Louisiana units had been sent to Braxton Bragg at Pensacola. Within two weeks of Twiggs' arrival the crack Washington Artillery, the 6th Louisiana, the 7th Louisiana, the 8th Louisiana, and Wheat's battalion had left New Orleans for Virginia.

New Orleans was in such a defenseless state that General Twiggs didn't quite know what to do first, but events, or at least rumors of events, soon pointed out his course of action. On June 7 a messenger from Adolphe Ducros' plantation at the mouth of Bayou Bienvenu brought word to General Twiggs that two fishermen had reported the arrival of two small war steamers in Lake Borgne and that "night before last they sent two boats towards the mouth of the bayou, as was supposed, for taking soundings." Twiggs immediately ordered a garrison to occupy the Martello tower at the mouth of the bayou.

A wild rumor began to spread immediately throughout the city that elements from the enemy's mosquito fleet had actually taken possession of the Martello tower at Bayou Bienvenu. Terming the rumor "false" and "silly," the *Picayune* told its readers that General Twiggs had requested it to state that Confederate troops of sappers and miners under Major M. L. Smith were at that very moment occupying the tower. With the rumor contradicted, New Orleans breathed more easily.[4]

General Twiggs had been in command of Department No. 1

46

barely ten days when the Common Council of the City of New Orleans expressed its confidence in the old soldier as a man of "integrity, sagacity, and nerve, so essential to a commandant." And it offered Twiggs "such facilities in the way of money" as he deemed necessary and it authorized a bond issue of $250,000 for the defense of New Orleans, expressing the belief that this amount was "amply sufficient to cover the costs of erecting fortifications at suitable localities."

But almost a month went by before Twiggs began to concern himself about fortifications. On July 9, he wrote the Secretary of War: "The defense of the city seems to me to demand immediate attention on the part of the commanding officer of Department No. 1." The public mind, he said, should have "not a doubt of its perfect security." And yet, Twiggs held back, because he did not "feel authorized to expend money for such purposes without the special orders of the Secretary of War." The old general told Secretary Walker that the face of the country had changed since the British tried to take New Orleans. Drainage, he pointed out, "had rendered many places formerly impassable sufficiently firm to support the march of troops." He said there were six or eight practical approaches to the city. "The citizens are very desirous to have the defense of these approaches attended to at once, and in this desire I participate."[5]

There were many avenues of approach to New Orleans for invading army or naval forces, and General Twiggs, although not able physically to go out and inspect them all himself, soon realized the inadequacies that had to be overcome to put the city in a substantial state of defense. There was the approach up the Mississippi River, past Forts Jackson and St. Philip, which were not ready to defend against an enemy fleet, either as to guns or to powder with which to fire the guns had they all been mounted in the casemates or on the parapets. Similarly, there was the approach downstream from St. Louis, but Federal vessels would have longer to travel on this route and could hardly be expected to advance down the river without an accompanying land operation by Federal armies. Nevertheless, if a Federal warship ran the Confederate shore batteries and appeared above New Orleans, the city would be absolutely defenseless.

Fort Macomb guarded Chef Menteur, and Fort Pike guarded the Rigolets, two passes leading into Lake Pontchartrain, the shores of which were barely five miles north of New Orleans. If either fort was reduced, the enemy could enter Lake Pontchartrain and reach land routes to the city. From Lake Borgne, east of New Orleans, lay the route the British took in December 1814. This was now defended by the Martello tower at the mouth of Bayou Bienvenu and by Battery Dupré, farther up the bayou. The Mexican Gulf Railroad to Proctorsville made possible the rapid movement of troops from New Orleans should a landing be effected in this area.

On Grand Terre Island, an old haunt of Laffite's pirates, Fort Livingston was situated where Barataria Bay empties into the Gulf. This fort defended the approach to New Orleans through a network of bayous, the successful navigation of which by an enemy would have called for traitorous assistance by native fishermen. Berwick Bay, where the western terminus of the New Orleans, Opelousas and Western Railroad was located, offered another, but more inaccessible, approach to New Orleans.

All of these fortifications formed the outer line of New Orleans' defense, and if General Twiggs could get the guns and powder and the men to fire them, the situation would improve considerably. But what of an inner line of defense? New Orleans had none. What of a barrier across the Mississippi to hold an enemy fleet under the fire of Forts Jackson and St. Philip? None had been started, despite General Beauregard's urging six months earlier.

General Twiggs, for all his honest efforts, was baffled by the tremendous task ahead of him, a task which at this late date would have taxed the physical strength of a man half his age. And while the old general's mental powers were in no way impaired, he was just not able physically to cope with the vast problems that the proper defense of New Orleans posed.

One of Twiggs' immediate concerns was the occupation of Ship Island, a dozen miles off the Mississippi Coast at Biloxi. This sandy stretch, about a mile across and nine miles in length, guarded the entrance into Mississippi Sound, where coastwise communications between New Orleans and Mobile were maintained. When Twiggs reached New Orleans, Ship Island was still unoccupied by Confederate forces, mainly because of a fantastic argument among Governor Moore, General James Trudeau of the Louisiana Legion, and the Confederate War Department.[6]

It all started on May 11, when Adjutant General Samuel Cooper telegraphed General Trudeau to occupy Ship Island with one regiment and two light batteries. Two days later, Secretary of War Walker attempted to speed up Trudeau: "You will proceed to organize your force as directed by the Adjutant General. It is most important that as little delay as possible shall intervene in your taking possession of Ship Island."

Trudeau telegraphed right back that Governor Moore had declined to allow his troops to leave the state with arms furnished by Louisiana. "Believing the occupation of Ship Island to be of the utmost importance, I will proceed at once to procure all we require. We have here 2000 men at Camp Walker. Can I take one battalion of that number? I think I can procure the material within four days."

On receipt of this, the Secretary of War wired Governor Moore on May 14 that General Trudeau had been ordered to Ship Island, but that he had reported that the governor had refused him ordnance for the expedition. "Will you please to explain what the difficulty is to which he refers, as it is not understood here. It is important for us to occupy Ship Island at once."

At the same time, Walker dispatched another telegram to Trudeau, stating that Montgomery authorities understood his force was organized and that if it was, he should proceed at once to Ship Island, notifying the Adjutant General when he was ready to move.

General Trudeau replied the same day: "My force is well disciplined, armed, uniformed, and organized. I am ready to leave for Ship Island at once. I can take a brigade if needed, but the Governor refuses to allow the ordnance and material to be used as directed by you."

One may imagine the Secretary of War's bewilderment on May

15, when this telegram from Governor Moore arrived at his desk: "I do not know of any command General Trudeau has except that of brigadier-general of militia. None of his military command has volunteered. I did not refuse to give ordnance. No application was made by him for ordnance. Had he applied for any, I should have refused them to him as brigadier-general of militia, for as such he does not need them. If General Trudeau has an appointment from the Confederate States, please inform us. I feel the necessity of occupying Ship Island, and will do all I can to aid it."

To this, doubtless after much headshaking, Secretary Walker replied that General Trudeau was offered the command of Ship Island by President Davis on his assurance that he had troops ready for service. "You state that he has no troops subject to his order," wired Walker. "If Trudeau is not sent to Ship Island, what is your proposition?" Walker apparently was not only befuddled but was beginning to get exasperated by the double talk, for he added: "State it distinctly, as prompt action is necessary." He told the governor that Trudeau had just wired that he was ready to move, but Moore still refused to permit him to take the arms.

The telegraph offices in New Orleans and Montgomery were busy the rest of the day sending messages from Moore to Walker and from Walker back to Moore and to General Trudeau. Moore wired that Trudeau was advertising in the afternoon papers for a regiment for twelve months' service. "He announced that he acts under your authority. Am I to understand that is so?"

Before Governor Moore got a reply to this telegram, he telegraphed again to Secretary Walker:

> I telegraphed you this morning that Trudeau had no command but that of a militia general. I telegraphed you this afternoon that he was advertising for recruits for twelve months. I do not believe he can raise a regiment in a month; probably not at all. I have no proposition to make about Ship Island. I have no doubt I can furnish whatever number of men for twelve months that may be needed. I am of the opinion that Ship Island ought to be garrisoned immediately,

and that a skillful officer should command. I have none such to offer; you have. It is not true that I have refused to allow General Trudeau to move with the arms of the regiment which he informs the Adjutant General he has. I have refused him nothing. He has not asked for anything. The fact is, in my opinion, that General Trudeau's men are a myth.

When Walker read this telegram, he figured that he had better bring the matter to an immediate close if he ever expected to get Ship Island occupied. He telegraphed Trudeau that his command of Ship Island was revoked and he wired Governor Moore informing him of the revocation. He then called on Moore to raise a force for Ship Island, suggesting that the Fourth Louisiana Regiment would be suitable. On May 17, the governor telegraphed Walker that "the Fourth Regiment will be ready to move to Ship Island today and tomorrow," and he sent a second wire, asking: "Is it advisable to occupy Ship Island without a battery of heavy guns? . . . Troops would be liable to capture." Walker, in a reply, ordered the Fourth Regiment to Ship Island as soon as mustered into service. He promised to send a 10-inch columbiad, two 68-pounders, besides some 32-pounders.

On May 18, President Davis, who doubtless was informed of the weird correspondence, received a telegram from Colonel Robert J. Barrow, commanding officer of the Fourth Louisiana Regiment: "I am told that the regiment which I have the honor to command, which is composed of gentlemen, is ordered to Ship Island. If you order me I am willing to storm the 'gates of hell,' but I do not wish to sacrifice my men. Will I have the means of protection?"

Meantime, in New Orleans, General Trudeau on May 15 and 16 disbanded his forces, "upward of 1,000 men . . . for twelve months," he wrote Secretary Walker on May 22, sending the letter by an officer to Montgomery because he felt that his "dispatches through the telegraph were not forwarded." Trudeau asserted that after receiving orders revoking his command, he had "proceeded at once to organize a regiment of 1,000 men for the war," and had so informed Walker on May 19 but had received no reply. "In the name of my officers and of the men under my command, I protest as a simple act of justice that His Excellency the President of the Confederate States be informed of the above facts. In behalf of my officers, I request you to assign us in a body to any duty in any capacity under the Confederate States for the time of the war."

By the time Walker received this letter, General Twiggs had already been assigned to New Orleans and machinery had been put into motion for the occupation of Ship Island. Adjutant General Cooper, on May 23, instructed Major M. L. Smith, ranking Confederate officer in New Orleans, to co-operate with Colonel Barrow "in all measures deemed necessary for the defense of the passes near that island leading into Mississippi Sound." Cooper stated that heavy ordnance had been ordered to Ship Island. Yet, when Twiggs took command in New Orleans on May 31, no move to Ship Island had commenced. One of Twiggs' first acts was to inform the War Department on June 1 that "troops stationed at Ship Island can be of no use except in defending that particular point. Indeed, without some heavy guns they could be taken by the Black Republican fleet at any time."

Twiggs looked around for heavy guns and discovered some naval guns at New Orleans, but when he tried to get them on loan from the Confederate Navy he was turned down. Accordingly, on June 18, in a letter to Secretary Walker, he was forced to confess: "I have not been able yet to garrison Ship Island for want of heavy guns. I have the troops for the purpose ready at Mississippi City, some ten or twelve miles distant. In the course of a week I expect to have some 38-pounders. When I get them immediate steps shall be taken to erect batteries on Ship Island. I applied to the Navy Department here for the loan of some heavy guns, but could not get them. I thought they might as well be at Ship Island in position as lying on the wharves of the city."

And so it was that after more than six weeks of hemming and hawing about occupying Ship Island, the island was still unoccupied. But not for long, for while the Confederates argued and talked and telegraphed, the Yankees moved. With a show of pique, the *Picayune* reported "the army at our doors" on June 25. "While we are remaining in fancied security, and boasting of the impossibility of the invasion of our shores by the enemy, a fleet takes possession of Ship Island and the sound, and cuts off our communication with Mobile," declared the paper. ". . . Where is our fleet of gunboats, and why are they permitted to lie idle when there is plenty of opportunity for them to exercise their skill and bravery by having a small tea party with the light craft of the enemy?" The next day the *Picayune* asked whether or not the military authorities had feasible means to halt the "petty scale annoyance" to small craft plying Mississippi Sound by sailing tenders of the blockading fleet. "It certainly could not involve a very large expenditure of money," the paper declared, "or the detailing of a very numerous body of men, to resist these petty harriers and to drive them out of our waters. Their presence is an intolerable insult, as well as injury, and should be borne no longer, especially as the means of ridding ourselves of it are abundantly practicable."[7]

General Twiggs' warning on June 26 against "communication of any kind and on any pretense with the Black Republicans" caused the citizens of New Orleans to speculate on the meaning of the order. The *Picayune* explained that it was to prevent all communication with the blockading vessels, and it commented: "If there are any spies among us, and report says that we are not free of them, we hope this will lead all loyal citizens to keep a sharp look-out for them . . ."[8]

On July 1, New Orleans was electrified to learn that the first Confederate man-of-war, the *Sumter*, commanded by Captain Raphael Semmes, had slipped through the Federal blockade at the passes and had gone to sea the day previous. The *Sumter*, a small packet steamer, had been outfitted in New Orleans and for nine days had bided its time at the Head of the Passes to make a dash to the sea. Taking advantage of the *Brooklyn's* pursuit of a sail, Semmes pushed down Pass a Loutre and into the open Gulf. When the Union vessel, three or four miles off, spotted the *Sumter*, Semmes had too much of a lead to be caught by the *Brooklyn*.[9]

On July 7, Confederate forces, 140 strong, landed on Ship Island, from which the Federals had departed. The Confederates had only two guns, but by July 15, Twiggs had eight 32-pounders and two navy columbiads mounted at the fort on Ship Island.[10]

Four days later came thrilling news: The Yankees had attacked Beauregard at Bull Run on July 18 and had met a bloody repulse. The first news was fragmentary but left no doubt as to the Confederate victory, for the Federals who had probed Beauregard's line at one of the fords retreated in discomfort to their base at Centreville. The next day, when the details came over the telegraph, New Orleans was swept into a frenzy of joyous excitement.

But the celebration was surpassed when word came late on July 21 that another southern victory had been gained on the plains of Manassas in a terrific battle from which the battered Federals had reeled back in a disorderly rout to the defenses of Washington. Throughout that whole sultry Sunday, New Orleans was keyed to a state of expectancy, and predictions were freely expressed that a furious general battle was under way.

Louisiana troops, New Orleans learned, had displayed great gallantry at Manassas, especially Major Roberdeau Wheat's Louisiana Tigers, Colonel Harry Hays' 7th Louisiana Infantry, and the Washington Artillery. But Wheat had fallen in a great demonstration of bravery and his life was despaired of. For days the newspapers were full of the victory at Manassas. But the *Picayune*, with profound judgment, warned: ". . . We must not suppose, in our exultations and our comfortings, that the winning of one great battle is the end of the war, or more than the beginning of an end which may be yet a long time off." This sobering advice was doubtless lost on many people, who were now substituting overconfidence for lethargy regarding the defense of New Orleans.[11]

The Common Council of New Orleans had been much concerned for some time over the apathy which settled over Louisiana after secession. A joint committee on defense set up by the two Boards of Aldermen was disturbed that, while other southern states had hastened to build defenses, "Louisiana alone seemed to rest in a perfect state of quietude." The committee was gravely concerned that as war became imminent "the State of Louisiana was still lying apparently dormant." Accordingly, the New Orleans administration, becoming "justly alarmed at the apathy of the State Government," decided it was high time "to take the defense of the city in its own hands." So on June 29 it established a commission of military and civil engineers "to thoroughly examine various approaches to the city" and to propose a plan of fortification.

On July 2, at a secret session of the Common Council, the commission's plan for fortifications to ring the city was adopted. Since 400 cannon were needed to defend the proposed works, the Common Council hurried a committee of J. O. Nixon, P. S. Wiltz, and Jules Benit to Richmond to try to procure them from Confederate authorities.

Because the plans of fortifications extended outside the city limits of New Orleans, the defense committee and the engineers conferred with Governor Moore and Colonel Hébert, who gave verbal approval for the work to begin. Two days later Governor Moore sent his approval in writing and an order authorizing Major Benjamin Buisson, president of the commission of engineers, "to take possession of such positions, lands, houses, or other property as may be necessary" to enable him to carry out the project of fortifications for New Orleans.

Armed with this authority, the commission of engineers took possession of certain lands on both sides of the Mississippi on July 16. The work started on July 18 at the Waggaman Plantation on the West Bank, above New Orleans, and by July 22 at all other sites. Both the defense committee of the Common Council and the commission of engineers were astounded that day when a letter arrived from Governor Moore announcing his "reconsideration" of the fortification project. "I now . . . revoke any authority you may have derived from me," wrote the governor. "I will hereafter authorize the location of any important work for the defense of the city, if it be approved by the Confederate Commander of this Department, but will not authorize any that has not his approval."

What caused Governor Moore to change his mind? Why, late in

July—six months after secession and three and a half months after Sumter—was there a city-state feud over where the fortifications around New Orleans should be placed? For one thing, there had been protests to Governor Moore from landowners above New Orleans and the Jefferson Parish Police Jury. Injunctions were sought to stop the work on certain properties, and some were granted on July 24. On the same day Messrs. Wiltz and Benit returned from Richmond with Jefferson Davis' assurances that he would immediately send armament to New Orleans for the fortifications. This information the defense committee and the commission of engineers construed as "tacit proof of his consent and approval of the projected fortifications." Accordingly, the defense committee sought an interview with General Twiggs and Governor Moore's Military Board to discuss the resumption of work on the fortifications.[12]

General Twiggs sent Colonel Hébert and Major Smith on an inspection of the fortification project, and they reported on July 27 that they found themselves in the unhappy position of having to approve plans with which they did not agree or to reject them and thus "deprive the city of works which in common with others we are anxious to see finished." They felt that the site below the city was not well chosen and that the location of the fort in Carrollton would not permit effective fire to bear on vessels coming down the Mississippi. "This work," they reported, "is intended to bear upon vessels approaching in the straight reach just above, and yet this very reach is masked by the point directly opposite." The officers reported that the best spot for the fort was a half mile upstream, "where its view is unobstructed and range given for the largest guns." These and other objections together with suggestions for the fortifications were embodied in two reports which General Twiggs forwarded to the War Department on July 30, stating: "The city authorities have, I understand, commenced their works both above and below the city. There is but little probability of the army engineers agreeing either in the location or the form of the works proposed by the engineers employed by the civil authorities. This is very unfortunate, as the time for preparation is getting so short."[13]

The defense committee, in the meantime, not having heard from General Twiggs, the Military Board, or Governor Moore, called on the governor, who promised a reply that day, July 30. Shortly after the meeting, the governor's letter arrived, enclosing a letter from General Twiggs to Moore, which read: "In answer to your letter . . . concerning fortifications proposed by a committee of the City Council, I would state that no plan of fortifications will be approved or sanctioned by me except such as may be prepared by or approved by the engineering officers of the Confederate army." In his letter to the defense committee, Governor Moore stated that "under the circumstances I do not consider myself warranted in giving my sanction to the works." The next day, July 31, the work on the fortifications was halted by the city authorities, who hotheadedly decided to go over Twiggs' head. Mr. Wiltz was authorized to telegraph Mr. Nixon, who was still in Richmond, "to get from President Davis his authority to proceed with said fortifications." But Mr. Nixon was on his way back to New Orleans and consequently did not receive the telegram.

There was a heated meeting of the Board of Aldermen on the night of August 6, and a compromise was reached allowing the Common Council to act as it saw fit.[14]

Three days later, on August 9, the Common Council authorized an appropriation of $100,000 to be put at General Twiggs' disposal "to be applied by him in such manner as he may deem proper, for the construction of fortifications to defend the approaches of the city." On August 20, General Twiggs addressed a letter to the Common Council: "Under your action . . . placing at my disposal the sum of one hundred thousand dollars for the purpose of constructing defences of the city, proposals were publicly invited for the execution of the work. I have now to inform you that contracts covering the whole work are entered into, the lines of defence defined, and that Major M. L. Smith, the chief engineer of this department, is ready to commence operation so soon as the amount referred to is placed subject to draft."[15]

Thus ended the time-consuming feud over the fortifications to defend New Orleans from a land attack. It was fortunate indeed, during the seven months from secession to late August, that President Lincoln did not launch an attack on New Orleans. But Mr. Lincoln had worries of his own, following the rout of the Federal Army in the Battle of Manassas.

5

☆ ☆ ☆ ☆ ☆

The Blockade Begins to Pinch

ON APRIL 15, 1861—THE DAY FOLLOWING THE SURRENDER OF FORT Sumter—President Lincoln proclaimed a blockade of southern ports, and on May 26 the *Brooklyn* anchored off Pass a Loutre and dispatched a boat to Fort Jackson to announce that the blockade of the port of New Orleans was in effect.

There was no immediate demand in New Orleans to do anything about the blockade. From Pensacola, General Braxton Bragg urged Governor Moore early in June to construct gunboats at once to operate on the lakes to keep open the communications between New Orleans and Mobile. Several gunboats were already under construction, but there wasn't any stepped-up shipbuilding program to meet the challenge of the Union war vessels which were choking the economy of New Orleans with their blockade.

Raphael Semmes, commander of the *Sumter*, chafing at not being able to put to sea immediately with his raider, recorded in his journal for June 1: "We are losing a great deal of precious time. The enemy's flag is being flaunted in our faces, at all our ports by his ships of war, and his vessels of commerce are passing and repassing, on the ocean, in defiance, or in contempt of our power, and, as yet, we have not struck a blow."

Although New Orleans itself was effectively sealed off by the blockaders at the passes, some goods, in small quantities and at irregular intervals, reached the city via blockade runners which ran into Berwick Bay, ninety miles to the west.[1]

Before the blockade was two months old, however, New Orleans began to feel the pinch, and the *Picayune* called for shipbuilding action:

> Besides the gunboats already under way, an additional force should at once be prepared for the defence of our river and Lake shore coast. This is a matter which demands the immediate attention of our sister States, Mississippi and Alabama. Let their citizens go to work, cut the timber and haul to the sea shore, ready for use, as was done during the war of 1812 on Lake Erie, and we can soon have enough gunboats afloat to protect the coast from Mobile to New Orleans. The engines of small steamers can be used for the gunboats, and thus a formidable force raised.
>
> Let the boats be built, and look to the Government for pay afterwards. There is no fear of the accounts not being paid.

Doubtless in answer to this piece came a letter signed "Hancock County," which stated that the towns of Pearlington and Gainesville, in Mississippi, had excellent facilities to build gunboats and were prepared to begin construction at once. "We have the timber, the mills, the boat yards, docks and ship carpenters, all on hand," stated the letter. "It may not be generally known that at both these places on Pearl River we are constantly building steamboats and schooners of the best live oak, cypress, yellow pine, white oak and cedar. Let the Confederate authorities or the Executive of Mississippi and Louisiana say the word, and by or before the 1st of January, Pearlington and Gainesville will fit out and complete any number of gunboats that may be needed."[2]

The Confederate government and the governors of Louisiana and Mississippi seem not to have availed themselves of these facilities to build what was essential to the defense of New Orleans—a large fleet of vessels actively to challenge the blockaders both in the Gulf and in Mississippi Sound.

There was, to be true, some activity by the Confederate Navy Department at New Orleans. On the authority of Secretary Mallory, Commodore Laurence Rousseau had purchased in March two ocean-going steamers, the *Habana* and *Marques de la Habana*, and had had them converted into warships. The former became the sea raider *Sumter*, which escaped the blockade on June 30, while the latter became the *McRae*, part of the river defense of New Orleans. Rousseau also contracted with a shipbuilder, John Hughes, to adapt a ferryboat, already on the ways at his Algiers shipyard, into a gunboat. Work was well under way when Commodore Rousseau—"the venerable . . . Rousseau . . . full of years, and full of honors," as Captain Semmes said of him—was summoned to Richmond to a desk job more suitable to his advanced age.[3]

To succeed Commodore Rousseau at New Orleans, Secretary Mallory sent sixty-two-year-old Commodore George N. Hollins, a Maryland-born sea dog bubbling with energy and bristling with fight. In the old Navy, which he joined in 1814 as a fifteen-year-old midshipman, Hollins had the reputation of being a brave, bold, and able officer and a thorough sailor. Hollins had sailed and fought with Stephen Decatur against the British and later against the Algerian pirates. In 1854, while commanding the *Cyane*, he shelled Greytown in Nicaragua in reprisal for outrages against Americans. The following year he was promoted to captain. He was commander of the *Susquehanna* at Naples, in May 1861, when ordered to report to the Secretary of the Navy. Upon his return to the United States he resigned his commission out of sympathy for the South. The Navy made it doubly official by dismissing him from service on June 1861. Two weeks later he was commissioned a captain in the Confederate States Navy. Almost at once, Hollins demonstrated why he had established a reputation in the United States Navy as a bold and aggressive fighter. He organized a raid to capture a Federal vessel in the lower Potomac, and with this vessel he seized two other Union ships. All three had cargoes useful to the Confederacy.[4]

Captain Hollins had a decided flair for the spectacular, and this was not lost on Secretary Mallory. Here was just the man to organize the naval defense of New Orleans, and Mallory dispatched him to the Crescent City with the rank of commodore. On July 31, Commodore Hollins took command at the New Orleans station. He was not long in augmenting his naval resources. He ordered the construction of two gunboats for service on the lakes and he purchased the *Florida* and *Pamlico*, also for duty on the lakes, and three river tugboats, which were converted into rams and named *Jackson*, *Ivy*, and *Tuscarora*. These commissions by Hollins, together with Commodore Rousseau's earlier contracts, represented the Confederate Navy Department's activities in New Orleans during the summer months and into the early fall of 1861.[5]

Early in August, General Twiggs proposed to the War Department that floating docks in New Orleans, of which there were six of immense size and strength, could be converted into floating batteries of tremendous power for a negligible cost. He was thinking of them especially to prevent Federal gunboats from descending the Mississippi to attack New Orleans from above. "These docks can be towed up to any point on the river where the channel is narrow and be made an impassable barrier to the vessels of the enemy," he wrote Secretary Walker. "They can be readily made impenetrable to boarders, and I think would effectually prevent any descent by way of the river." The letter bore the endorsement of Major General Leonidas Polk, commanding general of Department No. 2, strongly urging the immediate arming of the floating docks and the dispatch of them up the river as early as possible. Two weeks later, Twiggs got authorization from Richmond to convert the floating docks into batteries "at the earliest practicable moment." About September 1, work was started on two floating batteries.[6]

Meanwhile, private parties had been busy on two mysterious projects in New Orleans, spurred on by the Confederate government's offer of a bounty of 20 per cent of the value of all enemy heavily armed vessels destroyed. One of the undertakings, the idea of a shipowner and merchant, John A. Stevenson, was the creation of an ironclad ram from a river towboat. The other project was the idea of two marine engineers and machinists, James R. McClintock and

Baxter Watson, who conceived and began to build a submarine warship. Both vessels were "hush-hush" affairs and the New Orleans papers studiously avoided any mention of them. These various floating preparations by the Navy, Army, and private enterprise, however, did not satisfy the demand for small gunboats, which were an absolute necessity for coastal defense. More than a month later, the *Picayune* warned that the immense fleet of Union warships being fitted out in New York and Philadelphia was destined for New Orleans.[7]

The people of New Orleans were filled with anxiety, and there was good reason, for the blockade had wrecked the commerce of the Confederacy's greatest port and "business amounts to almost nothing." Shortages in everyday articles began to develop, and with the scarcity, prices began to soar. In early August, the *Bee* reduced its daily edition to a single sheet because of the depletion of its stock of newsprint, an expedient which other journals were compelled later to adopt as the blockade continued into the fall and winter months. Coffee drinkers—and who in New Orleans wasn't?—began to look for adulterants or substitutes, and the papers provided recipes as fast as they were called to their attention. One called for drying, parching, and grinding the seed of the okra plant; another called for using rye in the same way; a third called for slicing and toasting sweet potatoes, then grinding them in a mill; and a fourth employed a weed known as Indian or wild coffee, found all over New Orleans.[8]

The newspapers recommended "Southern Ink," manufactured in New Orleans by an enterprising housewife. However, attempts to meet an acute shortage in soap lagged. With no ship having arrived in New Orleans since May 29, it was natural that the stocks of northern and foreign goods in the city's shops should disappear. This was hailed, before many months, as a blessing in disguise, for it called for New Orleans to rally its own resources to serve and satisfy the city's needs during the period of blockade.[9]

Mayor John T. Monroe, reporting to the Common Council on the condition of the city in early October, noted the city's increasing self-sufficiency, taking special pride in the fact that New Orleans was well on its way to becoming an important arsenal for the Confederacy.

There was considerable enterprise shown in the manufacturing of arms and ordnance in New Orleans, or in the preparations to manufacture them. The first establishment to get under way was the gun-carriage plant which state authorities set up in February in the Custom House shops with John Roy in charge. By the end of June, the various workshops established in the Custom House were the centers of great military preparations for both the Army and Navy. By mid-July, T. K. Wharton, superintendent of the Custom House, recorded that all the ordnance work being done in his shops was now "of primary importance."[10] Leeds and Company, the most important foundry in the South after the Tredegar Works in Richmond, began to turn out war materials, castings for John Roy's gun carriages, water tanks for the *Sumter*, and shot and shells for the same sea raider. And shortly thereafter Leeds had begun to cast brass rifled cannon and eight-inch columbiads, the first ones being described by Wharton as "beautiful."[11]

In June, two Englishmen, Ferdinand W. C. Cook, an architect and engineer, and his brother, Francis, established a plant at No. 1 Canal Street to manufacture rifles on the Enfield pattern. The Cooks also manufactured swords and bayonets, and nothing was needed except capital to enable them to undertake a much greater expansion. In vain did the New Orleans press try to smoke out financial support for the Cooks. "If New Orleans capitalists would but increase the facilities of Cook's rifle factory . . ." lamented the *Bee*. But New Orleans capitalists apparently showed no disposition to invest in the project, a reluctance for which, perhaps, some explanation may be given. But it is beyond comprehension why, with a shortage of shoulder weapons in Louisiana, Governor Moore didn't move to have the state subsidize the Cooks' expansion.[12]

The blockade and the times proved stimulating to local inventors, and many came forward with blueprints and ideas for weapons that would make New Orleans safe—at least in the minds of their originators—from Black Republican incursions. A young machinist named Gilmore invented a Minié ball for use in smooth-bore muskets. Another mechanical-minded gentleman, named Copland, produced a windage stopper for use on rifled cannon. A new-style bayonet for use on a shotgun was devised by two men from St. Mary's Parish. A pike, with a scythelike blade to operate on a victim after he had been seized by a hook, was perfected by Captain Franz Beuter and adopted as the chief weapon for a company he was raising.[13]

A tool of war which seemed tremendously formidable to the *Crescent* was Arthur Barbarin's "submarine and subterranean torpedo," which in an experiment at Lake Pontchartrain blew a skiff to bits. Witnesses to the experiment were "sanguine that if a few large torpedoes were placed in the channel at the mouth of the river, in the bayous and in the Rigolets, approach to the city by a fleet would be impossible."

But the most talked about proposed new weapon was J. C. Wingard's new mounted rifle-gun, which reportedly would discharge 192 balls in one minute at a range as great as that of any gun then in use. Wingard's gun received the approval of General Twiggs, and the inventor set out to raise a thousand to fifteen hundred dollars for the construction of the gun.

Wingard's gun grew more formidable as the press and public discussed it, and eventually the Common Council appropriated $550 to assist Wingard in completion of his gun, but there is no evidence that the gun ever was perfected and put into use.[14]

Another military conversation piece was a bullet-making machine invented by Messrs. James R. McClintock and Baxter Watson, who were also engaged in building the submarine vessel. The machine could be constructed for two to three thousand dollars. "With it two men can turn out a thousand balls per hour, or with steam power it makes eight or ten thousand per hour," stated the *Bee*. "Thus one machine, worked night and day, could turn out 1,200,000 balls every week, more than enough to supply the Confederate armies in the most desperate and extended war conceivable."[15]

Meanwhile, long-deferred progress was being made in establishing the defenses of New Orleans, with General Twiggs, whose leadership was impaired by age and ailments, delegating most of the work to Major M. L. Smith. Contracts for building fortifications were let, and work started on August 22. Less than a month later, the *Picayune* assured its readers that "our fortifications were progressing rapidly, and . . . we shall soon be prepared to resist any force that the abolition despot, Lincoln, may send to invade our shores." The first guns from Richmond began to arrive in the middle of July—six 24- and 12-pound brass howitzers—and were mounted and outfitted in the Wharton-Roy workshops in the Custom House. By the third week in September, ninety-five heavy-caliber guns from Norfolk had reached the city. On the last day of September, the chain barrier across the Mississippi at Forts Jackson and St. Philip was in place. "Our defenses are improving daily," jotted Wharton in his journal.[16]

But Wharton, along with a lot of other citizens of New Orleans, must have been surprised and disappointed when the Confederate forces evacuated Ship Island in mid-September, presumably because the Union warship *Massachusetts* was preparing to shell the island. Wharton had supplied much heavy tackle, iron blocks, and other equipment to prepare the fortifications on Ship Island and he considered it "capably fortified" and able to "present a bold front." But in the view of the apparent urgency to occupy Ship Island several months earlier and the difficulty with which it was finally done, it seems strange that, at the first show of Federal force against it, it was given up without a struggle. Somewhere along the way, the Confederate thinking was pretty muddled regarding Ship Island. The Confederate force on Ship Island, if properly supported by naval vessels, could have prevented the use of the island as a base for the blockaders and later as the staging area for the invading army. Or at least the Confederates could have made the Federals pay something in time and material for the right to occupy the island.

General Twiggs, who had argued with Commodore Rousseau in July about the return of two heavy navy guns which had been loaned him for Ship Island, informed the War Department at the time that he could hold the island if he could keep the navy guns. Secretary of War Walker arranged with Secretary of Navy Mallory for Twiggs to keep the guns, yet even after this was arranged, Twiggs ordered the evacuation of Ship Island.[17]

It is no wonder that about this time complaints began to reach President Davis about General Twiggs' incapacity for the job to be done at New Orleans. On September 16, President Davis and his Cabinet "discussed Twiggs' inability to perform the duties of Major General at N. Orleans & the difficulty of finding a proper Genl," as Secretary Mallory noted in his diary.

The pressure for Twiggs' removal began to mount rapidly. The distinguished former governor of Louisiana, A. B. Roman, wrote with complete frankness to President Davis of "the feeling of uneasiness and apprehension which exists" as a result of "the infirmities of General Twiggs."

On September 20, Governor Moore wrote the President stressing the immediate need in New Orleans of "an officer . . . who, with youth, energy and military ability, would infuse some activity in our preparations and some confidence in our people." Moore told Davis that he had confided his views to General Van Dorn, who passed through New Orleans en route to Richmond, and had asked him to transmit them to the President. The governor closed with a plea that "this city, the most important to be preserved of any of the Confederacy, and our coast, the most exposed of all the states, be no longer neglected."

Two days later, Governor Moore wrote Benjamin in a gloomy vein: "Our fortifications are very backward. We have but one engineer here (Major Smith) and he is not an active one according to my judgment. I am not satisfied with our situation—*not at all*; and should we be attacked by any strong force, I am fearful of the result."

President Davis replied to Governor Moore on September 26, stating that from other sources he had learned that General Twiggs "has proven unequal to his command." President Davis shifted the blame to the people of New Orleans: "As in his selection I yielded much to the solicitation of the people of New Orleans, I think they should sooner have informed me of the mistake they had made." Davis informed Governor Moore he had directed that Mansfield

Lovell, a former army officer and deputy street commissioner of New York City, be appointed a brigadier general and assigned to New Orleans to take charge of the defenses of the city and the coast adjacent to it.[18] On September 25, General Lovell was ordered to report to General Twiggs in New Orleans. On October 1, Brigadier General Daniel Ruggles, who was with General Bragg at Pensacola, was also ordered to New Orleans.

General Twiggs eased a delicate situation on October 5 by writing to Secretary of War Benjamin as follows: "My health will not permit me to take the field. I would like an active and efficient officer to be sent to relieve me." President Davis immediately promoted Lovell to major general, and Benjamin replied to Twiggs: ". . . The Department learns with regret that the state of your health is such as to cause you to request to be relieved from active duty. Your request is granted, but you are expected to remain in command until the arrival of Maj. Gen. Lovell, who has been appointed to succeed you, and who leaves for New Orleans tomorrow."

The newspapers paid high tribute to the old soldier, not, to be sure, for what he achieved in command in New Orleans, but for his distinguished past. "His head is clear, his brain active, and his patriotism as fervent as of yore," said the *Crescent*, "but . . . the disabilities of disease preventing that personal and active attention which he deemed necessary to the requirements of the occasion, he asked to be relieved." The *Picayune* praised General Twiggs' "gallant spirit" and "incessant attention" and "immense labor" and "the sleeplessness with which he entered on the public service."[19]

Late in September, the people of New Orleans were diverted somewhat from their concern over the defenses of the city by the arrivals of Federal prisoners captured at the Battle of Manassas. By October 1, nearly 500 of them were behind the bars of the Parish Prison. Huge crowds turned out to see the arrival of the Yankees. The prisoners were bedraggled from travel and sullen and morose as they trooped through the streets to Parish Prison. The *Crescent* had a very low opinion of them: "There was nothing respectable in their carriage, and they wore more the air of thieves and pickpockets than soldiers . . . If old Abe's armies are composed of such material, the result of the conflict cannot be doubted. One Southern gentleman could run a score of them."[20]

Various activities aimed at providing relief for volunteers and their families were in full swing in New Orleans throughout the first summer and fall of the war. There were fairs and barbecues to provide funds, and sewing and knitting circles were formed to provide warm clothing for Louisiana troops during the coming winter. And a Free Market, the most successful of several in the Confederacy, was established to provide free food for the indigent families of soldiers in the field. Upriver planters and farmers sent foodstuffs and vegetables by steamboats to the Free Market, which was situated on Canal Street near the Levee. New Orleans citizens made cash contributions and benefits of many kinds and provided funds to purchase items that were not donated. The market, operated entirely with volunteer workers, was open Tuesdays and Fridays from 9 A.M. to 1 P.M. The Free Market opened on August 16 and 728 families with 1854 mouths to feed were supplied with food. Soon an average of 1500 poor New Orleans families were being fed by the Free Market. The people of New Orleans and the planters in the country gave generously to the Free Market. A thief, caught with a stolen barrel of flour, protested he had filched it for the Free Market.

The Free Market became every day more popular. Even a song, with words by J. W. Overall and music by a well-known local musician and composer, Theodore Von LaHache, was dedicated to the Free Market and published.[21]

All the while, as the summer moved into the fall, the pinch of the blockade tightened. There was, however, one marked benefit accruing from the blockade of the Mississippi River passes. "The health of the city was never in a better condition at this season of the year," reported the *Picayune* in mid-August. ". . . Is the blockade of our ports the cause of the absence of yellow fever?" A week later the same paper noted: "Thus far no signs of yellow fever." And in September it announced: "No single case of yellow fever, that we have heard of, has occurred this season."[22]

New Orleans people for a long time had been wondering when something was going to be done to drive the Federal blockading vessels away from the passes and to open the port of New Orleans. Because the newspapers were circumspect in their reporting, only a few behind the scenes knew what was being planned by old Commodore George Hollins.

6

Alias the "Turtle"

A SYNDICATE OF NEW ORLEANS BUSINESSMEN, HEADED BY A FORMER river captain, John A. Stevenson, had opened subscription books at the Merchants' Exchange on May 12, 1861, to raise $100,000 with which to purchase a powerful tugboat and convert it into a privateer. The first day $50,000 was subscribed, and apparently the other $50,000 was not long in coming in, for the work of converting the tug *Enoch Train* into an ironclad ram began shortly thereafter.

The *Enoch Train* was a twin-screw tug with a displacement of 385 tons. It was a single-decked, two-masted vessel, 128 feet long with a 28-foot beam and a 12½-foot draft. Constructed at Medford, Massachusetts, in 1855 as an icebreaker, the *Enoch Train* had for the past two years operated on the Mississippi River as a towboat.

Once on the ways, the *Enoch Train's* superstructure was removed and an arched roof of five-inch timber was constructed. Over this a layer of railroad iron three quarters of an inch to an inch thick was laid, and a heavy cast-iron prow was fitted below the water line. A single gun, operating through a sort of trap door, was mounted forward. When the job was completed, the new ironclad was fifteen feet longer, had a five feet wider beam, and four and a half feet greater draft than the *Enoch Train*. But for two smoke-stacks, the new vessel looked like a huge cigar.[1]

Although the whole operation was presumably clothed in secrecy, word of the "nondescript" soon began to get about. On July 11, the *National Intelligencer* in Washington carried a story that the Confederates at New Orleans had covered a powerful tugboat with railroad iron to attack the Federal blockaders at the mouth of the Mississippi. Lieutenant David D. Porter, who commanded the *Powhatan*, blockading Southwest Pass, had heard of the ironclad by July 19, for on that date he predicted to Flag Officer William Mervine that "there is no danger to be apprehended from the boat with the iron horn. She will likely never be finished, and if she is she won't come down here." About the same time, Kate Stone, on Brokenburn Plantation in northern Louisiana, recorded in her diary: "Mr. McGregor from New Orleans . . . was telling us the plan for blowing up the ship *Brooklyn* blockading the mouth of the river. The plan is to make a small tug entirely bomb and ball proof by covering her entirely with railroad iron corrugated, to run this little invincible right up to the ship, and to blow her up with a columbiad. It is a private enterprise but if successful the projector will receive a large sum from the government. I should not think they would live to come back."[2]

After the Confederate victory in Virginia, the ironclad got its name, *Manassas*, but already people in New Orleans were beginning to call it the "Turtle." As the summer wore on, the tales about the "Turtle" grew more fantastic. The *National Intelligencer*, quoting the New York *Commercial Advertiser*, relayed to readers in the Federal capital details about the "formidable instrument of destruction" being built at New Orleans. It told about the iron construction and the underwater ram, with a "formidable mass of iron . . . in the form of a knob." And then came awesome details of another frightful feature of the Confederate monster:

Beneath this knob, and beneath the surface of the water, two strong grapples have been arranged, so fashioned that upon colliding with a ship the claws will fasten into the sides of the vessel and take a firm hold. Protected by these grapples in a manner not unlike an insect's lance or sting, there projects an auger connected, by means of shafting, with an independent machine on the boat.

This instrument is intended to operate as follows: Upon the attachment of the grapples to the side of the attacked vessel, the auger will be set in rapid motion and bore its way into the side. When one hole has been forced through, the auger can be withdrawn, and, by means of an independent axle, the position will be changed so as to operate upon another portion of the ship; thus boring holes large enough to sink the vessel.

United States consul James H. Anderson in Hamburg forwarded to Washington early in September a description of the *Manassas* sent to an American in Hamburg from New Orleans, dated July 28. It read, in part:

The "Turtle" is a vessel of terrible engine power and construction . . . She is provided with a steam borer, or auger, about the size of a man's arm above the elbow, which, in a moment, bores a hole into the vessel. Twenty-five hose are kept to throw boiling water over the *Brooklyn* to keep all her hands from defending her. She is really a hellish engine . . .

Already several trials have been made with her, which have given complete satisfaction. Cannon balls of the size of a human head rebounded when fired upon her, producing no injurious effect. In fact, it is very difficult to hit her, she being very fast, and round, and so small a portion of her being above water. She is thoroughly protected by her iron coat.

This, of course, was a combination of imagination and misinformation, for it wasn't until about August 15 that the *Manassas* was launched in Algiers. And her trial run did not take place until almost a month later.[3]

Commodore Hollins, as a man of action, was impatient to make an attack on the Yankee blockaders and his plans were maturing when the *Manassas* was launched. He determined that the ironclad should be a part of his little fleet when he started down the river. But the *Manassas* was privately owned, and its owners had hopes of realizing much prize money by its use as a privateer against the Union blockaders.

Early in October, the blockaders had boldly sailed into the river and established themselves at the Head of the Passes, a broad and deep expanse of water fifteen miles from the bars. It was from the Head of the Passes that the river forked into its various routes to the Gulf, so by controlling the Head of the Passes, the blockaders had a much easier job to perform than by watching each of the several usable passes. The Federal vessels were thus concentrated at the small end of a funnel rather than scattered at the open end.[4]

Commodore Hollins stepped up his plans and decided to attack the blockaders at the Head of the Passes within the week. None of his preparations were broadcast, but they were soon generally well known in New Orleans and thereafter became "the engrossing theme of conversation on the streets." What did Hollins have to oppose the steam sloop-of-war *Richmond*, of 26 nine-inch guns, the *Vincennes* and the *Preble*, sailing sloops-of-war of 22 guns each, and the *Water Witch*, a steamer of 5 guns?

Hollins' little flotilla, which became known as the "mosquito fleet," consisted of the *McRae*, armed with six heavy rifled cannon and two howitzers; the *Ivy*, which carried a columbiad forward and a rifled gun aft; the *Calhoun*, Hollins' flagship which had two heavy guns; the *Tuscarora*, with an eight-inch columbiad forward and a rifled 32-pounder aft; the *Jackson*, with two long-range guns; and the cutter *Pickens*, with one eight-inch columbiad and four 24-pounder carronades.[5]

Commodore Hollins realized that he would be heavily outgunned by the blockaders; he simply had to have the ironclad *Manassas*, not just as a part of his flotilla, but as its most important unit. So he decided to seize her from her private owners. But just when Hollins seized the *Manassas*—at New Orleans before the expedition sailed, or at the forts as the time approached to attack—is not clear.

Alias the "Turtle"

James Morris Morgan, who was a midshipman on the *McRae* and a participant in the seizure of the *Manassas*, contributed a graphic picture of the episode in his memoirs, almost half a century later, but his narrative does not completely agree with contemporary newspaper accounts and it is possible that memory tricked him.

Morgan declared that the "patriotic owners" of the *Manassas* wanted to make a contract with Hollins for a large sum of money for every Federal vessel they would sink. Commodore Hollins' reply was to send over to the *Manassas* "a polite request" that the ram be turned over to him.

The answer from the *Manassas* was that Hollins "didn't have men enough to take her." The *McRae* then ranged alongside the ram and a boat was lowered. Lieutenant Warley ordered young Morgan to follow him into the boat and, accompanied by several seamen, they moved toward the *Manassas*. Morgan's story continues:

> On arriving alongside of the ram we found her crew lined up on the turtleback, swearing that they would kill the first man who attempted to board her. There was a ladder reaching to the water from the top of her armor to the water line. Lieutenant Warley, pistol in hand, ordered me to keep the men in the boat until he gave the order for them to join him. Running up the ladder, his face set in grim determination, he caused a sudden panic among the heroic crew of longshoremen who incontinently took to their heels and like so many prairie dogs disappeared down their hole of a hatchway with Mr. Warley after them. He drove them back on deck and then drove them ashore, some of them jumping overboard and swimming for it. With the addition of two fire rafts our fleet was now complete and we proceeded to the forts, where we anchored awaiting an opportunity to attack the enemy.

The *True Delta's* account of the incident said that the *Manassas* went down the river as a private enterprise, with agreement on board to a plan for everyone to share equally in whatever prizes the ram might gain. But at the forts, Commodore Hollins dispatched Lieutenant Warley to take possession of the "Turtle" in the name of the Confederate government. In vain did Captain Stevenson protest. Finally, with tears in his eyes, he resigned his command, and went ashore. Lieutenant Warley summoned the crew, read them his authority, and then informed the sailors that according to navy regulations and usage, all prize money gained would be divided among the entire fleet, whether won by the *Manassas* or any other vessels. This didn't suit the "Turtle's" crew, most of whom were out to turn an honest dollar while inflicting damage on the Yankee vessels. A dozen or so expressed immediate dissatisfaction and got their bags and left the *Manassas*. Lieutenant Warley, now in command of the ironclad ram, then secured volunteers from the other vessels in Hollins' little fleet to fill the vacancies.[6]

Commodore Hollins' expedition did not leave New Orleans in one group. On October 8, the *Ivy*, which had come up the river to be fitted with a rifle-gun, headed downstream again. It employed its early start to good advantage by harassing the blockaders at the Head of the Passes. The next day, Hollins sailed with the *Calhoun*, *Jackson*, and *Tuscarora*. The *Manassas* was to have left with Hollins, but it remained behind for emergency repairs. However, the "Turtle" was ready for action on the morning of October 10. At thirty minutes past noon, people thronged the Levee to see the ram "start on her destructive mission," and the crowd cheered enthusiastically as "she steamed down the river with fine speed."[7]

The entire city waited in a state of expectancy, hungry for word of a Confederate victory over the insolent Lincolnite blockaders. The departure of Hollins' "mosquito fleet" was of itself a tremendous morale lifter for New Orleans. It represented, at last, aggressive action against the blockading fleet after more than four months of astonishing passivity, while the commerce of the South's greatest city was suffocated.

Meanwhile, Captain "Honest John" Pope, who commanded the Federal blockaders at the Head of the Passes, began to panic a bit when the *Ivy* dropped down the river on the afternoon of October 9 and began peppering away at the Yankee ships, particularly his flagship, *Richmond*, and the *Preble*. As the *Ivy's* shot and shell passed 500 yards beyond the *Richmond*, while itself staying out of

range of the Federal guns, Captain Pope wrote a hasty dispatch to
Flag Officer W. W. McKean, commanding the Gulf Blockading
Squadron, declaring, "It is evident that we are entirely at the mercy
of the enemy. We are liable to be driven from here any moment,
and, situated as we are our position is untenable. I may be captured
at any time by a pitiful little steamer mounting only one gun." Pope
expressed the opinion that the *Ivy* was experimenting to get the
range of the Union vessels, "which they now have, and, of course,
will quickly avail themselves of the knowledge."

Despite his grave concern, Captain Pope did not take counsel
of his fears and place picket boats upstream to warn him of the
approach of Confederate vessels. Nor did he sit down and plan just
what he would do if Commodore Hollins did launch an attack on
the blockaders. When the attack did come, it came to Pope as a
surprise—"so suddenly that no time was left for reflection."[8]

Commodore Hollins, with his "mosquito fleet" and the *Manassas*
anchored under the guns of Fort Jackson, ready for action, decided
to attack Pope before daylight on the morning of October 12. He
called his officers together and unfolded his plan. The *Manassas*
would lead the way, and when contact was made with the enemy,
it would ram the most suitable target. Immediately after ramming
the enemy, the *Manassas* would send up a rocket, the signal for
the fire ships—three abreast, held together by cables—to be lighted.
Then Hollins' gunboats, particularly the *McRae, Ivy,* and *Tuscarora,*
would go into action.

The night was moonless and overcast, and Hollins cast off, with
no lights showing on the ships to disturb the pitch-black river.
Silently, but for the plop-plop of the paddle wheels, Hollins' little
fleet approached the unsuspecting blockaders, anchored at the Head
of the Passes, twenty miles below the forts. Aided by the five-mile
current, the *Manassas* outstripped the fleet, which followed in the
"Turtle's" wake in this order: first rafts, *McRae, Ivy, Tuscarora, Calhoun,* and *Jackson,* the last two in the rear because of the vulnerability of the former and the noisy exhaust of the latter.

Lieutenant Warley had as his first officer on the *Manassas* Charles
Austin, who knew every inch of the river. He piloted the ram him-

self, getting his view of the river through a four-inch opening in the forward hatch. The crew manifested no real fear, but on such a mission in an untried pioneer warship, the men could not but feel "the oppression of an awful suspense."[9]

Meanwhile, at the Head of the Passes, the *Richmond, Preble*, and *Water Witch* were anchored near the eastern bank while the *Vincennes* lay near the western shore, close to the head of Southwest Pass. A coaling schooner, the *Joseph H. Toone*, lay alongside the port side of the *Richmond*, while the watch on deck leisurely loaded coal. All was quite serene aboard the blockading vessels; no extra watch was kept, and no picket boats were out to sound the alarm should enemy ships loom suddenly out of the darkness.[10]

The *Manassas* was almost about to strike its prey before its presence was even hinted at. First Officer Austin himself was taken by surprise, as suddenly he discovered directly ahead the dim outline of a warship.

"Let her out, Hardy, let her out now!" he shouted to Engineer William Hardy, and the latter responded by throwing tar, tallow, and sulphur into the furnace to send the steam gauge to its highest point.

Just about this time, a midshipman on the *Preble* spotted the *Manassas* and dashed into the cabin of Commander French, awakening him with a shout: "Captain, here is a steamer right alongside of us." French, who had slept in his clothes, having been on deck much of the night, rushed from the cabin, noting through an open hole "an indescribable object not 20 yards distant."

It was 3:45 A.M. when the *Manassas'* iron nose struck the *Richmond* below the water line with the terrific impact of the speed of ten knots. Although the *Manassas* was discovered before it delivered the blow, the time interval was too short for any effective defense. And, indeed, Captain Pope was so taken by surprise that he had no immediate plan. He had the red danger signal flashed from the mast and ordered the entire port battery to open up on a target it could not see. The *Preble's* gun joined in a furious chorus. Meanwhile, the *Manassas*, having struck the *Richmond* abreast of the port fore channels, tore the coaling schooner away and forced a hole into the blockader's side. But the momentum of the blow was terrific for those on the *Manassas*, every man aboard being knocked down by the concussion. The ironclad "vibrated like an aspen." Austin ordered the engines reversed, and as the *Manassas* backed off, some of the crew heard distinct cries from aboard the *Richmond*:

"We're sinking!"

"She's going to blow up!"

"We're all lost!"

"Oh, my God!"

Bells clanged and foghorns sounded among the startled Yankee vessels as one by one they slipped their cables and got under way for Southwest Pass, in response to signaled orders from Captain Pope. First Officer Austin drew a bead on another vessel, this time the *Preble*, and sang out to Engineer Hardy again: "Now let her out, Hardy, and give it to her." But to the chagrin of Lieutenant Warley and all on board, Hardy reported that one of the *Manassas'* condensers had been broken by the shock, rendering one of the ship's two engines helpless. There was nothing for the *Manassas* to do but to circle away. It was then that the full blasts of the fire from the *Richmond* and *Preble* were directed at the ram. "Now the invulnerability of the *Manassas* was fairly tested," said a contemporary account of the action. ". . . The roar of the cannon was tremendous, and it seemed to those cooped up in the little ram as if all the thunderbolts of Jove were rained upon them."

In the heat of the action, the rocket which the *Manassas* was to fire to summon the rest of the fleet was not immediately fired. A midshipman, who had gone on top on the assignment, lighted the rocket, but in the excitement of the moment held on to the stick, so that the fire burned his hand and the rocket flew down the open hatch. Members of the crew, believing it to be an enemy shell, rolled over and piled into corners for protection. Relief overbalanced their sheepishness when they found out what it was.

All the Federal shots, except two or three, went over the *Manassas*, but one of them cut a smokestack cleanly away, and another shot knocked the remaining smokestack down over the vent of the first. Choking fumes from the tar, sulphur, and tallow the ram was burning soon spread through the *Manassas*, threatening to suffocate the crew. Despite the fact that enemy shells were still probing the darkness in search of the ram, something had to be done to cut away the wreckage. Engineer Hardy seized an ax and rushed up the companionway, brushing by Lieutenant Warley, who tried to stop him. First Officer Austin, realizing that Hardy could not stand securely on the ship's arched roof by himself and do the job, followed him up the ladder. While Austin held on to him, Hardy cut away the fallen chimney from its guys, opening the vent, "and the sulphurous smoke rushed out, just as those below were getting almost suffocated."

Meanwhile, the fire rafts were lighted and towed into action, but by the time they reached the scene, the *Preble*, *Vincennes*, and *Richmond* were moving down Southwest Pass in full retreat. The *Water Witch*, which behaved more admirably than the other Union vessels, avoided the rafts, which were blown ashore and harmlessly burned themselves out. With the prize schooner *Frolic* in tow, the *Water Witch* followed the other Federal warships down Southwest Pass as day began to break. At precisely the same time that all the Yankee vessels were hurrying down Southwest Pass, all of the Rebel vessels were moving upstream, and thus both forces were retreating from the scene of action.[11]

Captain Joseph Fry of the *Ivy*, who had had a hand in designing the *Manassas*, was considerably concerned for the ram during the firing. "My anxiety for the *Manassas* was intense," Fry wrote later. "I believed her calculated to run down a single vessel, not to sustain a cross-fire at a short distance directed at her sides. My delight was unbounded to see her slowly emerge from the smoke, an immense volume of it conveying the impression she herself was on fire. Her progress was so slow I was convinced she was crippled; but her commander declined my offer of assistance until she got aground. I then parted two lines in trying to get her off, and went in search of assistance."

Captain Fry discovered the *Tuscarora* also aground and was about to go to its assistance when the break of day revealed to him the Federal vessels in full flight down Southwest Pass. It occurred to Fry that in the daylight the Federals would realize the weakness of the attacking force and the *Richmond* might return to the Head of the Passes. So he started down the pass with the *Ivy* to engage the enemy until the *Manassas* and *Tuscarora* could get free.[12]

In the meantime, Captain Pope had signaled to the squadron to cross the bar, and the *Preble*, leading the way, cleared the barrier. The *Water Witch*, with the *Frolic* in tow, also made it across the sand bar. But the *Vincennes* stuck fast, its stern upriver, and almost immediately, the *Richmond* also ran aground, broadside.

Commander Robert Handy of the *Vincennes* dispatched a short note to Captain Pope on the *Richmond*: "We are aground. We have only two guns that will bear in the direction of the enemy. Shall I remain on board, after the moon goes down, with my crippled ship and worn-out men? . . . While we have moonlight would it not be better to leave the ship? Shall I burn her when I leave her?"

Captain Pope may have had moments of indecision when the *Manassas* rammed his ship, but he knew the right answers when he got Handy's message. He replied: "You say your ship is aground. It will be your duty to defend your ship to the last moment, and not to fire her, except it be to prevent her from falling into the hands of the enemy. I do not think the enemy will be down tonight, but in case they do, fight them to the last. You have boats enough to save all your men. I do not approve of your leaving your ship until every effort to defend her from falling into their hands is made."[13]

Meanwhile, before 8 A.M., Commodore Hollins returned to the Head of the Passes, and finding it free of the enemy, took possession of the coaling schooner and a cutter from the *Richmond* and some lumber which Pope had landed on the point of land between South Pass and Southwest Pass with the aim of setting up a battery to fire upstream. Hollins sent his little flotilla down Southwest Pass to engage the enemy, with the *Ivy* leading the way, followed by the *McRae* and the *Tuscarora*. A lively action followed, more noisy than damaging to either squadron. Confederate shells burst around the Federal ships, generally overshooting their mark, whereas the Union guns could not reach Hollins' vessels.[14]

During the furious exchange, Captain Fry of the *Ivy* had his clerk keep the score on the shots fired by the various vessels, and the report showed that the *Richmond* fired 107, the *Water Witch* 18, the *Vincennes* 16, the *Ivy* 26, the *McRae* 23, and the *Tuscarora* 6. Captain Fry claimed that some of the *Richmond's* salvos were fired after a white flag showed. He wrote:

> . . . A white flag was displayed by the *Richmond*. I was astonished beyond measure at this, and stopped my fire. Being in the presence of the commander-in-chief, I started to report the circumstances, when the flag was hauled down, the act being *preceded* by the discharge, as I believe, of an eleven-inch gun and her whole broadside. The only explanation of the flag to my mind was that the sloop-of-war being aground with her stern to us, the *Richmond* being also in the mud, they presumed our other steamers were armed with rifled cannon, and, being at our mercy, they meant to make an appeal to us to stay proceedings. When we started up the river, they fired their own broadsides, which appeared as if they had intended to decoy us within certain range of her guns . . .[15]

The *Vincennes* was unable to bring its broadsides to bear on the three Rebel gunboats during the fight because its nose was stuck fast on the bar. Commander Handy took down all the cabin bulkheads and ran two eight-inch guns out the stern port and fired away until the *Richmond* hoisted a signal, "Get under way," intended for the vessels outside the bar. But in some fantastic manner it was misread aboard the *Vincennes*. Seaman Nathaniel P. Allen, stationed on the poop deck to assist in signaling, was looking at the *Richmond* when he spotted the signal. "I . . . saw a flag—blue, white, blue— and I knew it to be No. 1 because I have studied the numbers on the paper inside the signal chest," he declared later in a sworn statement. Turning to the first lieutenant, Allen said: "The *Richmond* is signalizing," and added the signal was No. 1. The lieutenant looked into the signal book and then stepped up to Commander Handy: "It means to abandon ship." The seaman was ordered to answer the signal, which he did, and the *Richmond's* signal was hauled down.

Signal Quartermaster William Burrows of the *Vincennes* also said he saw a blue-white-blue flag and heard Seaman Allen report it. He saw the lieutenant look it up in the signal book and heard him tell Handy that it meant to abandon ship.

Handy was certain that he had been instructed to abandon his ship, a proposition which he had heartily favored from the moment the *Vincennes* had run up on the bar. He ordered a slow match to be put in the magazine and then gave the order to abandon ship. According to the log of the *Vincennes*, this was about 11:20 A.M. "Honest John" Pope's report, however, set the abandonment of the *Vincennes* at about "9 o'clock," at which time it was reported to him that several boats filled with men were leaving the *Vincennes*, some heading for the *Water Witch*, others for the *Richmond*. To his astonishment, "in a few minutes Commander Handy, with several of his officers, came on board, Commander Handy having wrapped around his waist in broad folds an American flag."

Pope asked Handy the meaning of this, and the latter replied that he had abandoned ship in obedience to Pope's signal. Pope insisted that no such signal had been sent. And Handy insisted right back that he had so read it and that he had lighted a slow match to the magazine. When, long past the time that the explosion should have come, nothing happened, Captain Pope ordered Handy to return with his men to the *Vincennes* and attempt once more to float her.[16]

By now, Commodore Hollins had called off his gunboats—to Captain Fry's disgust, because the *Ivy's* guns were then able "for the first time to hull the *Richmond* every time"—and was steaming proudly up to Fort Jackson, from where he telegraphed the dispatch which sent a thrill racing through New Orleans and, indeed, throughout the entire Confederacy.[17]

Commander Handy, still fearful that the Confederates might return and capture the *Vincennes*, asked Pope for permission to lighten the ship by tossing his guns and ammunition overboard, because "the vessel was of more value to the Government than the guns." Although he threw fourteen 32-pounders and all the shot for them, plus twenty-seven stands of grape, the *Vincennes* did not ease itself off the bar.

In this weird, fantastic incident, worthy of Gilbert and Sullivan treatment, a Union quartergunner stands out as the hero. He had followed Commander Handy's instructions to light a slow match to the magazine, but he didn't take the order too literally, for after he lighted the match, he immediately cut off the burning end and tossed it into the water. And so, in fact, there never was any danger of the *Vincennes'* being blown up.[18]

Captain Pope justified his actions as best he could. "My retreat down the Pass," he reported, "although painful to me, was to save the ships, by preventing them being sunk and falling into the hands of the enemy, and it was evident to me they had us in their power by the operation of the ram and the rafts. If I have erred in all this matter it is an error of judgment; the whole affair came upon me so suddenly that no time was left for reflection, but called for immediate action and decision." The commander of the *Richmond* regretfully informed Flag Officer McKean that "Handy is not fit to command a ship . . . He is a laughing stock of all and everyone," and stated that "everyone is in great dread of that infernal ram." To show that he had learned his lesson, Pope added: "I keep guard boats out up river during the night." But a few days later, because of reasons of health, Pope asked to be relieved of his command. Thus ended one of the oddest and most humiliating incidents of the Civil War—the incident which quickly became known as "Pope's Run."[19]

Meanwhile, New Orleans was thrown into a frenzy of delight when, late in the afternoon of October 12, newspaper extras and bulletin boards displayed a dispatch from Commodore Hollins dated at Fort Jackson at 2:30 P.M. It read: "Last night I attacked the blockaders with my little fleet, and succeeded, after a very short struggle, to drive them all aground on the Southwest bar, except the sloop-of-war *Preble*, which I sunk. I have captured a prize from them, and after I got them fast on the sand I peppered them well. No casualties on our side. A complete success."

People had scarcely talked about anything else, after Hollins' fleet went down the river, but the daring attack on the blockaders and the chances of its success. And now the news had come. "A general exultation and rejoicing pervades the city," wrote a young girl in her diary. T. K. Wharton, who had seen from the top of the Custom House the smoke of the gunfire at Southwest Pass, added a notation later when the news of the victory reached New Orleans: ". . . The joy here is intense."[20]

Hollins was serenaded by military bands at his headquarters in the St. Charles Hotel, and various military units paused to salute him as they marched past. A testimonial and a beautiful set of colors were presented to him by grateful citizens. A new company of volunteers called themselves the Hollins Guards. And Richmond rewarded the old sea dog by promoting him to the rank of flag officer.[21]

Hollins had reported sinking the *Preble*, and he did this on the assumption of Captain Fry of the *Ivy* that it was the *Preble* that the *Manassas* had rammed. "I . . . communicated to the flag officer . . . the intelligence of the *Manassas* having sunk the *Preble*, as it was not doubted she had gone down," Fry reported. But he was just guessing, and it wasn't a good guess. Later, on the authority of a doctor who had been taken aboard the *Richmond*, it was finally established that this was the Federal vessel that had been rammed.[22]

This called, of necessity, for a re-evaluation of the "great victory" for the Confederates at the passes. Hollins did not sink any Federal ships, and although his attack was humiliating to Union pride, it had no effect whatsoever on the blockade. The river was still closed tight, but the blockers henceforth did their blockading at the mouth of the passes, not returning again to the Head of the Passes. The important thing about Hollins' victory was its effect on morale in New Orleans. Here was something positive that had been done and it lifted the people out of the doldrums.[23]

7

Enter General Lovell

AS SOON AS THE NEW ORLEANS NEWSPAPERS REACHED BIVOUAC PLAN-
tation on Bayou Lafourche, Elise Ellis Bragg devoured them for
news of General Bragg and his forces at Pensacola. Whenever an
item seemed likely to be of interest to the general, she would pass
it on to him in her next letter. So it was, on October 13, that she
put down the *Delta* and began a letter to her husband: "Yesterday's
paper informs us that Captain Lovell—*Mansfield Lovell*, never
conspicuous that I am aware of, of doubtful attachment to our
cause, certainly *very slow* in joining us, has been raised to the same
rank as yourself & assumes this important command of two States!
While you are still confined to the petty province of Pensacola . . ."[1]

For reasons that probably went back to their days in the old
Army, perhaps even to the Mexican War, Braxton Bragg did not
hold Mansfield Lovell in high personal regard. And Mrs. Bragg
probably shared, or at least reflected, her husband's views. On
October 18, Mrs. Bragg wrote the general again: "Gen. Lovell has
not yet arrived. I presume he will make a great stir when he does
come. You know he is very fond of pomp and show."[2]

Actually, Major General Mansfield Lovell, C.S.A., had reached

New Orleans the previous day. Persons at the railroad station when the Jackson train came in marked his soldierly bearing as he descended from the car. Lovell, who reached New Orleans three days before his thirty-ninth birthday, was of average height with a trim, wiry physique. He had clear eyes and a drooping mustache, and his gait was that of a man in the prime of life and full of energy.

General Lovell received glowing press notices in New Orleans: "a man of much promise . . . remarkable for foresight, and exactly the general to calm the apprehensions and justify the hopes of the people to whose defenses he has been placed," and "able and accomplished" and possessed of "knowledge, experience, bravery and the unlimited confidence of the Government which has placed him here." What was the military background of the man Jefferson Davis had named a major general and picked to defend New Orleans?[3]

Mansfield Lovell was born in Washington on October 20, 1822. His father, Dr. Joseph Lovell, who had served as a surgeon during the War of 1812, had become Surgeon General of the United States Army. Orphaned at fourteen, he lived with a guardian in New York until a few months before his sixteenth birthday, when he was appointed to the Military Academy at West Point. He was graduated ninth in the class of 1842, one place below his friend and later associate, Gustavus W. Smith, who wrote of Lovell: "Gifted with fine physical, mental and social qualities, an independent and manly spirit made him prominent in a class remarkable for the number, ability and high character of its members."

Upon graduation Lovell was assigned to the Fourth Artillery, where he soon established himself "as one of the most promising young officers in the artillery." Serving under Zachary Taylor in the Mexican War, he was wounded at Monterrey. He later became chief of staff to General John Quitman and was at Quitman's side at the storming of the Belén Gate at Mexico City, suffering another wound as the city fell. Lovell was breveted to captain for his "skill and distinguished gallantry" in Mexico and that was the rank he held when he retired from the Army in 1854 to join General Quitman in the latter's projected Cuban expedition, which never materialized. Lovell, in the meantime, had married Emily M. Plympton, daughter of Colonel Joseph Plympton, and when the Cuban affair went up in smoke, he engaged in business pursuits in New York until 1858, when his old classmate Gustavus Smith, commissioner of streets in New York, invited him to become his deputy.[4]

Lovell and his friend Smith, a Kentuckian, were both sympathetic to the South when the Cotton States started the movement out of the Union after Lincoln's election. In January 1861, when Beauregard stopped in New York on his way to his brief tenure as Superintendent of West Point, he told Lovell and Smith that if Louisiana seceded he would follow it out of the Union. Both approved of Beauregard's proposed course and stated that if "they were similarly situated they would act in the same way."

Toward the end of February 1861, when President Jefferson Davis dispatched Captain Raphael Semmes to New York to buy arms, munitions, and ships, if possible, for the newly established Confederate States of America, he wrote Semmes: "Captain G. W. Smith & Captain Lovell, late of the U. S. Army and now of New York City, may aid you in your task; and you will please say to them that we would be happy to have their services in our army."[5]

A few days later, General Beauregard, writing from Montgomery to enlist Gustavus Smith's assistance in some purchasing, asked: "When shall we have the benefit of your services and those of Lovell?"

Smith's reply to Beauregard, after disposing of business, is revealing:

> You ask in your joint letter to Lovell and myself, "When may we expect your services?" &c. Neither he or I are citizens of the seceded states, but you know well what our views, opinions and sympathies are. . . . In a word, propositions from either Mr. Davis or his military representative, his Secretary of War, would, if up to our standard (as we understand it) be favorably considered and in all probability accepted. . . . But if L. and I are wanted we take for granted we will be invited.[6]

Sumter fell and the Union Army was routed at Manassas, but still Lovell and Smith retained their positions in New York. Meanwhile, General Joseph E. Johnston had recommended Lovell to President Davis as a competent division commander for the Confederate Army. It was not until September of 1861, however, that Lovell sold his house and other properties in New York and with his family made his way to Richmond, where he joined the Confederacy. He was appointed a brigadier general and assigned to New Orleans on September 25. Before Lovell was ready to leave Richmond, General Twiggs' resignation was accepted and Lovell was promoted to major general and appointed to command at New Orleans.[7]

Before leaving Virginia, Lovell went to Centreville to confer with his friend Beauregard about the situation at New Orleans. Beauregard told Lovell what he had told the authorities in Louisiana many months earlier: that steam vessels could run past Fort Jackson and Fort St. Philip unless the river was obstructed in a way to hold the enemy ships under the fire of the forts. As an experienced artillerist, Lovell agreed with Beauregard. The forts were established in the day of sailing vessels, which would have been sitting ducks to the gunners in the forts, as were indeed the British vessels which tried in 1815 to pass Fort St. Philip. But steam-powered gunboats were something else again, as both Lovell and Beauregard recognized.

In his final interview with President Davis, and later with Secretary of War Benjamin, before leaving Richmond, Lovell raised the question of his control over the Confederate naval units at New Orleans. As the commanding general of Department No. 1, which embraced the Confederacy's greatest city, Lovell felt that a unified command was the only way to defend New Orleans properly, and since he was responsible for its safety, he argued that he should dictate the use of all the available means of defense.

After Lovell left for New Orleans, both Davis and Benjamin became concerned over what the general's conception of his responsibilities was. On October 17, President Davis wrote General Lovell:

I am induced by the impression made on the mind of the Secretary of War, in a conversation which you had with him just before your departure, to write you on the subject of your relations to the officers of the navy. . . . The fleet maintained at the port of New Orleans and its vicinity is not a part of your command; and the purpose for which it is sent there, or removed from there, are communicated in orders and letters of a department with which you have no direct communication. It must, therefore, be obvious to you that you could not assume command of these officers and vessels coming within the limits of your geographical department, but not placed on duty with you, without serious detriment to discipline and probably injury to the public service.[8]

General Lovell was thus launched on his assignment with the feeling that the Richmond government had made his task all the more difficult by limiting his authority over all the available forces at New Orleans. However, this in no way affected the application of his energies to learning immediately just what the status of his department was. Lovell was appalled at what he found, and on the next day, October 18, he got off two letters to Richmond, one to President Davis and the other to Secretary of War Benjamin. To Davis, Lovell reported: "I arrived yesterday, and assumed command at once. I find great confusion, irresolution and want of system in everything administrative. Such executive work as has been confided to Major Smith has been faithfully done so far as it lay in the power of one man to do it. It will be a mountain of labor to put things in shape. The city has been almost entirely stripped of everything available in the way of ordnance, stores, ammunition, clothing, medicines &c. . . . Our main want at present is powder, and as so much of our defense is to depend upon heavy artillery, it will require a large stock for guns which consume 8 to 10 lbs. for each discharge. . . .

"Should you see in the New Orleans papers that we are well supplied with everything, you may regard it as a ruse. But every deficiency and want has been proclaimed from the housetops, until every boy in town knows just what we lack. This I may find it necessary to counteract by circulating contrary reports. You will always be advised of the *true condition* of affairs."

The fortifications below the city were nearly finished, Lovell reported, and those above New Orleans would be ready in two weeks. These he had already inspected, and the next two days he would spend visiting the defense east of New Orleans and on the opposite side of the river. He said New Orleans would "derive great benefit" from some eight- or ten-inch-shell guns mounted at the various forts to oppose northern gunboats under construction which would carry one or more guns of this description. "I do not like to call for them officially, unless I know they can be had, as it would be an unnecessary display of our deficiencies." Lovell stated that in order to keep state troops together and create some order and discipline, it might be necessary to muster them into Confederate service, even though he would have to rely on the shotguns and rifles of the people with which to arm them. In conclusion, Lovell said:

"But they will answer a good purpose behind entrenchments. I shall make the best shift I can, but if we can get some small arms, powder and money from the Government, within two weeks I should feel much relieved. Notwithstanding our deficiencies I have entire confidence in our ability to hold New Orleans against all comers."[9]

To Secretary of War Benjamin, General Lovell reiterated how New Orleans had "been greatly drained," and he asked that heads of bureaus be requested not to requisition anything else from New Orleans "until we have provided ourselves with a fair supply for the force required for the defense of this city." His two greatest needs, Lovell said, were an assistant adjutant general to do the paper work and saltpeter with which to manufacture powder. "While the first would greatly facilitate matters here," he said, "it is not indispensable—the latter is."[10]

A week later, after Benjamin had telegraphed that the War Department had sent within a month to New Orleans powder and saltpeter equivalent to 500 barrels of powder, Lovell wrote back that he had no correct returns of ordnance and ordnance store. Continuing, he said:

Admit, however, that we have 500 barrels. We have now at the various forts and approaches, two hundred and ten guns in position, and about one hundred more that we shall soon have in place; giving, in all, three hundred and ten guns, of the calibre of a twenty-four pounder, and upwards. The average charge, large and small, will be eight pounds for each gun, or two thousand four hundred and eighty pounds for a single piece round. Five hundred barrels contain fifty thousand pounds, which would give us twenty rounds per gun— not more than enough for an hour's fight. But the powder received from Memphis was quite worthless; more than thirty barrels invoiced to us have not arrived, and we loaned Com. Hollins the powder with which he made his attack on the vessels above the passes— We have, therefore, less than twenty rounds per gun. I am hurrying into operation two mills which will give us 6,000 or 8,000 pounds per day, if we can get the saltpetre . . .

The want of powder is our only glaring deficiency. I do not allow an ounce to be burnt unnecessarily, and am straining every nerve to add to our supply.

If I can get saltpetre, and the enemy will give us a few weeks, which I think he will do, we shall be pretty well prepared to defeat him. With one hundred rounds per gun, I should feel pretty safe."[11]

General Lovell's correspondence with Richmond in his first week in New Orleans shows how quickly and efficiently he sized up the situation, evaluating needs with the eye and knowledge of an experienced and energetic officer. Lovell's energy indeed was boundless, and after many hours spent in daily inspections of the various defenses of the city, he would return to his office to work at night as well.

During the first two weeks, the commanding general covered his department thoroughly. On the Mississippi Gulf coast, he found three regiments of troops badly armed and sorely in need of ammunition. One regiment had only enough ammunition to fire five rounds per man. He found the entrance to Pearl River unobstructed, as indeed, also, were entrances to all other inlets in the department. At the various forts, he found marked deterioration because of their having been unoccupied for so long. Forts Pike, Macomb, and Livingston were so dilapidated that in some places they were crumbling of their own weight.

At Fort Jackson and Fort St. Philip, below New Orleans, Lovell was impressed with what Colonel J. K. Duncan had done to put them in a state of preparation. But even here, he found the means necessary to make a proper defense sadly lacking. The ammunition was reported as so inferior as to give only half range to the guns. Lovell discovered that the all-important river obstruction at the forts, which he had discussed with Beauregard, was just about to be started.

In the environs of New Orleans, the fortifications, eight miles in total length, were still incomplete and not a gun was mounted, nor a magazine built. Lovell's inspection of the 100 old Navy guns which General Twiggs had received from Norfolk revealed that most of them were so worn as to be unfit for the friction tubes which were to fire them. Deficiencies in gun carriages, chassis, and gun implements—none of which had come with the guns from Norfolk—were rapidly being eliminated in the ordnance shops at the Custom House, where the technical skill of John Roy was much in evidence.[12]

This, then, was the state of things in New Orleans about November 1, 1861, more than nine months after Louisiana had seceded from the Union and six months after hostilities opened in Charleston Harbor. Despite Lovell's depressing appraisal, the New Orleans newspapers continued with optimistic reports of the city's state of affairs.[13]

Meanwhile, Lovell's appointment as a major general to command at New Orleans had stirred up considerable resentment in some quarters in Richmond. A clerk in the War Department in Richmond noted in his diary on November 1: "There is an outcry against the appointment of two major generals, recommended perhaps by Mr. Benjamin, Gustavus W. Smith and Gen. Lovell, both recently from New York. They came over since the battle of Manassas."

Brigadier General W. H. T. Walker, who had been transferred from the newly organized Louisiana Brigade so as to clear the way for President Davis' former brother-in-law, Colonel Dick Taylor of the 9th Louisiana, to become a brigadier general, bitterly denounced both Davis and Secretary Benjamin. But General Walker didn't stop there. In his indignant letter of resignation he brought General Lovell's name into the issue, complaining that Davis had promoted younger men over him: "Not content with putting my own *countrymen* over me, an office holder (Gen. Lovell, from New York City, who was there under pay of New York when our countrymen were gallantly fighting at Manassas and elsewhere) has been brought to the South and made Major-General . . ."

Most of the New Orleans newspapers printed General Walker's letter and made appropriate comments. The *True Delta* deplored Walker's "bad taste" and said that he was blinded by passion. It reminded its readers that many other Confederate officers were in the same category as "the distinguished officer . . . whose name is thus unkindly used." The paper saw no impropriety in President Davis' seeking out for the Confederacy good officers "who are recognized as being well disposed wherever they can be found, irrespective of birth place or connection . . ." The *Delta* declared Walker's letter had created among the public a false impression concerning General Lovell. But kindly words are frequently far from successful in wiping out erroneous impressions, and it is certain that General Lovell, almost from the very beginning of his command in New Orleans, was faced by a degree of public suspicion.[14]

That some of this doubt existed in high places, even as high as the governor of Louisiana, is quite possible. At any rate, Governor Moore received during the first two weeks of November three letters from General Braxton Bragg, who made no attempt to conceal his dislike and distrust of Lovell. The first letter was a copy of one Bragg had written Secretary Benjamin on behalf of Brigadier General Daniel Ruggles, who was irked by the fact that several younger officers, lately appointed, outranked him. Bragg said that when Ruggles was assigned to New Orleans it was hoped that the cause of Ruggles' complaint would be removed.

The day after General Bragg penned his lines to Benjamin, undercutting Lovell in Richmond, he wrote to Governor Moore with undisguised contempt for Lovell and with personal resentment that he had been given the command Bragg really wanted. "How do you get along with your new fledged Major General fresh from the lecture room of New York where he has been up to July instructing the very men he will have to oppose soon?" inquired Bragg. "I had confidence in him at one time but he forfeited it all by asking a price before he would come and when it was offered waited to see who was strongest or likely to succeed." Bragg contrasted Ruggles' actions with Lovell's, declaring that the former, a Massachusetts man, had promptly joined the Confederacy and "sacrificed all, commission, kin, property, all." Then Bragg gave words to the actual thoughts that had been on his mind for some time, ever since Lovell's appointment was announced: "The command at New Orleans was mine. I feel myself degraded by the action of the Government . . . Had the command been organized under proper hands three months ago, you would now be impregnable. As it is, I tremble for my home."[15]

Although Governor Moore may have privately made reservations concerning Lovell after receiving Bragg's letters, he seems to have kept an open mind regarding the commanding general. At any rate, if Bragg's criticism occupied the governor's thoughts for a time, there is no evidence that he ever actually questioned General Lovell's ability, capacity, and energy. And Governor Moore had almost daily opportunity to evaluate the general at first hand.

The "restless activity" of the department commander was noted and discussed by New Orleanians as Lovell worked day and night to make up the deficiencies which should have been taken care of months before he arrived. When his request to Colonel Josiah Gorgas, Confederate Chief of Ordnance, for ten-inch mortars and columbiads brought the reply: "None to spare at present," Lovell addressed himself to Braxton Bragg at Pensacola, with the same result. He then went to Leeds and Company and other New Orleans foundries and induced them to set up facilities to cast guns and also to manufacture shot and shell. He blockaded bayous and inlets which offered avenues of approach to New Orleans and completed telegraphic communication lines between the city and all points on the outer defense line from Fort Pike on the Rigolets to Brashear City on Berwick Bay. He set up a cartridge manufactory and got permission to use half of the new Marine Hospital for an arsenal. He constructed a rail link between the Pontchartrain Railroad and the Mexican Gulf Railroad, which would facilitate the movement of troops if the enemy effected a landing at Proctorsville on Lake Borgne. He secured chains and anchors to strengthen the barrier across the Mississippi at Forts Jackson and St. Philip.

The *Picayune* noted the new tempo of activities at headquarters and said that "Major Gen. M. Lovell is indefatigable, and his activity was fortunately infused in all the branches and numerous ramifications of his department."

An extra burden was thrown on Lovell, because Brigadier General Daniel Ruggles, who had arrived in New Orleans about the same time as the department commander, had become severely ill, and it was some weeks before he was able to assume any duties. In the meantime, Lovell had been much impressed with Colonel Johnson Kelly Duncan's efficient operations at Fort Jackson and Fort St. Philip. He wrote to President Davis urging strongly that Duncan be promoted to brigadier general. "He is worth a dozen of Ruggles," said Lovell, "and has rendered most efficient service, with a zeal, untiring industry, and ability which entitle him to your high consideration." He added that with more rank Duncan could assist him in organizing the department, "and I can assure you that help would not be unacceptable, as I have to keep driving all day and frequently the larger part of the night."[16]

8

The Tifts Build a Warship

A MONTH BEFORE GENERAL LOVELL TOOK COMMAND AT NEW ORLEANS, two strangers arrived in town from Richmond and began looking for a shipyard in which to build an ironclad warship. They were brothers, Nelson and Asa F. Tift, and they had just convinced Secretary of the Navy Stephen R. Mallory and a board of naval officers that their novel design for a warship had unusual merit.

The plan belonged to Nelson. He was a Georgia planter who early in the war hit upon the idea of constructing a warship out of ordinary pine timber and so designed that house carpenters instead of ship carpenters could build it. The reason this could be done was that there was no framing and no curves; all the surfaces of Nelson Tift's vessel were flat, or in straight lines, except the four corners that connected the two ends of the ship with the sides.

Being neither an engineer nor a shipbuilder, Nelson Tift discussed his proposed vessel with his brother Asa, whose many business interests included a ship-repair yard in Key West, Florida. He studied Nelson's plan for a warship and the model he had constructed and gave his warm approval.

The Tifts decided to go to Richmond and offer the vessel to their friend, and sometime business associate of Asa, Secretary Mallory. This they did in August 1861, stopping on the way to Richmond at Savannah and Charleston, where naval and military men to whom they exhibited the model approved heartily of the idea. So, too, did Secretary Mallory and the board of naval officers which he convened to examine the model and study the plans.[1]

Here, indeed, was not only a warship which would be built upon new principles but one that would be the greatest warship in the world. It was to be 260 feet in length with a beam of 58 feet and a hold of 15 feet. Its tonnage was to be 4000 and its speed 14 knots. Its iron sheathing would make it impregnable to any shot that could be fired at it, and its armament of twenty heavy guns would give it the most formidable firepower of all the warships afloat. An amazing innovation, designed many decades before its adoption in the modern American Navy, was the use of three separate engines, each driving a single propeller.[2]

On August 26, the Tifts made a generous proposal to Mallory: ". . . to give to the government the use of the invention and to superintend and direct, as your agents, the construction and completion of one or more such vessels, without pecuniary compensation from the government for our services, or any other reward than that which every citizen must feel who can, in any way, contribute to the defence of our country."

Should Mallory accept the offer, the Tifts wanted officers appointed to co-operate with them in the early and economical construction of this vessel. Mallory did not delay very long in accepting. He entered in his diary on September 1: "I have concluded to build a large warship at N. Orleans upon Nelson Tift's plan, & will push it." He matched those last words with action, for he got off a telegram the next day to Commodore Hollins in New Orleans instructing him to inquire as to costs, and time to manufacture them, of three high-pressure engines, three propellers of 11-foot diameter, and ten boilers. Hollins turned the telegram over to the indefatigable John Roy at the Custom House, and the latter sent a circular request for bids to the various machine shops and foundries in town.[3]

The Tifts received their instructions from Mallory on September 5, and they arrived in New Orleans on the 18th to build the *Mississippi*, the most formidable warship in the world.

Two days after their arrival in New Orleans, the Tifts were introduced by Commodore Hollins to John Roy, who recorded that he drove with the Tifts to the various foundries and machine shops with which they might have dealings, and "gave them all the information I could."[4]

More than that, the astute Roy pointed out a glaring error in the assigned boiler capacity for the vessel. Roy studied the boiler and horsepower data, did some rapid figuring, and showed the Tifts that the *Mississippi* required ten times the heating surface they had planned for it. They said that they had gotten their information from the engineer of the Navy Department, but they nevertheless accepted Roy's correction without any hesitancy. They wrote Secretary Mallory that the changes would necessarily increase the cost of the *Mississippi*, "but the efficiency of the vessel will be greatly increased by her greater steaming power, and she can carry two more heavy guns." Secretary Mallory approved.[5]

The Tifts wasted no time in getting started on the *Mississippi*. At first they tried to have the hull of their vessel constructed in one of the New Orleans shipyards, all of which were in Algiers, on the west side of the river across from New Orleans. But this would require transporting the timber across the river, an operation both delaying and expensive. And so the Tifts looked about for a suitable site and found exactly what they needed in Jefferson City, just above the New Orleans city limits. It was a tract of about four acres, right on the river, belonging to a wealthy property owner named Laurent Millaudon, who offered the Confederate government the use of his property until February 1, by which time the Tifts were confident that the *Mississippi* would be in operation against the blockaders.

The Tifts worked day and night to get their shipyard ready to begin work on their warship. Within ten days of their arrival, they had secured the land, purchased a steam engine and a sawmill, prepared blacksmith shops and carpenter shops, purchased some timber and contracted for more, and had let a $45,000 contract to Jackson and Co., of the Patterson Iron Works, to complete all the ship's steam machinery in ninety days, with a $5000 bonus if they came within that time.

The Tifts discovered that the Confederate government's credit was none too good in New Orleans, mainly because the Navy had been slow in paying in a number of transactions. In their first progress report to Mallory, in which they set forth their considerable accomplishments in ten days in New Orleans, the Tifts lectured the Secretary of the Navy mildly on payments of official debts.[6]

On September 27, the Tifts were joined by Joseph Pearce, acting naval constructor, who was assigned by Secretary Mallory to superintend the construction of the *Mississippi*. Pearce, whose chief responsibility was the construction of the hull, preparatory to putting on the iron, brought twenty ship carpenters with him from Richmond. In less than three weeks, everything was in readiness to start and, a foundation for the ship having been built, the first timber was laid on October 14.

Two weeks later, the Tifts reported to Mallory only "tolerable progress," blaming a lack of timber for preventing them from working as many men as they wished. They expected the lumber situation to improve within a week, but in the meantime work on the boilers and machinery was well under way. "We think that the boilers will be completed within two weeks, and will not delay the vessel. The engines will also be done we think in good time." They inquired of Mallory whether they could get flat iron to cover the *Mississippi* or should make preparations for covering it with railroad T iron. And they discussed the very important question of the shafts for the vessel, stating that they hoped to get the three nine-inch shafts in New Orleans, the middle shaft of 50 feet and the two side shafts of 40 feet each. But they told Mallory "to reserve the shafts you wrote of, to be used as a last resort." Mallory had suggested that the *Mississippi's* central shaft could be salvaged from another vessel in the vicinity of Richmond and that it could be reworked to specifications at the Tredegar Works in the Confederate capital. In the end, the Tifts had to depend upon Tredegar to produce the middle shaft; the other two were prepared in New Orleans.[7]

Meanwhile, another shipyard had been established immediately adjoining the shipyard of the Tifts, and work had begun on a second large warship for the Confederate Navy. On the same day that the Tifts reached New Orleans, Secretary Mallory signed a contract with E. C. Murray, a Kentuckian, to construct in New Orleans a 264-foot ironclad with a 62-foot beam to be known as the *Louisiana*. Whereas the Tifts had no boatbuilding experience, Murray came to Mallory with high recommendations as a boatbuilder and contractor with twenty years' experience and some 120 steamboats and sailing vessels to his credit.

The contract called for the *Louisiana* to be finished and turned over to the Confederate Navy by January 25, 1862, a little more than four months after the signing of the agreement. The total cost to the Confederacy was to be $196,000, paid in six installments of $24,500 each and a final payment of $49,000 on delivery of the vessel. There was a bonus-penalty clause: for every day earlier than January 25, 1862, that the *Louisiana* was finished, Murray was to receive $98, and for every day later, he was to be penalized $98. In case of unavoidable delays in receipt of materials, the penalty clause would not be invoked. Any rise above $60 per ton for iron would be assumed by the Navy Department.

Murray hurried to New Orleans, eager to get under way with his warship. Upon arrival he contracted for 1,700,000 feet of lumber and purchased the steamer *Ingomar* with the purpose of transferring her machinery to the *Louisiana*. He contracted for two propellers and two propeller engines and bought 500 tons of railroad iron at $65 a ton from the Vicksburg and Shreveport Railroad. He acted with such rapidity that, although the Tifts had had several weeks' start, Murray was able to begin work on the *Louisiana* on October 15, the day after the first timbers of the *Mississippi* were laid.[8]

Progress was satisfactory for two or three weeks. But on November 6 all the ship carpenters in New Orleans went out on strike for a $1.00-a-day increase in their $3.00 wages. This caused work stoppage not only on the *Louisiana* and *Mississippi* but on every other war vessel under construction in New Orleans, of which there were several in Algiers and on Bayou St. John, north of the city.

All the carpenters except the twenty workmen from Richmond

laid down their tools at the *Mississippi,* but Murray was able to induce the men working on the *Louisiana* to stay on the job, promising them that if wages were increased to $4.00 or $5.00 a day as a result of the strike, he would meet the raise. However, the next day, forty or fifty strikers appeared at the shipyard and forced the Richmond men to knock off on the *Mississippi.* The Tifts hastened to the authorities, and several ringleaders among the strikers were arrested.

Meanwhile, the strikers, their number increased to five or six hundred, threatened the carpenters on the *Louisiana* that if they did not quit working they would throw their tools into the river. Appeals to the strikers were fruitless. Their leaders said that they would go into the Army or serve the Confederacy some other way but they would not return to the shipyards for less wages than they demanded.

The strike did not meet with sympathy in New Orleans. The *True Delta,* usually a ready friend of labor, stated, on the fifth day of the strike: "This affair is becoming a serious matter. We will, as true chroniclers of public sentiment, tell our friends, the mechanics, engaged in this affair, that there is but one opinion with the public on the matter, and that is adverse to their actions at this time."[9]

The New Orleans shipbuilders were unanimous in favor of not meeting the carpenters' demands, and wanted to hold off until necessity compelled the men to return to work. But the Tifts and Murray, with urgency constantly being pressed upon them by Secretary Mallory, had other ideas.

"What do you propose to do?" Asa Tift asked the shipyard operator, Hughes.

"I can force these men back to work without the increase, if you don't interpose," replied Hughes.

"How long will it take?" inquired Tift.

"Two years ago there was such a strike as this," said Hughes. "The employers refused to allow the increase and finally the strikers came back."

"But how long did it take?" queried Tift.

"Six weeks," answered Hughes.

Tift agreed not to do anything for a couple of days. "We cannot wait any longer than that," he stated.

After six precious days were lost, with no work whatever on either the *Mississippi* or *Louisiana*, the Tifts and Murray decided that they could no longer let money stand in the way of pushing the work on the two ironclads. Accordingly, they agreed to the $1.00 increase in wages for the carpenters and work was resumed on the two vessels on November 12.[10]

Just about this time, in the face of mounting criticism of the Confederate Navy Department in the New Orleans press, Flag Officer Hollins purchased two steamboats, the *Grosse Tête* and the *Lizzie Simmons*, to add to his little flotilla of six improvised gunboats and six launches, all of which had a total of only thirty-seven guns.

Two floating batteries, the *New Orleans* and *Memphis*, constructed from dry docks, were being fitted out with twenty and eighteen guns respectively. Still on the ways in an Algiers shipyard was the *Livingston*, which was to carry six guns, while on Bayou St. John the *Bienville* and *Carondelet*, each also to carry six guns, were nearing completion. Also available to Hollins were two three-gun revenue cutters, the *Pickens* and the *Morgan*.

The floating batteries were the cause of considerable comment in New Orleans, and frequent mention of them appeared in the newspapers in the fall of 1861. General Twiggs, in August, had obtained authority from Richmond to convert two of the floating docks at New Orleans into batteries and work had commenced early in September. As the work progressed on the *New Orleans*, the first of the two floating batteries, enthusiasm mounted over their formidability. Thomas K. Wharton took particular pride in the floating battery, because the chassis and carriages for the guns were being constructed in his Custom House shops under the direction of John Roy. He visited the battery almost daily, taking visitors on occasion, and he duly noted the progress in his journal. On October 24 he recorded that the floating battery "will be ready immediately for active service." Two days later he "found it rapidly perfecting her armament" and declared: "She and her consort will be amply sufficient to keep every Lincolnite war ship out of our River."

The confidence that Wharton inscribed in his journal was matched in the public prints. The *True Delta* remarked the throngs that were drawn to the wharf to see the "formidable affair," which it characterized as "something in the way of improvised naval architecture that bids fair to awaken the echoes of the delta swamps and startle the alligators from their sense of propriety . . . The new monster . . . will be placed in charge of some volunteer company, who are expected to do wonders with her."

The public was permitted to inspect the *New Orleans* during the final stages of its completion, and on Sunday, November 17, a reception was held for the benefit of the Free Market. Thousands of people visited the floating battery and contributed $307.70 to the worthy cause. This marked the last time that the floating battery could be visited, because it was now ready for service up the river. Lieutenant John J. Guthrie commanded the floating battery and its complement of nine officers and a crew of about twenty-five. Shortly thereafter the *New Orleans* was towed up the river to Columbus, Kentucky, to join in the defense of the upper river, where the Fighting Bishop, Major General Leonidas Polk, was in command of Confederate military forces. The *New Orleans* reached Columbus on December 11.[11]

In the meantime, Flag Officer Hollins had also taken his mosquito fleet up the river, along with the ram *Manassas*, to join the Confederate forces at Columbus, where a Federal amphibious attack was momentarily expected. Thus it was that by the end of November 1861 New Orleans was bereft of Confederate naval forces except for those vessels on the ways—*Louisiana, Mississippi, Livingston, Bienville, Carondelet*—and the *Grosse Tête* and *Lizzie Simmons*, which were being converted into gunboats named *Maurepas* and *Pontchartrain* respectively. There was also the second floating battery, the *Memphis*, which was nearing completion in Algiers.[12]

Confederate authorities in Richmond, Secretary Mallory especially, were obsessed with the idea that the real threat to New Orleans was from upriver and not from the Gulf. The New Orleans newspapers directed sharp criticism at Mallory for not having provided naval vessels to break the blockade at New Orleans.[18]

By this time, however, New Orleans had at last awakened to the fact that it ought to start doing something itself to break the blockade and open the port to commerce. On October 27, the *Delta* reported that "some of our wealthiest and most public spirited citizens" contemplated building a fleet of ironclad vessels to be used exclusively in defending New Orleans and in raising the blockade. It continued: "It is proposed to effect a subscription of $2,000,000, and with that sum construct ten steamships . . . It is contemplated . . . to tender them to the Confederate government for the war, with the condition that they shall be employed at the mouth of the Mississippi River or in the neighboring waters of the Gulf."

Less than two weeks later, the *Crescent* reported that talk on the Exchange was lively on the subject of raising two and a half million dollars for the building of warships for New Orleans. On November 7, the Board of Assistant Aldermen passed a resolution appropriating $500,000 to build ironclads if the merchants of the city would put up $1,000,000 for the same purpose.

"Will our banks and capitalists now second practically and promptly the patriotic and enlightened action of the Board of Assistants, by taking double or treble the desired amount, which they can do without feeling it to the extent of a feather's weight?" inquired the *Commercial Bulletin*. "Will they do it, and do it without further delay?"

The *Picayune*, warmly supporting the appropriation and urging the Board of Aldermen to hasten to pass the measure of the Board of Assistants, called upon the Confederate government, the state of Louisiana, and the city of New Orleans to "fully come up to the requisitions of the exigency." It may be safely said that the *Picayune* reflected the general opinion of the man in the street in New Orleans at this time, when the commerce of the city had been choked out of existence by the six-month blockade of the mouth of the Mississippi.

These were fine, brave actions, but they should have been started back in June, when the blockade was begun in earnest.

In mid-December, the Louisiana legislature got around to considering an appropriation to build a navy to defend the state. Two bills, one for $1,000,000 and the other for $2,500,000, were introduced in the Senate. The first bill ultimately passed in the upper chamber but was defeated in the House of Representatives, presumably as a needless expenditure.[14]

The Confederate Navy's resources in New Orleans were negligible almost to the point of nonexistence when Lieutenant Beverly C. Kennon was assigned to the city. Kennon, an old Navy man, was an energetic individual who spurned rules and regulations as so much entangling red tape, which prevented things from being accomplished. Commodore Hollins assigned him to the ordnance department about August 1, and Kennon had a real job on his hands because there was no ordnance in New Orleans to take charge of and no preparations had been made for manufacturing anything. When the *McRae* was commissioned there were no cartridge bags for it and Kennon had to have them made.

Working without any assistance, and under trying conditions, for the facilities for manufacturing items for the Navy were scattered all over New Orleans, Kennon accomplished wonders. He made models for shells and shell shot; he had shells made for muskets and Mississippi rifles; he caused hand grenades, filled with guncotton and Greek fire, to be manufactured; he invented and had manufactured liquid shells for rifles and other guns. Kennon ordered guns to be cast and made extensive purchases of block tin, zinc for powder tanks, flannel for cartridge bags, and that very precious commodity, powder, at highly favorable prices. He made submarine batteries and proved their effectiveness by blowing up a scow in Lake Pontchartrain. But Lieutenant Kennon made one grievous error. He bought most of these articles without authority to do so, and this brought down upon his head charges from Richmond of reckless extravagances. When Kennon's expenditures and purchases contracted for approached a million dollars, it was too much for Secretary Mallory and he ordered Kennon out of New Orleans.

The *True Delta* got wind of this, and on November 1, under the heading "Let Well Enough Alone," it voiced its disbelief that the Navy would remove Lieutenant Kennon, whose "service as an officer and head of the ordnance department . . . has been a steady theme of commendation of all citizens who honor efficient service unobtrusively performed." Pointing out the necessity of Kennon's staying on the job, the *True Delta* expressed the hope that Commodore Hollins "will energetically protest against such a deprivation as the removal of so accomplished an officer at this time would be." Kennon got Hollins' permission to stay on; in fact, he got Hollins' repeated permission to remain in New Orleans and continue the ordnance operation, in the face of repeated orders for him to leave New Orleans. Finally, the sixth or seventh time that Secretary Mallory ordered him off the job, Kennon left New Orleans on November 28.

Some of Kennon's purchases, deemed extravagant by Mallory and his Navy Department advisers, were, in fact, extremely sound in the light of rising prices. Speculators in New Orleans were not above buying up strategic articles needed by the Confederacy and later offering them at extortionate prices. Secretary Mallory was quite irked when Kennon paid 30 to 40 cents a yard for flannel, which later sold for $2.00 to $2.50 a yard. Zinc, which he purchased at 20 cents a pound, went up to 87 cents, and block tin, for which he paid 25 cents, later soared to $5.00 a pound.

Kennon went to Richmond, where he found himself much in disfavor. He was reassigned to serve on the navy school ship *Patrick Henry* under men whom he outranked, and refusing to do this, he resigned his commission in the Confederate Navy.

Lieutenant R. D. Minor, who had been sent from Richmond to investigate the ordnance situation in New Orleans, reported on December 2 that "Lieut. Kennon has collected a large amount of stores, and deserves credit for his energy in doing so, but from what I can ascertain the prices charged by those who have furnished them is very high, and, in some instances not only exorbitant, but out of all proportion." The Navy Department seemed disposed to accept the implication of extravagance on Kennon's part and ignored his energy and ingenuity in creating an ordnance stockpile where not the semblance of one existed before.[15]

Meanwhile, the ship carpenters had returned to work after the six-day strike, and more than 200 of them were engaged on the *Mississippi*. The naval constructor, Joseph Pearce, was extremely pleased at the progress, for in thirty days the body was made and the floor put into the vessel. And thirty days after that, the *Mississippi* was three feet high. The Tifts, too, seemed satisfied with the way the work was going, for on November 21 they reported to Secretary Mallory as follows: "We are progressing very well with our structure; today we will complete the fourth streak of timber all around, and the next week we will have the sides up to eight feet. We fasten, caulk, paint, and finish perfectly as we advance."

Expenses on the *Mississippi* up to this time had reached $78,-226.73, the Tifts told Mallory. Progress was such that on December 6 the Tifts wrote Mallory that they expected the *Mississippi* to be ready by February 1. Optimism was still expressed on December 26, when they informed the Secretary of the Navy that they had begun that day to lay down the gun deck. "We shall make rapid progress until the structure is completed."[16]

Work on the *Louisiana* went on, but not without some annoying delays in the delivery of lumber and of the railroad iron, with which the sides were to be sheathed. In the latter instance, Murray waited two weeks for the iron after he was ready to put it on.

Although the citizens of New Orleans were quite conscious of the fact that two giant ironclad war vessels were being built in adjacent Jefferson City, nothing beyond veiled hints about either vessel got into the newspapers until the Algiers *News Boy* scooped the city dailies with a fairly accurate description of the *Mississippi*. The *Delta*, on November 29, quoted the Algiers *News Boy* at length, much to the disgust of the *Crescent*, which said:

"Our contemporary in Algiers has given a full description of the shipyards at Jefferson City which have been copied by our city papers, so that the Hessians will know all about the great vessel in the course of progress. It does not make much difference, as the Yankees spies are no doubt among us. . . ."[17]

9

☆ ☆ ☆ ☆ ☆

New Orleans Awaits Invasion

THROUGHOUT THE SUMMER AND EARLY AUTUMN OF 1861, NEW ORLEANS had viewed the blockade with a complacency that is incredible when one considers that the Mississippi River was the city's commercial life line. New Orleans had geared its thinking, generally, to the Confederate philosophy that King Cotton would eventually bring England and France, but especially England, around to recognizing the South's independence. For months and months, many people expected British warships to appear off the mouth of the river and raise the northern blockade. And although nothing of the sort happened, New Orleans still held itself in a state of expectancy regarding foreign intervention on behalf of the Confederacy.

But as the winter approached and articles became even scarcer, as prices soared and money became tighter than ever, people began to complain, and the complaints soon found their way into print.

"Let us confess it frankly, we have not here, in New Orleans, made exertions such as the occasion called for and as opportunities favored, in respect to the relief of the vast commercial interests centered in and radiating from this city," admitted the *Delta*. The *Commercial Bulletin* also called on New Orleans to do something in its own behalf. The Algiers *News Boy*, chiding New Orleans for its "do-nothing policy," pointed out that other southern cities had done much in their own behalf.[1]

People began to complain of the high prices, all the more unbearable with the trade and commerce at a standstill and money hard to come by. Soap which formerly sold for $5.00 for a forty-pound box was selling for $19, and flour was going at $20 a barrel. Prices of medicines mounted, and quinine and other drugs were frequently stolen and offered for sale at fantastic prices. Coffee went to $1.00 a pound—various substitutes or "lengtheners" were used abundantly—and a single candle cost twenty cents. Ice was so scarce that the *Picayune* reported signs in some barrooms reading: "Gentlemen will refrain from eating ice left in the glass after drinking." The milliners and dressmakers of the city were thrown into a state when it became known that there was a shortage of pins. And a shortage of newsprint caused some of the papers to reduce their size and others to prepare for such an eventuality. Other shortages provoked some amusing comments, such as the *Picayune*'s on the scarcity of pomades, scented soaps, perfumes, essences, hair oils, and other articles of daily use by well-groomed ladies and gentlemen:

> The persons most cruelly affected by this state of things, are perhaps those who use hair dyes. . . . When the four districts of the city are thrown into the greatest excitement by the painful report that there is not a single bottle of dye stuff left in any shop, all those disguised denizens will turn up, like so many ghosts, and surprise us with their white locks and gray beards, looking for the first time, just as old age, cares, dissipation, sickness or hard work have made them . . .[2]

Not averse to turning an honest dollar or two, even at the expense of the city's safety, speculators bought up articles and materials needed for defense purposes and jumped the price tags exorbitantly. One glaring instance was publicized by the Algiers *News Boy* and reprinted by the *Picayune*. When it became known that a long heavy chain was required by the military authorities and that there was in New Orleans no such chain, "an eminent and patriotic house . . . whose names are found on all patriotic donations lists" procured a chain of the required size and length in Mobile for five cents a pound, delivered in New Orleans. "It was then offered to the Government at the modest price of 15 cents a pound—only two hundred per cent profit on iron." Shortly after his arrival, Lovell had reported to President Davis that speculators were endeavoring to secure materials needed by the government. "The first operation I can fix on them," he wrote, "I shall publish their names to the community."[3]

Money was tremendously tight in New Orleans in the fall of 1861. A friend of a northern Louisiana planter wrote that he had tried in vain for two days to raise money but gave it up and that a friend had tried without success to borrow $2000 for 30 days, offering 7 per cent interest and collateral double the value of the note. "Merchants tell me that such times have never been seen here, it exceeds even 1837, and growing worse . . . A great many houses have already suspended and if times don't get better pretty soon others will have to follow. The papers are careful and don't speak of the number that have suspended . . ."

Small coins practically disappeared from circulation and coffee-houses and saloons and even merchants issued change in the form of tickets good in trade. These were put into circulation, as were tickets for the new streetcar system, and they soon acquired the picturesque name of shinplasters. George W. Cable, who was a boy in New Orleans during the Civil War, wrote of shinplasters: "The current joke was that you could pass the label of an olive oil bottle, because it was greasy, smelt bad, and bore an autograph—Plagniol Frères, if I remember rightly. I did my first work as a cashier in those days, and I can remember the smell of my cash drawer yet. Instead of five-cent pieces we had car-tickets. How the grimy little things used to stick together! They would pass and pass until they were soft and illegible with grocers' and butchers' handling that you could tell only by some faint show of their original color what company had issued them. Rogues did a lively business in 'split tickets,' literally splitting them and making one ticket serve for two."

On all sides there were calls for abatement of the shinplaster nuisance, and doubtless among the voices raised against them was that of the divine who, according to the *True Delta*, "took up a collection in church, last Sunday, for the purpose of distributing temperance tracts and was appalled to find the contribution plate full of tickets for drinks, representing every coffee house in the city."[4]

New Orleans, which began hunting spies immediately after secession, was still at it in the fall. "It is high time that we looked about us," said the *Picayune*, "and knew who is among us." There were still numerous cases of persons being committed to jail as "dangerous and suspicious characters," or "using incendiary language and being an Abolitionist." An old fisherman was jailed on suspicion of "having a little too much to do with the Lincolnitish fleet outside."[5]

When a ban was placed on the oyster traffic because it was believed the Barataria fishermen were bringing New Orleans newspapers to the blocking vessels, the price of oysters went up 50 per cent. This drew the criticism of the *Delta*, which complained that "if we are to undergo the sufferings of a besieged city, we do not expect our friends to beleaguer us." Reports were current that spies in the city were daily stuffing newspapers into bottles and floating them down the river to the Federals, who thus learned "by bottle express" what was going on in New Orleans almost as quickly as the subscribers.[6]

Charles Ellis, a race track operator, who was "supposed to be an abolitionist or Lincolnite," was seized, taken into the swamps, tarred and feathered, and threatened with death if he made any identifications. Unintimidated, Ellis promptly swore out charges against his half dozen assailants, one of whom was a city magistrate. The men charged presented alibis and countercharged that Ellis was an abolitionist. For two weeks the two cases dragged on. Mayor Monroe, who tried the cases, in the end acquitted everybody.

Another spy *cause célèbre* concerned an elderly man named Daniel Hand, whose arrival in the city in mid-November was followed by a dispatch from Chattanooga to Mayor Monroe de-

nouncing him as a spy. Hand, described as a "gentleman of educa-
tion and fine deportment," claimed to be wealthy, with millions of
dollars' worth of property in Georgia and South Carolina. After his
arrest, Mayor Monroe did not know what to do with him or why
he should be held. The *Picayune's* account of the disposal of the
matter is amusing:

> Mr. Hand, the mysterious traveler, the alleged Lincoln spy,
> the millionaire, the citizen of Georgia, and the supposed
> President of two Societies of Abolitionists in New York, was
> a much embarrassing man for our authorities. Arrested by the
> Mayor, on the strength of a denunciatory telegram from Chat-
> tanooga, he was handed over to the Governor, who turned him
> over to the Provost Marshal, who passed him over to another
> functionary, who gave him in charge to Mr. Thomas B. Lee,
> who took him up to Augusta, in Georgia, and handed him
> over to the Mayor there, who not knowing what to do with
> the prisoner, telegraphed yesterday to the Mayor here, asking
> him what the charge was against the prisoner. Mr. Monroe
> replied the prisoner was a spy.

Because of so much spy talk and admonitions from the press that
suspicious people should be watched closely, Governor Moore in
October ordered that no one could leave the city without a pass-
port. This caused inconvenience to many, with grumbling and irritation sometimes accompanying it.[7]

On November 18, the people of New Orleans had something else
over which to be indignant, for on that day the newspapers carried
the first account of the seizure on the high seas of the Confederate
commissioners to Europe, James Mason and John Slidell. In the late
summer Mason, a Virginian, and Slidell, former senator and Demo-
cratic boss of Louisiana, had been appointed to go to Europe, the
one to England, and the other to France, to plead the Confederacy's
cause. With their families, Mason and Slidell had run the blockade
to Havana, where they took passage on an English ship, the *Trent*.
The U.S.S. *San Jacinto*, commanded by Captain Charles Wilkes, intercepted the *Trent*, and Mason and Slidell were removed over the

English captain's protest and taken to Fort Warren as prisoners. The New Orleans newspapers were filled with invectives against the Lincoln government for the seizure of the two commissioners, and the people freely expressed the thought and hope that England would take steps to punish the insolent Yankee for the insult to its flag. Some expected England to go to war against the North; others felt recognition and the raising of the blockade could not be far off. "Speculations on the probable course of Great Britain in regard to the gross outrage upon her flag, were innumerable," declared the *Crescent*. But it warned the public not to arouse false hopes of "evidence of friendship on the part of England to the people or Government of the Confederate States." Since the war began, England has "expressed neither sympathy, nor extended any encouragement or support."[8]

The good health that had been noted in New Orleans in the summer still prevailed in the fall, and the fact that the blockade had kept out yellow fever was implicit in the vital statistics for 1861, which showed that from May to October—the normal yellow-fever season—there were 913 fewer deaths in the city than for the same period in 1860. The absence of an epidemic served to encourage the people.[9]

Meanwhile, General Lovell, having made a whirlwind tour of all points of defense in his department within the first two weeks of his arrival in New Orleans, worked feverishly to remedy the glaring deficiencies he had noted. New Orleans had become a veritable military camp since September 28, when Governor Moore, in his capacity of commander in chief, issued a proclamation setting forth rules and instructions for the organization of the militia. The result was that thousands "who were willing enough to do military duty, but were too lazy to drill" found themselves compelled to volunteer or enter the militia. However, hundreds were still shirking their duty, the *Crescent* said, calling for "more energetic means . . . to compel them to obey the requirements of the law."[10]

Four camps were established around New Orleans. Camp Chalmette was pitched on the old battleground of 1815 below the city, and Camp Benjamin was set up on the Gentilly road, close to the tracks of the Pontchartrain Railroad. Above the city, just below Carrollton, Camp Lewis was laid out among the live oaks of Greenville, while above Carrollton was situated Camp Roman. In addition, in the late afternoons the Levee for blocks was covered with soldiers drilling and maneuvering while admiring crowds of spectators looked on.

The military ardor of the troops sometimes overflowed, and there were many instances of fights and brawls among the various companies, and sometimes blood was shed, heads bashed, and soldiers even shot or stabbed to death. Duels between militia or volunteer officers and their men were occasionally reported in the daily press, one being between a private and his militia colonel. The private, a leading merchant, absented himself from a parade "on account of his objecting to the uniform chosen by his officers." Promptly arrested, the incensed private immediately sent a challenge to his colonel, which the latter accepted with alacrity. The duel was fought with officers' swords, and after both were slightly wounded, they agreed that their honor had been satisfied. Another duel had a slightly different outcome from a similar beginning. After both parties, again a colonel and a private, had obtained satisfaction by drawing blood, the colonel, having proven his bravery as a gentleman, then had the private summoned before a court-martial for violating military law. "We know of several duels fought lately by gentlemen of the militia," commented the *Picayune*, "and not one had ever thought of screening himself behind his rank."

Many of the militia and volunteer officers attended Captain Oscar Platosz's military school, which he held at the Armory for battalion classes and at the Varieties Theater for company school and sword and bayonet exercises. Others, unable to take instruction from Platosz, carried in their pockets cheap editions of Hardee's tactics for self-study. Well-to-do parents frequently had their sons privately tutored in military drill, as, for instance, did Judge Edwin T. Merrick with his seventeen-year-old son, David, to prepare him for a commission.[11]

Everywhere one turned, he encountered marching soldiers and

heard drum and fife corps or military bands blaring away. Sunday was no exception, and it became necessary for orders to be issued to the militia to play no music as units marched past churches during the time of divine service. When the troops were all collected for a review by Governor Moore and General Lovell and their staffs, as they were on November 23, the enthusiasm of the public knew no bounds.[12]

Many of the troops were poorly armed, or not at all, and many were in need of training. General Lovell set up a two-gun mock battery in Lafayette Square, just across from his Camp Street headquarters, and began the training of artillery officers and noncoms in the handling of big guns. When General Ruggles regained his health, General Lovell placed him in charge of all Confederate troops in the city. He continued to press upon Richmond the advisability of elevating Colonel J. K. Duncan to the rank of brigadier general.

Lovell expected the Federal attack on New Orleans to come in January, and he devoted himself incessantly to getting New Orleans ready for the blow. By December 5 he had reported in detail to Secretary of War Benjamin on the state of Department No. 1, its troop dispositions and its forts and fortifications, and he said that within a few weeks "New Orleans will be a citadel." On the exterior line of defense from Calcasieu Bay to the Mississippi Gulf coast at Pass Christian, he had 4500 men, while the interior line around New Orleans was manned by 3500 troops. He also had 6000 volunteers in the city itself. "With 15,000 men," Lovell told Benjamin, "I can defend the city against any force that can be brought, unless we are attacked on all sides at once." Lovell had established at the various bays and inlets, the back doors to the city, a small number of troops and guns in newly constructed works. These included two substantial defensive points at Berwick Bay—Fort Berwick and Fort Chêne—each defended by a company and armament of a 32-pounder and four 24-pounders.

The real keys to the defense of New Orleans were the permanent forts—Jackson, St. Philip, Livingston, Macomb, and Pike. At Fort Livingston, on the Gulf at the entrance to Barataria Bay, Lovell had four companies, totaling 300 men, and 15 guns, including a rifled 32-pounder, an 8-inch columbiad, seven 24-pounders, four 12-pounders, and two howitzers. Fort Macomb, guardian of the Chef Menteur pass from Lake Borgne into Lake Pontchartrain, was defended by 250 men and 30 guns, of which twenty-one were 24-pounders. At the Rigolets, Fort Pike was defended by 350 men and 33 guns. Twenty of these were 24-pounders, but also included in Fort Pike's armament were two 32-pound rifled guns.

The chief defensive positions at New Orleans, of course, were Fort Jackson and Fort St. Philip, which guarded the broad highway of the Mississippi at Plaquemines Bend, 75 miles below the city. Here Lovell had ten companies, totaling nearly 1000 men, and 115 guns of a variety of calibers. Fort Jackson's armament consisted of six 42-pounders, twenty-six 24-pounders, sixteen 32-pounders, two 32-pound rifled guns, three 8-inch columbiads, one 10-inch columbiad, ten 24-pound howitzers, two 48-pounders, two 8-inch mortars, and one 10-inch mortar—a total of 69 guns. At Fort St. Philip were six 42-pounders, nine 32-pounders, twenty-two 24-pounders, four 8-inch columbiads, one 8-inch mortar, one 10-inch mortar, and three field guns, making in all 46 guns.

The raft, or barricade, across the river just below the forts, which was talked about in February and left unconstructed until late summer, had been in place since September, before Lovell's arrival. However, Lovell had anchored it more securely and it now formed a complete obstruction. It was securely chained to both banks and held by fifteen anchors weighing from 2500 to 4000 pounds each and laid in twenty-five fathoms of water with sixty fathoms of strong chain. The raft was supported by enfilading fire from Fort Jackson, direct fire from Fort St. Philip.

The interior line of defense consisted of formidable earthworks with ditches, which, with the intervening swamps, made a complete continuous line around the city. Where the works touched the river, on both sides, strong points were set up, and preparations were under way to install powerful batteries to cover the river. These were to consist of ten or more 32-pounders or 42-pounders. And where the Carrollton line met the river, an obstruction was being built to block the passage of ships descending the river.

At Proctorsville, on Lake Borgne; at Tower Dupré, at the mouth of Bayou Bienvenu; and at Battery Bienvenu, where Bayou Mazant meets Bayou Bienvenu, General Lovell stationed a company each, the armament at these land approaches to New Orleans being six, five, and ten guns, all but two being 24-pounders.

General Lovell was quite satisfied with the way things were going at New Orleans, particularly in the light of the state of affairs when he arrived in October. In less than two months he had created order out of confusion and had organized the defenses and readied them for action. He was confident that he could hold New Orleans indefinitely, provided he could be assured of sufficient powder and provisions. "I am endeavoring silently through other parties, to induce holders to lay in not less than 60,000 barrels of flour, of which the city consumes about 800 per diem," he wrote Benjamin. "This with beef cattle from Texas and from Mississippi via Mandeville, would enable us to stand a siege of two or three months, if it should be necessary."[18]

The crying shortage was powder. Two powder mills were now in operation in New Orleans, one at the barracks below New Orleans and the other in the old Marine Hospital building, across the river from New Orleans in Gretna. Although Lovell had the other ingredients for making powder, sulphur and charcoal, his need for saltpeter was all the more acute. In an effort to solve his problem, Lovell invited Major George W. Rains of the Ordnance Department to New Orleans to confer with him relative to securing supplies of saltpeter from abroad. Lovell suggested, Rains concurred, and Secretary Benjamin approved a plan to charter the steamship *Tennessee*, then lying idle in the river, and send it through the blockade to Liverpool for a cargo of saltpeter to be delivered at any Confederate port into which the vessel could run. But the scheme was never developed, because the Federal blockade, which had prevented all ships from entering the river since May, proved too tight for the *Tennessee* to escape.

Early in December, Lovell moved a third powder mill from

Handsboro, Mississippi, to New Orleans, and as it had a capacity of about 1500 pounds a day, this increased the need for ever greater quantities of saltpeter.[14]

The shortage of powder in New Orleans was even more keenly felt by Flag Officer Hollins; his little fleet depended on Lovell for whatever it could get. The latter gave Hollins four tons of powder but was not inclined, under the conditions, to meet any other requisitions the Navy presented. Hollins then appealed to Richmond to have Lovell release more powder.

Lovell told Hollins that he would manufacture powder for him if the latter secured the saltpeter. Hollins advertised on December 15 for sealed bids on delivery of 400 tons of saltpeter, or any lesser quantity. This was either unjustified optimism or just a shot in the dark, for General Lovell himself, on December 27, was still asking Benjamin in Richmond for more saltpeter.[15]

At this stage the powder crisis in New Orleans was sharpened by a midnight explosion on December 28, which shook buildings all over the city, upsetting furniture and shattering windowpanes. There were actually two blasts, and the shock was too great and too sudden to be mistaken for anything but what it was—the blowing up of the powder mill in the old Marine Hospital across the river. "A pillar of flame shot up to the sky," said the *True Delta*, "for an instant illuminating the whole heavens, and then came the noise and the shock." The *Delta* reported "houses were shaken, doors opened, windows broken and gas lights extinguished." The *Crescent* said: "The explosion was tremendous, destroying the building and shaking the earth for miles around . . . thousands of buildings were shaken as with the throes of a not very moderately mild earthquake." T. K. Wharton, who lived in a section not very distant from the explosion, was awakened by the violent shaking of his house. When he went to the front door "the great wreath of smoke rolling up from the direction of the river and the strong fumes of sulphur" told him at once that the powder mill had blown up. No lives were lost, fortunately, but 8000 pounds of powder were destroyed, along with the mill. Luckily, Lovell had taken out 4000 pounds—the daily capacity of the mill—the day of the explosion.

The cause of the explosion was not determined, yet the *True Delta* was convinced it was no accident, but "the diabolical work of some incarnate fiend," and it called for the hunting down of "traitors in our midst."[16]

Meanwhile, New Orleans had been full of invasion gossip for several weeks. On December 3, about 1900 Federal troops, under Brigadier General John W. Phelps, arrived at Ship Island and, aided by naval vessels, began to disembark. It took almost three days for the men and equipment of the 26th Massachusetts and the 9th Connecticut regiments, plus a battery of artillery, to get ashore on the sandy island, which one northern officer described as "barren enough to deserve the name of 'Misery Island' which name it rec'd by some of the men." It was not long before the Yankee arrival at Ship Island was noted in the New Orleans papers, as was indeed General Phelps' bombastic and completely unauthorized proclamation "to the loyal citizens of the Southwest," in which he denounced the institution of slavery in sharp terms. When a copy of Phelps' proclamation came into its hands, the *Crescent* said he ought to be promoted at once. "He is evidently as big a fool as Lincoln and as great a scoundrel as Seward," the paper commented.[17]

About the time the people of New Orleans began reading of the Yankees on Ship Island, they also read articles about the warships that the Federals were building at St. Louis, notably the *Benton*, which was 186 feet long, pierced for 18 heavy guns, and scheduled to pay New Orleans a visit. The *Delta* also reported on December 15 that a mortar fleet was being prepared in the East River shipyards in New York.

Naturally, New Orleans hummed with conversation about the huge Federal preparations and, as is usual in such instances, there were all varieties of opinion: Was New Orleans the target? Or was it Mobile? Didn't the Federals have to reduce Pensacola before they could launch an attack on New Orleans? The *Crescent* summed up all the gossip and talk neatly: "The Yankees are coming in great force, and to cut a long argument short, we have merely to repeat the talk: are we prepared?"

General Lovell thought that he was prepared, for he so addressed himself to Secretary of War Benjamin on December 29: "The enemy has now at Ship Island twenty-two vessels, large and small, and is landing troops in large numbers . . . They cannot take New Orleans by a land attack with any force they can bring to bear."[18]

10

The Ambitious Lieutenant Porter

EIGHT MONTHS EARLIER, ON APRIL 15, 1861, EDWARD BATES, MR. LINcoln's Attorney General, had gone to the cabinet meeting with a long memorandum, which he submitted to the President.

On the day previous, Fort Sumter had fallen, and Lincoln had already issued his call upon the states for 75,000 volunteers to suppress the rebellion in the South.

Attorney General Bates' memorandum proposed the closing of the southern ports and the effective guarding of the mouth of the Mississippi to prevent all ships from leaving or entering the river. "It is my opinion [we] ought to take and hold with a strong hand, the City of New Orleans," wrote Bates. "And that, I believe, can be done, without much fighting provided the plan be judiciously matured, & the preparations be made with intelligence, secrecy and celerity . . . If regular war be inaugurated, in the valley of the Mississippi, we *must* command the mouth of the river. . . ."

Bates declared that the blockading of southern ports, especially from Charleston to New Orleans, cutting off all their sea commerce, would be the "easiest, cheapest & most humane method of restraining those States and destroying their confederation."[1]

Such was also the opinion of old General Winfield Scott, commanding general of the United States Army, who believed that the South could be brought to terms by strangulation. His "Anaconda Plan" called for a naval blockade of the entire Confederate coast and a southward drive down the Mississippi Valley to New Orleans by the Army. The Confederacy thus would be cut in half and the blockade of its entire perimeter would be complete. Not until then would Scott make a direct assault on Richmond, the southern capital. He wanted to put the squeeze on the South before launching a major campaign.[2]

But the public and the press had picked up Horace Greeley's "Forward to Richmond" chant, and Scott was helpless to stem the pressure on Lincoln to move on Richmond before adequate preparations were made to deliver decisive blows against the South. Old Scott was considered a "fuddy-duddy," a bumbling old hero, who had been so long away from the smell of powder that he had lost his zest for fighting. Reluctantly, "Old Fuss and Feathers" ordered General McDowell to strike at Beauregard's line behind Bull Run, and the Federal rout on the Plains of Manassas on a steaming, dusty July Sunday resulted from the impetuous movement.[3]

From the very beginning of hostilities, the importance of seizing New Orleans was very much in Mr. Lincoln's mind, not only from the memorandum that Attorney General Bates had submitted on April 15, but from General Scott's studied program of crushing the Confederacy by steady, constant, and slowly constricting pressure.

The President was not alone in thinking about New Orleans. A board appointed by Secretary of the Navy Gideon Welles also recommended measures for effectively blockading the coast bordering on the Gulf of Mexico, and discussed New Orleans and its water approaches at great length. The board, which consisted of two naval officers, Captain Samuel F. Du Pont and Commander C. H. Davis; an Army Engineers' officer, Major J. G. Barnard; and the head of the United States Coast Survey, A. D. Bache, concluded after much study that the conquest of New Orleans is "incompatible with the other nearer and more urgent naval and military operations in which the Government is now, and will be for some time hereafter engaged."

The board, in its report of August 9, 1861, continued as regards an attack on New Orleans:

> It is an enterprise of great moment, requiring the cooperation of a large number of vessels of war of a smaller class, but of formidable armament, a great many troops, and the conduct of sieges, and it will be accomplished with slow advances . . . We recommend, therefore, that the subject of the capture of New Orleans be deferred for the present; be deferred at least until we are prepared to ascend the river with vessels of war sufficiently protected to contend with the forts now standing and the temporary fortifications which, in the event of invasion, would be established at every defensible point . . . Instead, then, of presenting a plan for the capture of the city of New Orleans, we shall offer one for shutting it up, for suspending its trade, and obstructing the freedom of its intercourse with the ocean and with neighboring coasts, feeling assured that the moral effect of such a course will be quite as striking as that of its possession by the United States.[4]

Had this sort of thinking come to the attention of Lieutenant David Dixon Porter, commanding the *Powhatan* on blockade duty off Southwest Pass, he would have exploded with characteristic contemptuous comments about old fogies in the Navy who concentrated on dreaming up ways of obstructing action instead of going ahead and getting a job done. More than a month before the board's memorial was submitted to Secretary Welles, Porter reported to his commanding officer, Flag Officer William Mervine, how easy it would be to take New Orleans.

"There is a field here for something to do," wrote Porter on July 4. "The steamers they have up the river could be captured by a proper combination of force, and we could very easily be in possession of the lower part of the river and cut them off from important supplies . . . The sooner we get in with our forces and prevent them from putting up forts at any of the Passes the sooner this war will be brought to a close. I am an old cruiser in this river, and know every inch of the ground. I assure you that any expedition up the river is an easy thing for vessels not drawing over 16 feet . . ."

Later in July, Midshipman John R. Bartlett of the *Mississippi* visited Porter aboard the *Powhatan,* and as they walked up and down the quarter-deck Porter aired his views on the Navy Department's strategy.

"He was very much exasperated," Bartlett said later, "that the department at Washington delayed sending vessels of proper draft to enter the river, and said that if he had half a dozen good vessels he would undertake to run by the forts and capture New Orleans."

Porter, of course, was on solid ground. New Orleans, in July 1861, was virtually defenseless, and neither the forts nor the river defenses were in any condition to repel any sort of attack pushed with boldness and energy. There was no obstruction in the river at that time, although it had been suggested by Beauregard and others many months before. Not later, as Gideon Welles' board recommended, but now was the time to dash up the river and put New Orleans under the guns of the fleet.

"Porter's clear professional insight saw not only the feasibility of the enterprise, but its overwhelming strategic importance," wrote one of his biographers. "It was not merely the moral effect of the conquest of the great commercial seaport of the South; it was the stupendous strategic effect of opening a highway from the Gulf to the Ohio . . . and cutting in halves the territory of the Confederacy."[5]

Oddly enough, Porter did not make any suggestion of an attack on New Orleans in writing on July 5 to his friend Gustavus V. Fox, Assistant Secretary of the Navy. Rather, he needled Fox about a promotion.

As to the Commission business promised to the individual who does take a fort, I think it better to wait until I get the one which has been due me for *five* years. After I get that, it will do to try and earn another one, for it might be handed

me as a reward for taking somebody's Fort. A man doesn't
associate down here with alligators, sand flies, mosquitoes
and rattlesnakes for nothing, he soon gets his eye teeth, and
gets wide awake—take a fort indeed![6]

Although forty-eight-year-old David Dixon Porter had spent
thirty-two years in the Navy, he was still a lieutenant in 1861, and
this fact irked him considerably. He was a man of overweening
ambition, full of energy, bold both in thinking and in action. He
inherited, said those who knew him best, a family failing for treat-
ing the truth, if not lightly, at least advantageously to himself, and
he developed to the point of artistry the knack of making himself
the hero or central figure in relating the history that was being made
around him. "Old Father Neptune"—Gideon Welles—summed him
up neatly in his diary: "He has . . . stirring and positive qualities, is
fertile in resources, has great energy, excessive and sometimes not
overscrupulous ambition; is impressed with and boastful of his own
powers, given to exaggeration in relation to himself—a Porter infirmity—is not generous to older and superior living officers, whom
he is ready to traduce; but is kind and patronizing to favorites who
are juniors. Is given to cliquism, but is brave and daring like all his
family."

On another occasion, Welles recorded of Porter and his occasional
stretching of the truth: ". . . David was not always reliable on un-
important matters, but amplified and colored transactions, where
he was personally interested especially . . . I did not always consider David to be depended upon if he had an end to attain, and
he had no hesitation in trampling down a brother officer if it would
benefit himself."[7]

Porter was given leave from the Navy in 1849, after twenty years
of service, to take command of a merchant steamer, the *Panama*,
and later the *Georgia*, which made regularly scheduled trips between New Orleans, Havana, and New York. This was under a
Navy Department policy of detaching young officers to the merchant
service to acquaint them with steam navigation. Before Porter returned to active Navy duty in 1855, his frequent trips to New Or-

leans had made him thoroughly familiar with the Gulf waters and the Mississippi River. Porter, indeed, could without exaggeration claim—and did claim—that he was an authority on steamship operations in the Mississippi River.[8]

A man of ideas, Porter lost no time, after Gideon Welles was established in the Navy Department, in presenting to the secretary some of his schemes for improving the Navy. He had no scruples about bypassing channels, and on at least five occasions in 1861, Porter wrote directly to Welles, perhaps with the studied purpose of keeping his name before the head of the Navy Department.

From Washington, on March 12, Porter suggested to Welles that the sides of existing naval vessels be sheathed with "longitudinal bars of wrought iron rounded on the top, and bolted through the sides of the ship: the bars to be of a sufficient size to resist any size shot—I propose that these bars shall be at *least* two inches wide at the top, ten inches deep, and two and a half inches at the base, to be three inches apart."

Before Father Neptune—he had taken over the Navy Department on Lincoln's inauguration only eight days earlier—had time to digest this proposal, Porter came up with another idea on March 14, suggesting for the Navy a new kind of propeller which he modestly identified as "an invention of my own."[9]

Whatever impression Lieutenant Porter made on Welles with these ideas, he very shortly fell out of favor by engaging in what the secretary later called an "irregular cruise on which he had been improperly sent." This "irregular cruise" was a secret project which not only had the blessing of Lincoln but which was put into motion by the signed orders of the President himself.

This caused complications in which Porter found himself with conflicting orders, one from the President and the other from the head of the Navy Department. Welles, on President Lincoln's authority, dispatched a naval expedition to the relief of Fort Sumter. But Secretary of State William Seward, without consulting either the Navy or War Departments, arranged with the President to send a secret naval and military expedition to Florida to reinforce and secure Fort Taylor at Key West, Fort Jefferson at Dry Tortugas, and Fort Pickens at Pensacola. Lieutenant Porter, as a friend of the moving spirit of the affair, Captain Montgomery C. Meigs of the Army, consulted with Seward. After all three called on Lincoln at the White House, Porter wound up as commander of the *Powhatan* in the Florida expedition although Welles had already assigned the *Powhatan*, under Captain Samuel Mercer, to the Sumter relief fleet.

Porter's willingness to join in the project—one of the conditions of which was that the Secretary of Navy was not to be told of the expedition—and his actual participation therein were not calculated to win for him the favor of Gideon Welles. The latter did not hide his indignation over Seward's trespass into the Navy Department's precincts when he finally heard of the affair, and he went protesting to Lincoln.

Porter reached Fort Pickens, at the entrance to Pensacola Bay, on April 17, but was restrained from attempting to attack Pensacola for fear of bringing on hostilities, which, of course, had broken out five days earlier in Charleston Harbor.[10]

Lincoln's blockade order of April 19 did not reach Fort Pickens until May 12, and the *Powhatan* was ordered on blockade duty, first to Mobile Bay, and then, on May 30, to the mouth of the Mississippi, where it blocked the entrance to Southwest Pass. The *Powhatan* had hardly dropped anchor before Porter took up his pen to write to Gideon Welles, not through channels but directly, motivated in all probability by the desire to re-establish himself in the eyes of the Secretary of the Navy. "I cannot impress upon the Department too strongly the importance of having plenty of Coal Vessels at the points here, where steamers of the Navy are blockading." He also urged that small, light-draft steamers be procured to patrol the many inlets on the Louisiana coast.[11]

While on blockade duty at Southwest Pass, Porter conceived a bold plan to capture the Confederate ships *Ivy* and *Sumter*, the latter biding its time in Pass a Loutre to make a dash to sea. Porter's account of this operation reflects his boundless confidence and eagerness for action:

The enemy are beginning to make some demonstrations; the *Sumter* has come down within 10 miles of us, but owing to the current has been beyond the reach of our boats. An armed tugboat called the *Ivy* is employed in attendance on this vessel, and I think they are putting up batteries at what is called the Passes. Wishing to get hold of this *Ivy* I fitted out an expedition up the river under the command of Lieutenant Watson Smith, who was directed to proceed at night to the telegraph station, seize the operator, cut the wire, and with thirty-five picked men, well-armed and concealed, seize the *Ivy* when she came as usual to the dock. The vessel did not come down as usual. The position was seized and all my directions carried out, and on the third day, after the men had laid patiently concealed, a mail steamer came down and landed on the opposite side of the river. Mr. Smith could stand it no longer, and with 16 men stowed away in the bottom of the old deck boat, he proceeded under sail across the river, but as he was almost near enough to board her, the boat started off under a full head of steam, gave the alarm up the river, and everything in the shape of a steamer (man-of-war and all) immediately got underway and have not shown themselves since. My intention was to seize the *Ivy*, put 200 men in her at once, carry the *Sumter* by boarding, and proceed to New Orleans under the disguise of the secession flag, and burn the *Star of the West*. The only thing that prevented this was the want of one more minute in time, for the boarding was almost accomplished.[12]

When Porter wrote this he was unaware that a few nights earlier the *Sumter* had slipped out to sea and had already begun its depredations on northern merchant vessels. But on August 13, the *Powhatan* intercepted the *Abby Bradford* trying to enter the river, and from its papers Porter learned that it had been captured by the *Sumter* and turned into a blockade runner; also that the *Sumter* was at Puerto Cabello, Venezuela, and short of coal. All this Porter related the same day in a letter to Secretary Welles, stating: "I sail tonight for Pensacola to report the circumstances to the Flag Officer & hope to induce him to let me go in search of the *Sumter*."

When Porter reached Pensacola on August 16, Flag Officer Mervine gave him permission to give chase to the *Sumter*, and after fueling up, the *Powhatan* steamed off at once. "In withdrawing the *Powhatan* from her station, I have departed from the letter of my instructions," Mervine wrote Welles, "but the object sought to be obtained in arresting the depredations of that piratical craft upon our merchant marine, will, I hope, justify the measure and meet with your approval."[13]

Although Welles did not enjoy the idea of weakening the blockade at the Mississippi, he realized that the North desperately needed a victory of some kind. The fall of Sumter had been followed by the loss of the important Norfolk Navy Yard and then, in July, had come the morale-shattering rout at Bull Run. Now northern papers were full of the activities of the rebel raider *Sumter* against northern merchant ships. If Porter could capture the *Sumter*, there would be something to cheer about at last.

Porter never did catch up with Raphael Semmes and his raider, but he made a good try of it, picking up the *Sumter's* trail and following it tenaciously. But while the chase was on, the victory the North had needed for so long finally came. On August 31, the Union Navy scored a great success at Hatteras Inlet, North Carolina, which not only bolstered northern morale but caused concern to sweep through the Confederacy.

In New Orleans, people read the news uneasily and the newspapers asked questions: "Has the capture of the North Carolina forts brought its useful lesson to those in charge of our defenses?" inquired the *Crescent*. "This city is beginning to be seriously alarmed at the want of preparation for the immense fleet which are now ready to invest New Orleans," stated the Algiers *News Boy*. "What is to be done?"[14]

Porter finally gave up his pursuit of the *Sumter*, putting into St. Thomas on October 10. The *Powhatan*, which had been in bad shape for months, was practically useless for further service until repairs were made. So Porter sailed for the Gulf, where the *Pow-*

hatan arrived off Southwest Pass on October 25. Flag Officer William W. McKean, commanding the Gulf Blockading Squadron, ordered Porter to take his ship to New York for repairs. At his old blockading station Porter got the word that he had been promoted to commander in his absence, his new rank dating from April 22. Commander Porter sailed north with his old tub, and on November 9 the *Powhatan* came to anchor at the Brooklyn Navy Yard.[15]

Two days earlier Captain Samuel F. Du Pont gave the Union another important victory at Port Royal, demonstrating what some military and naval men had been contending ever since the war started: Wooden vessels under steam could pass shore batteries.

11

A Plan—But Whose?

THE APHORISM THAT "HISTORY IS SOMETHING THAT DIDN'T TAKE PLACE written by a man who wasn't there" would apply to the rival claimants for suggesting the Union attack on New Orleans but for one fact: most of those who made claims or for whom claims were made were there. Commander David Dixon Porter passed it off as his idea. Horace Greeley credited it to the controversial Ben Butler. Butler's biographer, James Parton, asserted that Secretary of War Edward Stanton and General Butler concocted it at a conference.[1]

Gideon Welles, Secretary of the Navy, declared flatly that Porter had no more to do with proposing the attack on New Orleans than did Butler, and that gentleman had nothing to do with it. And as for Stanton's part in suggesting it, Welles pointed out that Navy Department plans for the attack were launched two months before Stanton entered Lincoln's Cabinet. He credited the idea to "the Department," but Gustavus V. Fox, Assistant Secretary of the Navy, claimed it was he who proposed the attack on New Orleans, and the testimony of Postmaster General Montgomery Blair and Admiral George Dewey, the hero of Manila Bay, who as a young officer participated in the New Orleans expedition, supports his claim.

Nine years after the "great event second only to the final surrender of Lee," Fox recalled to Welles incidents connected with the plans to capture New Orleans. Welles, who was preparing two articles on "Admiral Farragut and New Orleans" for the magazine *Galaxy*, wrote to Fox on June 10, 1871, for all the information his wartime assistant could recall about the expedition.

Fox replied a week later with a ten-page letter, the first several pages being devoted to a denunciation of Porter, who, he said, "has attained the heights of his ambition by means which have brought him into general contempt and he has lost the happiness he had when we took him by the hand . . . Finally Porter, so soon as we leave Washington, and to his young officers, claims to have conceived the plan of a naval ascent of the Missi. Well may we exclaim with Pilate, 'What is truth?'"

Immediately after the capture of Port Royal on November 7, Fox reminded Welles, "I suggested to you a naval attack upon New Orleans." He recalled that he had said that from his experience on the Mississippi the forts below New Orleans would present no great difficulty to steamers passing their line of fire at night. Also, that the river was too deep and too powerful for permanent obstructions and that because of the low banks, effective batteries could not be brought to bear on ships ascending during the spring freshets. Once New Orleans had fallen to the navy gunboats, 10,000 army troops would be sufficient to occupy the city.

"You adopted this plan at once," Fox reminded Welles, "and it was discussed and approved at a meeting held at Genl. McClellan's house . . . present Mr. Lincoln, yourself, Genl. McClellan and the writer. The Navy Dept. were to go forward with their preparations and the Army force was promised by Genl. McClellan when wanted. From this interview the Navy Dept. dates its efforts and in secret, but continuously, progress was made."

Fox recalled that Major Barnard, McClellan's chief of engineers, considered it absolutely essential that both Forts Jackson and St. Philip be captured by a joint Army-Navy operation before any attempt was made to go up the river above the forts. "The answer to this was obvious," wrote Fox, "it gave up our plan for theirs and turned over the direction of it to the War Dept."

David Dixon Porter now came into the story. Fox told Welles:

> With your consent I informed Lieut. David D. Porter of the contemplated attack and offered him a command in it. He agreed with the Ch. Eng. of the Army of the Potomac that the forts ought to be reduced before passing. On the 30th of Nov. 1861 he and I met at Judge Blair's and had a long discussion in regard to the matter—I maintaining the joint project, as one within our means, whilst a reduction of the forts required iron clads and a larger Army force than we could probably get. Lieut. Porter thought the forts could be destroyed with mortars and offered to command a special mortar flotilla to be attached to the squadron. This compromise met with your approval, though it was determined to keep in view the original plan, provided a commander could be found who would make it his own.[2]

Gideon Welles' story of the conception of the expedition against New Orleans was printed in two installments in *Galaxy*, November and December 1871. Although Welles told Fox in a letter on July 8, 1871, that "I am unable . . . to specify when we first considered the subject of an expedition to . . . New Orleans," in his *Galaxy* articles he stated that as soon as arrangements for Du Pont's attack on Port Royal were completed, and before his squadron had actually sailed for Hampton Roads, "the attention of the Department . . . was intently directed toward New Orleans, the most important place in every point of view in the insurrectionary region. . . ." Neither the Army nor the Administration entertained any idea at the time of a naval conquest of New Orleans.

Welles wrote that "in general and desultory conversation" with naval and military men, "the passage of the forts and the capture of New Orleans was spoken of as a desirable but not a practical naval undertaking." But when navy warships steamed repeatedly past the Rebel batteries at Hatteras and Port Royal and reduced them without serious injury to the vessels, the idea of an attack on

New Orleans gained favor in the Navy Department "until the conclusion was reached that it was not only practicable, but the best step that could be taken for perfecting the blockade, getting possession of the river, and to aid in suppressing the rebellion."[3]

Lincoln was informed of the Navy Department's views, Welles declared, regarding New Orleans and its belief that the Hatteras and Port Royal expeditions had proved that steam had revolutionized naval warfare. If the forts were passed, Welles told Lincoln, New Orleans was sure to fall. Welles wrote that Lincoln "became deeply interested, but was at first somewhat incredulous as to the feasibility of the enterprise." The Hatteras and Port Royal successes "inspired the President with confidence in naval management and naval power, and with very little hesitation he came into the project."

It was at this time that Commander Porter returned to Washington, Welles wrote, and the Navy Department "was glad to avail itself of his recent observations and of whatever information he possessed in regard to the river and the forts." Porter was then taken into the Navy Department's confidence, Welles stated.[4]

"He entered with zeal into the views of the Department, but expressed great doubts whether the forts could be passed until reduced or seriously damaged," stated Welles. "This he said might be effected by a flotilla of bomb-vessels with mortars, which could in forty-eight hours demolish the forts or render them untenable . . . and as a mortar flotilla would furnish additional power and would probably render success more certain, it received favorable consideration from the President and Secretary of the Navy, and was adopted as part of the program."

President Lincoln arranged a meeting at General McClellan's home, Welles wrote, and Commander Porter attended along with the President, Welles, Fox, and McClellan. Welles said that Fox and Porter called at his house for a conference before going to McClellan's. Fox, be it recalled, did not list Porter as being present at the meeting, which Welles said in his *Galaxy* article took place on the evening of November 15.[5]

McClellan endorsed Porter's mortar-flotilla scheme and agreed to furnish 10,000 men to garrison the forts and occupy New Orleans after it had been captured. With that, preparations for the campaign against New Orleans were in motion. At least that was the way the Secretary of Navy says it got under way. But not Commander David Dixon Porter. His version (of which there are two accounts, varying slightly in detail, but not in point of view) was quite different. And, being published after the death of Lincoln, Welles, Fox, and Farragut, it did not admit of rebuttal by any other principal actor in the expedition.

"While I was at the entrance to the southwest pass of the Mississippi, I had ample opportunity to find out much that was going on at the forts and in the city of New Orleans," declared Porter. "Upon reaching home in the *Powhatan*, I proceeded to Washington, and found everything at the Navy Department as calm and quiet as if we had nothing to do but blockade the Southern ports."

This was a ridiculous exaggeration, if for no other reason than that the news of Du Pont's victory at Port Royal reached Washington that very day, causing considerable elation all over the capital, even in the "calm and quiet" Navy Department.

It was on November 12 that Commander Porter found himself in the anteroom of the Secretary of the Navy, awaiting an opportunity to see Welles. In one version of his story Porter said that he could not obtain an interview with Welles because, he soon discovered, he was out of favor. In the other version, he credited his long wait at Welles' door to the fact that "in those days it was not an easy matter for an officer, except one of high rank, to obtain access to the Secretary of the Navy."

Porter had cooled his heels in Welles' office most of the morning when Senator John P. Hale of New Hampshire and Senator James W. Grimes of Iowa walked into the office. After greeting the commander warmly, they inquired about his cruise. "During this interview I told the Senators of a plan I had formed for the capture of New Orleans, and when I explained to them how easily it could be accomplished, they expressed surprise that no action had been taken in the matter, and took me in with them at once to see Secretary Welles."

To Porter's surprise, Father Neptune received his errant subordinate kindly and listened attentively to all he had to say. At the conclusion, Welles remarked that the matter should be laid before President Lincoln immediately, whereupon, says Porter, "we all went forthwith to the Executive Mansion, where we were received by Mr. Lincoln."

Porter outlined his plan: A fleet of fast steam warships, drawing no more than 18 feet of water, carrying about 250 guns, to run past Forts Jackson and St. Philip at night after a flotilla of mortar vessels had bombarded the forts to silence or neutralize them. A body of troops would follow the fleet in transports to occupy New Orleans and the forts after their capture. Lincoln listened interestedly, until Porter had finished.

"This should have been done sooner," declared the President. "The Mississippi is the backbone of the Rebellion; it is the key to the whole situation. While the Confederates hold it they can obtain supplies of all kinds, and it is a barrier against our forces. Come, let us go and see General McClellan."

At this juncture, stated Porter, Secretary of State William Seward arrived at the White House, and he joined the group as it proceeded to General McClellan's home at Fourteenth and H streets. (Recall that neither Fox nor Welles mentioned Seward as being present.)

General McClellan greeted the President and others affably, and warmly shook the hand of Porter as an old acquaintance.

"Oh," exclaimed Lincoln, "you two know each other! Then half the work is done."

Then the President explained to General McClellan the purpose of the visit:

"This is a most important expedition. What troops can you spare to accompany it and take possession of New Orleans after the Navy has effected its capture?"

Lincoln talked on a while and then said: "Now, time flies, and I want this matter settled. I will leave you two gentlemen to arrange the plans, and will come over here at eight o'clock this evening to see what conclusions you have arrived at."

In one version, Porter said that it took two days for McClellan to settle the matter; in the other he stated:

> So General McClellan and myself were left alone to talk the matter over, and we soon determined upon a plan of operations. At eight o'clock that evening the President returned to General McClellan's headquarters, and was informed that the general could spare twenty thousand men to accompany a naval expedition to New Orleans, and that they would be ready to embark as soon as the naval vessels could be prepared.
>
> The President then directed the Secretary of the Navy to have the necessary number of ships ready. This duty was assigned to Assistant Secretary Fox, who took hold of the matter with his usual energy, and soon assembled a squadron adequate to the occasion.[6]

Thus did Commander Porter describe the genesis of the New Orleans campaign in a manner far different from the way Gideon Welles and Gustavus V. Fox did. While there were undoubted errors in details, one cannot believe that either would deliberately distort the facts, especially as at the time Welles' *Galaxy* articles were published, Porter was able to nail any misrepresentations. Why didn't he do so at the time?

"In reference to Mr. Welles' narrative in the *Galaxy*," Porter wrote years later, "it would be charitable to suppose that age had impaired his memory, although his mind was vigorous to the end . . . I never noticed the article, thinking myself strong enough to defy such attacks, nor would I let my friends publish the papers in my possession that would have refuted Mr. Welles' statement."

Yet after Lincoln, Welles, Fox, and Farragut had all died, Porter produced a narrative in which he credited himself not only with awakening the Navy Department to the importance of attacking New Orleans but with providing the very blueprint for the expedition.[7]

After the plan to attack New Orleans, whatever its source, had been decided upon, it next became necessary to pick a commander for it. And here again the stories vary.

Said Assistant Secretary Fox: "In casting about for a suitable commander I could only say that Captain Farragut, though not a young man, stood high in the Navy. The importance of obtaining his views as to the plan proposed led to entrusting Lt. Porter with a confidential mission to him . . ."

Said Secretary Welles: "I am not aware who first named Farragut . . . His course in leaving Virginia the day after the passage of the secession ordinance warmed me to him. . . ."

Said Commander Porter: ". . . The next thing to be done was to select an officer to command the naval forces. Mr. Fox named several, but I opposed them all, and finally urged the appointment of Captain D. G. Farragut so strongly that I was sent to New York to communicate with him on the subject. The result was the acceptance by Farragut of the command—a command assuring his reputation, which no man ever more deserved." Farragut was the foster brother of Porter, having been adopted by the latter's father before Porter was born.

Thus did Porter, having already claimed the credit for thinking up and providing a plan for the New Orleans expedition, now assert that it was he who named the man to command it. In another place, Porter amplified this claim: "Mr. Fox and myself had often discussed the matter. He had had in mind several officers of high standing and unimpeachable loyalty; but, as I knew the officers of the Navy better than he did, my advice was listened to, and the selection fell upon Captain David Glasgow Farragut."

Postmaster General Montgomery Blair gave the credit to Fox, who, he said, prevailed upon Welles to choose Farragut because his conduct in leaving Norfolk showed "great superiority of character, clear perception of duty, and firm resolution in performing of it."[8]

David Glasgow Farragut's name stood thirty-seventh on the list of navy captains that Welles and Fox scanned closely. When they came to his name, Welles recalled an incident that took place during the Mexican War.

"I had met and been favorably impressed by Captain Farragut some fifteen years previously, during the Mexican War, when I was officiating in the Navy Department as chief of a naval bureau," wrote Welles. "He at that time made what was considered a remarkable proposition to the then Secretary of the Navy, John Y. Mason, which was a plan to take the castle of San Juan d'Ulloa. I was present when he stated and urged his plan. It was characterized by the earnest, resolute, and brave daring which at a later day was brought out . . ."[9]

Farragut was born in the vicinity of Knoxville, Tennessee, on July 5, 1801, of Spanish origin. During his childhood the family moved to New Orleans. It was there that young Farragut's father did a service of kindness to Commodore David Porter's aged father when the latter fell ill near Farragut's home. In gratitude, Commodore Porter offered to adopt young David Farragut, and so it was that at the age of nine Farragut found himself a midshipman, serving under his adopted father. During the War of 1812, Farragut was with Commodore Porter aboard the *Essex*, and he was only thirteen when the *Essex* valiantly engaged two British ships, *Cherub* and *Phoebe*, in an unequal engagement in the harbor of Valparaiso.[10]

During his midshipman days, Farragut served in the Mediterranean and later was attached to the United States consulate in Tunis, where he learned to speak Italian, French, Spanish, and Arabic. When the Mexican War broke out, he sought active service, but the best he could get was blockade duty. Farragut established the Mare Island Navy Yard in California in 1854.

At the time Virginia seceded from the Union in April 1861, Farragut was living in Norfolk, awaiting orders. He was outspoken in his opposition to secession, which gained for him the advice that people who felt that way would not find living in Norfolk very agreeable. "Very well, I can live somewhere else," Farragut replied, and he packed off to New York, establishing himself and family at Hastings-on-Hudson.

Farragut was appointed a member of a naval board for the retirement of officers, and he was engaged in that duty at the Brooklyn Navy Yard when Secretary of the Navy Welles decided, at Fox's urging, that perhaps this quiet, unassuming captain was just the man for the New Orleans expedition. Welles questioned a number of navy men about Farragut and all spoke well of him. Welles himself already entertained a high regard for Farragut for a number of reasons: "Farragut was attached to no clique, which is sometimes the bane of the navy, was as modest and truthful as he was self-reliant and brave, had individuality, and resorted to none of the petty contrivances common with many for position and advancement . . . Farragut had a good reputation, had been severely trained and had always done his duty well . . ."

Yes, Welles thought, this could well be the man the Navy Department wanted to capture New Orleans. "It now became important to ascertain the ideas, feelings and views of Captain Farragut himself, and this, if possible, before informing him of the expedition, or committing the department in any respect," wrote Welles. "Nothing . . . was put on paper which related to the actual destination of the expedition, and every movement was made with caution and circumspection. Under these circumstances it was thought best to entrust Commander Porter with a confidential mission to proceed to New York on business relating to the mortar flotilla, and while there to ascertain, in personal interviews and conversations on naval matters and belligerent operations generally, the views of Captain Farragut on the subject of such a programme and naval attack as was proposed by the Navy Department, without advising him of our object or letting him know that the Department had any purpose in Porter's inquiries or knew of them."[11]

Porter's instructions for interviewing Farragut were verbal ones. But he received written orders on November 18 to visit Philadelphia and New York to see if schooners purchased by the Navy were suitable for mortar vessels. He was also to inspect ironclad vessels being built at Philadelphia, New York, and Mystic, Connecticut, while on his trip.[12]

It is not certain when Porter interviewed Farragut, but one of the latter's biographers sets the date "about the middle of December." Considering how important it was to secure a commander for the expedition, it is difficult to believe that almost an entire month elapsed from the date Porter was ordered to New York until he fulfilled the most urgent part of his mission. At any rate, they met at the Pierpont House in Brooklyn, two strangely contrasting figures: Farragut was clean-shaven, while Porter, his junior by a dozen years, wore a thick black beard.

In his private journal, Porter recorded the interview. He found Farragut, he wrote, "the same active man I had seen ten years before. Time had added grey hairs to his head, and a few lines of intelligence, generally called 'crow's feet,' round his eyes. Otherwise he seemed unchanged. He had the same genial smile that always characterized him and the same affable manner which he possessed since I first knew him . . ."

The usual small talk out of the way, Porter asked Farragut what he thought of the naval officers who had joined the Confederacy.

"Those damned fellows will catch it yet," exploded Farragut.

"I am glad to hear you talk that way," said Porter. "Would you accept a command such as no officer in our navy ever held, to go and fight those fellows whose conduct you so reprobated?"

"What do you mean?" said Farragut.

"I will tell you nothing until you have answered my question," replied Porter. But he quickly added, exceeding greatly his instructions from Gideon Welles: "I am empowered to offer you the best command in the navy, if you will go in against the Rebels and fight them to the last."

"I cannot fight against Norfolk," replied Farragut slowly, in a sad voice.

"Then you are not the man I came after," snapped Porter, "for Norfolk will be the very place to be attacked first, and that den of traitors must be wiped out."

This was a cruel test to which Porter put Farragut, for Mrs. Farragut had relatives in Norfolk and some of the old captain's most intimate friends lived there. Torn between affection for his own people in the South and an innate devotion to duty, Farragut listened for nearly two hours while Porter tried to convince him that it was not wrong for him to fight against his. kinsfolk. Farragut was conscious, too, that he had sworn to serve the United States, "honestly and faithfully without any mental reservation, against all their enemies."

Suddenly Farragut jumped to his feet. "I will take the command," he said, "only don't you trifle with me."

"You will hear in twenty-four hours what your fate will be," said Porter as he bade Farragut good-by.[13]

In one of his published accounts, Porter says he wired the Navy Department: "Farragut accepts the command, as I was sure he would."

How much of this one may believe, it is hard to say. It is incredible that Porter, sent on a secret mission with instructions not to commit the Navy Department in any way whatever, should have exceeded those instructions in offering a high command to Farragut. By the same token, how could he send a telegram to Secretary Welles announcing Farragut's acceptance of a command which Welles had not authorized him to offer?

Farragut's account of this interview, in marked contrast to Porter's flamboyant narrative, abounds in simplicity:

"*My* first intimation of the attack [on New Orleans] was a message through him [Porter] from the Department to know if I thought New Orleans could be taken, to which I replied in the affirmative. The next message was to know if I thought I could take it, to which I answered that I thought so and if furnished with the proper means, was willing to try. Upon this I was ordered to Washington . . ."[14]

Welles' order detaching Farragut from the New York retiring board and directing him to report personally to the Navy Department was issued on December 15. Farragut reached Washington on December 21, and Fox, under instructions from Welles to have a "free, social and discretionary talk" with him before Farragut talked to the secretary, took him to the home of Postmaster General Montgomery Blair.

Blair said that the meeting took place after breakfast at his home on December 21, and years later he recalled the incident in this way:

After breakfast, in my presence, Mr. Fox laid before him the plan of attack, the force to be employed and the object to be obtained, and asked him his opinion. Farragut answered unhesitatingly that it would succeed. Mr. Fox then handed him the list of vessels which were being fitted out and asked him if they were enough. He replied that he would engage to run by the forts and capture New Orleans with two-thirds of the number. Mr. Fox told him more vessels would be added to these, and that he would command the expedition. Farragut's delight and enthusiasm was so great that when he left us Mr. Fox asked if I did not think he was too enthusiastic. I replied that I was favorably impressed and was sure he would succeed.[15]

Welles was impressed with Farragut's enthusiasm and his "unqualified approval of the original plan" of the Navy Department. Farragut agreed emphatically that it was the only way to get to New Orleans. Welles was delighted. "In every particular, he came up to all that was expected and required," wrote the Secretary of the Navy. "To obey orders, he said, was his duty; to take any risk that might be imposed upon him by the Government, to obtain a great result, he considered obligatory; and believing it imperative that a good officer and citizen should frankly but respectfully, communicate his professional opinions, he said, while he would not have advised the mortar flotilla, it might be of greater benefit than he anticipated, might be more efficient than he expected, and he willingly adopted it as part of his command, though he apprehended it would be likely to warn the enemy of our intentions."

Farragut, indeed, was lukewarm to the idea of Porter's mortar flotilla. In a letter to Welles, in 1869, he reminded the former Secretary of the Navy that when he was ordered to Washington before the New Orleans expedition, "the Department informed me I should have all the vessels I desired and many more, including a number of mortar boats. To this I replied, that I did not want the *latter* as they would be more in my way than otherwise, as I felt satisfied they would be an impediment in my mode of attack . . . But as the

Department seemed to think they were indispensable . . . I made no further objection."

Welles was much impressed by Farragut's "modest self-reliance," and he was pleased when he said that he expected to pass the forts and restore New Orleans to the United States, or never return. Welles recognized at once that Farragut "considered himself equal to the emergency and to the expectation of the Government."

Although it was not until two days later, on December 23, that Welles told Farragut to hold himself in readiness to take command of the West Gulf Squadron and the expedition to New Orleans, he undoubtedly gave him some assurances at their interview, for Farragut wrote Mrs. Farragut:

". . . Went to see Mr. Fox and Secretary Welles. Now to begin, you must keep your mouth shut and burn my letters for perfect silence is to be observed—the first injunction of the Secretary. I am to have a flag in the Gulf and the rest depends upon myself . . ."[16]

12

Outfitting the Fleet

BIOGRAPHERS OF DAVID DIXON PORTER HAVE TENDED TO EXAGGERATE his part in outfitting the mortar flotilla which he had suggested as an arm of the naval force to attack New Orleans.

For instance, J. R. Soley wrote: "In the details of preparation Porter had a large share. The mortar-flotilla was created out of nothing, and the department left the supervision of this branch of the work entirely to him. He had to purchase and fit out twenty large schooners, each one mounting a heavy 13-inch mortar and two 32-pounders."

And Richard S. West wrote: "During the months of preparation Porter divided his time between the Navy Department and New York City, where he pushed the work of purchasing suitable schooners and getting them outfitted . . ."[1]

The fact is, that all but two of the schooners used by Porter in his mortar flotilla were purchased before mid-October by the navy purchasing agent in New York, George D. Morgan, while Porter was still at sea in the *Powhatan*.[2]

No doubt, as befits a highly competent commander of a fleet, Porter was kept busy during the period of preparations, but to say that the Navy Department "left . . . the work entirely to him" is far from true.

Lieutenant Henry A. Wise of the Naval Ordnance Bureau did a remarkable job of co-ordinating the efforts of Knap, Rudd and Company of Pittsburgh, which cast the 13-inch mortars and shells, and Cooper, Hewitt and Company of New York, which undertook the production of the mortar beds.

And both Secretary Welles and his assistant, Fox, took active parts in getting the machinery to move and keeping it moving. The result was that the expedition was at sea, heading for the rendezvous at Ship Island, considerably less than three months from the date Porter was sent to New York to sound out Farragut. It was quite a remarkable job that the Navy Department did, and Commander Porter, of course, shared in it, but to give the impression that he did it all is a complete distortion, in no way supported by the records.

Porter got his orders on November 18 to "proceed to Philadelphia and examine at those places the schooners purchased by the government, whether any of them are suitable for bomb vessels." At Philadelphia, Porter found two schooners at the Navy Yard that suited him, the *Adolph Hugel* and the *George Mangham*, and he wired the Navy Department on November 20 to that effect and that he wanted two mortars with beds and platforms sent for them. Lieutenant Wise of the Naval Ordnance Bureau wired back on November 21 that Porter was authorized to take the schooners and the bureau would immediately issue orders for mortars, carriages, and ammunition.[3]

The next day, Wise, who was then acting chief of the Ordnance Bureau, wired more explicitly to Porter, who was still in Philadelphia:

Immediately upon the receipt of your communication of the 20th instant, the Bureau made application to the Army Ordnance for the two 13 in. mortars you required, and a telegraphic order was dispatched to the Fort Pitt Foundry to forward the mortars together with 500 shells, with the *utmost possible dispatch* to the Philadelphia Yard. At the same time, Mr. Knap of Pittsburgh has been authorized to procure the models of the mortar bed and platform and will personally attend to the execution of the work in the promptest manner practicable.

Wise's instructions to Charles Knap, a member of the firm of Knap, Rudd and Company, who also acted as a Navy Department agent on occasion, were dispatched on November 23. He was to proceed to New York at the earliest moment and procure fifteen wrought-iron beds for heavy 13-inch mortars in accordance with the models he had procured, and speed was paramount.

Knap lost no time in enlisting the services of his friend Abram Hewitt, and Cooper, Hewitt and Company took the job on a nonprofit basis, securing the assistance of other iron manufacturers in the New York area in turning out various parts for the mortar beds. On December 4, within ten days of Knap's visit, Hewitt wrote him: "We hope to finish the 15 beds in three weeks."

Meanwhile, Porter, having left Philadelphia, visited briefly at the Brooklyn Navy Yard, where he found that schooners already purchased by the Navy Department were admirably suited for the mortar flotilla. Then, following his original instructions, he went to Mystic, Connecticut, to inspect and report on an ironclad under construction there. On November 24, from Mystic, he wrote General McClellan: "I have selected a beautiful lot of vessels . . . If I can succeed in getting the flotilla up in the manner I desire, and obtain the command of it, I think it will prove the most formidable arm of offense yet put afloat."[4]

On November 25, Secretary Welles wrote Commander Henry H. Bell at the Brooklyn Navy Yard, approving the choice of the schooners for the mortar flotilla. The nineteen schooners, ranging in length from 89 feet to 114 feet, in tonnage from 150 to 349 tons, and in cost from $6000 to $16,000 each, had been purchased by the Navy Department in October or even earlier. By November 4, eleven of the nineteen were listed as ready for service and the other eight in various stages of preparation. While several of the schooners drew ten or twelve feet of water, the majority drew seven, eight, or nine feet, and thus they would offer no problem in getting across the bar at the mouth of the Mississippi.

The nineteen vessels, excluding the costs of outfitting and arming, cost the Navy Department $170,000. The vessels, with their tonnage, were: *Norfolk Packet* (349); *Horace Beals* (296); *T. A. Ward* (284); *Sea Foam* (264); *Henry Janes* (260); *Racer* (252); *Sidney C. Jones* (245); *John Griffith* (240); *Sarah Bruen* (233); *Sophronia* (217); *Matthew Vassar* (216); *C. P. Williams* (210); *Arletta* (200); *Para* (200); *Oliver H. Lee* (199); *William Bacon* (183); *Maria J. Carlton* (178); *Orvetta* (171); *Dan Smith* (150). The *Adolph Hugel* and the *George Mangham,* both about 275 tons, joined the flotilla later.[5]

Although Gideon Welles had enjoined strict secrecy on all aspects of the New Orleans expedition, it was not long before the New York newspapers got wind of the mortar-fleet preparations at the Brooklyn Navy Yard. Horace Greeley's New York *Tribune,* on November 29, carried the following story:

A Mortar Fleet of Schooners—The visit of Capt. [*sic*] D. D. Porter of the Navy to this city, last week, was in connection with the outfit of a small mortar fleet. Upward of 15 schooners, of from 250 to 300 tons burden each, are at present undergoing novel modifications at the ship yards on the East River and being fitted for coast service. They are strengthened with additional beams and knees, and have extra deck for their armament. They are to be built up solid in front, where an enormous mortar, weighing 25,000 pounds, will be mounted.

The enormous shock from the discharge of a 13-inch mortar will require the greatest degree of firmness in a ship to resist it successfully, hence the determination to build their small vessels solid in front . . . No other armaments will be placed on board, although some of the vessels have been fitted to carry four guns . . . other vessels are being inspected in the Eastern States by Capt. Porter, who will be in command of the fleet. Directions have been given to use all possible diligence in completing these vessels, as they are intended for immediate service. They have, therefore, been divided among almost as many ship-builders as there are vessels. The armament for these schooners is being prepared at Pittsburgh.[6]

Did Porter leak information to Horace Greeley about the flotilla and his possible command of it? Someone did, for Porter did not get his official orders from Welles until December 2, to "proceed to New York . . . for the command of the bomb vessels now being fitted for sea by Commander H. H. Bell." Thus Porter's orders were not dispatched until four days after the *Tribune's* article identified him as the mortar flotilla commander.[7]

On December 3, Lieutenant Wise rushed a telegram to Knap, Rudd and Company: "Be pleased to make for this department as early as practical, twenty-one 13-in. mortars, of the same model, as those recently sent from Pittsburgh to Navy Yard New York . . . Also two hundred & fifty shells for each mortar . . ." Two days later, in reply to a telegram from the Ordnance Bureau, Commander Bell reported that two mortar schooners were ready to receive their mortars and that eleven other vessels would be ready by December 8.

Apparently, the rapidity with which the schooners were being prepared at New York prompted the Navy Department to enlist McClellan's assistance in speeding up delivery of the mortars. It appears that McClellan was prevailed upon to release to the Navy mortars originally ordered for the Army, and permit the Navy to repay the loan when its order was completed by the foundry. This assumption is based upon a telegram which Lieutenant Wise sent to Knap, Rudd and Company on December 8: "Use every possible exertion to forward the nineteen mortars ordered for New York by Genl. McClellan. Employ special agents if necessary and push the mortars and bombs on without a moment's delay as the vessels will all be ready for them within eight days." Obviously, the mortars which Wise on December 8 urged the foundry to "push . . . on without a moment's delay" could not have been mortars which he ordered on December 3. On this point, Welles wrote in 1871:

". . . I have an impression that we borrowed some mortars of the Army to hasten matters."[8]

Meanwhile, Abram Hewitt had not been idle concerning the beds and platforms for the mortars. He pushed the work along not only at the Cooper, Hewitt foundry but at the other foundries to which he had farmed out the construction of various parts. On December 19, he was able to ship two mortar beds to the Philadelphia Navy Yard for installation on the two schooners which Porter had selected there. And on January 6, not many days beyond the three weeks in which he had hoped to complete the job, Hewitt wired Lieutenant Wise: "We have now delivered fifteen of the mortar beds, and the remaining six beds will be completed this week."[9]

If David Porter was not involved in every phase of the outfitting of the mortar flotilla, as claimed by both himself and his biographers, he was nonetheless kept busy. On December 21, Welles instructed Porter to send officers to New England to enlist sailors for the mortar flotilla. The men were to enlist for the war and thereby receive two months' pay in advance. At Brooklyn Navy Yard, Porter had already been enlisting acting masters and acting master's mates, and early in January he began training them in their duties. Every morning at nine o'clock, they assembled at the Lyceum at the Navy Yard for instruction. By January 17, 1862, nearly 100 officers, chiefly acting masters and acting master's mates, had already reported for duty. Within a few days 280 seamen had enlisted for Porter's mortar flotilla.[10]

When it was evident in mid-December that good progress was being made in getting the mortar schooners ready and the work on the mortars and mortar beds was advancing rapidly, the Navy Ordnance Bureau had turned its attention to getting mortar shells for the flotilla. On December 12 an order for 5000 more, over and above what had already been ordered, was sent to Knap, Rudd and Company, and on December 21 this firm was instructed to "continue the manufacture of 13-inch bombs until the aggregate number reaches fifteen thousand." Additional orders were placed elsewhere.

A little more than a month later, as January was drawing to a close, Lieutenant Wise wired Porter to inquire if he had received enough mortar shells to put on board the schooners. Porter replied that he had 10,000 mortar shells on hand, which was "5000 more than the schooners can carry. They carry 250 each." Wise telegraphed back: "Orders will be given to charter a vessel and ship all the mortar shells that you do not take in the squadron, to a certain point where you are going. Two thousand in addition will follow."[11] Porter had selected as his flagship the 600-ton sidewheeler *Harriet Lane*, which was transferred from the Revenue Service. Five other gunboats, to tow the mortar schooners and also to protect them, were attached to the flotilla. These were the *Owasco*, a new gunboat of 507 tons, mounting two guns; three converted Staten Island ferryboats, *Clifton*, *Jackson*, and *Westfield*; and a new side-wheeler, the *Miami*.

The mortar schooners and their steam consorts were nearly ready to sail about the time Farragut received his first official orders to command the expedition. On December 23, Welles had told Farragut to hold himself in readiness to take command of the West Gulf Squadron and had said that the *Hartford* would be assigned to him as his flagship.

On January 9, 1862, Secretary Welles gave the official word to Farragut: "You are hereby appointed to command the Western Gulf Blockading Squadron . . . When the U.S. steam sloop of war *Hartford* shall be prepared in all respects for sea you are authorized to hoist your flag on board of that vessel . . . Further instructions will be issued before your departure."

Farragut meanwhile had invited Commander Henry H. Bell, whose name had been suggested to him by Porter as one eager for the assignment, to join the expedition as fleet captain. The flag officer had already dropped in at Philadelphia Navy Yard to have a look at the *Hartford*. This screw sloop-of-war, barely three years old, was of 1990 tons and carried 24 guns. Its length was 225 feet, its beam 44 feet, and its draft was a few inches in excess of 16 feet.[12]

Upon receipt of his order, Farragut went immediately to Philadelphia, where he received a second order from Welles, dated January 13: "So soon as the *Hartford* is ready for sea, you will proceed with her to Hampton Roads, Virginia, reporting your arrival to the Department, and there await further instructions."

On January 19, the *Hartford* was commissioned, and to the top of her mast went Farragut's square blue flag. Several delays in taking on powder and also the ice and bitterly cold weather encountered in the Delaware River held up the *Hartford*, and it was not until January 29 that Farragut reported his arrival at Hampton Roads. "You can better imagine my feelings at entering Hampton Roads as an enemy of Norfolk than I can," Farragut wrote his wife. "But, thank God, I had nothing to do with making it so."[13]

At Hampton Roads, Farragut found two dispatches from Secretary Welles. The first, dated January 20, ordered Farragut to put to sea as soon as possible and make for the Gulf of Mexico, where Flag Officer W. W. McKean would turn over to him thirty vessels, which would comprise his West Gulf Blockading Squadron. In addition, the mortar fleet under Commander Porter, with its steamers, was assigned to Farragut, Welles stated. And then came a peremptory order:

When the formidable mortars arrive, and you are completely ready, you will collect such vessels as can be spared from the blockade and proceed up the Mississippi River and reduce the defenses which guard the approaches to New Orleans, when you will appear off that city, and take possession of it under the guns of your squadron, and hoist the American flag thereon, keeping possession until troops can be sent to you. If the Mississippi expedition from Cairo shall not have descended the river, you will take advantage of the panic to push a strong force up the river to take all their defenses in the rear. You will also reduce the fortifications which defend Mobile Bay and turn them over to the army to hold. As you have expressed yourself satisfied with the force given to you, and as many more powerful vessels will be added before you can commence operations, the Department and the country will require of you success . . . operations of a minor nature . . . must not be allowed to interfere with the great object in view, the certain capture of the city of New Orleans.

Destroy the armed barriers which these deluded people have raised up against the power of the United States Government, and shoot down those who war against the Union, but cultivate with cordiality the first returning reason which is sure to follow your success.[14]

Welles' second letter to Farragut, dated January 25, stressed the importance of "a vigorous blockade at every point" of Farragut's command, which was from St. Andrew Bay in Florida to the Rio Grande. "By cutting off all communication," wrote Welles, "we not only distress and cripple the States in insurrection, but by an effective blockade we destroy any excuse or pretext on the part of foreign governments to aid and relieve those who are waging war upon the Government."

Farragut promptly assured Welles that "the wishes of the Department shall be carefully carried out to the best of my ability, and that there will be no lack of exertion on my part to secure the best results for the Government and the country." That same day, January 30, Welles ordered Farragut to sail for the Gulf, touching at Port Royal en route. Because he was awaiting ordnance stores, Farragut did not weigh anchor until February 2, but three days later he reported himself at Port Royal. The *Hartford* arrived at Key West on February 11, and on February 20, Farragut reached Ship Island.

Commander David D. Porter, his mortar schooners and steamers having sailed several weeks earlier for Key West, boarded the *Harriet Lane* in Washington on February 11 and headed for the rendezvous in the Gulf. The Navy's expedition against New Orleans was now under way. But what of the Army's share of the project?[15]

It will be recalled that General McClellan in mid-November had promised 10,000 men to occupy New Orleans after that city had fallen before the Navy's attack. But in the pressure of affairs nearer home for the Army, McClellan seems to have put it out of his mind immediately.

Meanwhile, the politician turned major general, Benjamin F. Butler, had begun to outlive his usefulness in the East. He had wrangled with Governor Andrew of Massachusetts over raising troops in that state, and his military exploits to date had not inspired the Regular Army with any confidence in his ability. Besides, his high rank created problems among professional military men who were his subordinates, and General Butler's imperious nature was an ever-present source of embarrassment to President Lincoln and his Cabinet. If a place could be found for Butler, a long distance off, it would make many people in Washington happier.

Such a place was soon available. In November the Confederates had evacuated Ship Island and units of the Federal blockading fleet had occupied it. Years later, Gideon Welles recalled that "all would be relieved were this restless officer [Butler] sent to Ship Island or the far Southwest, where his energy, activity and impulsive force might be employed in desultory aquatic and shore duty in concert with the Navy." General Butler was ordered to occupy Ship Island, and the first elements of his troops under Brigadier General John W. Phelps—1908 strong, "including servants"—arrived there on December 3.[16]

As yet, Butler, who was still in Washington, had not the vaguest idea of the naval expedition to New Orleans. His biographer, Parton, however, tells dramatically how Butler and Secretary of War Edward Stanton initiated the New Orleans adventure, an utterly fanciful tale, which Butler himself did not relate in his autobiography.

During a conference, about January 10, 1862, Parton's tale goes, Stanton suddenly asked Butler:

"Why can't New Orleans be taken?"

Butler, "thrilled to the marrow" by the question, bellowed his reply: "It CAN!"

"This was the first time New Orleans had been mentioned in General Butler's hearing, but by no means the first time he had thought of it," declared Parton. "The secretary told him to prepare a programme . . ."

McClellan, said Parton, was also asked for an opinion, but he said that it would take 50,000 men to take New Orleans and they could not be spared.

"But now General Butler, fired with the splendor and daring of the new project, exerted all the forces of his nature to win for it the consent of the Government," declared Parton. "He talked New Orleans to every member of the cabinet. In a protracted interview with the President, he argued, he entreated, he convinced. Nobly were his efforts seconded by Mr. Fox, the Assistant Secretary of the Navy, a native of Lowell, a schoolmate of General Butler's. His whole heart was in the scheme. The President spoke, at length, the decisive word, and the general almost reeled from the White House in the intoxication of his relief and joy."

Welles effectively scuttled this fable in his *Galaxy* article:

> The truth is, the President, instead of being urged, entreated, and at length convinced, in January, as stated, had "spoke the decisive word" as early as the middle of November, had many interviews with the Secretary of the Navy in regard to it, had examined charts and been made acquainted with the opinions of the Army Engineer, General Barnard, and advised that the auxiliary bomb flotilla proposed by Commander Porter should be adopted, before Mr. Stanton was a member of Mr. Lincoln's cabinet. Mr. Fox, who is represented as *seconding* General Butler, had been engaged for many weeks in earnest, incessant labors and preparatory arrangements before General Butler was let into the secret . . ."

Welles declared that Butler's Ship Island expedition was about to go up in smoke when the Navy Department got wind of it. Butler himself had told his friend Gustavus Fox that orders for reinforcements to Phelps had been revoked. Fox hastened at once to Secretary of War Stanton's office. Stanton was astonished to hear that preparations had been afoot for more than two months to launch a naval attack on New Orleans.

"An attack upon New Orleans by the Navy?" he exclaimed, seizing Fox's hand. "I never have heard of it. It is the best news you could give me."

Fox explained that the approximately 2000 men that Butler had already sent to Ship Island, and the reinforcements for which orders had been canceled, were part of the 10,000 troops McClellan had promised in November, with the full knowledge and approval of Mr. Lincoln.

Stanton immediately sent for McClellan, who agreed that he had committed the Army to support the Navy with troops as soon as the expedition was prepared. "So quietly had the preparations progressed," wrote Welles later, "and so little had he been consulted in this naval expedition, that General McClellan was surprised when informed of the facts, the progress that had been made, and that Flag Officer Farragut had been selected and received his orders."[17]

On February 23, McClellan issued orders to Butler, naming him "to the command of the land forces destined to cooperate with the Navy in the attack on New Orleans." His force would include 14,400 infantry, 275 cavalry, 580 artillery, for a total of 15,255 men. And Butler was authorized to borrow temporarily two regiments, one from Key West and the other from Fort Pickens, to bring his troop total to 18,000.

"The object of your expedition is one of vital importance—the capture of New Orleans," wrote McClellan. "The route selected is up the Mississippi River, and the first obstacle to be encountered (perhaps the only one) is the resistance offered by Forts Saint Philip and Jackson. It is expected that the Navy can reduce these works. In that case you will, after their capture, leave a sufficient garrison in them to render them perfectly secure . . . Should the Navy fail to reduce the works, you will land your forces and siege train, and endeavor to breach the works, silence their guns, and carry them by assault. . . ."

McClellan, in a general order the same day, created a new military department, the Department of the Gulf, stating that the headquarters would be movable, wherever the commanding general, General Butler, might be.[18]

Butler called on Secretary Stanton and found President Lincoln with him. He told them of his orders, whereupon "Mr. Stanton was overjoyed," Butler wrote later. "The President did not appear at all elated." On taking his leave, Butler said to the Secretary of War:

"I am going to take New Orleans or you will never see me again."

"Well," replied Stanton, in Lincoln's presence, "you take New Orleans and you shall be a lieutenant general."

On February 25, General Butler, with his wife and some staff officers, and 1600 troops, sailed for Ship Island on the steamer *Mississippi.*

Flag Officer Farragut was already in Gulf waters; Commander Porter, aboard the *Harriet Lane,* was nearing Key West; and now General Butler was on the high seas. The New Orleans expedition was in full swing and the stage was being set at the mouth of the Mississippi for some of the most dramatic moments of the war.

In Washington, as Butler sailed away, many officials felt relieved. General McClellan's father-in-law, R. B. Marcy, expressed it neatly:

"I guess we have found a hole to bury this Yankee elephant in."[19]

13

New Orleans Becomes Jittery

"THE FIRST OF JANUARY, 1862, FINDS US UNSUBDUED," DECLARED THE New Orleans *Crescent*. "It finds us in better condition than ever for a successful defence of our independence. It finds us with more men in the field than ever before, more guns, more munitions of war, a naval service gradually enlarging, and the sympathies of the nations of Europe on our side. It finds us, in fact, 'masters of the situation.'"

This, of course, was sheer whistling in the dark as far as New Orleans itself was concerned, for despite leaks in the blockade by ships occasionally running in and out of Berwick Bay, the commerce of New Orleans was paralyzed. The *Crescent*, less than a week later, modified its claims sharply by blaming Confederate or Louisiana authorities for lack of boldness as regards the blockade at the mouth of the Mississippi. It said that there had not been a day since October 12, when Commodore Hollins chased the blockaders out of the river, that vessels could not have gone to sea out of the Mississippi. "But what evidence have we to furnish the great powers of Europe of the ineffectuality of the blockade, publicly and openly?" it asked. "Not an iota." The *Crescent* was ill informed on this point, however. While it was true that the blockade kept ships from reaching New Orleans, some vessels did escape from the city and out through the passes. On November 23, the schooner *Break of Day* went to sea through Pass a Loutre, and six days later the steamer *Vanderbilt* escaped by the same exit. On January 4, the *Calhoun* ran the blockade, but later was abandoned and then captured by the Yankees, who promptly put it into blockade duty. At the time the *Crescent's* piece was published, other ships were under the guns of Fort Jackson, awaiting an opportunity to slip away.[1]

Judging from press comments in New Orleans as the first anniversary of secession neared, people were growing impatient, especially at the Confederate authorities' devotion to the idea that European intervention was imminent. "The Confederacy must work, and prepare and fight as though it were to be alone on this continent with its enemy," said the *Picayune*, "and had to depend on its own strength and endurance alone to uphold itself." The *Commercial Bulletin* was even more emphatic:

The situation of this port makes it a matter of vast moment to the whole Confederate State that it should be opened to the commerce of the world within the least possible period . . . We believe the blockading vessels of the enemy might have been driven away and kept away months ago, if the requisite energy had been put forth. We have waited in vain for the Navy Department of the Confederate Government to perform the service, and equally in vain have been our expectations of any relief from abroad . . . For more than six months past . . . the blockade has remained, and the great port of New Orleans has been hermetically sealed to the commerce of the world all that time, and may continue so for six months longer unless we ourselves break the seal. Here is the pinching point. Shall we permit the port to remain closed six months longer without making a bold, vigorous, aye a desperate effort to open it? We say not, and we believe this is the voice of almost the entire community . . .

The *Delta*, voicing impatience at the lack of "form, compactness and efficiency" in the city's militia, called for "less parade and more work." It complained that "we have let months and months of precious time slip away for naval armament . . ." Editor John Maginnis, of the *True Delta*, never a timid soul, expressed his disgust at the way things were going by calling upon the people to agitate to make New Orleans a free city, under the protection of the Confederacy, "but separate, distinct and independent in all things from the protecting power."

The *Crescent*, if not contradicting itself, again diluted its New Year's Day confidence less than two weeks later when it complained that the authorities had neglected Lake Borgne and Lake Pontchartrain:

> That the Mississippi Sound could have been kept clear, that communications with Mobile maintained, there is not a shadow of a doubt. Who is or are to blame can be asked and readily answered, that is, the Secretary of the Navy of the Confederate States. The Hessians have not had over twenty guns afloat on Mississippi Sound at any time up to the present . . . Twenty gun boats could have been on the lakes weeks ago, and Mississippi Sound been too warm a place for the Hessians . . .[2]

Just a few days earlier Secretary of War Benjamin had written General Lovell expressing the hope that he could do something "to check the enemy and encourage our people on the sea-coast of Mississippi." His letter crossed one from Lovell in which the latter reminded Benjamin that in their final conversation in Richmond he had warned "that if the protection of the navigable streams running up into the country was removed from my control it would in all probability not be properly arranged in connection with the land defenses, while the general commanding the department would be considered by the people at large as responsible for inroads into the territory of his command. This is just what has happened."

Lovell explained that he would have long since had light-draft armed vessels or launches at many points along the coast, "had I not kept in view your expressed wish that all clashing, even in appearance, should be avoided between the two armed services." He added that he had larger forces on Lake Borgne than the Navy, "kept up under the name of supplying our forces on the sound," the vessels ostensibly being armed for their own defense.

In conclusion, Lovell again asked Benjamin for what he had sought in vain in October prior to assuming command at New Orleans: "I hope that, in connection with Mr. Mallory, you may be able to devise some plan by which either the entire matter may be placed under my control or the naval officer in command may have orders to afford such aid as I may officially require of him. The blame of want of protection will rest upon me in any event, and I should therefore have some power to say what should be done."[3]

New Orleans was just as sensitive to spy rumors in January 1862 as it had been in the summer of 1861. On January 3, General Lovell ordered the censorship of outgoing letters, an action which most people readily agreed was demanded by the crisis. About a week later the city was swept with fantastic rumors which apparently fell on the ears of those expecting the direst things to happen. Noting the excitement that swept the city, especially among the timid, the *Picayune* commented: "Every day they hear one thousand alarming rumors, and their wonder is, every morning they were not made prisoners of war during their sleep, by an invading army."

The *Commercial Bulletin* took cognizance of the spy fever:

Dame Rumor—This respectable lady was unusually busy all last week, and kept the military, their wives, and sweethearts in a perfect state of excitement, the whole time. Every possible idea that could enter the head of credulous people seemed to have been hatched up and enlarged, and if Gen. Lovell and Governor Moore were to do half what it was reported they were about to do, they would soon become the most remarkable men of the age.

It remained, however, for the *Crescent* to list some of the rumors that had been called to its attention, but as its tone was facetious, it is likely that it was indulging in a bit of journalistic satire. Here are some of the things the *Crescent* said the people were worried about: Yankees at Milneburg, just five miles from town; armed organization of abolitionists in Metairie, a suburb, who plan to burn the city and murder the women and children; General Lovell has asked Governor Moore for 40,000 men; the ram *Manassas* has accidentally blown up; the Yankees have taken Baton Rouge and released the prisoners from the penitentiary on promise of their cutting the levee; the Yankees are digging a tunnel into New Orleans; guns have been stolen from the forts and General Lovell had to replace them with water pipes.[4]

A rumor circulated in the Louisiana legislature that Federal officers had slipped into New Orleans in disguise on January 8, when a review of troops was held in celebration of the anniversary of the Battle of New Orleans. The *Delta* declared the rumor utterly baseless and "of the same character with hundreds of others that have been in circulation by gossipmongers or evil-disposed persons." It said that the military authorities investigated the report and "it proved to be a dream or imagination of some too imaginative person."

Nevertheless, the story came to the attention of the New Orleans correspondent of the Charleston *Courier*, which printed it under a January 18 New Orleans date line. The story, quoted in the New York *Tribune*, and doubtless other northern papers, said:

We have the story in circulation, and it seems to be pretty well authenticated, that three officers from the Union fleet paid our city a clandestine visit, disguised as oystermen, on the 8th. What was to be accomplished by the hazardous adventure passes our comprehension, unless it was to communicate directly with the stationary spies here, of whom there are many, no doubt, and perhaps to witness the spectacle of the celebration of the anniversary . . . with a view of measuring our military strength. Before leaving, one of them dropped a note in the Post Office to a military officer, with whom he was formerly acquainted, bantering him upon the laxity of our guard, and promising another call at an early day, under circumstances not constraining a masquerade.

Apparently General Lovell put more stock in the story than the New Orleans newspapers did, for on January 15 he inquired of Secretary of War Benjamin what to do if he caught a Federal officer spying: "It was reported yesterday that Lieutenant Foster, of the United States Navy, had been in the city as a spy some days since. Should I arrest a Federal officer under such circumstances, is he to be punished with death?" Benjamin answered: "If you arrest a Federal officer as a spy he is to be put to death without the slightest hesitation."

A few weeks later, perhaps the most startling rumor of them all spread through the city. It was that General Beauregard had been killed and that his body had been brought secretly to New Orleans and just as secretly buried at Terre-aux-Boeufs, with only the family and a few trusted friends present.[5]

General Lovell had more on his mind than running down rumors. For one thing, he was trying to get back some troops that he had loaned to General Polk on a purely temporary basis. Lovell complained to Secretary Benjamin on January 8 that despite the distinct understanding that he would get the troops back when the enemy appeared in the vicinity of New Orleans, all he got was a telegram from Polk stating that he had asked the War Department to send some troops to Lovell in place of his two regiments and that Benjamin had agreed to this. Lovell expressed the hope that this was untrue, and for a very good reason. "The troops I sent him are natives of this part of the country, and cannot be replaced with others," wrote Lovell. "The third Mississippi regiment is composed largely of the fishermen, oystermen and sailors of Bay St. Louis, Biloxi, Ocean Springs, etc., and are well acquainted with all the inlets, bayous and soundings of that intricate and difficult coast and can be of more service there than any other body of men." Lovell said that he had written General Polk, insisting upon the return of the 3d Mississippi and also the 13th Louisiana regiments, and he begged Benjamin, even if he authorized Polk to keep the 13th Louisiana, that he would order the Mississippi regiment to return at once. Lovell made no attempt to disguise his irritation at General Polk's action. "He does me great injustice," said Lovell, "by leaving me till this late hour under the impression that when I wanted those two regiments they should be returned . . ." Benjamin, a week later, ordered the Mississippians back to Lovell. About this time, the promotion of Colonel J. K. Duncan to brigadier general, which Lovell had sought for several months, came through and Lovell appointed General Duncan to the command of all the coastal fortifications in the department.[6]

On January 14, Benjamin sent telegraphic orders to General Lovell to seize fourteen steamboats and steamships at New Orleans and impress them for the public service, their value to be determined by disinterested and trustworthy parties. Lovell, in the dark as to the purpose of the seizure, telegraphed back the next day that the order had been carried out, and he followed on January 16 with a letter confirming the seizure of the *Mexico, Orizaba, Texas, Charles Morgan, Florida, Arizona, William Heines, Atlantic, Austin, Magnolia, Matagorda, William H. Webb, Anglo-Saxon,* and *Anglo-Norman.* He recommended that the *Galveston* be substituted for the *Atlantic,* which was small and in poor shape.

Lovell, who placed the vessels in the charge of Flag Officer Hollins until further orders, discovered the seizure had broken up a projected plan to outfit some of the vessels as warships for the state of Louisiana. "In this connection," he wrote Benjamin, "permit me to call attention to Captain Higgins, who lately resigned with a view of fitting out some of these vessels for war purposes under State Authority. This seizure puts an end to his business. He is an officer of the old Navy, of experience, skill and high reputation as a bold and efficient officer. His services would be of great value in assisting to fit out a fleet here and in fighting it afterwards."[7]

Seizure of the vessels created considerable stir in New Orleans. What in the world, people asked, did the War Department want with steamships? The *True Delta* fairly exploded:

The consternation this produced among the shipping men and cotton dealers can be more easily imagined than described. Suffice it to say, that it beggars description, and all the more so, as a war department is rather an unusual avenue through which to direct naval affairs. Mr. Mallory in Richmond, Commodore Hollins here, must derive peculiar satisfaction from finding Colonel Benjamin and General Lovell discharging duties usually believed to appertain to their cloth, but which, we suppose, they are not deemed eligible to discharge. The whole thing is so funny and eccentric, that we believe there is some truth in the story circulating that it is in contemplation to organize, for blockade service, a corps of horse-marines.

The *Delta* took the *True Delta* to task the next day, stating that there had been a general understanding among the press, for obvious reasons of public policy, that no mention of the seizure would be made. "It seems, however," it declared, "that there are those among us who consider it proper, perhaps a duty, to apprise the enemy of every important military movement made here . . . No good can be accomplished by the self-imposed reservation of one portion of the press, while another is performing espial offices for the enemy."

About ten days after Benjamin's telegraphed orders, Lovell received an explanatory letter from the secretary stating that Congress had provided $1,000,000 for floating defenses on the western rivers to be spent at the President's discretion by either the War or Navy Departments. Obviously, the force intended would be a "peculiar" one. "It is not to be part of the Navy, for it is intended for service on the rivers, and will be composed of the steamboatmen of the Western waters," declared Benjamin. "It will be subject to the general command of the military chief of the department where it may be ordered to operate, but the boats will be commanded by steamboat crews, who will be armed with such weapons as the captains may choose, and the boats will be fitted out as the respective captains may desire."

Mr. Benjamin then outlined the ingenious plan for encasing the bows of the ships in iron and running down or running over at high speed the gunboats and mortar boats with which the Yankees planned to attack the Confederacy's river defenses. In the judgment of both President Davis and Congress, these Federal vessels, because of their iron plates and peculiar construction, offered little chance to the Confederate forces to arrest their descent of the river by shot and shell. However, their weight, unwieldy construction, and slow speed render them vulnerable "to the mode of attack devised by the enterprising captains who have undertaken to effect their destruction." The secretary continued:

> Captains Montgomery and Townsend have been selected by the President as two of those who are to command these boats. Twelve other captains will be found by them and recommended to the President for appointment. Each captain will ship his own crew, fit up his own boat, and get ready within the shortest possible delay. It is not proposed to rely on cannon, which these men are not skilled in using, nor on fire arms. The men will be armed with cutlasses. On each boat, however, there will be one heavy gun, to be used in case the stern of any of the gunboats should be exposed to fire, for they are entirely unprotected behind, and if attempting to escape by flight would be very vulnerable by shot from a pursuing vessel.

Benjamin called on Lovell to give the project his full co-operation, because "prompt and vigorous preparation is indispensable." The river fleet, he said, while aimed at operations on the upper Mississippi, "may prove very formidable aids to your future operations in the lower part of the valley." The sum of $300,000 was being placed to Lovell's credit, Benjamin stated, for outfitting the vessels. He was advised to "allow a very wide latitude" to the captains in preparing their ships, but at the same time to prevent "throwing away money in purely chimerical experiments" and checking "profligate expenditures."

General Lovell must have read this letter with astonishment and much shaking of his head. A few days later, he wrote Secretary Benjamin urging that some competent person have general control of the fleet in fitting it out and in establishing rules and orders for its control and management. "Fourteen Mississippi River captains and pilots," he observed dryly, "will never agree about anything after they once get under way."

A board appointed by General Lovell to appraise the steamers set the value at $900,000, but by replacing several of the more expensive ones with cheaper vessels that would just as well serve the purpose, Lovell reduced the cost to $620,000. This, he told Benjamin, he needed at once, because the owners were clamoring for their money. "The parties annoy me considerably," he said.[8]

About this time, Colonel St. John Liddell, Louisiana planter turned soldier, arrived in New Orleans on a troop-seeking mission for General Albert Sidney Johnston. Liddell had gone first to Richmond, where in mid-January he had an interview with President Davis, presenting General Johnston's request for reinforcements.

"My God!" exclaimed Davis. "Why did General Johnston send you to me for arms and reinforcements, when he must know that I have neither? He has plenty of men in Tennessee and they must have arms of some kind. Shotguns, rifles, even pikes, could be used. We commenced this war without preparation and we must do the best we can with what we have at hand."

Liddell remarked that perhaps troops from Charleston, Savannah, Pensacola, and even New Orleans might be spared.

"Do you think those places of so little importance that I should strip them of troops necessary for their defense?" asked Davis.[9]

Nevertheless, Liddell must have received some encouragement from President Davis to try to get some troops from General Lovell, for within two weeks he was in New Orleans conferring with the commanding general of Department No. 1.

"There is the probability of an immediate movement of Buell and Grant against Johnston," Liddell said. "If you can possibly spare some troops from your command you should do so quickly, sending them to Kentucky."

Lovell listened as Liddell posted him on the state of affairs in Johnston's army and the great need for reinforcements.

"I'll do it," Lovell reluctantly agreed. "But I must be the judge of the necessity of my troops being there. I do not wish to be cheated again of any portion of my command. General Polk requested reinforcements from me, which I sent, with the understanding that they were to be kept no longer than absolutely necessary. But afterwards, Polk, not wishing to return them, had obtained the consent of the War Department to keep them altogether. I will not be cheated out of my troops again."

"How would it sound, General Lovell, for General Johnston, at the distance he is from you, to insist on being the judge of your necessities in New Orleans before he would aid you?" asked Liddell.

"Well," replied Lovell, "I will send a staff officer to inquire into the facts, and afterwards send the troops if I find they are needed."[10]

Colonel Liddell later called on Governor Moore to urge him to telegraph President Davis for authorization to use the idle steamboats at New Orleans to transport the commands of General Van Dorn and General Price from Arkansas to General Johnston in Tennessee.

"This will be sufficient to bring it to the notice of Mr. Davis," pointed out Liddell. "He might then take immediate action, otherwise the chance may escape his attention."

Liddell explained to Governor Moore the sheer necessity of getting reinforcements to Johnston at once:

"Time and celerity of action are with us and delay might be fatal, even to New Orleans and Louisiana, for the possession of the Mississippi River will follow failure on our part."

Governor Moore hesitated a moment and then declined to do anything in the matter. "I have nothing to do with the military," he said.

Liddell then called on Judge E. W. Moïse, state attorney general and one of Governor Moore's close 't advisers, entreating him to use his influence on the governor to send the telegram to Davis.

"The governor has been repeatedly snubbed by the President,"

173

answered Moïse in a quick and decided tone, "and will not subject himself to any further indignities from that quarter."

Liddell was "shocked at the vindictive absurdity of the excuse, when disaster was threatening the very existence of State and City."

"Well, I would take a thousand snubbings to save the cause," responded Liddell.

Moïse gave a determined shake of his head, saying as he turned away: "The governor will not, and it is useless to talk further about it!"

Liddell could not fathom such a state of affairs. "What folly!" he thought. "These two big men . . . engaged in keeping up absurd and nice points of etiquette."[11]

New Orleans enthusiastically celebrated the first anniversary of secession. But the public celebration took place on January 27, because the twenty-sixth, the actual date, was a Sunday. That is, everybody except the Orleans Guards celebrated it a day late. This unit voted unanimously to observe Secession Day on the anniversary date, drawing praise from the *True Delta* for "thus worthily commemorating a great day, while rebuking the Sabbatarian puritanism which would convert their city into a pitiful imitator of fanatical Boston." The *True Delta* was joined in these sentiments by the Abbé Napoléon Perché, editor of *Propagateur Catholique*, who inquired why patriotic rejoicings of the day would be a profanation of the Sabbath.

The city was decked with flags and colors and there was a "grand military turnout" on Canal Street. The newspapers estimated that from 10,000 to 15,000 troops participated in it. The *Commercial Bulletin* expressed "confidence in the ability of our city's troops to defend their homes from desecration," but it was with regret and discouragement that it noted "thousands of men idly looking on" who should have been in uniform. Although the regiments were out in only half strength, said the *Crescent*, the first observance of Louisiana's Independence Day passed off "most creditably, and afforded a fair opportunity for prediction as to what it will be in the future, when it shall come to our children and our children's children to show their gratitude to the patriotic men who dissolved connection with the Yankee despotism." The *Delta* called the observance "truly a grand, impressive and magnificent one," and the troops strung out along the length of Canal Street made "one of the grandest and most impressive military spectacles ever exhibited in this country." At noon, the Orleans Artillery fired a 21-gun salute in Jackson Square. "The cost of this firing, about seventy dollars, was subscribed by patriotic gentlemen in and out of the company," declared the *Delta*.[12]

The enthusiasm over the anniversary of secession had not subsided when sobering news reached New Orleans. The *Picayune* printed on January 29 an article from the Richmond *Examiner*, which quoted the Washington *Star* as follows:

It is now publicly announced that Commander Farragut is to command the great expedition that is to operate on the western part of the gulf. It may be stated that the fleet will consist of the *Richmond*, *Pensacola*, and other large steam frigates, a great number of gunboats, and some twenty or thirty vessels carrying mortars and thirty-two pounders. The opinion is expressed in naval circles that few fortified places can hold out against such an expedition.

This brought forth salvos of criticism from the New Orleans press. The *Delta* opened fire by deploring the fact that Confederate gunboats in the river and the lakes had done nothing to justify the high hopes placed in them. "There is no doubt but that much discontent is felt and expressed on account of the abortive character of all the enterprises that have been undertaken by this department," complained the *Delta*. "The enemy's cruisers, often small and detached vessels, come into the river and into the bays, where they might be attacked and captured, and yet our gunboats remain in port, or closely hug the shore, and our officers seem to have a pleasant and jolly time of it." The *Crescent* declared that but for "the inefficiency and weakness of the Navy Department of the Confederate States, the port of New Orleans might, on this day, have been opened to the commerce of the world. As it is, all we have to do is to go to work and do the opening ourselves."[13]

What progress had the Navy Department at New Orleans made in the face of gathering Federal fleets outfitting for operations in the Gulf of Mexico? On January 18 the *Bienville* was launched on Bayou St. John and a week later the *Trent* came off the ways on the same stream. Both were expected to be ready for service on the lakes within three weeks. "The Lincolnites may expect some fun when all our gunboats are finished," predicted the *Commercial Bulletin.*

Large and approving crowds witnessed the launching of the two lake gunboats, but they were nothing compared with the turnout at Jefferson City on February 6, when the giant ironclad *Louisiana* was launched. Thousands of people lined the levee and cheered as the formidable craft, gaily decked in Confederate and Louisiana flags, sliding broadside into the river, was christened with champagne. "Everyone present seemed to be impressed with the idea that she might safely be called the Invincible," said the *True Delta.* "As to her dimensions, armament, engines, and such particulars, we do not deem it proper to say anything." The *Louisiana*, which was begun on October 15, thus hit the water a little more than three and a half months after the first timbers were set down. But there was much to be done, particularly sheathing the vessel with its railroad iron and installing the machinery. And contractors for the latter piled delay upon delay.

In the adjoining shipyard, Nelson and Asa Tift pushed the work on the *Mississippi.* At the time that the *Louisiana* was launched, the woodwork on the *Mississippi* was complete and the boilers had been installed. But the central shaft which Secretary Mallory had undertaken to have the Tredegar Works turn out was still in the Richmond foundry, and the machinery for the *Mississippi* was being as slowly produced in New Orleans as that of the *Louisiana.*

The ship carpenters' strike in November, delays in arrivals of materials, military drills which took workmen off the job, all combined to slow down the progress on the two ironclads upon which so much dependence was placed for the defense of New Orleans.[14]

In early February, New Orleans received word that its favorite son, General P. G. T. Beauregard, had been shifted to the West from Virginia,[15] but the ardor with which this was received was chilled when the news arrived that Fort Henry, on the Tennessee River, had fallen to the Yankee army, supported by gunboats. This was a severe and unexpected loss, but the *Crescent* refused to be alarmed by it:

> On the contrary, our confidence in the success of our cause is greater than ever. We are sure of eventual triumph . . . convinced that the hour is not very far distant. A few reverses will do us good by teaching us wholesome lessons. A long career of uninterrupted successes had the natural effect of making us boastful, arrogant, and over-confident. We trust we are now cured; and that we will gird up our loins; deliberately and determinedly, to drive the abolition hordes from our borders, or perish in the attempt . . . We must all put our shoulders to the wheel with an invincible will to conquer. Nothing more is required, and nothing else will answer.

The fall of Fort Henry had its repercussions in other than emotional ways in Department No. 1. On February 8, Secretary of War Benjamin wrote General Lovell to dispatch 5000 troops to Columbus, Kentucky, to reinforce that point, which was threatened by superior Federal forces. "The menacing aspect of affairs . . . has induced the withdrawal from points, not in immediate danger, of every man that can be spared . . ." wrote Benjamin. "New Orleans is to be defended from above by defeating the enemy at Columbus; the forces now withdrawn from you are for the defense of your own command, and the exigencies of the public defense allow us no alternative." To prepare Lovell for the order, Benjamin also telegraphed him that he had written him "to send immediately 5000 of your best equipped men to Columbus, to reinforce General Beauregard."

On February 12, Lovell wrote Benjamin that General Ruggles and his entire brigade of five regiments, with a field battery, would leave in two days, but he made no attempt to disguise the reluctance with which he yielded his troops. "I regret the necessity of sending away my only force at this particular juncture," wrote Lovell, "and feel sure that it will create a panic here, but will do my best to restore confidence by a show of strength." Lovell told Benjamin that he would do his best to organize a force for the defense of New Orleans' inner lines from the volunteers and militia of the city and state. "Unfortunately," said Lovell, "the legislature passed a law at its late session reorganizing the whole militia, which has to be done at a very inconvenient moment, but I am in hopes that most of the volunteers will elect their company and field officers on the instant, so that we shall soon have a force on land."[16]

Lovell's fears of panic in New Orleans on the withdrawal of 5000 trained and equipped troops were not groundless, for New Orleans was already in a jittery state of mind. Among things—other than the bad news from Tennessee—not calculated to improve morale in New Orleans was the report of a ship captain just arrived from Mississippi Sound that 65 Federal vessels were at Ship Island, and a wild rumor that the Federals had landed troops at Terre-aux-Boeufs, barely ten miles below the Chalmette battlefield where Andrew Jackson had beaten the British. No wonder the *True Delta* declared: "The disposition is strong in this city to give way to panic. Every piece of adverse news fabricated by ignorance, manufactured by sordid speculators on public credulity to sell, or naturally happening in the vicissitudes of war, is greedily seized upon, devoured and again reproduced with marvelous rapidity and distorted into every fantastic shape the terror-stricken mind can possibly impart to it."[17]

A significant indication of the state of morale in New Orleans was the growing undertone of distrust among influential citizens concerning the Confederate command at New Orleans. This last was implicit in an ordinance passed by the Common Council creating a Committee of Public Safety, composed of sixty-three leading citizens, and in a lengthy comment in the *True Delta* calling for public support of General Lovell:

> Nothing is wanted to harmonize the whole and render this city impregnable but the fullest and most perfect confidence

in the capacity, determination and reliability of the generals intrusted with our defense and protection . . . Our generals must be left to manage their professional duties in the manner they judge to be the best, and they must have an ungrudging and generous support in all they do, if our city is to be preserved, and this revolution—of which this is the heart and soul—be a success. If any person or persons have complaints to make of these soldiers upon whom so heavy a responsibility rests, let him or them aggrieved carry their charges directly to their superiors for arbitration . . . We accept the eminent military and naval men sent here to direct the defensive operations of the place with confidence, because it is proper and wise to do so, and we respect them and will do all in our power to strengthen their endeavors to discharge their duties satisfactorily, without cavil or complaint; and we are persuaded that unless this conduct be followed by everyone, nothing but division, heart-burnings, disasters, and disgrace will follow. We are thus emphatic because we have reasons to apprehend that a disposition to meddle with and trammel the generals . . . exists, and the time to discourage and correct the tendency is at the very start, before mischief is done, or bad feelings engendered. Generals Lovell and Ruggles are entire strangers to us, unknown to us, even by sight; but the president has sent them to us, as possessing his fullest confidence, and no citizen who is animated by love for the cause or devotion to his country, will countenance or tolerate any cabals to annoy or to dictate to them.

A few weeks later, Mrs. Braxton Bragg wrote General Bragg that "Lovell is more & more distrusted, persons are open & plain in the expression of their opinions of him—it will in time of danger, be followed by *open mutiny.* Duncan would be far better—in him there is confidence."[18]

The Committee of Public Safety called on Lovell and offered him both financial help and personal assistance. At the same time they inquired into many aspects of the defense of New Orleans, which

Lovell was, however, unwilling to discuss with so many people. Doubtless some members of the committee, resenting Lovell's non-committal attitude, contributed to the grumbling when the general refused to take them into his full confidence.[19]

A week after the fall of Fort Henry, the people of New Orleans learned that the Federals were attacking Fort Donelson, on the Cumberland River, and the first reports were favorable to the Confederate defenders. The *Crescent* rejoiced over "highly gratifying" news, but it cautioned the public not to "rejoice unduly," for while it thought the victory was with the defenders and "that the sunlight of success shines upon our cause," it reminded its readers that it does not follow that "they are to have perpetual sunlight." When New Orleans learned that Fort Donelson, like Fort Henry, had fallen, the city "was thrown into a tempest of excitement."

A flood of abuse was poured upon the head of General Albert Sidney Johnston. The *Delta* commented that Johnston "abandoned a position of masterly inactivity at Bowling Green, and commenced a movement which has resulted in scattering his forces in a manner as inexplicable as . . . it is melancholy and disastrous." The *Crescent* agreed with the *Delta*, and denounced Johnston scornfully:

> Gen. Johnston, no doubt, fortified Bowling Green scientifically. No doubt he evacuated that town scientifically. Very likely he displayed masterly science in his retreat. Quite possibly everything was done in strict accordance with the rules laid down at West Point. But, while he was fortifying a post only to evacuate it when the enemy made certain movements, it does seem to us that he might have displayed a little common sense, and obstructed the channels of the Tennessee and Cumberland rivers . . . We care not what Gen. Johnston's strategy may have been. He left the main artery to the heart of the Confederacy open to the enemy . . . What he should have protected, he left unprotected, and what he did attempt to defend, he had to abandon.

The *Crescent* then blasted Secretary of Navy Mallory as "the cause of many of the disasters that have latterly overtaken us," declaring that it was "his fault that we are so wretchedly helpless on the water." Subsequently the same paper called on President Davis to put Beauregard in command in Tennessee and assign Johnston somewhere else, because "neither the army nor the people have confidence in him as a chief."

The *True Delta* stood alone in defending General Johnston and put the blame on "the sleepers at Richmond." It noted that, among the city's uneducated, who had never heard of Fort Donelson, a rumor had spread that the Yankees had captured Donaldsonville, an upriver town between New Orleans and Baton Rouge. The *Picayune* declared that "our first duty . . . is to strive to be calm." Continuing, it said:

> The lesson of the hour is increased vigilance, determination, courage, and patriotic devotion to duty. A war like that we are waging, a war for independence, for liberty, for existence, is a battle to be fought out, in the face of all discouragements, despite all disappointments, despite all reverses. All is not lost, while courage, resolution and patriotism remain, and have their sway in hearts determined to be free . . . Now is the hour when every man should resolve to stand in his own lot, and maintain to the last utterance. Are we ready? Are we determined? Are we resolved, as one man, to do, and if need be, to die, in the defence of the independence we have declared . . . ?[20]

There were, however, in New Orleans, large numbers who definitely were not resolved to die for the defense of a southern independence in which they had no real concern. These were the foreigners, who had organized themselves into military companies for service in New Orleans. Now, under the recently passed militia law, these foreign companies feared that Governor Moore would order them out of the city for duty.

There was considerable distress among the foreign element, especially the British. Acting consul George Coppell had reported early in January to the Foreign Office that all business was dead in New Orleans. With work unobtainable, many Britishers, once well off, were now almost destitute. "Many men have been compelled to join the Army as the only means of now obtaining a livelihood for their families," said Coppell. Many British subjects, he also reported, had asked to be sent home, but because of the expense this was impossible. He suggested that a small vessel could be chartered to take home those "who are anxious to avoid starvation, and, perhaps, taking part in this Civil War to defend their homes, which only exist in name here."

On February 13, two days before the new militia law went into effect, there was considerable concern among the British and other foreign elements in New Orleans that Governor Moore would repudiate his assurance, given the previous September, that the foreign companies would be used only for city defense or as a local police force. Coppell sent Lord Russell in the Foreign Office a copy of the militia law, which, he pointed out, "irrespective of nationality brought within its provisions every able-bodied man in the State."

Governor Moore, the day before the militia law went into effect, notified the commanding officers of the foreign companies that he could not make any exceptions in their case and that they would be placed on the same footing as the militia and volunteer companies. "This . . . would have subjected foreigners not only to very great inconveniences in the event of being ordered away from the City," Coppell informed the Foreign Office, "but they might be compelled to take an active part in a contest in which they would be looked upon as traitors and rebels, without having the defense of their homes and property as an excuse."

The commanding officers of the British companies called upon Coppell and demanded the protection that it was in the consulate's power to give. They declared that they would not serve in bodies in the way Governor Moore wanted but would disband and be forced into the militia.

Coppell, knowing that there were many French and Spanish subjects in New Orleans in the same position as the British, arranged a conference with the French and Spanish consuls to take joint action in the matter. The consuls of Austria, Bavaria, Prussia, Belgium, and Italy joined in signing a letter to Governor Moore in which exception was taken to the new militia law and stating that in case of its enforcement against foreigners the various consuls would be compelled to protest against it and against any interference with rights already conceded to foreigners.

Although the consuls' letter was written and delivered on February 14, it was not until February 18 that Governor Moore replied. "The Executives of the several states of the Confederate States of America are not charged in any manner with the relations which these states bear to foreign powers, and should you be dissatisfied with the conclusions at which I have arrived, your complaints will of course be governed by the settled usage of international intercourse," wrote Governor Moore. "I do not anticipate, however, that there will be any difficulty in satisfying the non-naturalized residents of New Orleans that I shall require nothing from them more than the duty they owe to the state whose laws protect them, and which is exacted of them by the laws of nations."

The governor recalled his promise to the foreign companies made when "we were in no danger of invasion." There was hardly the possibility then that the militia would be needed for active service in the field. "The condition of affairs is now changed," wrote Moore, "and the probabilities are every day increasing that the Militia will be required in the field." He felt compelled to withdraw the exemption given to foreign citizens from service outside the limits of New Orleans; otherwise they would remain in absolute inaction at a time when their homes were threatened, a condition, the governor said, "as inconsistent with their obvious duty as I believe it to be with their national gallantry." Governor Moore said that the defense of New Orleans would not be within its limits "but outside of them and behind her fortifications." The governor said that he did not expect to order a single soldier from New Orleans elsewhere. "I shall not exact from the foreign population any service not within the interior lines," Governor Moore added.

The British consul reported that Governor Moore's answer was deemed "as favourable as we could expect," and he had advised the British commanders, who were satisfied. Coppell concluded his report, written on February 19, by summing up the military situation at New Orleans: ". . . Land and naval forces of the United States are concentrating in great numbers on and about the Islands near this State. Heavy rains which have fallen lately and filled the swamps may impede land operation for the present, but an attack on this City is expected and active preparations are making for its defense."[21]

This was by no means the end of agitation by foreigners to avoid military service in New Orleans. On February 27, the newspapers carried an invitation from the "British Neutrality Association" to a meeting that night of "British subjects who desire to maintain the neutrality enjoined upon them by their government."

The *True Delta* declared that "such a publication has created a general disgust in the minds of every decent man in this city who owes allegiance to the British crown." It asked if the decent British citizens are going to "permit themselves to be compromised by irresponsible parties, who, in this perilous crisis, are trying not only to divide and distract our community, but, perhaps, to create a revolution within a revolution in our midst." It called for the arrest of everybody connected with the British Neutrality Association, even at the risk of war with England. The *Delta* likewise denounced the group and said that the law required military service of foreigners and "all the resolutions of public or private meetings will not relieve them from this plain obligation of international law."

The British Fusiliers were quick to repudiate the British Neutrality Association, calling its proceedings "uncalled for, ungrateful and illegal." They were joined by the British Guard and other British units, which in one way or another sought to dissociate themselves from the neutrality movement.[22]

During the height of the discussion over the foreign companies and militia service, the call came in from General Beauregard for 5000 volunteers to join his army immediately. Governor Moore published a bombastic proclamation to "Fellow Citizens and Soldiers," stating that General Beauregard had called on him for 5000 troops "to defend the Mississippi Valley, and with it your loved state, this beautiful city, and, more than all, our homes and those dearer than all else, save honor." The proclamation continued:

The laggard and the dastard await the foe at the very shrine of the sanctuary. It is the part of the brave and noble-hearted to meet him at the threshold or beyond it. . . . An insolent and powerful foe is already at the castle gate . . . In the name of all most dear to us, I entreat you to go to meet him. A brave General, our fellow citizen, calls for you, and his patriot heart feels you will come . . . Fathers, husbands, brothers, lovers, your country calls you! Citizens, your property and your rights are in danger! Will you not go? The hour for glorious action is upon us—let it not pass unheeded by . . . Upon volunteering, you will be ordered to Gen. Beauregard . . . and in a few weeks, when the necessity is past, you will return victorious or leave your name as martyrs embalmed in our hearts.

This alternative to a victorious return apparently induced some reluctance among potential volunteers, who were not anxious to become embalmed in anyone's heart. Accordingly, volunteering was slow; some were unwilling to go at all while others were willing to go for only ninety days; still others professed to be fearful of leaving New Orleans undefended. To the latter, the *Delta* addressed itself: "Those who seek to excuse their reluctance to respond to the call of Gen. Beauregard for reinforcements, by the pretense that our city is in danger from the enemy now off our seacoast, have no authority or countenance from Gen. Lovell or Gov. Moore for any such plea of apprehension. Gen. Lovell has no doubt of his ability to defend this city against any such attack as may be meditated, with the remainder of the force that will be left in the city after the quota demanded by Beauregard shall be sent. He thinks, as all sensible men do, that New Orleans is in greater danger from the advance of the enemy at Nashville than from the enemy now at Ship Island . . . There is no foundation whatever, therefore, for the report that Gen. Lovell disapproves of the dispatch of forces to the aid of Beauregard."

Lovell's true feelings, however, were not reflected by this and other newspapers' efforts to encourage volunteers for Beauregard's army. Having sent off eight regiments and two batteries, in addition to 500 shotguns and one million cartridges, Lovell had reason to feel that his department was being raided. "People are beginning to complain that I have stripped the department so completely," he wrote Secretary of War Benjamin on February 27, "but I have called upon Governor Moore for 10,000 volunteers and militia for State Service."

Thinking in terms of a land attack against New Orleans by the Federal troops on Ship Island, General Lovell added:

> Raw troops, with double-barreled shotguns, are amply sufficient to hold our intrenchments against such troops as the enemy can send to attack them. Besides, I regard Butler's Ship Island expedition as a harmless menace so far as New Orleans is concerned. A black Republican dynasty will never give an old Breckinridge Democrat like Butler command of any expedition which they had any idea would result in such a glorious success as the capture of New Orleans. He will not have 10,000 men for a demonstration by land upon any of the Gulf cities.[23]

What General Lovell did not know when he wrote that letter was that Flag Officer Farragut was already at Ship Island to organize the naval expedition against New Orleans and that Commander Porter's mortar flotilla was just a few days' sailing distance away from the rendezvous, and General Butler, with the first of the land force reinforcements for the New Orleans adventure, was at sea, steaming for the Gulf of Mexico.

14

Farragut Enters the River

FLAG OFFICER FARRAGUT WAS IMPATIENT TO GET GOING. ON HIS ARRIVAL at Ship Island on February 20, 1862, he wrote Secretary Welles that all he was waiting for was the arrival of Porter's "bombards" and the heavy warships *Pensacola* and *Richmond.*

It did not take long for Farragut and his predecessor in the western Gulf waters, Flag Officer William W. McKean, to effect the change of command, after which Farragut began in earnest the preliminaries to setting into motion his expedition against New Orleans.

On February 22, he sent a Coast Survey man to sound the passes at the mouth of the Mississippi and to place buoys to mark the safest channel. At the same time, he issued orders to Captain Craven of the *Brooklyn* to seize the telegraph station at the Head of the Passes and to cut the telegraph line to New Orleans. Both assignments were executed with dispatch.

Farragut busied himself at Ship Island, as he awaited Porter's mortar flotilla, with a thousand and one details, perhaps the most important being the securing of coal from the Army. He borrowed 800 tons, all the Army had at Ship Island, and he warned Welles that if coal supplies were not hurried to him, he would be seriously embarrassed.[1]

On March 3, Farragut reported the arrival of the *Pensacola* at Ship Island, its engine in a "lamentable condition," and he received word that the *Richmond* had gone on a reef off Key West, but without serious damage, and would soon report to him. Farragut was determined to have the *Pensacola* in his fleet, although the engineer of the vessel claimed that there was danger of the engine breaking all to pieces. To put it in repair would take a minimum of three weeks and to do the job properly would require six weeks. "I have therefore determined to run her down to the river under sail," said Farragut, "and if the engines will not perform the duty of running her up, and I can get her over the bar, I will tow her, for I cannot dispense with her battery."[2]

Farragut grew impatient awaiting Porter. "As soon as Commander Porter arrives with his gunboats I shall commence operations," he told Welles on March 3. On that date, Porter and his flotilla were at Key West. Porter had reached there on the *Harriet Lane* on February 28, finding all but three of the mortar schooners in port ahead of him. But only one of his steamers, the *Owasco*, had reached Key West. While awaiting the arrival of the missing vessels, Porter ordered mortar drills for the flotilla and found them "very creditable to the officers in charge."[3] When his flotilla was finally at full strength a couple of days later, Porter sailed to join Farragut.

Farragut, meanwhile, left Ship Island for the mouth of the Mississippi, sixty miles away, leaving a brief order to Porter: "You will find me at Pass a Loutre or in the Mississippi, anxiously awaiting your arrival." The flag officer also sent a raiding party to Biloxi, a dozen miles away on the mainland, to seize the latest New Orleans papers in the post office. When Farragut read of the fall of Fort Donelson and the Confederate surrender of Nashville, he was impressed with the urgency of striking his blow at New Orleans. "There is a great fear of everything at New Orleans," he wrote, "so that I think they are becoming very demoralized, and there could not be a better time for the blow to be struck by us, and you may depend upon its being done the moment the mortar boats arrive."[4]

Farragut issued his general order to the fleet on March 5, giving detailed instructions on how to prepare the vessels for service in the Mississippi River and how to act in battle. "Send down the topgallant masts, rig in the flying jibboom, and land all the spars and rigging except what are necessary for the three topsails, foresail, jib, and spanker," he specified. "Trice up to the topmast stays, or land the whiskers, and bring all the rigging into the bowsprit, so that there shall be nothing in the range of the direct fire ahead." One or two guns were ordered mounted on the poop and topgallant forecastle, and howitzers were to be placed in the foretop and maintop. Grapnels were to be available at all times for towing off fire rafts. Vessels were to be trimmed "a few inches by the head so that if she touches bottom she will not swing head down the river." If a vessel's machinery were damaged, under no conditions would an attempt be made to turn the ship's head downstream. Rather, it should "back and fill down under sail." Farragut covered many other details in his order, details for repairing damage to the ships during battle, details on fire fighting and water supply, details on boarding ship, details on firing the guns effectively. "No Vessel," he warned, "must withdraw from battle under any circumstances without the consent of the flag officer . . . I wish you to understand that the day is at hand when you will be called upon to meet the enemy in the worst forms of our profession. You must be prepared to execute all those duties to which you have been so long trained in the Navy, without having the opportunity of practicing. I expect every vessel's crew to be well exercised at their guns, because it is required by the regulations of the service, and is usually the first object of our attention, but they must be equally well trained for stopping shot holes and extinguishing fire. Hot and cold shot will no doubt be freely dealt us, and there must be stout hearts and quick hands to extinguish the one and stop the holes of the other."[5]

When Farragut's officers read that order, they realized that the old flag officer meant business. While devoting himself with boundless energy to the task at hand, the flag officer exuded confidence in the successful outcome of the great adventure. Some of this confidence was expressed by Farragut in a letter to Gustavus Fox on March 5: "That I will be able to carry out the wishes of the Department I have little doubt if I am spared, and if I am shot someone will, I trust, as I will make provisions for all the contingencies I can."

The "wishes of the Department" had been restated by Gideon Welles in a recent letter, in which he had also sent Farragut detailed information on Forts Jackson and St. Philip, as supplied by Brigadier General John G. Barnard. "The most important operation of the war is confided to yourself and your brave associates," Welles declared. ". . . The Department relies upon your skill to give direction to the powerful force placed at your disposal, and upon your personal character to infuse a hearty cooperation amongst your officers free from unworthy jealousies. If successful, you will open the way to the sea for the great West, never again to be closed. The rebellion will be riven to the centre, and the Flag, to which you have been so faithful will recover its supremacy in every State."[6]

But while Farragut was cool and confident and went about his preparations with methodical thoroughness, the Navy Department had been thrown into dismay by a letter he had written from Key West, weeks earlier, asking for light-draft ships. Gustavus Fox did not grasp Farragut's purpose of using the shallow-draft vessels to tighten the blockade off the many bayous and inlets that broke up the irregular Louisiana coast. Much concerned, Fox hurried off a confidential letter to Commander Porter: "A cold shudder ran through me . . . I trust we have made no mistake in our man, but his dispatches are very discouraging. *It is not too late to rectify our mistake.* You must frankly give me your views from Ship Island, for the cause of our country is above all personal considerations . . . I shall have no peace until I hear from you."

It was not until more than a month later that Porter was able to answer Fox's letter, and he did so with characteristic candor that did not preclude undercutting the superior officer whom he had recommended to command the expedition. "Yours of the 24th has been received," he wrote Fox, "and I hasten to answer it . . . If as you suppose there is any want of the proper qualities in the Flag Officer it is too late now to rectify the mistake; but as yet I see no reason why he should not be competent to do all that is expected of him. I never thought Farragut a Nelson, or a Collingwood; I only consider him the best of his rank and so consider him still; but men of his age in a seafaring life are not fit for the command of important enterprise, they lack the vigor of youth." Porter promised Fox that he would straighten Farragut out. "Farragut . . . talks very much at random at times, and rather underrates the difficulties before him, without fairly comprehending them," he told Fox. "I know what they are and appreciate them, and as he is impressionable hope to make him appreciate them also."

Porter wrote Fox again a couple of weeks later, declaring that Farragut was "full of zeal and anxiety, but has no administrative qualities, wants stability, and loses too much time in talking. Everyone likes him personally. He is as brave as anyone." But by the time Fox had received these two letters, he and Secretary Welles doubtless had had enough opportunity to re-evaluate Farragut's worth on the basis of his dispatches, which made it very clear that he was bristling with energy, determination, and confidence.[7]

Meanwhile, Farragut had been waging a ceaseless struggle against the mud barriers at the mouth of the Mississippi River, where he arrived with the *Hartford* on March 7. The five-fingered delta of the Mississippi created enormous bars at each of the entrances of the river, and these, because of constant shifting, were great hazards to navigation for vessels of heavy draft. Whereas his lighter vessels would have no trouble in crossing the bar at either Pass a Loutre or Southwest Pass, the two usable entrances into the river, Farragut was much concerned about his bigger ships, which would draw sixteen, eighteen, or more feet of water.

For three days, Farragut tried to get the *Brooklyn* over the bar at Pass a Loutre, but she stuck fast in the mud and for seventeen hours defied all the tugging and pulling efforts to free her. Finally, on March 11, the *Hartford* succeeded in dragging the *Brooklyn* into deep water, and Farragut gave up the idea of trying to enter Pass a Loutre. He then steamed around to the western side of the delta to Southwest Pass, where the *Brooklyn* crossed the bar on the first trial, grounding for about an hour some distance inside the barrier. The *Hartford*, to Farragut's relief, had no difficulty in crossing the bar. Together the *Brooklyn* and *Hartford* steamed to the Head of the Passes, which, by March 15, was already occupied in force by Union vessels.

For while Farragut was concerned with his heavier ships, the gunboats *Kineo*, *Kennebec*, and *Winona* had entered the river and had anchored at the Head of the Passes. Moreover, Fleet Captain Henry H. Bell had already fired the first shots in the New Orleans campaign. On March 12, Bell, in the *Winona*, led the three gunboats up the river on a reconnaissance. About 10:45 A.M. they spotted a Rebel steamer coming downriver. The latter turned and headed back upstream. A chase developed, and when it became evident that the gunboats were not gaining on the Confederate vessel, the *Winona* and *Kennebec* tried the range of their 20-pounder Parrotts, firing two shots each. As the Rebel ship was estimated to be two and a half to three miles away, the effect of the shots could not be determined and the firing was discontinued. But the shooting phase of the campaign had begun.

After getting the *Brooklyn* and *Hartford* into the river, Farragut ordered the *Colorado*, *Pensacola*, and *Mississippi* back to Ship Island to be lightened so as to be able to cross the bar. He felt confident that the two latter vessels would make it, but the *Colorado*, which drew twenty-three feet of water, was out of the question. Still, he had to make the attempts, as he confided to his wife: "Success is the only thing listened to in this war, and I know that I must sink or swim by that rule. Two of my best friends have done me a great injury telling the Department that the *Colorado* can be gotten over the bar into the river, and so I am compelled to try, and take precious time to do it. If I had been left to myself, I would have been in before this."[8]

Farragut went to Ship Island on March 17 to supervise the preparations, but he was not long in abandoning the idea of trying to get the *Colorado* into the river. However, as the *Mississippi* and *Pensacola* drew eighteen feet of water, another attempt would be made with them, after they had been lightened of everything except the coal necessary to fuel them. Even then, as Farragut wrote Welles, the two ships "will . . . have to be pulled through at least 1 foot of mud by the tugs."

Before Farragut left the Passes, sixteen of Porter's mortar schooners had arrived there, and he was pleased to find at Ship Island that the other mortar vessels were on hand and that the last of Porter's steamers, the *Clifton* and the *Westfield*, for whose safety there had been concern, had also arrived. Commander Porter lost no time in beginning his operation. ". . . The *Westfield* and *Clifton* . . . were set to work the moment they arrived," Porter wrote Welles, "and in eight hours we had towed into the river, across the bar, the 21 vessels in the Mortar Flotilla, the *Harriet Lane* and *Owasco* assisting."[9]

Meanwhile, in New Orleans, a crisis was rapidly developing. Prices of necessities soared and many shopkeepers were refusing to accept Confederate currency except at large discounts. Speculators were rampant, even "speculators in tears," who, according to the *Delta*, were buying up all the mourning goods in New Orleans, because "they expect the city to be filled with grief and wailing . . . Hence the opportunity to turn an honest penny."[10]

Almost daily, Lovell reported to Benjamin on March 6, prominent citizens urged him to declare martial law in New Orleans. Lovell, believing that more inconvenience than good would result, had resisted these importunities. He asked Benjamin for his opinion on the propriety of martial law for the city. However, before Benjamin could reply, the situation changed rapidly. The draining of men and material from New Orleans had set people to talking. "Persons are found here who assert that I am sending away troops so that the city may fall an easy prey to the enemy," complained Lovell to Benjamin. The next day he wrote the secretary that "loud complaints are made on all hands." Lovell protested that "the fleet threatening us below is much more formidable than that above, and I object strongly to sending every armed vessel away from New Orleans at this time."

Moreover, the accumulation of driftwood and the strong current in the river had broken the obstruction below the forts, at the very time that Union vessels in large number had entered the river. When the raft showed signs of weakness late in February, because of the high water and the vast amount of drift, Lovell employed steamboats and skiffs to remove the drift, but as fast as it was removed, the high water brought in more and more, and so the attempt was given up. The raft gave way at various points, and by the end of the first week of March, the main chains snapped, and the raft, upon which so much depended to hold the Federal vessels under the fire of the forts, ceased any longer to be an obstruction. Lovell applied to the Common Council of the city for funds and $100,000 was turned over to him to restore the raft. Under the flood conditions this was found impossible, but a makeshift obstruction was made of part of the old raft and some schooners anchored and fastened together by chains.[11]

By now, affairs both inside and out of the city made it evident to many in New Orleans that the time had come for martial law to be proclaimed. The newspapers discussed the question openly, and on March 11 the *Delta* predicted that General Lovell would proclaim martial law the next week. The following day, the *Picayune* said: "We are gratified to be able to say, that the authorities will, very soon, proclaim martial law in this city . . . and also to state that there is perfect accord between the civil and military powers in regard to the necessity . . ." That very day, a telegram was dispatched to President Davis over the signatures of Governor Moore, Attorney General Moïse, and General Lovell: "In our opinion the writ of Habeas Corpus should be suspended immediately in New Orleans. We beg that you will declare martial law here at once or authorize General Lovell to do so. Answer."

President Davis' reply came the next day, authorizing martial law not only for New Orleans but also for the nearby parishes of Jefferson, St. Bernard, and Plaquemines. On March 15, Lovell issued his martial-law order embracing the four parishes. All grown white males, except unnaturalized foreigners, were ordered to take the oath of allegiance to the Confederate States. All persons unfriendly to the Confederacy were ordered to leave without delay. All places selling liquor must close at 8 P.M., under penalty of permanent closing and confiscation of the liquor. Persons newly arrived in New Orleans with no ostensible business or any interest in the city or state must satisfy the provost marshals of their good intentions or leave New Orleans immediately.

As provost marshals for New Orleans, Lovell named William Freret, first district; Cyprien Dufour, second district; Pierre Soulé, third district; and Colonel H. D. Ogden, fourth district.

"The Gentlemen named as Provost-Marshals in the four districts of the city are well-known and prominent citizens and will discharge their duties, we are sure, with firmness, discretion, and fidelity," said the *True Delta*. The *Crescent* said that General Lovell could not have made better selections, for the provost marshals "enjoy the full confidence of the good people of New Orleans in all respects and they will discharge their duties faithfully, ably and patriotically."

There was general concurrence that Lovell's choice of men to enforce martial law was a good one, and hope was expressed on all sides that the provost marshals would do something "to protect the citizens of New Orleans from the rapacity, avarice, and monopolizing of forty or fifty (or less) individuals." Flour soared to an unheard-of twenty-two dollars a barrel. Speculators were going up the river and buying hogs for nine cents a pound and selling them for fourteen cents at the stock landing. A temporary cattle shortage sent the price of beef up 50 per cent.[12]

Lovell's declaration of martial law was followed by an order that all males above the age of sixteen should register with the provost marshals and that all arrivals from northern states since May 21, 1861, must procure permits to remain. "Circumstances have rendered these measures necessary for our safety and success," Lovell's order read, "and it becomes each and every good citizen to contribute all in his power to the promotion of such a desirable end."

To Secretary of War Benjamin, General Lovell elaborated on these "circumstances." Writing a week after he had proclaimed martial law, Lovell said:

Affairs here . . . reached a crisis . . . and it became necessary for some one to seize the helm with a strong hand, or we should have had trouble, perhaps bloodshed, between men who were all friendly to the cause. A city composed of such heterogeneous elements as this, with an excitable population, who are easily led into excesses, is difficult to govern, as there are so many interests to consult, each jealous of the other. This rendered the appointment of provost marshals a matter of great difficulty, more especially as I know that there were large and influential associations in existence whose leaders were desirous to take control. The universal approval of my appointments throughout the city and the satisfaction and quiet so apparent to all lead me to infer that the difficulty has been entirely solved, and everything seems to have settled back into its proper channels. We shall encourage our friends, root out our enemies, guard the public interests and keep the speculators in hand. No movement has been made since martial law was proclaimed that has not been received with approval by the people at large. I feel that the administration and our cause has been saved from a terrible embarrassment here in New Orleans.

In the same letter, Lovell told Benjamin that because there were thirteen Union ships already in the river and an attack on the forts was imminent, he had kept six steamers of the Montgomery or River Defense Fleet at New Orleans to assist in repelling an attack. "The people of New Orleans thought it strange that all the vessels of the Navy should be sent up the river," declared Lovell, "and were disposed to find fault with sending in addition fourteen steamers, leaving this city without a single vessel for protection against the enemy . . ."

Lovell then launched an attack on the bureaucracy at Richmond, which demanded estimates of requirements which it was impossible to make "because we are called upon here from all quarters to furnish everything—powder, food, equipments, and ordnance stores of all kinds." He said that he needed money in large amounts and at once for the commissary, ordnance, quartermaster, and medical departments at New Orleans to meet the demands from both within and without Department No. 1. "Bragg telegraphed today for 500,-000 pounds of hard bread, yet the estimate of my commissary, approved by me, has been returned from Richmond for details of what we would require. Such red tape will kill us." Poor Lovell, he had a thousand details to look after, details with no immediate bearing on the defense of New Orleans against the Union fleet gathering at the mouth of the river. "My position here is one of labor and difficulty," he told Benjamin.[13]

Among Lovell's chief concerns, with Farragut's powerful fleet assembling at the Head of the Passes, was the question of whether the formidable ironclads, *Louisiana* and *Mississippi*, would be ready to meet the Union threat.

The *Louisiana* was much further advanced than was the *Mississippi*. It had been launched early in February and structurally was approaching completion. But there were delays in getting its machinery installed, and precisely when it would be ready for action could not be determined.

As for the *Mississippi*, the concern over the center shaft, which was being fabricated in Richmond, became, by March 15, a pressing one. In mid-January, Secretary Mallory had written the Tifts that the shaft was still in the hands of the machinists and would be forwarded as early as possible. But two months later, when the *Mississippi* was ready to receive the shaft, not only had it not arrived but it had not even been completed by the Tredegar Iron Works in Richmond.

The exchange of telegrams and letters by the Tifts and Mallory tell a frustrating story of the delays which plagued the construction of the *Mississippi*:

February 22, Tifts to Mallory: "It is unfortunate we have not the shaft, as we could put it on one of the engines at once."

March 14, Tifts to Mallory: "When may we expect the shaft? We need it now."

March 15, Mallory to Tifts: "The Tredegar Works have disappointed us terribly. The shaft is not ready, although promised from day to day, may not be ready for a week. If you can supply its place do so immediately—work night and day to get your ship done, without regard to expense."

March 17, Mallory to Tifts: "The shaft will leave in two days . . ."

March 20, Mallory to Tifts: ". . . Shaft leaves in two days . . ."

March 21, Tifts to Mallory: "Shaft will be in time if sent through without interruption."

March 22, Mallory to Tifts: "The shaft leaves on Monday morning, the 24th, complete; a beautiful piece of work."

March 22, Tifts to Mallory: "Hurry the shaft with special agent; we can't launch without it."

March 23, Tifts to Mallory: "Everything is being done possible until the shaft arrives; can it come by special train?"

April 3, Mallory to Tifts: "Has the shaft arrived, and is it all right?"

Mallory, in every message, exhorted the Tifts to speed the work on the *Mississippi*:

"Work night and day to get your ship done, without regard to expense."

"Can I do anything to expedite your ship? Work day and night if possible. How near is she done?"

"Please advise me of progress and push on . . . day and night."

"Strain every nerve to finish ship. Expend money to encourage mechanics if essential to speedy completion. Work day and night."

"Spare neither men nor money to complete her at the earliest moment. Cannot you hire night gangs for triple wages?"[14]

Farragut, sensing quite correctly the state of uneasiness that existed in New Orleans, wrote confidently to his wife: "We have the stampede on them now." But he still had to solve the problem of getting his big ships across the bar. And next to mud at the entrance to the Passes, Farragut's chief concern was the astonishing shortage of coal for the expedition. Where was the coal that the Navy Department had ordered to him? Why hadn't a stockpile already been built at Ship Island? Why weren't coal boats arriving regularly from the East?

Commander Porter commented to Fox on the coal situation at

Ship Island, again feeling no hesitancy at taking pot shots at his commanding officer. "I don't know whose fault it is," he wrote, "but we are *without coal* . . . Farragut could not know the wants of this squadron. It is true that a wise man would have provided against all contingencies, but as I said before I only considered Farragut the best of his rank, his administrative abilities are not of the first order."

With Farragut preoccupied with too much mud and not enough coal, it was fortunate, as his biographer, Charles Lee Lewis, aptly put it, "that during the delays and disappointments incident to the struggle against the mud, Farragut did not know what Fox and his own subordinate officer, Porter, were writing about him 'confidentially.'"

The critical coal situation was shortly thereafter relieved by the fortuitous intervention of General Benjamin Butler, who took pride that his foresight in thinking of ways to save the government money made it possible for him to assist Farragut out of his difficulty. Butler had chartered a large number of ships for his Ship Island troop movement under an agreement that the ships would return to their home ports in ballast.

"Now the usual way of ballasting a ship is to fill it up with stones," Butler explained later, "take them to the end of the voyage, and then throw them overboard. But I had to return the vessels in ballast. I saw that anthracite coal was steadily rising in the market when our equipment was forwarded from Boston, and I assumed that if I ballasted all my ships with anthracite coal the coal would be worth more when it got back to Boston after having gone down to Ship Island, than it was when I put it on board, and so something very considerable might be saved to the government. I had therefore directed my quartermaster to buy coal enough and put it on board to ballast all the ships on their return voyage."

When Farragut told Butler of his plight, the general, in one of his expansive moods, put his coal ballast at the service of the flag officer.

"I guessed that somebody might want coal and so I brought a quantity with me," Butler told Farragut. "I have twenty-five hundred or three thousand tons that I can let you have as fast as you can put it on board your ships, and I will ballast back with dry sand if I can find nothing else."

"Why, this is almost providential," said Farragut.

"Yes," replied Butler, "I provided it."

"But how can you in the Army let the Navy have the coal?" asked Farragut. "Your army regulations are against it, are they not?"

"I never read the army regulations," declared Butler, "and what is more I shan't, and then I shall not know I am doing anything against them. If the Navy uses the coal for the benefit of the government, I, as a lawyer, know that the government will never get the pay for it out of me again."[15]

Butler's offer greatly relieved Farragut's mind, and shortly thereafter the arrival of some of the long-delayed coal ships removed the problem altogether. Farragut could now concentrate on getting the *Richmond, Mississippi,* and *Pensacola* across the bar. The *Richmond,* on March 22, tried to enter Pass a Loutre, but having twice run aground, it backed off, put on sail, and started the engine at full speed, but to no avail. Commander Alden gave up the try and the next day went to Southwest Pass, where three or four fruitless attempts were made, on each of which the *Richmond* stuck three or four feet in mud. On March 24, the *Mississippi* and *Pensacola* arrived off Southwest Pass in time to see the *Richmond* succeed in backing off the bar and steam out a bit to get a good start. Then, with a good head of steam, the *Richmond* raced at the bar and crossed without sticking.

The three days that were consumed in getting the *Richmond* into the river were nothing to the time required to pull the *Mississippi* and *Pensacola* through the mud. Both vessels drew eighteen feet of water, the *Mississippi* forward and the *Pensacola* aft, and Farragut did all in his power to tip them to seventeen feet. To add to the difficulties of the barrier, a furious gale blew for several days. To Farragut's dismay, both vessels stuck firmly in the mud and for days nothing could budge them, although the services of the smaller gunboats and Porter's steamers were employed in tugging and pulling. On March 28, Farragut wrote one of his officers at Ship Island:

"We are still tugging at the *Pensacola* and *Mississippi* to get them over the bar, and I am much disheartened by the many trials without success, but live in hopes that a southerly wind will raise the tide on the bar a few inches higher."

It took ten days to get the *Mississippi* into the river and about two weeks to get the *Pensacola* across the bar. It was not until April 8 that Farragut reported to Fox, in an unofficial letter, that the job was done. "I am able at last to announce that the *Mississippi* and *Pensacola* are over the Bar, thanks to the Tugs and the exertions of Captain [*sic*] Porter and Renshaw and Baldwin of the *Westfield* and *Clifton*," wrote the flag officer. "We had a strong Southerly wind yesterday, which raised the tide, and they brought the *Pensacola* over by main force."

Porter did, in fact, play an important part in getting the two ships into the river, and characteristically, in relating the details to his friend Fox, he resisted valiantly any inclination to modesty. He wrote, also on April 8:

At last the *Mississippi* and the *Pensacola* are over the bar and up to Pilot town. The former I brought over four days ago, after the hardest work I ever had in my life, owing mostly to my not having entire control. The latter I got over the first time she was put in my hands, and after they had dismissed the pilots . . . who, it has long been apparent to everyone, were entirely unfit for the business. We have with our steamers got everything through. Without us they would have been still at anchor, outside the bar. I got so disgusted at times, that I declared I would not go near one of them, but Sam Phillips Lee persuaded me to pocket my disgust, and take them in whether they would or not. An hour after I anchored the *Pensacola*, the Flag Officer told me he was all ready and waiting for me! Good, that, was it not? Not coal enough on hand to move the ships, *Mississippi* and *Pensacola* entirely empty and mortar steamers all out. I told him I was ready to start in *half an hour!* which was true, for we had spanking fair wind up the river and the schooners all have sails . . .

Farragut could not do anything until the ships were over, and the ordnance ship is still to be lightened before she can pass the bar.

In his manuscript journal, Porter played a variation on this theme of how he came to the rescue of the grounded warships: ". . . I assert that without my aid they would not have succeeded in getting across . . . Farragut never once thanked me publicly or privately."[16]

Forty-seven days after he arrived at Ship Island in the *Hartford*, Farragut at last was in the river with his formidable fleet assembled at the Head of the Passes. He had conquered the mud, and the coal crisis had passed. He still was sorely in need of hospital stores. "The Surgeons tell me that there is not enough material to dress wounds of 100 men properly for a week," he complained to Fox. "I hope it may be on its way, as I have often told you, many are to be hurt in this attack, and they should be properly cared for."[17]

Why, one may well ask, was Farragut's crossing the bar not challenged by the Confederates? With the work on the *Louisiana* and *Mississippi* lagging, Richmond's one strategy should have been to purchase time by upsetting Farragut's timetable. But did this occur to President Davis or Mallory? Apparently not, for Mallory ordered the navy vessels up the river, and it was only by Lovell's physical detention of six of the River Defense vessels that there was anything afloat at New Orleans at the time when Farragut was massing his fleet at the mouth of the river.

But Farragut did not have shells to contend with in his struggle with the mud, and now the preliminaries were over. Every effort in the fleet from now on would be directed toward crashing the barrier in the river below Forts Jackson and St. Philip and passing the blazing guns of the forts themselves.

In the meanwhile, Brigadier General Johnson K. Duncan and his officers and men had worked at the forts to the point of exhaustion preparing for the now certain attack on New Orleans from the sea. Duncan, who commanded all the coast defenses of Department No. 1, had hastened to Fort Jackson late in March when Lieutenant

Colonel Higgins informed him that the enemy's fleet was crossing the bars and entering the Mississippi River in force.

Duncan found upon arrival at Fort Jackson that backwater resulting from the excessively high river and continuing strong easterly winds had flooded the fort. The parade plain and the casemates were submerged to a depth of from three to eighteen inches and, notwithstanding the valiant efforts of officers and men, the water daily gained on them. By isolating the magazine and pumping day and night, it was only by the greatest exertion that the water could be kept out. Living conditions in the fort were almost unbearable, and officers and men, obliged to live in the submerged casemates, were in constant discomfort from wet clothes and feet, thus exposing themselves to the danger of sickness. To a lesser degree, the backwater had created a similar condition in Fort St. Philip, across the river.

It was under such miserable conditions that the men at the forts built platforms and mounted three 10-inch and three 8-inch columbiads, a rifled 42-pounder, and five 10-inch seacoast mortars which had just arrived from Pensacola, following the Confederate evacuation of that place, and two rifled 7-inch guns which General Lovell had temporarily borrowed from the Navy in New Orleans. The old water battery below Fort Jackson, which had never been completed, was prepared to receive some of these guns, and mortar-proof shell rooms and magazines were constructed within the battery.

Because of their vulnerability to the vertical fire of the mortar shells, all the main magazines at both forts were covered with sandbags to a considerable depth. The garrisons worked in shifts day and night until the job was accomplished. Both officers and men responded cheerfully although they were almost worn out by the intensity of their labor, the pressure of being virtually in the sight of the enemy, and the difficulties and discomfort caused by the water in the forts.

To Duncan's chagrin, no sooner were the borrowed navy guns mounted than he received telegraphic orders to return one of them at once to New Orleans to be mounted on the ironclad *Louisiana*.

In vain did he remonstrate, and so, with great difficulty, the gun was dismounted and sent up the river to the city.

In the meantime, Duncan had called on Lovell for some additional troops. The Chalmette Regiment, about 500 strong, under Colonel Ignace Szymanski, was sent to the quarantine station six miles above the forts to guard against Federal troops landing there through the many bayous and canals connecting the river to the bays to the east. In addition, Captain W. G. Mullen's company of scouts and sharpshooters, about 125 men, was placed in part in the woods below Fort Jackson, with the remainder on the other side of the river below Fort St. Philip.

Four steamers of the War Department's River Defense fleet, improvised into warships by the addition of cotton bulkheads and fitted with iron prows for ramming, had been sent down to the forts by General Lovell. These were the *Warrior, Stonewall Jackson, Defiance,* and *Resolute,* commanded respectively by Captains Stevenson, Philips, McCoy, and Hooper. Also sent down to cooperate with General Duncan in the defense of the forts were the *Governor Moore* and *General Quitman,* two steamers outfitted by the state of Louisiana. Commanding the latter was Captain A. Grant, while the skipper of the *Governor Moore* was Captain Beverly Kennon, erstwhile naval ordnance officer at New Orleans, who had resigned his Confederate commission rather than serve under subordinates. Kennon had returned to New Orleans and offered his services to Governor Moore. To this little flotilla were added the ram *Manassas,* the famed "Turtle" which had caused a panic among the Federal blockaders at the Head of the Passes back in October, and the Confederate States steamer *Jackson,* under the command of Captain F. B. Renshaw.[18]

Duncan gave clear and precise instructions to Captain Stevenson, who commanded the River Defense Fleet, to keep his ships in constant readiness at all times for the enemy's approach. "Should he attack, all of your fleet must be kept above the raft, and such of your boats as have stern guns should lie in the middle of the stream, above the raft and without the field of our fire, and use these guns against the enemy," Duncan directed. "Should any boat of the enemy by any means get above the raft, you must instantly ram it with determination and vigor at all risks and every sacrifice." Duncan also ordered Stevenson to keep one of his vessels constantly below, night and day, to observe the movement of the Federal warships and give the signal if the enemy started up the river in force. And to Captain Stevenson, General Duncan also entrusted the entire control of the large number of fire rafts, loaded with combustible material. These were tied to the banks above the two forts, from where on a moment's notice they could be towed into the current, set ablaze, and turned loose upon the enemy. The fire rafts had a dual purpose—to set the Union vessels afire and to light up the river so the gunners in Fort Jackson and Fort St. Philip could better see their targets.

The obstruction across the river now consisted of a line of schooners anchored at intervals, with bows upstream, and chained together stem, stern, and amidships. As an additional hazard to the propellers of the enemy vessels, all rigging and cables were left to trail astern of the schooners.

But a severe windstorm on April 10 and 11 seriously damaged the schooner raft, parting the chains and scattering the schooners, and, to make matters worse, carelessness in handling the fire rafts resulted in further damage to the obstruction.

Down at the Head of the Passes, twenty miles away, Flag Officer Farragut, with all his gunboats and mortar vessels in the river, was almost ready to make his move against New Orleans. "By gradual and regular approaches, he carefully closed upon the forts day by day . . . ," recorded General Duncan.[19]

15

If There Had Been Radio

IF RADIO HAD BEEN INVENTED IN 1861, THE CIVIL WAR WOULD HAVE had, even as World War II, its Edward R. Murrows, Eric Sevareids, Cecil Browns, Howard K. Smiths, and William L. Shirers, with on-the-spot broadcasts of what was happening while it happened. One can imagine a network announcer of the period calling in special observers stationed at vital points in the theater of war. Radio commentators in New Orleans; at Forts Jackson and St. Philip, which defended the Mississippi River approach to the city; with Farragut's fleet at the Head of the Passes; and on Ship Island, which served as a staging area for Ben Butler's troops, would have furnished listeners, North and South, with graphic pictures of the meaningful event unfolding before their eyes.

Let us then tune in an imaginary broadcast on a day in 1862, when April approached its midmark:[1]

"And now, we take you to Ship Island."

"This is Ship Island, a barrier of gleaming white sand, nine miles in length and about a mile wide, where Union troops under General Benjamin Franklin Butler are staging for the New Orleans expedition.

"Ship Island gets its name, not, as many think, because it is shaped like a ship, but because it provided a safe anchorage for the large French vessels in 1699, being called by Iberville *Ile aux Vaisseaux*, or Island of the Ships. Ship Island lies about twelve miles off the Mississippi coast, in front of the little town of Biloxi, and it is about sixty miles from the mouth of the Mississippi River, where Flag Officer Farragut's fleet awaits his signal to assault Forts Jackson and St. Philip.

"Ship Island is barren and deserves the name of 'Misery Island,' given to it by some of the soldiers quartered here.

"The story is being repeated that when General Butler came ashore on March 23, he received a salute from the fort at the western tip of the Island, but no cheers from the men greeted his ears. Rather, he heard a dirge from the band that participated in the burial of a poor fellow of the 30th Massachusetts. There is considerable grumbling among the officers and many are threatening to resign their commissions and go home. Loud and deep are the imprecations heaped upon General Butler. One officer, thoroughly disgusted, told me: 'May God help us in the hour of trial, for if such men are to be our generals we can expect only disaster unless an overruling power interferes in our behalf.'

"Several days later, this same officer confided in me again, expressing disgust at what he called 'the corruption and political intriguing that crops out in every department of the expensive and unprofitable expedition.' The officer continued: 'It does seem as though the expedition was put on foot to enable knaves and political demagogues in particular to rob the government in the most unscrupulous manner. Such things are truly disheartening. The men who have sacrificed home, friends, business, everything for the cause of their country are compelled to remain silent and see their energy, labor, and patriotism diverted from its true channel and applied to the unholy purpose of building up an old broken-down, worn-out political demagogue. In view of this, I am not surprised that men lose their energy and their devotion, that officers resign, that everybody grows sick and tired of the business.'

"There are other evidences of lowered morale on Ship Island.

Some of the men have absented themselves from drill without leave. Grumbling is widespread because orders to prepare to embark are no sooner given them than they are countermanded. One day, recently, the line was formed five times and as many times dismissed. The men keenly resent the indecision and feel that they are being trifled with and as a result are losing much of their interest in the service, and this is not confined to the ranks alone.[2]

"We now return you to . . ."

"That was a report from Ship Island, where Union forces under General Butler await embarkation to participate in the attack on New Orleans. And now, for a report from the beleaguered city itself, we take you to New Orleans."

"Excitement over the great battle of Shiloh is still much in evidence in New Orleans. For several days trainloads of wounded have been arriving here. Many Orleanians have gone to Corinth, Mississippi, to care for wounded relatives or to bring back for burial in the city the bodies of their dead.

"Tremendous joy pervaded the city when the first word of the battle reached New Orleans on April 7, carrying with it the news of a great Confederate victory. Typical of the extravagant claims made on the basis of this first information was this in the *Picayune*: 'The night of our disasters has passed, and the sun of victory has begun to dawn on the armies of freedom . . . It is with inexpressible joy that we announce, through our numerous dispatches from the seat of war, the repulse and dispersion of the Federal army of invasion in Tennessee. The details are wanting, but the victory of southern arms is complete, and, we may venture to say decisive.'

"However, more sobering news, the death of General Albert Sidney Johnston and the subsequent retirement of General Beauregard with the Confederate Army to Corinth, arrived several days later to dampen the enthusiasm. Later the casualty lists brought grief into many New Orleans homes.

"Huge crowds congregated around the bulletin boards of the newspapers and the telegraph office on St. Charles Street, eager, anxious, fearful, as they sought information about husbands, fathers, sons, brothers, and sweethearts. The war indeed is getting closer to New Orleans.

"The shock and surprise of Confederate failures on the upper Mississippi, the most recent being the fall of Island No. 10, have created considerable concern in the city, and the evacuation of the Confederate positions along Bull Run by the Army in Virginia caused many to despond over the southern cause. A speech at the St. Charles Hotel last month by William L. Yancey, former Confederate Commissioner to Europe, who had run the blockade into Berwick Bay, carried little hope of any helpful intervention by England or France. Mr. Yancey told his audience that he came back convinced that the South had no friends in Europe and must fight the battle alone.

"New Orleans today is an armed camp. Tents have been pitched in the various squares of the city and troops are constantly drilling there, and in the streets and on the Levee, while crowds of citizens look on. Every evening large groups of the latter gather at Lafayette Square to hear a concert by the military band. Picturesque uniforms fill the streets, especially those of the European Brigade, which contains French, Spanish, Italian, German, Scandinavian, and Portuguese battalions.

"At the camps on the outskirts of the city, Camp Benjamin on the Gentilly road and Camp Lewis at Greenville, just below Carrollton, military activity continues and large crowds from the city have been taking the trains on weekends to visit the camps.

"Martial law, in effect for about a month, has generally been well received in the city. There has been some grumbling here and there, but for the most part it has operated smoothly. True, there have been some incidents, one of which recently involved a clash of authority between the city police and a patrol of the provost marshals, with the result that Chief of Police McClellan was jailed on orders of Provost Marshal Cyprien Dufour. An amusing incident occurred when a woman opened her barroom at one o'clock in the morning and was promptly arrested for violating the 8 P.M. curfew. She argued that the law stated the hour when barrooms must close but did not specify when they could open.

"Despite the shortages caused by the war and the presence of the enemy in the vicinity, New Orleans is doing its best to keep up the reputation it always had of being the gayest city in the American states. A perusal of the advertising columns of the New Orleans papers reveals that hardly a day passes without a concert, a ball, or a theatrical performance. We are speaking of public amusement, but there are private *soirées dansantes* or *chantantes* that have become a new and attractive feature of New Orleans' social life. Recently, the *Picayune*, chiding those melancholy people who keep aloof from society because of hard times and retire at eight or nine o'clock in the evening, noted that 'the world outside is now just as merry as it ever was, ere the Northerners blockaded the mouths of our noble river.'

"However, on Mardi Gras, March 4, masquerading was forbidden by order of Mayor Monroe, and the Mistick Krewe of Comus did not emerge from its Carnival den to parade through the streets of the city in the final gay fling before Lenten austerity prevailed. Because of the war and the difficulties it presented, the Archbishop of New Orleans released Catholics of the city from the usual Lenten fast.

"Some weeks ago, General Beauregard issued a call to Louisianians for plantation, church, and other bells to be contributed to the Confederacy to be melted down into cannon. The response has been excellent and there are now more than 200 bells collected at the Custom House, their total weight exceeding 22,000 pounds.

"A drive for old iron is under way under the auspices of the Committee of Public Safety. It will be melted into cannon, bombs, and balls and all the newspapers exhort their readers to bring old stoves, old plows, old pieces of iron of all descriptions to the foundries. One paper, the *Crescent*, went so far as to urge that if the need for iron grows, fences and railings and even the statues of Andrew Jackson in Jackson Square and Henry Clay in Canal Street be sacrificed to make cannon.

"People of New Orleans are talking confidently of an ally soon to join them in the defense of the city against the Union invaders—Bronze John, Yellow Jack, yellow fever. People everywhere—in the streets, on the exchanges, at the clubs, at home—speak of the approaching yellow-fever season and the effect it will have on the unacclimated Northern soldiers. The *Delta* predicted: 'Warm weather is rapidly approaching, and the deadly heat of the Gulf and Lake coasts, combined with pestilence, will soon commit more ravages than a dozen battles.' The other newspapers have picked up the idea and state that if the Federals are going to strike at New Orleans they had better hurry before yellow fever strikes first.

"New Orleans is very sensitive to spies, and a day doesn't go by that someone is not arrested as one. Several weeks ago, an attempt was made to fire the warship *Mississippi* while the hands were at dinner, and the newspapers have called for greater vigilance in ferreting out the spies in the city.

"Spies within, the enemy without, and pressures on the Confederacy in general are not the only things weighing on the minds of the people of New Orleans at the moment. There is genuine concern felt here over the exceptionally high water in the river. Last month, just above Carrollton, there was a serious threat of a crevasse, and several days ago strong winds sent water over the levee at several points in the city.[3]

"And that's the story from inside New Orleans. We now return you to . . ."

"On April 13, 1862, gunboats of the fleet of Flag Officer David Glasgow Farragut made their first attack on Fort Jackson, seventy-five miles below New Orleans. For an eyewitness account of this attack, we now take you to Fort Jackson."

"For the first time since it was built, Fort Jackson, one of the strong defenses of the Mississippi River, below New Orleans, was, on Sunday last, under fire.

"Availing ourselves of a courteous invitation, we accompanied a pleasant party to the forts, leaving the city in a steamer, on Saturday night, and arriving after some detention by a fog on the river, in the forenoon of the next day. Just as our boat touched the landing, we heard the drum beat 'the long roll,' while a bugler standing on one of the bastions sounded the call to quarters. At this summons, many of the soldiers who had been engaged outside set off at double-quick and made their way to the interior of the fort. When we entered, we found the various companies drawn up in line or on their way to the casemates and the parapets. Soon all were in place beside their guns, ready for the threatened conflict, while General Duncan and his assistant officers were seen pacing the parapet, spyglasses in hand, casting eager glances to the point of woods about two miles down the river, and behind which they could already discern the masts of the oncoming enemy vessels.

"At this moment a red flag was raised over the Confederate banner, by way of a signal to St. Philip opposite that the enemy was approaching, and immediately the blue-crossed, white-starred battle flag was run up on the staffs of both forts.

"Meantime, the several gunboats lying off the forts formed in readiness to take part in the contest. One of these went down on a reconnoitering expedition, and having neared the·point of woods that yet hid the boats of the enemy from our sight, returned, but not without being honored on her passage with a compliment or two from the guns of Farragut. She accomplished her return without injury. Soon a black hulk was seen to emerge beyond the woods, making her way toward the left bank of the river. Having attained what she probably considered an eligible position for her purpose, she came round, and presented her broadside to the fort, being then about two miles distant.

"A few moments of eager expectation, and a flash, followed by a puff of smoke, was seen to issue from one of her guns, and then there came whizzing and hurtling through the air, heard by all, and seen by many in its course, the first shot ever fired at Fort Jackson. It was a very creditable line shot—a shell—and passed critically near the position of those who were watching its destination. It passed over the fort, and fell between its walls and the river, smashing a small footbridge and making a formidable splash in the mud and water thereabouts. The next was aimed with about the same degree of precision, and fell beyond the wall, within a few feet of the outer bastion facing the river. Some portions of the exploded shell were secured by the spectators as relics.

"Some twelve shells in all were bestowed upon us from different positions in the course of the forenoon, including one fired from behind the woods, doubtless a mortar shell. This described a lofty curve and in mid-air it exploded, the fuse being too short to carry it to its destined goal. Two of the shots came in very dangerous proximity to our pretty steamer, which lay at the landing, one passing directly over the pilothouse and the other dropping into the water just astern. And another shell passed clear over the river, beyond St. Philip, into the prairie, and others were thrown, all without accomplishing their hostile intent.

"All this, of course, was done mainly by way of getting the range, though it is not to be doubted that every shot was intended to tell. From St. Philip some six or seven of the enemy's vessels of different classes were plainly seen, and from Jackson the masts of the flagship of the fleet, with the gridiron flaunting at the peak, were visible over the tops of the woods.

"There were but three responses made on our side to these repeated compliments of the enemy. But these were all most elegantly turned. After the gunboat that opened the ball had amused herself a while in this way, a seven-inch rifle was brought to bear on her, and though not as effectively as desired, yet showed good practice, and was flatteringly prophetic of a 'better next time.' At all events, the enemy deemed it prudent to retire for the time, and, as he was making his way across to the point of woods to seek shelter, he was greeted with two more messengers that very closely approached, if, indeed, one of them did not hit him.

"Taken all together, though but a reconnaissance on the one side and a ready and prompt reception on the other, it was a brisk little affair and greatly interested the spectators during the two hours or so it lasted.

"Though the enemy did not pay any further attention to the forts during the day, he was not idle. Captain Mullen's company of sharpshooters were annoyingly about, among that long reach of woods to which we have referred as skirting the river below the fort. Rumor reached us, in the course of the day, that an epauleted Federal had been picked off by the rifle of one of these bushwackers to whom the officer presented a tempting mark as he stood on the quarter-deck of one of the vessels. And this may be the reason why, at intervals for several hours, there was a cannonading kept up by the enemy's gunboats upon the woods. The grape and canister were very freely distributed among the trees and underbrush, but we fancy with little effect.

"There is a prevalent impression in both forts that the grand drama, of which this little affair was but the prelude, may commence in earnest any day, but undoubtedly in the course of the current week. The strong impression left upon our minds by the manner in which Fort Jackson deported herself on the occasion of her first fight was that the enemy will have to make a better fight than we think he will or can to run that gantlet successfully.

"We abstain from going into particulars as to the force and the armaments at Forts Jackson and St. Philip. It is enough for our present purposes to say that we believe them to be abundantly sufficient for the work that lies before them.[4]

"And that's the story from Fort Jackson. We now return you to . . ."

"From Fort Jackson, we now take you to the Head of the Passes, in the Mississippi River, where a formidable Federal fleet awaits the order to launch its attack on New Orleans."

"Here at the Head of the Passes, a state of expectancy prevails. The coolest and calmest man in the fleet is Flag Officer David Glasgow Farragut, a bundle of energy, enthusiasm, and confidence. The flag officer is always on the move, overseeing everything in person, breathing an air of confidence and imparting a spirit of efficiency. Rowed by sailors, he goes from ship to ship from early dawn to dark, infusing his enthusiasm into the officers and men. Sometimes the flag officer hails a vessel and asks how things are going; on other occasions he climbs over the side to see for himself. Farragut's energy and activity and promptness of decision and action are the talk of the squadron, and his winning smile and charming manner have made him popular with all, especially the younger officers, who marvel at his agility. To one of these the flag officer solemnly stated that he always turned a handspring on his birthday and should not consider himself old until he was unable to do it. Farragut's constant supervision is keeping subordinate commanders and deck officers always on the alert, for they don't know at what moment the flag officer's barge may come alongside a vessel.

"It is a formidable fleet that Flag Officer Farragut has here poised at the Head of the Passes, just twenty miles down the river from Forts Jackson and St. Philip. First there are the screw sloops *Hartford, Pensacola, Brooklyn,* and *Richmond,* all around 2000 tons, carrying among them a total of 93 guns.

"The side-wheeler *Mississippi,* 1692 tons, carrying 17 guns, and three screw corvettes—*Oneida* (1032 tons and 9 guns), *Varuna* (1300 tons and 10 guns), and *Iroquois* (1016 tons and 7 guns)—complete Farragut's heavy ships.

"Then there are nine screw gunboats, dubbed 'the ninety-day gunboats' because they were built, outfitted, and commissioned in ninety days, each of 507 tons and carrying two guns. These are *Cayuga, Itasca, Katahdin, Kennebec, Kineo, Pinola, Sciota, Winona,* and *Wissahickon.*

"Thus Flag Officer Farragut has 17 warships with which to try to pass the forts, the fleet having a total number of 154 guns.

"To these, of course, must be added Commander David D. Porter's mortar flotilla of twenty schooners and seven steamers. Each mortar schooner carries a 13-inch mortar, and fifteen of them are also armed with two 32-pounders as well. The steamers, all but one of which are side-wheelers, have a total armament of twenty-seven guns.

"The flag officer has stimulated great enthusiasm among the various commanders, and each has contributed some ingenious idea which has been adopted by the entire fleet. Every vessel is as well prepared as the ingenuity of her commander and officers could suggest, both for the preservation of life and of the vessel, and perhaps there is not on record such a display of ingenuity as has been evinced in this little squadron. The first was by the engineer of the *Richmond,* Mr. Moore, who suggested that the sheet cables be suspended up and down on the sides in the line of the engines, which was immediately adopted by all the vessels. The links of the cable are of iron an inch and a half in diameter, and each strand or bight is lapped over the next, the links fitting between each other so that it makes an almost continuous coat of mail, extending about two feet below the water line.

"Great quantities of sand have been taken aboard the ships and placed in bags which have been stacked around the engines and machinery, in the propeller wells, between the guns and in the bulwarks, under the topgallant forecastle, and in other spots where the sandbags will afford extra safety to the ships and the men.

"To protect the men during battle from sparks, splinters, or pieces of timber falling from above, nettings made from large ropes have been spread above the decks. The ships have been smeared with mud or painted mud color, so as to merge with the river and the darkness when the attack is made. And to make it easier to locate in the dark the tools and implements used in firing, the gun carriages and decks have been whitewashed.

"Everything is in readiness for the attack on the forts, and confidence and determination pervade the entire fleet. Flag Officer Farragut exemplified this recently when a French squadron which had been allowed to go to New Orleans came down the river and passed out to sea. After exchanging salutes with the *Hartford*, the French admiral signaled, with reference to the forts, 'You will find them very strong.' To this message, Flag Officer Farragut replied, 'I shall take them by audacity.'

"And that's the story from Farragut's fleet at the Head of the Passes on the eve of the launching of the Federal attack on Confederate New Orleans.[5]

"We now return you to . . ."

GENERAL JOHNSON K. DUNCAN
He gallantly defended the forts below New Orleans and surrendered them
only after large numbers of his troops mutinied in Fort Jackson.

FLAG OFFICER DAVID GLASGOW FARRAGUT
A bold, brave, and determined man who never thought for a moment that
he would not succeed in running past the forts.

OFFICIAL U. S. NAVY PHOTOGRAPH

DAVID GLASGOW FARRAGUT

GENERAL DAVID E. TWIGGS

He was old and infirm and the post of commander in chief at New Orleans was too much for him, and so in October 1861 he asked to be relieved.

GENERAL MANSFIELD LOVELL

He arrived too late at New Orleans and had too little to meet the Federal attack. Despite a clean bill from a court of inquiry into his conduct at New Orleans, Lovell was made a scapegoat for its fall by Jefferson Davis.

COMMANDER DAVID DIXON PORTER

He claimed credit for many things, but no one could take from him the fact
that he was a fighting man, full of energy, initiative, and originality.

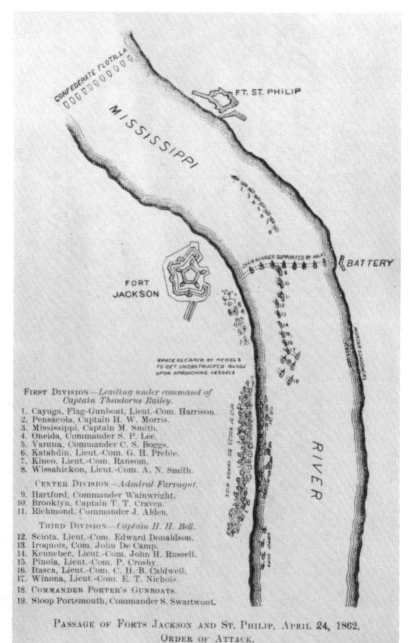

FIRST DIVISION—*Leading under command of Captain Theodorus Bailey.*

1. Cayuga, Flag-Gunboat, Lieut.-Com. Harrison.
2. Pensacola, Captain H. W. Morris.
3. Mississippi, Captain M. Smith.
4. Oneida, Commander S. P. Lee.
5. Varuna, Commander C. S. Boggs.
6. Katahdin, Lieut.-Com. G. H. Preble.
7. Kineo, Lieut.-Com. Ransom.
8. Wissahickon, Lieut.-Com. A. N. Smith.

CENTER DIVISION—*Admiral Farragut.*

9. Hartford, Commander Wainwright.
10. Brooklyn, Captain T. T. Craven.
11. Richmond, Commander J. Alden.

THIRD DIVISION—*Captain H. H. Bell.*

12. Sciota, Lieut.-Com. Edward Donaldson.
13. Iroquois, Com. John De Camp.
14. Kennebec, Lieut.-Com. John H. Russell.
15. Pinola, Lieut.-Com. P. Crosby.
16. Itasca, Lieut.-Com. C. H. B. Caldwell.
17. Winona, Lieut.-Com. E. T. Nichols.
18. COMMANDER PORTER'S GUNBOATS.
19. Sloop Portsmouth, Commander S. Swartwout.

PASSAGE OF FORTS JACKSON AND ST. PHILIP, APRIL 24, 1862.
ORDER OF ATTACK.

FARRAGUT'S ORDER OF ATTACK

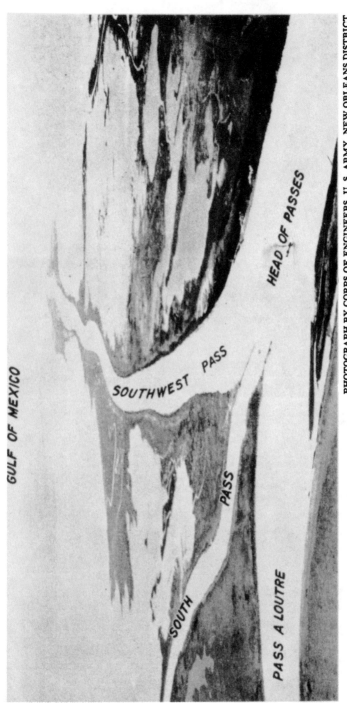

THE HEAD OF THE PASSES

Here the ironclad *Manassas* threw a Federal flotilla into a panic in October 1861. Later Farragut's gunboats entered the river through Southwest Pass, while Porter's mortar vessels came through Pass a Loutre.

ONE OF PORTER'S MORTAR VESSELS AND ITS LETHAL
13-INCH MORTAR

For nearly six days and nights, almost ceaselessly, Porter's mortars blasted the Rebel forts.

GUNBOAT *CAYUGA*

It is fighting its way through the Confederate River Defense Fleet above the forts.

FARRAGUT'S FLEET AT THE MOUTH OF THE MISSISSIPPI
Sketch by an officer of the Mississippi for Harper's Weekly.

THE *MANASSAS*

Called the "Nondescript" and "Turtle" by the people of New Orleans, this was the first ironclad vessel ever to engage in combat. It chased the Federals out of the river in October 1861 and fought valiantly in the passage of the forts by Farragut.

PASSAGE OF THE FORTS

Showing the *Manassas* about to ram a Federal warship.
As visualized by lithographer Charles Parsons.

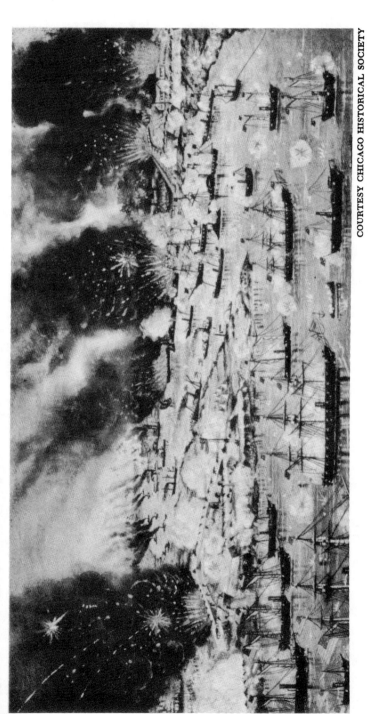

FARRAGUT'S FLEET PASSING FORT JACKSON AND FORT ST. PHILIP

From an oil painting by J. Joffray.

AS A FRENCH ARTIST "SAW" THE PASSAGE OF THE FORTS

From Le Monde Illustré, *Paris.*

THE DEMAND FOR THE SURRENDER OF NEW ORLEANS

A defiant rabble lined the wharves when Captain Theodorus Bailey and Lieutenant George Perkins came ashore from the *Hartford* to demand the surrender of New Orleans.

This engraving by Samuel Sartain was from a drawing by F. B. Schell.

FARRAGUT'S FLEET ANCHORS BEFORE NEW ORLEANS

Citizens put cotton to the flames on the Levee.

Sketch from Harper's Weekly.

16

The "Bummers" Open Up

THE CIVIL WAR IS FULL OF INSTANCES IN WHICH MILITARY INTELLIGENCE was neglected, broke down completely, or was nonexistent. Braxton Bragg wondered what was on the other side of the mountain at Chickamauga, but did not send scouts to find out. At Shiloh, the Confederate Army edged to within a couple of miles of Sherman's lines when he was assuring Grant that he didn't anticipate any enemy attack in the immediate future. At Gettysburg, Lee and Meade virtually stumbled on each other because neither had exact information as to the other's whereabouts. The Richmond government had almost a whole year between Manassas and the Peninsula campaign to map the terrain over which the defense of Richmond would be fought. And yet, because adequate maps were not available, Stonewall Jackson got lost moving into the Seven Days' Battle.

There was no such lack of intelligence of the enemy aboard Flag Officer David G. Farragut's flagship, the *Hartford*, anchored a relatively few miles below Forts Jackson and St. Philip, the prime targets in the Federal assault on New Orleans. As one student of the campaign put it, "he could not have had more information concerning the enemy had he been working a war-college map problem in tactics."[1]

To begin with, Farragut had precise information on the two forts from a memorandum prepared by Brigadier General J. G. Barnard, chief engineer of the Army of the Potomac, and forwarded to the flag officer by Secretary Welles early in February.

Farragut doubtless spent many hours studying the lengthy memorandum of General Barnard, who, many years before the war, had been actively engaged in strengthening and improving the forts as a collaborator of the then Major P. G. T. Beauregard. The flag officer learned that Fort Jackson was "a bastioned pentagon, with fronts of about 100 yards . . . built of brick and . . . in good condition . . . surrounded by a wet ditch." He noted that "the two curtains bearing on the river are casemated for 8 guns each," and that because "the traverse of a casemate gun is but 60 degrees . . . there is a sector of 12 degrees in front of the central water bastion which is not touched by casemate fire." Farragut also read that "parapets of the two water fronts are arranged to receive 22 channel-bearing guns," whereas "the parapets of the other fronts receive 16 more barbette guns, a portion of which bear indirectly upon the channel." Farragut gathered that a water battery to the east of Fort Jackson would probably be in action against his fleet, for "the earthwork had been entirely completed, parapets formed, etc. . . . at the time it went in rebel possession." What was most important information to the flag officer was that Fort Jackson was arranged for a total of 127 heavy guns and that the river at that point was 700 yards wide. The flag officer doubtless noted with interest General Barnard's concluding comment on Fort Jackson:

> In the center of Fort Jackson is a defensive barrack of decagonal shape. It is intended to be made bombproof by covering the 1-foot square timbers of the ceiling with earth. Probably the rebel garrison has done this. This building will accommodate 400 or 500 men. As there is besides a great deal of bombproof shelter in the casemates and galleries, the garrison is well sheltered from a bombardment.

Turning his attention to Fort St. Philip, Farragut learned that this irregular quadrilateral work of about 150 by 100 yards, originally built by the Spaniards but brought to its present shape during the War of 1812, was arranged to receive "20 heavy guns bearing directly upon the channel." Two external batteries, mounting 52 guns, brought to 72 the channel-bearing guns at St. Philip. Farragut was warned he could expect plenty of hot shot, as "there are furnaces for nearly all the batteries at both forts." General Barnard's memorandum outlined Farragut's task in detail:

> . . . It is not a trifling undertaking to pass so large a number of guns at such close quarters. (Fort St. Philip is about 700 yards higher up the river than Fort Jackson; the distance between the nearest salients of the main works is about 1,000 yards.) From a point in the river 1½ miles from the lowest battery of Fort Jackson to another 1½ miles above the nearest upward-bearing batteries we shall find a distance of 3 miles to be traversed, 2 miles of which under the fire of 100 to 125 guns and the other 1½ miles under that from 50 to 100. Now, against the current of the river this distance will not be performed by the majority of the steamers of a squadron in less than twenty-five minutes or a half-hour. With hot-shot thrown by this armament . . . I should look upon the daylight passage as too hazardous to be undertaken . . . Such an attempt should be made at night, when the distant fire must be very uncertain.

General Barnard expressed great doubt that any obstruction, such as a raft, in the river at the forts could be maintained in high or even moderately high stages of the river, but if the Rebels could keep an obstruction intact, "the forcing of a passage would become almost impractical."

"Would it be prudent . . . supposing these works to be at all formidably armed, to force a passage, leaving them behind intact, while the fleet advanced on New Orleans?" asked Barnard. Answering his question, he continued: "I think not, unless perchance, in conjunction with an attack to be made on this city by a large land force from Lake Borgne or Pontchartrain; but it is as hard to get a land force from these lakes as to take the Forts . . . A fleet cannot maintain itself long above these works unless the city of New Orleans is captured and held by us."[2]

This information, and considerably more, together with General Barnard's opinions and suggestions, was thoroughly digested by the flag officer. From New Orleans papers, Farragut had fairly accurately gauged the state of morale in the city; from fishermen he acquired useful information concerning the river raft, the Confederate naval complement at and above the forts, and the vessels being built at New Orleans. Two fishermen reported on March 16 that the armed steamers at New Orleans had been sent up the river, that the *Manassas* was giving out, but that two more rams were under construction in the city.

But Farragut wanted firsthand information on the nature and condition of the raft, the range and caliber of the guns at Fort Jackson and Fort St. Philip, and what naval support the Confederates had at the forts. So, as early as March 28, while the struggle to pull the heavy ships through the mud continued, Fleet Captain Henry H. Bell steamed up the river aboard the *Kennebec*, accompanied by the *Wissahickon*, and took a good look at the forts and the raft of schooners. He drew the fire of both Fort Jackson and Fort St. Philip, and then, "having observed all that was distinctly visible," he steamed back down to the Head of the Passes. Bell did not fire a shot, because, as he reported, "the range of our guns [was] no better than theirs."[3]

Flag Officer Farragut himself went up for a look on April 5, accompanied by Captain Bell and his volunteer signal officer, B. S. Osbon, who was also correspondent for the New York *Herald*. Farragut, aboard the *Iroquois*, accompanied by other gunboats, steamed to the vicinity of the forts, reconnoitering from noon to 4 P.M. Fort Jackson opened up on the *Iroquois*, firing seven shells, which, though they came close, inflicted no damage. Seated on the foreyard with Captain Bell, Farragut was undisturbed as the shower of iron dropped around the *Iroquois*. "He was as calm and placid as an onlooker at a mimic battle," Osbon recalled later. A young officer recorded the amusement among the sailors of the fleet when some of Farragut's staff dodged and ducked as some of the shells came close. But the flag officer, he noted, was imperturbable, with his glass in hand, calling out occasionally: "There comes one! There! There!" When a shell splashed into the water at fairly close range, Farragut remarked: "Ah, too short; finely lined though!"

On April 13, Farragut went up to the forts again, this time on Porter's flagship, the *Harriet Lane*, with two gunboats in support, and a lively exchange of shots took place between the vessels and Fort Jackson. Day by day, Farragut thus accumulated data on the ranges to the forts and the range of the forts' batteries.[4]

But before launching his attack, the flag officer was to have more precise information on which Porter would base his mortar bombardment of the forts. This was secured by a Coast Survey party, under F. H. Gerdes. Porter had had the foresight to request Professor A. D. Bache, superintendent of the United States Coast Survey, to assign a survey party to the New Orleans expedition. Gerdes and his assistants, J. G. Oltmanns, T. C. Bowie, Joseph Harris, and R. E. Halter, arrived in the river on the Coast Survey steamer *Sachem* on April 11, and Porter immediately requested Gerdes to supply a reliable survey of several miles of the river below Fort Jackson and Fort St. Philip and including these fortifications.

At daybreak on April 13, Gerdes and his assistants began their work. For five days, under fire of the forts and from sharpshooters on the shores, they labored. Their difficulties were increased by the destruction by the Confederates each night of the marks and signals that had been placed during the day. To circumvent this, Gerdes had numbered posts set in the riverbanks, camouflaged with grass and reeds, so that the Rebels could not find them in the dark.

Each night, after returning to the *Sachem*, Gerdes mapped the day's work, and in the end he turned over to Farragut and to Porter "a reliable map of the river and the shores from the 'Jump' to and including Forts Jackson and St. Philip, with their outworks and water batteries; the hulks, supporting the chain across the river, and every singular and distinguishable object along its banks."

Gerdes' account of making the survey is interesting:

> The survey was made by triangulation carried forward simultaneously on both sides of the river. Two coast survey signals were found, the "Jump telegraph post," and "Salt-work's chimney top," of which the geodetic relations were known, and the work was founded upon a base line connecting these two points . . . The angular measurements were made with all kinds of instruments found suitable to the locality. Only a few of the stations were on solid ground, nearly all the shore being overflowed. Frequently the members of the party were compelled to mount their instruments on the chimney tops of dilapidated houses. In other places boats were run under overhanging trees on the shore, in which signal flags were hoisted, and the angles measured by sextants.

At Porter's request, Gerdes furnished him with points along the riverbank a hundred or hundred and fifty meters, on both sides of the river, so that the mortar vessels could be placed at given distances from the forts. Farragut warmly congratulated Gerdes for the "intrepidity, determination, system and dispatch" with which he had accomplished his important mission. And Porter praised the "great coolness and precision" with which the mortar-boat positions were established.[5]

On April 15, before Gerdes had completed the survey, Porter towed three mortar schooners into position 3000 yards' distance from Fort Jackson, "to try their range and durability." In his official report, Porter wrote: "I found the range satisfactory, and had no reason to doubt the durability of the mortar beds and foundation. I received but little encouragement from anyone about the success of the mortars, it having been confidently predicted that 'the bottoms of the schooners would drop out at the tenth fire.'"

In his manuscript journal, Commander Porter expanded on this experimental mortar practice:

> On the 15th of April, 1862, I towed one of the schooners to within two miles of the forts and opened a slow fire to ascer-

tain ranges. As I learned afterwards Governor Soulé [Pierre Soulé was not governor of Louisiana] and a party of his friends were at the fort enjoying a look at the "Yankee fleet." When the mortar first opened they stood quietly on the ramparts, watching its effect. Soon there was a stir among the spectators, for a shell fell right on the parapet near them and exploded.

The parapets were immediately cleared. A second shell, fired minutes later, fell on the drawbridge and nearly destroyed the communications with the main land.

A third also exploded inside the works and pieces of it were taken to New Orleans as specimens of Yankee oppression.

I don't know what effect it had on General Lovell, but he and his friends made no more visits to the forts.[6]

Porter and his "bummers," as the sailors of the fleet called the mortar schooners—"Porter's chowder pots" was another name—were now ready for action. He had not wasted his time while waiting for Farragut's vessels to get into the river, and the thirteen-man mortar crews had been kept busy drilling at the mortars and engaging in target practice.

Hour after hour, the commanders of the various mortar schooners had drilled their men in the manual of the mortar:

"Silence!

"Cast loose and provide!

"Train! (Right or left)

"Serve vent and sponge!

"Load!

"Elevate!

"Prime!

"Ready—Fire!

"Mortar front!

"Secure!"

And at the Head of the Passes, while awaiting the order to move up the river, the mortar crews got in some actual practice, ramming home the twenty-pound powder charges, cutting fuses, loading the

216-pound shells into the mortars, and firing into the marshes. As the mortars went off, the crews stood on tiptoe with mouths and ears open, as the manual prescribed, "to lessen the shock of the discharge and the concussion on the ear."

This was the first opportunity for the "bummers" actually to fire, for while at sea on the way to Ship Island, the schooner commanders were under strict orders not to fire the mortars for fear of capsizing the vessels. Acting Master George W. Brown, commander of the *Dan Smith*, who fired the first practice shot at Southwest Pass, described the experience:

> My vessel was alone; others either had not arrived or had already gone up the river . . . In port we had exercised the crews in the manual, but not one of the mortars had been fired, and were going into action, as I thought, "blind."
>
> Considering my "sea-orders" over, and as I was the senior officer present . . . I thought I would assume command (of myself) and try the mortar in earnest; so we went through all the preparations for action; loaded the mortar with a full-service charge of twenty pounds of powder, cut a fuse for four thousand yards, and, after several changes of sighting, one and then the other, I gave the order to fire. The crew, according to the manual, had been taught to "stand in the rear of the piece on tip-toe, with mouth and ears open"; but, as this was real and I didn't know what the thing would do, I ordered them farther away, while I, with my officers, noted the time of flight of the shell; after which I took a survey of the deck. The mortar had recoiled off the turntable back against the side, driving the rear of the carriage into the water-ways, and listing the vessel about 10 degrees. The concussion had taken nearly every door off the hinges, the arms-chest and round-houses collapsed, and other slight damage . . . For my discovery I was rewarded with a "day off," and breechings were ordered to be fitted on the mortars of all the vessels. This heretofore had been deemed unnecessary.[7]

Commander Porter, in the days that followed, was highly pleased with the mortar crews, as he told his friend in the Navy Department, Gustavus Fox: "I have made some beautiful practice though only at short ranges, everything works well in the Flotilla . . . the gun practice is perfect." Porter had divided the mortar flotilla into three divisions, under the commands of Lieutenants Watson Smith, K. R. Breese, and W. W. Queen. He was more than satisfied with the efficiency the young officers demonstrated, so it was with supreme confidence—"I have great hopes of the Mortars," he wrote Fox —that Porter awaited Farragut's order to commence the bombardment of the forts.

On April 16, the day after Porter had made his trial shots at Fort Jackson, the flag officer moved up his fleet and told Porter to commence operations as soon as he was ready. All the next day, the masts of the mortar schooners were dressed with bushes and small trees so that they would merge into the trees behind which they were to be placed, thus rendering them invisible to observers in the Rebel forts. Porter had picked an ideal spot for the mortar flotilla under the lee of a thick wood closely interwoven with vines and presenting in the direction of both Fort Jackson and Fort St. Philip an impenetrable jungle for three hundred yards, through which shot and shell could hardly pass. From the beshrubbed mastheads of the mortar vessels, both forts could be seen, but from the forts, Porter's schooners could not be detected, so well were their masts camouflaged. By nightfall of April 17, all was in readiness for the mortar assault which Porter had promised Gideon Welles would reduce the forts in forty-eight hours.[8]

At the very time that Commander Porter was readying the mortar flotilla for the attack, Governor Moore in New Orleans was frantically wiring Jefferson Davis to countermand orders sending the *Louisiana*, still not finished, up the river. Orders had come a week earlier to the naval commander at New Orleans, Commander W. C. Whittle, to send the *Louisiana* with all dispatch up the river. Amazingly, Secretary of Navy Mallory was still convinced that the greater danger to New Orleans was from above and not from below.

Governor Moore, caught up by the excitement in New Orleans over the preliminary firing at the forts, telegraphed President Davis on April 17:

> Forts bombarded an hour and a half yesterday. General Duncan telegraphs none of our guns will reach them. Commodore Whittle has orders from Secretary Navy to send the *Louisiana* to Tennessee. Duncan and Higgins both telegraph she is absolutely a necessity at the forts for the safety of New Orleans, and that it is suicidal to send her elsewhere. With the enemy's plan of attack, our safety may depend upon her timely arrival there. I earnestly beg her destination may be changed, and protest against her being sent up the river. Excitement among the people great on the subject.

President Davis, with an astonishing unawareness of the situation at New Orleans even as the formidable Federal fleet was poised to open a devastating attack on the forts, telegraphed in reply:

> . . . The wooden vessels are below; the iron gunboats are above. The forts should destroy the former if they attempt to ascend. The *Louisiana* may be indispensable to check the descent of the iron boats. The purpose is to defend the city and valley; the only question is as to the best mode of effecting the object. Military men must decide, and today their discretionary power has been enlarged.[9]

There was no logical reason for President Davis to have been so out of touch with the New Orleans situation, for General Lovell had wired Secretary of War Randolph on April 11: "With forty vessels in the lower river, please protest in my name against sending the *Louisiana* up the river." And on April 15, he informed the Secretary of War that twenty-seven vessels were in sight of the forts and that "the enemy is preparing for a formidable attack." The same day that Governor Moore and Davis exchanged telegrams concerning the *Louisiana*, General Lovell, after consultation with Commander Whittle, wired Secretary Randolph begging "that Captain Hollins may be allowed to remain in command afloat, at least until he can strike a fair blow at the enemy, which he is ready to do."[10]

The old sea dog, who had chased Federal vessels out of the river in October, was itching for another scrap below New Orleans. When Commander Whittle telegraphed him early in April that the enemy was in force at the mouth of the river and begged him to come down, old Hollins, at Fort Pillow, Tennessee, telegraphed Secretary of Navy Mallory on April 9 that his vessels might render good service at the mouth of the river and that he awaited an answer. Mallory wired back an emphatic refusal the next day. After expressing hope that the *Louisiana* would join Hollins "immediately" and the *Mississippi* "at the earliest moment," Mallory's telegram stated: "Your proposition to quit the enemy and go to the mouth of the Mississippi cannot be entertained. You must oppose his descent of the river, and his movements of vessels and troops at every step."

But Flag Officer Hollins hadn't waited for Mallory's reply. Leaving four vessels at Fort Pillow in command of Commander Pinckney, he headed down the river in the *McRae*, pausing at Baton Rouge to telegraph Mallory on April 10 that he had acceded to Whittle's plea and was en route to New Orleans. "Fleet is on its way up the river," he told Mallory. "Will you order mine down the river? I can render effective service below."

To this, Mallory angrily replied in a telegram on April 11, which he sent to New Orleans ahead of Hollins' arrival. He wired:

Your dispatch received yesterday, proposed to abandon opposition to the enemy's descent of the river by your fleet, and to carry your fleet to the mouth of the river. This proposition is totally inadmissible; every effort that nautical skill, invention, and courage can put forth must be made to oppose the enemy's descent of the river, and at every hazard.

You inform me that you have gone to New Orleans at the urgent request of Capt. Whittle. You will therefore send these orders to the senior in command of your squadron by telegraph. The *Louisiana* must join your squadron at the earliest practicable moment.

Hollins reached New Orleans with definite ideas of what he would do if Mallory consented for his other vessels to join him. His plan was simple, but audacious. He would go below the forts and attack Farragut's fleet with his gunboats, which would have on each side a fire raft, heavily loaded with wood, tar, and other combustibles. Since the enemy vessels were so numerous and most of the fleet would be at anchor, Hollins reasoned that his sudden appearance with fire boats would create a panic and that the Federal vessels would run afoul of each other and become so confused as to administer little serious damage to the attackers. Moreover, Hollins considered that since all his guns were forward, and all his vessels were completely guarded with iron on their bows, he could fire with effect as he moved downstream, whereas the Federal gunboats could not use their guns until they turned broadside, which would have thrown them across the river, crowding them together in confusion and presenting excellent targets for Hollins' gunners and the fire rafts as well.

Hollins doubtless discussed his plan with Governor Moore, General Lovell, and Commander Whittle, to whom he showed Mallory's telegram forbidding his proposed movement down the river, for all three telegraphed Richmond to let Hollins remain in New Orleans and make his projected dash at the enemy. There was no direct reply to their request, but an answer came in unmistakable terms: Flag Officer Hollins was ordered by President Davis to report in Richmond immediately to serve as the head of the board to examine midshipmen![11]

Stephen Mallory's obsession that New Orleans was threatened much more seriously from above than from below seems to have been transmitted to President Davis. For on the very eve of the Union attack on the city's main defense, seventy-five miles down the Mississippi, Richmond showed an astonishing lack of appreciation of the gravity of the situation on the lower Mississippi.

Neither Mr. Davis nor Mr. Mallory came to grips with reality, but the defenders in the forts soon were compelled to do so.

At 6 A.M. on April 18, when pious Orleanians were already beginning their Good Friday visits to the various churches of the city, the *Owasco* got under way with orders from Commander Porter to proceed up the river to the designated positions of the mortar vessels and shell the riverbank to clear the bushes of any riflemen who might possibly be lurking there. Shortly thereafter the *Westfield*, *Clifton*, and *Miami* began towing the mortar schooners into place.

As the vessels arrived they were assigned positions previously marked by the Coast Survey party and each commander was given the precise range to each fort from his place in line.

The first division of Porter's mortar flotilla, commanded by Lieutenant Watson Smith, skipper of the *Norfolk Packet*, and consisting of the *Oliver H. Lee, Para, C. P. Williams, Arletta, William Bacon*, and *Sophronia*, was placed in closest range to the forts, the head vessel being 2850 yards from Fort Jackson and 3600 from Fort St. Philip, the others dropping into line close to each other. Next in line, on the west bank of the river, was Lieutenant K. R. Breese's third division, consisting of the *Horace Beals, John Griffith, Sarah Bruen, Racer, Henry Janes, Dan Smith, Sea Foam*, with the *Orvetta*, from the second division. To the east bank of the river, Porter assigned Lieutenant W. W. Queen's second division, consisting of the *T. A. Ward, Maria J. Carlton, Matthew Vassar, George Mangham, Sidney C. Jones*, and *Adolph Hugel*, with orders to direct their fire against Fort Jackson.

There were many doubters in Farragut's fleet as to the practicability of Commander Porter's "bummers," but no one could deny that Porter went about his business with confidence and precision. Even the scoffers admired the way in which he got his mortar schooners into line. "They looked very pretty," conceded a sailor on the *Hartford*, "as they ranged along the shore in line of battle, with their flagship, the *Harriet Lane*, at their head."[12]

Farragut ordered three gunboats, the *Iroquois, Cayuga*, and *Wissahickon*, upstream to cover the mortar fleet and draw the fire of the forts away from Porter's vessels. At precisely what hour the mortars opened the bombardment of the forts is not known, for Commander Porter does not state it in his report and the logs of the various mortar vessels give a wide range of times from 8 A.M. for the *C. P. Williams* to 2:35 P.M. for the *Sea Foam*. It is quite evident that sometime between nine and ten o'clock most of Porter's mortar vessels were in action, for General Duncan, Confederate commander at the forts, reported that "at 9 A.M. the enemy opened upon Fort Jackson with his entire mortar fleet of twenty-one vessels and with rifled guns from his gunboats."[13]

When Porter gave the signal to commence firing, the bummers opened in order, each one firing every ten minutes. Soon the air was filled with mortar shells arching their way toward the forts. These responded with rapid fire, but without attaining at once an effective range. Not being able to see the mortar schooners masked by the point of woods at the river bend, and finding the bummers on the east bank of the river at extreme range of their guns, the forts directed the greater part of their fire at the Federal gunboats, which now included the *Sciota* and the *Kennebec*.

The mortar vessels on the west bank of the river, their view of Fort Jackson from the deck being obscured by the point of woods, could sight their guns only from the mastheads. "Many curious expedients were resorted to to obtain correct firing," said Porter, "expedients very creditable to the intelligence of the commanders of the vessels." One of these expedients is interestingly described by Acting Master George W. Brown, who commanded the smallest schooner in the mortar flotilla, the *Dan Smith*:

> When we were firing, I took my position at mast-head, where I could see the forts and trace the flight of our shells, and did the sighting of the mortar at an elevation of about seventy feet above it. Different methods were adopted for this purpose on the various vessels. It was thought, before we commenced, that we could use a compass, and from the mast-head give the course to fire; but the concussion unhung the compass-cards, so that it was abandoned, and we, as was often the case, were left to our own resources. I adopted parallel

bars, taking two pieces of scantling. The upper one I had on the cross-trees; the other suspended from and parallel to that near the deck, weighted so as to keep it steady. I sighted and pointed the upper one for the fort; the officer in charge on deck sighted the mortar by the lower one. When the mortar was fired, the little vessel would settle down in the water nearly a foot, career over a streak or two, and shoot astern, bringing a heavy strain on the hawser and chain, and switch us poor fellows at the mast-head round so that at times it was a question whether we would stay there . . . Our vessels were moored close together, each with her head a little off shore, so that each fired over the quarter of the one ahead, and, as they fired at an angle of forty-five degrees, the line of fire was not far from our positions at the main mast-head, and I frequently felt the windage of the shell from the next in line and the concussion was very severe upon us . . .[14]

Far down the river, officers and sailors climbed the rigging and stood on the crossarms of the other warships of the fleet to watch the fireworks. "We can see the shell exploding all around the forts and they are striking around our vessels and some of them have been hit," noted one seaman in his journal. "The air is full of shell, it is a beautiful sight, it has been Bom Bom all day." An assistant engineer aboard the flagship *Hartford* thought the "bomb firing . . . only middling as far as we can judge from the view we have, many of the shells going wide of the mark." Fleet Captain Henry H. Bell thought that Porter's flotilla "generally fired well, but mostly to the left and too far."

Actually, neither Porter nor anyone else knew what effect that first day's firing had on the forts at that time, but at Fort Jackson the men were kept almost as busy putting out fires as they were manning the batteries. Early in the day quarters in the bastion were set ablaze and burned down, and quarters outside the fort met the same fate. Also set to burning was the citadel in the center of the fort; several times the fire was extinguished, only to start again when another shell struck. "The mortar fire was accurate and terrible," reported General Duncan, "many of the shells falling everywhere within the fort."[15]

But the guns of the forts kept blazing away, and eventually those of Fort Jackson began to get in some telling blows. A 120-pound shell ripped through the cabin of the *T. A. Ward*, damaging the magazine and coming out close to its water line. The *George Mangham* received a 10-inch shot near the water line, whereupon Commander Porter, to the disgust of their officers, ordered both vessels to drop back two hundred yards, thus throwing the enemy out of range. But this wasn't discovered by the forts for a couple of hours.

Fort St. Philip's batteries, firing at extreme range, had little effect on the Union vessels, which responded with a few rifle shells at long intervals but otherwise ignored this fort to concentrate on Fort Jackson. A 13-inch mortar in Fort St. Philip—the only gun of this caliber at the forts—became useless after the thirteenth round, when the bed broke and deposited the mortar upon the ground.

Throughout the afternoon, the monotonous boom-boom of the mortars continued, punctuated by the guns of the gunboats and the responses from the forts. A cheer went up in the early afternoon when the *Iroquois*, which had been firing with great efficiency, shot away the flagstaff at Fort Jackson. There was more cheering from every vessel when a gunboat came up the river late in the afternoon with the information that Norfolk had fallen to the Union forces and that the *Merrimac* had been taken.[16]

At five o'clock, it was observed from the bombarding fleet that Fort Jackson was in flames and the guns of the fort had fallen silent. The citadel was burning again, and this time more furiously than ever, and it became impossible to put the fire out. Porter, not realizing the extent of the damage in Fort Jackson, ordered the firing to cease shortly after sunset. In doing so, he made "the only mistake that occurred during the bombardment," as he later admitted. "Had I known the extent of the fire I should have proceeded all night with the bombardment, but the crews had had nothing to eat or drink since daylight," reported Porter. He also did not want to engage in night firing until he had determined how much, if at all, the mortar beds and vessels had suffered.

When the bummers ceased firing, the citadel was, in the words of General Duncan, "one burning mass, greatly endangering the magazines, which at one time were reported to be on fire." Many of the troops and most of the officers lost clothing and bedding in the fires, which added to the discomfort of already uncomfortable conditions, due to the overflow of water and the steady day-long mortar fire and shell and shot from the Federal gunboats.

During the night the fire blazed, a column of flame and smoke rising high above Fort Jackson. When the fire was discovered by the fleet downstream, a band aboard one of the ships struck up "Hail Columbia" and "Dixie," and there was cheering from every vessel. Porter, however, and doubtless others in the fleet, mistook the blaze for a fire raft which had either run ashore or had been ignited to light up the river.[17]

Porter's guess was not far wrong, because an abortive attempt was made to send a fire raft down among the Union ships. General Duncan's disgust at the bungling was undisguised. "I endeavored to get the naval forces to carry down fire barges against the enemy so as to disperse them," reported Duncan, "but they were all let go above the raft, and with such a lack of judgment that they only lodged under the forts, and did not reach the enemy."

General Duncan estimated that the mortar vessels had fired 2997 shells at the forts, but this was more than double the number Commander Porter reported, in evaluating the first day's fire by the mortar flotilla. "We fired on this day over 1400 bombshells, many of which were lost in the air, owing to bad fuzes," stated Porter. "No accident of any kind occurred from careless firing, and after a careful examination the vessels and mortar beds were found to be uninjured."[18]

Meanwhile, in New Orleans word of the bombardment spread rapidly, and all day long, as people made their Good Friday religious duties, the constant inquiry was for news from the forts. At night, huge and nervous crowds gathered on Canal and St. Charles streets, expressing, as the *Bee* said the next day, "vivid excitement."

The paper added: "Thus far we see no cause for such a high degree of anxiety." The *Delta*, on the other hand, did not minimize the threat to New Orleans. "It would be grossly delinquent in our press to attempt to disguise that the enemy is making tremendous exertions with extremely formidable appliances to get possession of the Mississippi River," said the *Delta*, "and that in consequence of these efforts, New Orleans is in serious peril. It is well for our citizens to know these facts and to look at them squarely—to face them like men, earnest, sensible, resolute, calm and courageous men . . . The defense of the river should at this conjuncture be the paramount object of their concern. Upon its defense hangs the fate of New Orleans and the Valley of the Mississippi . . . Let not history look back with scorn upon the puny efforts of New Orleans to defend herself from invaders."[19]

Several hours after dark on the eighteenth, Porter sent a specialist in submarine operations, Julius H. Kroehl, to reconnoiter the river obstruction, with a view to blowing it up the next night. Flashes on the shore at regular intervals and the cries of sentries, some of which seemingly came from the hulks in the obstruction, together with the rising moon, frightened the expedition off.[20]

Before the people of New Orleans read their newspapers on April 19, Commander Porter, seventy-five miles down the river, had opened up again with the mortar bombardment. The bummers began lobbing shells into Fort Jackson at 6:30 A.M., but it was not until two hours later that Farragut sent the gunboats into action in support of the mortar flotilla. The forts responded vigorously, and whenever a gunboat showed itself around the point, the fire was so hot it retired quickly. Fleet Captain Bell, observing the bombardment, thought the Rebels were firing "beautifully and with effect." This became very evident about 9 A.M., when the mortar schooner *Maria J. Carlton* was sunk by a shell which passed through her deck, magazine, and bottom. (She was one of the six mortar vessels originally placed on the east bank, but shortly after daylight Porter had them towed across the river to join the rest of the flotilla.) The gallant master of the *Carlton* fired his mortar for the last time as the damaged vessel went down. Masts and rigging of the advanced mortar vessels took a severe pounding from the forts, and the mortar on the *Arletta* was knocked out of commission for nearly three hours by a shot that struck the mortar bed.

Porter complained of bad fuses which caused the shells to explode too soon in the air. To remedy this, he scrapped the plan to time the burst and inserted full-length fuses to burst after the shell had hit the ground. The effect "was like that of an earthquake" as the bombshells plunged eighteen or twenty feet into the wet and soft ground and, "exploding after some time, lifted the earth up, and let it fall back into place again." A surprisingly large number of mortar shells fell within Fort Jackson, whose terreplein, parade plain, parapets, and platforms were considerably cut up, while much damage was also done to the casemates. The enemy's fire, which General Duncan acknowledged as "excellent," was a constant threat to the magazines, and one shell actually penetrated a casemate containing fixed ammunition. Five guns in Fort Jackson proper and two more in the water battery were disabled during the second day's bombardment, which, reported Duncan, "continued very regularly and accurately all night."

Meanwhile, early in the afternoon, the *Oneida* became a prime target of Fort Jackson. First its jibstay was shot away, and then two blasts of 10-inch solid shot ripped out planking on both sides of the vessel, with flying splinters seriously wounding nine men.[21]

Sixty miles away, on Ship Island, Mrs. Benjamin F. Butler, the general's wife, heard the "distant sound of heavy artillery." She was uncertain whether it was at Mobile or at the Mississippi River forts. "I think the firing must be at Mobile, some vessels, maybe, trying to run the blockade," she wrote her daughter. "It would seem impossible that the sound should reach us from the Mississippi sixty miles distant . . ."

It is probable that the persistent booming of the guns was also heard in New Orleans, only fifty air miles away, but at any rate, fear and anxiety raced through the city's streets during the second day of the bombardment. "Excited rumors without a shadow of foundation can now be expected to circulate pretty freely," warned the *Delta*. ". . . No credence should be given to them, nor should anyone contribute to circulate them." But people did believe the rumors and passed them on to others. Soon New Orleans was a city gripped almost in panic. The *True Delta* resorted to strong medicine to rally the flagging spirits:

> We are in possession of information from Forts Jackson and St. Philip which we deem neither prudent nor advisable to give publicity to. We will, however, say this much, that our authorities—nay, every man in the city who professes to have a heart or a soul within him—should prepare to meet the coming issue with unblenched faces. The hour is rapidly approaching when the question will be solved whether or not New Orleans will be a conquered city. The issue is now to DO or DIE. Who will be so craven as to falter?[22]

All night of the nineteenth, the mortars fired away, illuminating the heavens brilliantly, and men in the fleet could clearly follow the flight of each shell. Young George Dewey recalled years later how, "at regular intervals of about ten minutes, a mortar shell would rise, its loop in the air outlined by the burning fuse, and drop into the forts." Surgeon Jonathan Foltz, aboard Farragut's flagship, the *Hartford*, heard "the dull, heavy boom of 'the bummers' . . . rolling over the smooth waters of a lovely spring night" and prayed fervently to God to "soon put a stop to this horrible civil war and make us again a united, free and happy people." At Fort Jackson, General Duncan fumed as he recorded that "failures again were made in sending down fire rafts."[23]

At 4:10 A.M. on Easter Sunday, April 20, a mud-bespattered figure in red cap and shirt and brown trousers hailed the mortar schooner *Norfolk Packet* from the bank, asking to be taken aboard. He said that he was a deserter from Fort Jackson, whereupon he was immediately taken to Commander Porter, aboard the *Harriet Lane*. The deserter claimed to be a Union man, a Pennsylvanian and a former member of Dan Rice's famous shows, who had been compelled to join the Rebel forces in New Orleans. He told a tale of great destruction in Fort Jackson, of hundreds of bombshells falling into the fort, of casemates broken in, of citadel and outbuildings burned, of magazines endangered, and levees cut, and the men dispirited and demoralized. Although Porter at first greatly doubted the man's story, he was eager to accept it at face value, for the forty-eight hours in which he had promised to reduce the forts had passed.

"After bombarding the fort for three days I began to despair of taking it, and indeed began to lose my confidence in mortars," Porter admitted. He took the deserter to Farragut, boarding the flagship at 7:40 A.M., where the man told his story all over again to the flag officer. Under questioning he told how, during the previous night's firing, a shell fell at nine o'clock at the magazine door and exploded, tearing away the cotton bales which protected it and causing consternation for fear that the magazine would explode. During the confusion, the deserter slipped out of the fort, crossed the moat in a skiff, and made his way through the swamps to the mortar boats, the flashes from the mortars guiding him to the flotilla.[24]

Farragut listened attentively to the deserter's story and then, after Porter left to return to the mortar flotilla, he signaled for the commanders of all vessels to come aboard the *Hartford* for a conference.

From the beginning, Farragut had not had much faith in the mortars, and he was impatient at the delay that the prolonged bombardment imposed upon him, for he was brimming with confidence in himself and in his ships and in the men who manned them. Just a few days earlier he had written his wife: "Men are easily elated or depressed by victory. But as to being prepared for defeat, I certainly am not. Any man who is prepared for defeat would be half defeated before he commenced. I hope for success; shall do all in my power to secure it, and trust to God for the rest."[25]

17

The Hour of Decision

AFTER THREE DAYS OF INTENSE ANXIETY, NEW ORLEANS ON EASTER Sunday was full of agitated, nervous people ready to believe almost any rumor, however farfetched, which circulated through the city. In vain did the *Bee* warn the people to remain calm and to ignore the rumors, many of which, it said, were doubtlessly started and spread by disguised enemies in the city. To illustrate how groundless rumors start, the *Bee* cited one that spread rapidly that General Paul Juge of the European Brigade had been arrested, when in fact it was a man named Ned Judge who had been jailed for petty larceny.

On every lip was the same anxious question: What news from the forts? Some, perhaps, found reassurance in the *True Delta's* assertion that despite the fact that the enemy had expended 370,000 pounds of gunpowder and one thousand tons of iron, "he had accomplished nothing." The *Delta* printed the same information as coming from a "prominent officer" at Fort Jackson and quoted him: "I never heard of such a bombardment. There is no such recorded in history . . ." The *Picayune* attributed to another officer the statement that for nearly seventy hours the Federal mortar vessels and gunboats had kept up a steady fire day and night, averaging five shells a minute. "We suffer much from want of sleep," the *Bee* quoted a third officer at Fort Jackson, "but the satisfaction of doing our duty imparts to us superhuman strength."[1]

The *Delta* published an exchange of reassuring telegrams between General Lovell and General Duncan aimed at bolstering morale in New Orleans, and commented: "Our people, we are persuaded, possess as much nerve as any to be found in the world. But it cannot be disguised that, for some days past, they look with painful concern to the defense of the forts below against the furious and incessant bombardment of the enemy's fleet . . . For a time the danger was undefined, mysterious and fearful . . ."

With an offhand calmness that the situation belied, the *Crescent* said: "We have not much to fear from the dozen or so of the mortar vessels now bombarding the forts below . . ." Doing its bit to restore calm to the city, the *Commercial Bulletin* assured its readers that "from the most reliable intelligence which we have been able to obtain, we think the enemy has made very little progress in his work, while we have sunk or disabled quite a number of his boats." Continuing, it said: "Only the lower Fort has been disturbed at all. We have reason to believe that we have powers of resistance which have not yet been called into action, and we hope soon to make the enemy rue the day he ever entered the mouth of the Mississippi. We prefer to let him learn our meaning in another way."[2]

This cryptic reference, of course, was to the two ironclads, *Louisiana* and *Mississippi*, which everybody in town knew were nearing completion. The *Louisiana* had been launched many weeks earlier, but work on its motive power was still under way. On April 19, Commander Whittle ordered the *Louisiana* down to the forts at once, it being evident that in its incomplete condition it could not go upstream.

The *Louisiana* had to be towed down the river by two tenders, which not only served as tugs but as quarters for the officers and crew and mechanics who were taken down the river to continue work on the vessel at the forts. There were many "bugs" in the ironclad's machinery, and the best use to which the *Louisiana* could be expected to be put was as a formidable floating battery to support the forts if Farragut attempted to run past them.

Mistakes had been made, too, in mounting the *Louisiana's* sixteen guns, some being too high and some too low, and it took considerable time and effort to rectify the errors in the ironclad's batteries.[3]

The day before the *Louisiana* left New Orleans the *Mississippi* was finally launched after considerable controversy between the Committee of Public Safety and the Tift brothers. At the end of February, Joseph Pearce, naval constructor of the *Mississippi*, had urged the Tifts to launch the vessel, because of the rising of the river and the danger of soft ground under the ship's foundation. Nelson and Asa Tift made an examination, which indicated to their satisfaction that the foundation was stable and no apparent danger existed. A month later, on March 27, Pearce had written the Tifts, again urging the immediate launching of the vessel, because of "the accumulation of the immense weight." He stated: "The interest of the Government demands it. The water is still rising, and I fear the ship will settle on her ways; and if this should be the case we will have trouble to get her off. Again, if she was afloat I would put on the iron, which is not prudent to do now. The foundation is getting softer every day, and I can see no reason why she will not settle . . ." The Tifts then made another examination and once again were satisfied that there was no settlement or injury to the *Mississippi*. "We felt confident to launch her then would delay the completion of the vessel a month," they wrote Secretary of Navy Mallory.

The discussion came to the attention of the Committee of Public Safety—the Tifts said that Pearce and others went to the committee and reported that the vessel was endangered by not being launched —and a subcommittee called on the Tifts and urged them to launch the *Mississippi*. A member of the committee later testified that the Tifts "positively refused." The Tifts told Mallory that they gave the committee a "polite reception." The result of the interview was to cause considerable excitement in New Orleans and to raise in some minds prejudicial opinions against the Tift brothers.

For weeks the Tifts held out, but mounting public opinion finally compelled them to give in. The Committee of Public Safety was on the verge of making a public announcement of the entire affair, when one of its members received a private note from General Lovell stating he was apprised of their intentions but that he would not permit the publication, as it would acquaint the enemy with "our weakness." Finally, on April 18, the day Porter opened his mortar bombardment of the forts, the launching was begun. But all efforts resulted only in failure, for the more the steamers tried to pull the ironclad into the river, the more firmly did the *Mississippi* settle on her ways. The next day the steamers were discarded and hydraulic rams were used to push the warship into the river.

And so, on Easter Sunday, April 20, the *Mississippi*, now afloat, was being rushed to completion. Naval officers and seafaring men who saw the vessel agreed, the Tifts wrote Mallory, that the "*Mississippi* was the strongest and . . . most formidable war vessel that has ever been built." In two weeks, the Tifts promised, the ironclad would be completed and ready for action.⁴ If time could be purchased—if Fort Jackson and Fort St. Philip could hold out until the *Louisiana* arrived—if Farragut could be held to a stalemate until the *Mississippi* could join in the battle, New Orleans could be saved.

Meanwhile, aboard the *Hartford* that Easter Sunday, all the commanders of the Federal fleet, except the three whose gunboats were covering the mortars, gathered in the flag officer's cabin. Porter, with whom Farragut had conferred already that morning, was not at the meeting, but Lieutenant J. M. Wainwright, commander of the *Harriet Lane*, attended. Porter later wrote Gustavus Fox that ". . . Farragut has been pleased to consider me as an 'outsider' and has not deigned to invite me to his public councils."

Farragut opened the conference by unfolding his plan of operations, illustrating it with charts and maps, after which he assigned a place to each vessel during the forthcoming attack. After some discussion, Commander James Alden of the *Richmond* asked permission to read a memorandum which, he said, Commander Porter had asked him to present.

The memorandum, undated but obviously written before Farragut had gotten all his vessels into the river, was a long one, setting forth Porter's ideas on how to capture New Orleans. He urged that the chain across the river remain untouched until the mortars began firing, a condition that already existed. A demand on the forts to surrender should be made, and were it refused, the mortar vessels should keep two mortars in the air all the time. Porter suggested two methods of attack:

> One is for the vessels to run the gantlet of the batteries by night, or in a fog, the other to attack the forts by laying the big ships close alongside of them, avoiding the casemates, firing shells, grape and canister into the barbette, clearing the ramparts with boat guns from the tops, while the smaller and more agile vessels throw in shrapnel at shrapnel distance, clearing the parapets and dismounting the guns in barbette. The larger ships should anchor . . . the smaller vessels to keep underway, and be constantly moving about, some to get above and open a cross fire; the mortars to keep up a rapid and continuous fire, and to move up to a shorter range.

Porter was all for capturing the forts first, before moving up the river, because if the fleet ran past the forts, the mortar flotilla would be left behind, unprotected, unless they were towed by the gunboats, a hazardous, as well as a slow, undertaking. A final suggestion called for a joint operation by the Army and Navy against Fort St. Philip, which Porter assured was "practicable." Commander Alden finished reading the memorandum and folded it and returned it to his pocket. Fleet Captain Henry Bell suggested to Alden that Porter's memorandum more properly belonged in the possession of the flag officer, whereupon Alden turned it over to Farragut.

Referring to the barrier, Farragut stated that Porter had agreed that morning that the time was propitious to break the chain and scatter the hulks and that an expedition for that purpose was planned for that very night. Regarding Porter's objections, Farragut said he saw no danger to the mortars after the fleet passed the forts. It was necessary for a successful land attack on St. Philip that his gunboats cover the landing from the Gulf in the neighborhood of the Quarantine, seven miles above the forts.

Some of the commanders thought that trying to pass the forts was "a hazardous thing . . . as being out of reach of supplies." Farragut had an answer for them: ammunition was being rapidly consumed and no supply was at hand; something had to be done immediately. "I believe in celerity," said the flag officer.[5]

After the council broke up, Farragut issued, under the date of April 20, the following general order:

The flag-officer, having heard all the opinions expressed by the different commanders, is of the opinion that whatever is to be done will have to be done quickly, or we will be again reduced to a blockading squadron without the means of carrying on the bombardment, as we have nearly expended all the shell and fuzes and material for making cartridges. He has always entertained the same opinions which are expressed by Commander Porter—that is, that there are three modes of attack [Farragut seems to have included Porter's original plan to reduce the forts by mortar fire exclusively with the two Porter listed in his memorandum], and the question is, Which is the one to be adopted? His own opinion is that a combination of two should be made, viz: The forts should be run, and when a force is once above the forts to protect the troops, they should be landed at Quarantine from the Gulf side by bringing them through the bayou, and then our forces should move up the river, mutually aiding each other, as it can be done to advantage.

When, in the opinion of the flag-officer, the propitious time has arrived, the signal will be made to weigh and advance to the conflict. If, in his opinion, at that time of arriving at the respective positions of the different divisions of the fleet we have the advantage, he will make the signal for "Close Action," No. 8, and abide the result—conquer or to be conquered—drop anchor or keep underway, as in his opinion is best. Unless the signal above mentioned is made it will be understood that the first order of sailing will be formed after leaving Fort

St. Philip, and we will proceed up the river in accordance with the original opinion expressed.

The program of the order of sailing accompanies this general order, the commanders will hold themselves in readiness for the service as indicated.[6]

The order out of the way, Farragut wrote Secretary Welles a letter and, had Father Neptune received it before news of the victory, he would have torn off, as one of Farragut's biographers picturesquely put it, "his newest glossiest wig and trampled it underfoot in his consternation and agitation."

"The officers do their duty well, but I regret to say that I do not find myself half supplied with anything," complained the flag officer. "My shells, fuzes, cylinder cloth and yarn to make the cylinders are all out and should be at this moment entirely unable to continue the bombardment, so far as my squadron is concerned, were it not for the fuzes, etc., sent to Commander Porter, I would have been on the parish."

But for help from General Butler, Farragut went on, the fleet surgeons would not have had materials to dress little wounds. Despite his requisition on the Medical Bureau, there was not a piece of muslin in the fleet. "I asked for the shells I wanted and other ordnance stores, and I am told that my demand is out of the question, and now I find myself dependent upon the Army for everything; and General Butler has been most generous—he gives everything in his power. I mentioned these facts to show I am driven to the alternative of fighting it out at once or waiting and resuming the blockade until supplies arrive."[7]

On the night of April 20, Farragut dispatched an expedition, under Captain Bell's command, to go up the river and sever the obstruction and make a passage for the fleet. As usual, Commander Porter claimed it was his idea. In his manuscript, Porter wrote:

> I had in my part of the expedition, a person named Kroehl, who came out with me for the purpose of blowing up obstructions. I made a proposition to Farragut to fit out a party to

blow up the vessels the rebels had anchored in the channel, with chains from one to the other. This he consented to. I selected such volunteers as offered, from my part of the squadron . . . When all preparations were made I reported to Farragut, "I will go tonight." What was my surprise when the Flag Officer said to me, "Captain Bell will go in command of the expedition." To this I replied, "Then I don't go unless you order me." I thought this the unkindest thing Farragut had ever done . . . Every officer connected with the boat expedition as I planned it, declined going when Captain Bell took charge and that was the only satisfaction I had.[8]

Captain Bell boarded the *Pinola*, and at 10 P.M. that gunboat and the *Itasca*, all lights concealed, steamed noiselessly up the river past the fleet, their low hulls barely visible in the dark to the men who peered from the sides of the other vessels. "It was a wild night . . . dark, rainy, with half a gale of wind blowing down the river," one of the anxious watchers on the *Richmond* recalled. "But few of us in the fleet went below that night, for we were all impressed with the importance and danger of the work . . ." On board the *Pinola* was Julius Kroehl, Porter's petard man, with five 180-pound charges of powder, reels of insulated wire, and batteries. Nobody on the *Pinola* had any confidence in Kroehl or his machines, but that gentleman, one of the officers noted, "had an idea he was going to do great things."

As the two gunboats went up the river, Porter's bummers opened up furiously, each crew sending a shell on its way to Fort Jackson as rapidly as the mortars could be safely loaded and fired. Frequently there were as many as nine shells in the air at one time. From the deck of the *Pinola*, one young officer was fascinated by "the little brilliant meteors continuously circling in the air."

At ten-thirty the *Pinola* crashed into the raft, damaging its port-bow bulwark. The gunboat was secured to the nearest hulk and immediately men jumped aboard to place the petards, under Kroehl's directions, one over the bow and another over the stern moorings and a barrel of powder onto the midships cable. "At this moment a rocket went up on shore, lights were shown along the batteries, and immediately they opened fire in the direction which we were," a participant in the expedition wrote. "We kept perfect silence knowing it to be our only safety. They fired high though the shot came whizzing by very disagreeably. Soon they ceased firing thinking no doubt it was a false alarm, particularly as they could not distinguish our vessels from their own hulks."

Preparing the charges took about ten minutes, after which the *Pinola*, in backing off, fouled itself with the hulk. This caused more delay, but finally the *Pinola* glided free.

"Explode!" Captain Bell ordered Kroehl.

"The conductor is broken," replied the petard man.

"Explode the second one then," commanded Bell.

There was a moment's hesitation, and then Kroehl shouted back: "That one is also broken."[9]

Upon hearing this, Bell abandoned the "powder-barrel part of the plan" and looked about for the *Itasca*. As the *Pinola* approached the obstruction a second time, a boat from the *Itasca* came alongside with the information that she was stuck fast on the left bank of the river and needed assistance. The *Itasca* had gone alongside one of the hulks and "unincumbered by a petard man had sensibly gone to work and unshackled the chains binding her schooner thus opening the desired channel." The current swept the *Itasca*, along with the hulk, close to the shore, where the gunboat ran aground. The *Pinola* went at once to the aid of the *Itasca*, but a 9-inch hawser which was run to her broke and the *Pinola* drifted downstream. Back it came a second time, passing an 11-inch hawser to the grounded gunboat, but once more the hawser snapped. The third try, with a 13-inch hawser, was successful, and the *Itasca* was afloat again.

Lieutenant Charles H. B. Caldwell, commander of the *Itasca*, decided to inspect the opening in the obstruction before dropping down the river to rejoin the fleet. "Having succeeded in making a clear passage for the fleet to pass over the chains," he recorded in the ship's log, "we proceeded to return, and in running close by another schooner ran on a chain and carried it away breaking the schooner partially adrift and carrying away some booms astern moored by chains to the schooner, thus still more effectually clearing the passage."[10]

Meanwhile, down the river, frightening excitement seized the whole fleet. The crews saw the rocket go up and heard the booming of the guns of the forts, indicating that the expedition had been discovered. Minutes of fearful expectation lengthened into hours, and the well-disciplined crews began to murmur at the seeming inactivity of the fleet. At 12:30 A.M. an officer from the *Pinola* boarded the *Hartford* to report to Farragut that the *Itasca* was stuck in the mud and needed assistance. This only added to the tension aboard the flagship. At last a light, then another, was seen coming down the river and the two gunboats appeared in the darkness, gliding to their anchorages.

"Captain Bell went up last night to cut the chain across the river," Farragut wrote his wife. "I never felt such anxiety in my life as I did until his return. I was as glad to see Bell . . . as if he had been my boy. I was up all night, and could not sleep until he got back to the ship."[11]

But Farragut did not get much sleep at all that night, because at 2:30 A.M. a large fire raft came down upon the fleet, causing considerable confusion. Ships' bells sounded the call for fire quarters and the various gunboats in the path of the fire raft maneuvered to avoid it. The raft passed between the *Hartford* and the *Richmond*, great flames licking up in the strong wind as high as the masts. So intense was the heat that men on both ships could hardly look over the side until it passed. The *Kineo* drifted into the *Sciota* and became fouled and both gunboats drifted into the *Mississippi*, the *Sciota* losing its launch and cutter and suffering other damage. At this moment the fire raft struck the *Sciota* on the port bow, setting the ship on fire in two places, but the fire was quickly extinguished. Meanwhile, both boats from the *Iroquois* were sent out to tow the fire raft away from the fleet, and while the operation was under way, one of Porter's steamers, the *Westfield*, ran into the *Iroquois*.[12]

It was a very chaotic situation that one fire raft, unsupported by naval vessels, was able to create in the fleet. Fortunate, indeed, it was for Farragut that aggressive old Flag Officer Hollins had not prevailed upon Richmond authorities to let him bring his fleet down the river to attack the invaders. Hollins had a plan that would have employed fire rafts in great number, supported by his little flotilla. Probably, the very least he would have accomplished would have been to get fire rafts down among the Union vessels in such numbers as to threaten Farragut with disaster. At any rate, such an operation would have thrown Farragut off schedule and would have purchased precious time for the completion of the formidable ironclads, *Louisiana* and *Mississippi*.

But Hollins was ordered to Richmond and General Duncan could get no effective co-operation from the River Defense Fleet, which was charged with sending down fire rafts. On the night the *Itasca* cut the barrier, Duncan complained that "no barges were sent down to light up the river or distract the attention of the enemy at night." Captain Stevenson, who commanded the River Defense Fleet, had also been instructed nearly two weeks earlier by General Duncan to "keep one of your boats constantly below night and day," and had he followed instructions, the *Pinola* and *Itasca* would probably have been driven off, without accomplishing their purpose, Duncan asserted, stating: "The raft after this could not be regarded as an obstruction."[13]

All night of that eventful Easter Sunday the mortars kept up an incessant fire, and the monotonous bombardment now had become a commonplace within the fleet. "This bomb fire at first . . . was a matter of constant interest, and the top-mast heads . . . were thronged with anxious spectators," recalled an officer. "But as no perceptible effect was produced on the forts by the bombardment, we soon lost our curiosity and came to the conclusion that after all this was simply to be the overture, but the real work would remain for us to accomplish." Lieutenant Dewey recalled that the men of the fleet "were too busy to sleep much, but we were soon so accustomed to the noise, and so dog-tired when we had a chance to rest, that we could have slept in an inferno."

As for the mortar crews, they had little rest and few satisfactory meals for three days and nights. Accordingly, Porter divided the three divisions into three watches of four hours, firing from each division about 168 times a watch. This gave the exhausted gunners some rest, and when their firing period ended, they would slump to the deck and fall asleep in their tracks. "Overcome with fatigue, I had seen the commanders and crews lying fast asleep, on deck with a mortar on board and the vessel next to them thundering away and shaking everything around them like an earthquake," reported Porter. A mortar-vessel captain said that his men became so worn and sleepy that "nothing short of a kick would rouse them when it came our turn to fire."

Far down the river, the noise and shock of the unbroken firing shattered windows at the Balize, thirty miles distant, and jarred Ben Butler's transports, many miles downstream. An officer of a Massachusetts regiment noted in his diary: "This is a sabbath day but the thunder of the Bombardment and the excitement incident thereto, does not comport our quiet New England Sabbath."[14]

On April 21, there was no appreciable letup in the fire from the mortar flotilla. It went on day and night, disabling several guns in Fort Jackson. These were repaired as rapidly as was possible under constant bombardment. The first cheering note for the much harassed garrison in Fort Jackson was the arrival of the *Louisiana* during the night, news which General Duncan received with "extreme pleasure," for he hoped to make the necessary repairs to the fort under cover of the ironclad's heavy guns. The forts that day delivered a fire on the head of the first division of Porter's flotilla that was "very rapid and troublesome." Two mortar ships—the *Para* and *Norfolk Packet*—had rigging and masts cut up or carried away as 125 shots fell close to the vessels in the space of an hour and a half. To protect the forward vessels, Porter ordered three of them to a new position, much to the chagrin of their commanders.

Early on April 22, General Duncan met with Commander Mitchell, who explained that the *Louisiana's* motive power would not, in all probability, be completed within any reasonable time. Accordingly, Mitchell told Duncan, the ironclad could not be considered as "an aggressive steamer or . . . brought into the pending action in that character." Duncan urged that the *Louisiana* be used as "an ironclad invulnerable floating battery" and that she be placed below the raft, close in to the shore on the Fort St. Philip side, "where her fire could dislodge the mortar boats from behind the point of woods and give sufficient respite to Fort Jackson to repair *in extenso*."

The need for relief from the ceaseless mortar shells was indeed acute, as may be gathered from General Duncan's estimate of the situation: "Fort Jackson had already undergone and was still subjected to a terrible fire of 13-inch mortar shells, which it was necessary to relieve at once to prevent the disabling of all the best guns at that fort, and, although Fort St. Philip partially opened out the point of the woods concealing the enemy and gallantly attempted to dislodge him or draw his fire, he nevertheless doggedly persisted in his one main object of battering Fort Jackson."

Not satisfied to rest on his verbal plea to Commander Mitchell, General Duncan sat at his desk and "earnestly and strongly" put his views into a letter. Mitchell replied almost immediately, putting on paper what he had earlier told Duncan and rejecting the suggestion that the *Louisiana* be placed below the raft in its present state, but assuring Duncan that "the very moment I can venture to face our enemy with any reasonable chance of success . . . I will do it."

Duncan replied at once. "It is of vital importance that the present fire of the enemy should be withdrawn from us, which you alone can do," he wrote. "This can be done in the manner suggested this morning, under cover of our guns, where your work on the boat can still be carried on in safety and security. Our position is a critical one, dependent entirely upon the powers of endurance of our casemates, many of which have been completely shattered and are crumbling away by repeated shocks; and therefore I respectfully but earnestly urge again my suggestions of this morning upon your notice. Our magazines also are in danger."

Upon receipt of Duncan's second note late on the twenty-second, Mitchell conferred with Commander Charles F. McIntosh, captain of the *Louisiana*, Lieutenant Thomas B. Huger of the *McRae*, Lieutenant A. F. Warley of the ram *Manassas*, and his own aide, Lieutenant George S. Shryock, all of whom sustained his views of not committing the *Louisiana* in its present state of incompletion. Early the next day, April 23, Commander Mitchell addressed himself a second time to General Duncan, sending him the naval officers' opinion and adding:

I feel the importance of affording relief to your command as soon as possible, but, General, at the same time I feel I know the importance to the safety of Forts Jackson and St. Philip and the city of New Orleans, of having this vessel in proper condition before seeking an encounter with the enemy. If he seeks one, or attempts the passage of the forts before this vessel is ready, I shall meet him, however unprepared I may be. We have an additional force of mechanics from the city this morning, and I hope that by tomorrow night the motive power of the *Louisiana* will be ready, and in the meantime her battery will be in place and other preparations will be completed so as to enable her to act against the enemy. When ready you will be immediately advised.[15]

Meanwhile, the bombardment continued day and night, sometimes being so heavy that observers could count as many as nine shells at the same time flaring through the air after dark. Butler said he once counted eleven mortar fuses burning at the same time. At Fort Jackson the casemates were very much cut up by the bummers' fire, but the guns kept up a vigorous response, concentrating their fire on the point of woods which sheltered the mortar vessels. General Duncan again was irritated by the "little or no success in sending down fire barges as usual." Mitchell had informed him that the towboats *Mosher* and *Belle Algerine* were in no mechanical condition to perform the job, and a third little tug, *Music*, was likewise in bad condition. "This does not excuse the neglect, however, as there were six boats of the river fleet available for this service, independent of those alluded to," said Duncan, "and fire barges were plentiful."[16]

But that strange ward of the War Department, the River Defense Fleet, commanded by Captain John A. Stevenson, was in no mood to take orders from the Confederate Navy. On April 21, Captain

Stevenson wrote Commander Mitchell that he had received orders from General Lovell to place himself and his command under Mitchell's orders. But he added:

> Every officer and man on the river-defense expedition joined it with the condition that it was to be independent of the Navy, and that it would not be governed by the regulations of the Navy, or be commanded by naval officers. In the face of the enemy I will not say more. I will cooperate with you and do nothing without your approbation, and will endeavor to carry out your wishes to the best of my ability, but in my own way as to the details and the handling of my boats. But I expect the vessels under my charge to remain as a separate command. All orders for their movements addressed to me will be promptly executed, if practicable, and I undertake to be responsible for their efficiency when required. I suppose this is all that is intended by the order of Major-General Lovell, or that will be expected from me by you.

Mitchell forwarded a copy of this extraordinary letter to Duncan at Fort Jackson, disassociating himself from any connection with Stevenson: ". . . Notwithstanding General Lovell's order . . . this letter so qualifies my authority as to relieve me from all responsibility as to the movement of the vessels of the river fleet . . ." And so, at a time when all things pointed to an imminent assault on the forts by Farragut's entire fleet, there was no agreement between the Confederate Army and Navy commanders at the forts or between the Confederate Navy and the War Department's River Defense Fleet.[17]

Unable to change Commander Mitchell's mind about placing the *Louisiana* where it could enfilade the mortar boats, Duncan appealed to General Lovell in New Orleans. On the morning of April 23, Lovell called on Commander Whittle, virtually begging him to instruct Mitchell to accede to Duncan's urgent plea.

"I am satisfied that by placing the *Louisiana* on the Fort St. Philip side, about half a mile below the raft, where she would be under the protection of the cross fire of both forts, she could enfilade the position of the enemy's fleet and drive them off, when the men in the forts could get some rest and make repairs," declared Lovell.

"I have every confidence in the officers in command of our fleet below," replied Whittle, "and I do not like to interfere with them."

"Mitchell has already refused to make the desired change," stated Lovell. "And as chief in command I ask that it be done."

"The vessel isn't entirely ready with her motive power," said Whittle, "and by placing her there I am afraid she will be lost."

"I don't ask that the *Louisiana* be sent down amid the enemy's fleet," stressed Lovell, "but that she be towed down and placed in position as a battery. And the necessity is such that it will be better to lose the *Louisiana* than the city of New Orleans."

Almost reluctantly, Commander Whittle wrote out a telegram to Mitchell and handed it to Lovell, who read:

> Can you not occupy a position below Fort St. Philip, so as to enfilade the mortar boats of the enemy and give time to the garrison to repair damages at Fort Jackson? See General Duncan on the subject. Higgins will go and point out the position. As I understand it, it is covered by the fire of the two forts, and would require that the bomb vessels should be readjusted to get your range. Strain a point to effect this.

When Lovell handed the telegram back to him, Whittle asked: "Will that do?"

"Nothing short of placing the *Louisiana* in the position indicated will answer my purpose," said Lovell. "I am going down in a special boat to the forts this afternoon. Why don't you come and judge for yourself?"

Undoubtedly to Lovell's astonishment, Whittle replied that his business in the office was such that he could not spare the time. What in the world could have been so important in the office of the Confederate naval commander at New Orleans that he couldn't spare the time from his desk to go to the point of attack at the critical moment in the campaign?

Meanwhile General Duncan made a final effort of his own to induce Mitchell to move the *Louisiana* and then gave up. Having noticed that the enemy had sent up a small boat on the St. Philip side and planted a series of white flags, Duncan passed the information on to Mitchell. "It is the probable position of his ships in the new line of attack, which, in my opinion, he contemplates for attacking Fort Jackson with his larger vessels," he wrote. ". . . Please keep the river well lit up with fire rafts tonight, as the attack may be made at any time."

Shortly before 11 P.M., Commander Mitchell telegraphed Commander Whittle that he would take up a position the next night to act in daylight against the mortar boats, and that he was communicating this fact to General Duncan.

In addition to General Duncan's written request to Mitchell, Lieutenant Colonel Edward Higgins, commander at Fort Jackson, sent two verbal messages to the navy commander during the day and early evening urging him to move the *Louisiana* to a spot where it could engage the mortar flotilla. Higgins was in Duncan's office when a naval officer arrived with Mitchell's message that he would place the *Louisiana* at the desired position in twenty-four hours.

"Tell Commander Mitchell that there will be no tomorrow for New Orleans unless he immediately takes up the position assigned to him with the *Louisiana*," Higgins told the officer. "If he does not do so the city is gone, and he will be responsible to the country for its loss. The forts are powerless to prevent it."[18]

Duncan and Higgins had shrewdly assessed Farragut's intentions. In fact, the impatient flag officer, unimpressed by the effect of the mortar fire, had planned his move against the forts on the night of April 22–23 but had postponed it because the ship carpenter and assistants of the *Mississippi* had gone down the river and Captain Melancton Smith was reluctant to go into battle without them.

Surgeon Jonathan M. Foltz remarked on April 17 that the flag officer "is anxious to make the attack upon the forts without waiting for the action of the mortar fleet. He is brave—impulsive." Some weeks earlier he had characterized Farragut as a "smart little sailor man" and "a bold brave man, full of fight but evidently does not know what he is going about." Foltz noted that many of Farragut's officers doubted that the wooden ships could pass the fire of the forts. "They are impassable by ships alone, they say. If the attempt is made, we shall probably have another disaster at a moment when all north of us is progressing so favorably. Wherever my brave brother officers and shipmates will go I will go to take care of them, but I pray God that we will not be led to defeat."[19]

Farragut had no misgivings about defeat, but he had plenty about delay. And yet Commander Porter in his manuscript journal describes a conversation with Farragut which is so fantastic as to be suspect. "The mortar ammunition was growing scarce and I did not feel that the crews could stand it much longer," wrote Porter. ". . . I determined to go and have a plain talk with the Flag Officer." Porter wrote that he stated "exactly how matters stood," asserting that the batteries at Fort Jackson had been damaged enough to justify an attempt to pass the forts, that Fort St. Philip was a "poor affair," that ammunition was running short, and finally that "the rebels were gaining time to get their heavy iron-clad, the *Louisiana*, down, which if placed a little below the forts would drive the mortars out of their position . . ." According to Porter, the following conversation ensued:

Farragut: "How can I attempt this thing when I am strongly opposed by some of the leading officers of the fleet? I am willing to go at any time, but I must listen to these people. Craven is putting me back all the time, and I have had to tell him that I wanted no more of his croaking, and that he was demoralizing the whole fleet. Other officers are lukewarm, and when I ask their opinions, shrug their shoulders and say they are ready to obey my orders."

Porter: "But Flag Officer, why not be governed by the opinions of Alden, Melancton Smith, De Camp, Bailey, Harrison and men of that stamp? All my officers are ready and desirous to go at any moment and remember the Secretary of the Navy says 'you must run risks to achieve great ends.'"

Farragut: "All well for *you* to talk, Mr. Captain, but I have all the responsibility and you have none."

Porter: "Yes I have. I have the responsibility that everyone in the fleet has. I am responsible that you don't fail, through want of exertion on my part, and it is my duty to exert myself and counteract those who will get us back to the mouth of the river if they can."

Farragut (after more talk by Porter): "What do you advise me to do?"

Porter: "Call a Council of your commanders and let each man put himself on record . . ."

Farragut: ". . . I think myself that it is time we should go to work."[20]

From this account, Porter would have us believe that Farragut was vacillating, and unwilling to take responsibility for the attack, and that he only did so at Porter's urging. However, quite a different story is told by Farragut's signal officer, B. S. Osbon. According to Osbon, after four days of the mortar bombardment, Farragut "could no longer control his expression of its uselessness."

When Porter came aboard the *Hartford* on April 22, the flag officer said:

"We are wasting ammunition and time. We will fool around down here until we have nothing left to fight with. I'm ready to run those forts now, tonight."

Porter pleaded for still a little more time. "Wait one more day, Flag Officer," he urged, "and I will cripple them so you can pass with little or no loss of life."

"All right, David," agreed Farragut. "Go at 'em again and we'll see what happens by tomorrow."

The next day, April 23, Porter came aboard the *Hartford* again, "downcast," recorded Osbon, "but still anxious to continue the bombardment."

"Look here, David," said Farragut. "We'll demonstrate the practical value of mortar work."

Turning to Osbon, who had been originally sent to him by Porter, the flag officer ordered: "Mr. Osbon, get me two small flags, a white one and a red one, and go to the mizzen topmasthead and watch where the mortar shells fall. If inside the fort, wave the red flag. If outside, wave the white one."

Turning to Porter with a smile, Farragut said: "You recommended Mr. Osbon to me, so you will have confidence in his observations.

Now go aboard your vessel, select a tallyman, and when all is ready, Mr. Osbon will wave his flags and the count will begin."

Osbon took his post and the mortars opened up vigorously. "It kept me busy waving the little flags," he recalled, "and I had to watch very closely not to make mistakes. On the deck, 'way aft, Farragut sat, watching the waving flags and occasionally asking for the score. The roar became perfectly deafening, and the ship trembled like an aspen. At last . . . the tally sheet was footed up, showing the 'outs' had it, by a large majority."

This was all the evidence that Farragut needed. "There, David," he said, when Porter reboarded the *Hartford*, "there's the score. I guess we'll go up the river tonight."[21]

In his official report of April 30, 1862, to Secretary Welles, Porter inserted an astonishing statement: "On the 23rd I urged Flag-Officer Farragut to commence the attacks with the ships at night, as I feared the mortars would not hold out." A qualm of conscience must have seized Porter later, for on May 10 he wrote his friend Gustavus Fox asking that the sentence be deleted from his report. "Though this is so, it won't do in a public dispatch to say so," he wrote. "It looks as if I was trying to make capital which I am not in the habit of doing—let Farragut have all the credit he can get."

The Navy Department, as Secretary Welles put it after the war, "declined to mutilate and change the record, and omit a statement, the truth of which was deliberately and secretly reaffirmed by the author." Welles also said that if Porter had sent his report through channels to Farragut, the statement would never have appeared, and moreover, Farragut "needed no urging from anyone to move—certainly not from one who from the first had advised that the forts should be reduced before the passage of the fleet was attempted."[22]

On the afternoon of April 23, the flag officer made the rounds of his fleet to see that all was in readiness and to learn positively that each commander understood the orders for the attack. Farragut's visit to each vessel was reassuring. "Everyone appeared to understand their orders well," noted the flag officer, "and looked forward to the conflict with firmness, but with anxiety . . ." Farragut sent instructions to Commander John De Camp of the *Iroquois*, who commanded the gunboats guarding the mortar flotilla, neither to risk his vessels nor to waste ammunition, "as it is my intention to pass up tonight." And the flag officer issued also a general order that two perpendicular red lights hoisted at the peak of the *Hartford* would be the signal to get under way and proceed at once up the river. "The division led by the flag officer will be the red, that led by Captain Bailey blue, and that of Commander Bell red and blue," the order read. "The leading division will not use their port guns, and the flag officer's division will not use their starboard guns in ascending the river, for fear of firing into each other."

Before sundown, the ships began to take their positions as indicated in the diagram which Farragut had supplied each commander. Captain Bailey's division, led by the *Cayuga*, anchored in a column along the right bank of the river while the other divisions took up positions on the left bank. Captain Bailey and Lieutenant Harrison addressed the officers and men of the *Cayuga* on the quarter-deck immediately after the vessel was in position. Captain Bailey spent part of the night steaming up and down his division to satisfy himself that nothing was amiss.[23]

Shortly before 8 P.M., Farragut ordered Lieutenant Caldwell of the *Itasca* and Acting Master Jones to go up the river in a ten-oared boat, to inspect the raft at the forts. More than three hours later, the party returned, and at 11:10 P.M. Farragut learned that the river was all clear for the passage of the fleet.

From the quarter-deck of the *Hartford*, Farragut watched the preparations among his ships. Suddenly, he turned to his signal officer, Osbon, and asked:

"What do you estimate our casualties will be, Mr. Osbon?"

"Flag Officer, I've been thinking of that," replied Osbon, "and I believe we will lose a hundred."

Farragut looked at Osbon in surprise, for this was a small percentage of the four thousand men in the fleet.

"No more than that?" asked the flag officer. "How do you calculate on so small a number."

"Well, most of us are pretty low in the water, and, being near, the enemy will shoot high," explained Osbon. "Then, too, we will be moving and it will be dark, with dense smoke. Another thing, gunners ashore are never as accurate as gunners aboard a vessel. I believe a hundred men will cover our loss."

"I wish I could think so," said Farragut. "I wish I could be as sure of it as you are."

A few moments later, Osbon studying the sky to determine weather prospects for the attack, suddenly saw a great bald eagle circling above the fleet.

"Look there, Flag Officer," called Osbon, pointing to the eagle. "That is our national emblem. It is a sign of victory."[24]

There was not much sleep in Farragut's fleet that night. When the hammocks were piped down after dark, the crews were told they would be called at midnight, not with the customary noisy signals, but quietly, and the seamen sought whatever sleep the thought of the coming event would allow them.

An officer on the *Richmond* described the solemn moment in the wardroom at the evening meal, and doubtless similar scenes were enacted on every other vessel in the fleet. He wrote:

> There was none of the merry jesting that usually marked our meals, and when the table was cleared every officer went to his stateroom, and I think each of us wrote some lines to his nearest and dearest in anticipation of what might happen before we saw another sun. I know, at least, that I wrote such a letter. The lights were extinguished and all was quiet throughout the ship; such absolute quiet as is never found except just before a battle.

On the *Pensacola*, Lieutenant Francis A. Roe recorded his feeling in his diary:

> Our people view this conflict as most desperate . . . I see no want of determination on the part of our people. But I look for a bloody conflict. These may be the last lines I may ever write. But I have an unflinching trust in God that we shall plant the Union flag upon the enemy's forts by noon tomorrow. I trust in Almighty God for the results. If I fall, I leave my darlings to the care of my country.[25]

Thus did the awesome before-the-battle stillness envelop Farragut's fleet as it lay at anchor in the dark river under a moonless sky.

And in New Orleans, on that fateful night of April 23–24, morning newspapers were "put to bed" containing a message of encouragement from heavily bombed Fort Jackson to the nervous, rumor-ridden city:

> God is certainly protecting us. We are all cheerful, and have an abiding faith in our ultimate success, which I deeply regret is not altogether the case in the city.
>
> A people in earnest, in a good cause, should have more fortitude.
>
> We are making repairs as we can. Our best guns are still in good working order.
>
> The health of the troops continues to be good, and they are generally in better spirits than even in more quiet times. So much for discipline.
>
> From 22,000 to 25,000 13-inch mortar shells have been fired by the enemy, thousands of which have fallen within the Fort. They must soon exhaust themselves. If not, we can stand it, with God's blessing, as long as they can.

The dispatch was signed by General Duncan, who, early on the morning of April 24, noting activity among the Union vessels as he peered into the dark from the parapet of Fort Jackson, sent a last, desperate appeal to Commander Mitchell: "You are assuming a fearful responsibility if you do not come at once to our assistance with the *Louisiana* and the fleet. I can say no more."[26]

18

Farragut Runs the Gantlet

SHORTLY BEFORE ONE O'CLOCK ON THE MORNING OF APRIL 24, HOT coffee and hardtack were served the men of the fleet. Many grumbled because grog was not distributed, but Flag Officer Farragut would not hear of it. Final preparations for battle were made aboard each ship as carpenter gangs prepared plugs and patches to stop shell holes and gunner's mates busied themselves looking after the lock strings of the guns, filling the division tubs with water for use in case of fire, or to drink, and putting buckets of sand in the rear of the guns to be scattered over the deck should blood make it slippery.[1]

Although the stars were out, it was a dark, moonless night and the air had a bite in it. But despite the chilliness, many of the gunners came to their stations stripped to the waist, their monkey jackets knotted by the sleeves, hanging loosely around their necks. Guns were cast loose and prepared for action, and crews stood silently awaiting developments. In the engine rooms, the engineers of the fleet had not been idle, for a heavy pressure of steam was on.[2]

On the stroke of two o'clock, Signal Officer Osbon hoisted to the *Hartford's* mizzen peak two red lanterns, the signal to weigh anchor, and almost immediately the little *Cayuga* got its anchors up and steamed off into the darkness. Captain Bailey's division, formed in a close line on the extreme right, followed the *Cayuga* as it led the fleet like a pilot fish up to the Rebel barrier below the forts.[3]

As the warships glided silently past the *Hartford*, Farragut, "calm and cheerful," responded to Signal Officer Osbon's announcement of each vessel with a cordial "All right," or "Thank you, sir." However, when the *Pensacola* fumbled with its anchor and delayed getting under way, the flag officer lost his composure and fumed at Captain Morris. "Damn that fellow!" he exploded. "I don't believe he wants to start."

Meanwhile, the *Louisiana* was still in her old position above Fort St. Philip, all of General Duncan's importunities to Commander Mitchell having been in vain. The unfinished ironclad was surrounded by her tenders. The other ships of the Confederate fleet—with the exception of the *McRae* and the turtleback *Manassas*, which were just above Fort Jackson with steam up, ready for instant action—lay above the *Louisiana*. And moored to the shore were numerous fire rafts ready for the torch.

The *Cayuga* moved noiselessly through the barrier at 3:30 A.M., and shortly thereafter a sergeant in the water battery of Fort Jackson directed Captain William B. Robertson's attention to "several black, shapeless masses, barely distinguishable from the surrounding darkness, moving silently, but steadily up the river." Robertson knew what that meant and so did General Duncan, who hurriedly scrawled his final plea to Mitchell to come at once with the *Louisiana*.

Captain Robertson looked hopefully for the illumination by the fire rafts, but "not a torch had been applied to a single fire-raft, and not one of them had been started from their moorings." Early that night, on instructions from Lieutenant Colonel Higgins, Robertson had prepared for this movement by the Yankee fleet. His guns were loaded, his gunners ready. It took only a moment for the guns to be trained upon the two leading Federal vessels, and at 3:40 A.M. Fort Jackson's water battery "thundered its greeting to the enemy."

Immediately, Fort Jackson and Fort St. Philip opened up with roaring salvos, and Farragut's ships, their guns silent up to now, responded with broadsides, the flashes of their guns lighting up the river luridly and revealing more distinctly the outlines of the attacking warships. The awesome grandeur of the scene was a vivid memory of Captain Robertson:

> I do not believe there ever was a grander spectacle witnessed before in the world than that displayed during the great artillery duel which then followed. The mortar-shells shot upward from the mortar boats, rushed to the apexes of their flight, flashing the lights of their fuses as they revolved, paused an instant, and then descended upon our works like hundreds of meteors, or burst in mid-air, hurling their jagged fragments in every direction. The guns on both sides kept up a continual roar for nearly an hour, without a moment's intermission, and produced a shimmering illumination, which, though beautiful and grand, was illusive in its effect upon the eye, and made it impossible to judge accurately of the distance of the moving vessels from us; and this fact, taken in connection with their rapid and constant change of positions as they speeded up the river rendered it very difficult to hit them with our projectiles.[4]

When the forts opened up their fire on the *Cayuga*, young Lieutenant George H. Perkins, who was in charge of steering the gunboat, was almost blinded by the explosions. Noticing, however, that the guns of the forts were aimed for midstream, he steered the *Cayuga* close under the walls of Fort St. Philip. At 3:45, the *Cayuga* opened on the fort with grape and canister, and for fifteen minutes there was a furious exchange at close range. At 4 A.M., its masts, rigging, and hull riddled by forty-two shots, the *Cayuga* passed the line of fire of Fort St. Philip and found itself alone in the midst of the Rebel fleet.

Originally, Farragut had planned to employ two columns of vessels abreast in his rush past the forts, but because of the narrowness of the opening in the barrier, the flag officer decided there would be less chance of getting fouled by the hulks and chains if the advance was made in a single column, and he issued new verbal instructions to this effect.[5]

At 3:30, the *Hartford* was under way, leading the *Brooklyn* and *Richmond* and Captain Bell's gunboats, *Sciota, Iroquois, Kennebec, Pinola, Itasca,* and *Winona,* "into the black folds ahead, through which the flash and thunder came back incessantly." Gun crews lay flat upon the deck as the flagship felt its way through the opening in the barrier and came simultaneously into the dense smoke and the range of the forts. While shells burst about the *Hartford* and solid shot screamed overhead, Osbon hoisted the largest American flag aboard at the peak and then sent smaller flags to the top of the fore- and mainmasts.

"Why do you do that?" called the flag officer, mindful that a ship did not fly colors at night.

"Flag Officer," shouted back Osbon, "I thought if we are to go down, it would look well to have our colors flying above the water."

"Very well," replied Farragut, doubtless pleased at the inspiring irregularity. Shortly after, the *Brooklyn* and *Richmond,* and the gunboats astern that could make out the *Hartford's* flags through the thickening smoke, broke their colors.

Although all of Bailey's first-division vessels were supposed to clear the barrier before Farragut's division pushed through, there was a foul-up. The *Brooklyn,* which started astern of the flagship, collided with the *Kineo,* in line in Bailey's division, almost capsizing the little gunboat.

As each vessel steamed into range of the forts and responded with broadsides, the already tremendous tempo of the battle was stepped up. The *Richmond* passed so close to Fort Jackson that a stone could have been tossed into the fort, and after raking it with grape and canister, it crossed the river to engage Fort St. Philip. A gun-crew captain, about to fire his gun, had his head carried away by a solid shot, and as he fell, the lock string in his hand discharged the gun. A gunnery officer had his right arm torn off by an exploding shell, and a young master's mate, hurrying up to the topgallant forecastle with a message for Commander Alden, barely had touched his cap in salute when a rifle ball struck him in the forehead and killed him instantly.

On board the *Pensacola*, Lieutenant Francis A. Roe, piloting the vessel in place of Captain Morris, whose eyesight was weak, stood on a fire-swept bridge, abaft the mainmast, in close range of Fort St. Philip's guns. A signal quartermaster at Roe's side had a leg shot off and his boy aide was swept away. Shells burst all about Roe, and although the right leg of his pantaloons and drawers was cut away at the knee and the skirt of his coat was cut in a strip, the young pilot escaped unscathed.[6]

As the battle reached its peak, Porter's mortar flotilla delivered a furious fire, filling the starlit sky with deadly shooting stars and little comets of destruction. But despite the withering bombardment of the bummers, Fort Jackson's guns laid down a frightful barrage through which the fleet had to pass and Fort St. Philip joined valiantly in creating the fiery gantlet for Farragut to run. One of General Butler's officers, viewing the attack from a distance, wrote: "Combine all that you have heard of thunder, add to it all that you have ever seen of lightning, and you have, perhaps, a conception of the scene . . ." An officer on the *Hartford* thought "it was like the breaking up of the universe with the moon and all the stars bursting in our midst." To Farragut himself "it was as if the artillery of heaven were playing upon the earth."[7]

The flag officer, having climbed to the *Hartford's* port mizzen to see above the smoke the progress of the battle, stood with his feet on the ratline and his back against the shrouds. Oblivious to the shells bursting around him, Farragut "stood there as cool and undisturbed as if leaning against a mantel in his own home." It had taken twenty-five minutes for the *Hartford* to get into position opposite Fort Jackson, during which time, by the flag officer's order, it had held its fire. But now it opened up, first with its bow guns, and then it engaged Fort Jackson with its port battery. A galling fire from Fort St. Philip sent shots crashing into the hull and spars and whistling through the rigging.

At first the forts fired high, but soon shot, shell, grape, and canister were bursting all around the *Hartford*. A shell struck the mainmast on a line where the flag officer stood in the mizzen rigging. Signal Officer Osbon hurried to Farragut and begged him to come down. Farragut brushed aside the plea.

"We can't afford to lose you, Flag Officer," argued Osbon. "They'll get you up here, sure."

Osbon had loaned Farragut a pair of small opera glasses, which were handier up there in the rigging than the flag officer's binoculars. So Osbon took another tack.

"Flag Officer, they'll break my opera glasses if you stay up here."

Farragut held out the opera glasses to Osbon, who exclaimed: "Oh, damn the glasses! It's you we want. Come down!"

In a few moments Farragut agreed to leave the perilous position, and hardly had he reached the deck again when a shell exploded and cut away much of the rigging where he had stood.

The *Hartford* steamed on steadily, but so thick was the smoke it was difficult to steer. At 4:10 A.M., the flagship was between the forts, caught up in an action at once general and terrible. Thicker and faster came shot and shell from the forts, while the *Hartford* answered with grape, canister, and shrapnel, which swept the parapets of Fort Jackson. Signal Officer Osbon painted a graphic picture of the action:

> It is quite out of the question to give any idea of the fire at this time, or of the night picture we made there in the midst of flame and smoke and iron hail . . . A shell burst on our deck . . . I ran forward to see what damage had been done, when the wind of another shell carried away my cap . . . We were struck now on all sides. A shell entered our starboard beam, cut our cable, wrecked our armory and exploded at the main hatch, killing one man instantly, and wounding several others. Another entered the muzzle of a gun, breaking the lip and killing the sponger who was in the act of "ramming home." A third entered the boatswain's room destroying everything in its path, and exploding, killed a colored servant who was passing powder.

Death and destruction seemed everywhere. Men's faces

were covered with powder—blacked and daubed with blood. They had become like a lot of demons in a wild inferno, working fiercely at the business of death.

Five minutes later, in veering to avoid a fire raft, the *Hartford* struck a shoal and ran aground close under the guns of Fort St. Philip. The *Hartford* pounded the fort with its starboard battery, while howitzers in the tops swept the parapets, but the flagship's position was indeed a critical one as the Confederate tug *Mosher* shoved the blazing raft under the *Hartford's* port quarter.[8]

In an instant, the *Hartford* was ablaze all along its port side, halfway up to the main and mizzen. For a moment, Farragut thought it was all up with the flagship, and Lieutenant Albert Kautz, hurrying across the deck, saw the flag officer with clasped hands above his head and heard him exclaim: "My God, is it to end in this way!" Quickly recovering, Farragut cried out: "Don't flinch from that fire, boys! There is a hotter fire than that for those who don't do their duty."

The flames and the heat drove the men from the port guns, and without occupation in a critical situation, gun crews and officers were thrown into the greatest confusion. "For a few moments, it looked like every one for himself," recalled Bartholomew Diggins, a young seaman. "My youthful emagination [*sic*] of hell did not equel [*sic*] the scene about us at this moment . . ." The men moved excitedly and purposelessly about the deck. Seeing a master's mate grab up a grating from the main hatch, presumably to support himself in the water, Diggins, "thinking the mate knew more about those things than me," grabbed up a grating himself and prepared to jump into the river if the ship got too hot.

But Diggins had not moved very far before he heard a calm but authoritative voice over the din. Through the thick smoke he discerned the tall, straight form of Commander Wainwright moving slowly through the disorganized crew, Flag Officer Farragut at his side. Giving commands through a speaking trumpet, Commander Wainwright quickly restored morale: "Take your places at fire quarters!" Wainwright's calmness, his assurance, his dignified bearing, all gave confidence to the men. In a matter of seconds, they jumped to their stations, and fire hoses were played upon the blazing rigging and the burning side of the *Hartford*. About this time, however, a new danger threatened the flagship, for a shell exploded in the cabin, setting the ship's interior on fire, a fact that became known only when smoke and flames burst through the windows.

Surgeon Jonathan Foltz, although kept busy below deck in the *Hartford's* improvised hospital, experienced the full drama of "a scene which has never been surpassed and seldom equaled," with "the din, the roar, the crash, the whistling of balls, the bursting of shells, the crashing of masts and timbers, the shrieks of the wounded and dying, our ship on fire in two places . . ."[9]

Meanwhile, Signal Officer Osbon had an idea to rid the *Hartford* of the fire raft, still in contact with the burning vessel. Rolling some 20-pound rifle shells across the deck, he knelt down to uncap them, just above the raft. The heat was so great that Osbon covered his head with his coat as he went to work. Farragut, seeing him on his knees, called out:

"Come, Mr. Osbon, this is no time for prayer!"

"Flag Officer, if you'll wait a second, you'll get the quickest answer to prayer ever you heard of."

Osbon then rolled three of the shells over the side into the fire raft. There was a tremendous explosion, and in a moment the fire raft went down with a big hole in it.

By now, vigorous fire fighting under Lieutenant Thornton's able command had extinguished the blaze and fire no longer was a hazard to the *Hartford's* existence. But despite the constant efforts of the engineer to back the *Hartford* out into the stream, the flagship was still stuck fast in the mud, a perfect "sitting" target for the fire of both forts.

Commander Wainwright hailed the engine room and called for the chief engineer. Mr. Purdy, an assistant, answered the call.

"Are you doing all you can with the engines?" inquired the skipper. "You know we are in a bad way if she don't back off."

"The throttle is wide open on the engines, sir," replied Purdy.

"Is there any way you can increase the power?" demanded Wainwright.

"By reducing her water, which would endanger the boilers," answered Purdy.

"Well, try anything to get her afloat," ordered Wainwright.

Purdy nodded and returned to the engine room to manage the operation himself. In a few moments the ship commenced pumping and the vibration became so great that the men on deck could scarcely hold their feet. After moments that seemed interminable, the *Hartford* at last came free and backed out into the main stream, while a spontaneous cheer went up from all the men. Then the gunners returned to their guns as if nothing had happened, and once more the *Hartford* was blazing away in concert with the other vessels, whose guns kept up an incessant roar.[10]

Meanwhile, most of the vessels in the fleet had passed through the barrier and made a running fight by the flaming guns of the forts. But three of the gunboats were unsuccessful. The *Kennebec* struck one of the hulks and entangled itself in the raft, and as dawn was breaking when it finally got free, its commander prudently decided against trying to pass the forts in daylight. The *Itasca*, badly crippled when a 42-pounder from Fort Jackson struck her boiler, drifted out of action down the river. The *Winona*, also fouled by the raft, made a bid to run the forts as day broke, but so hot was the fire from both it gave up the attempt and retired down the river.[11]

Two of Farragut's larger vessels, the *Brooklyn* and the *Mississippi*, had dangerous moments. The *Brooklyn*, after its brush with the *Kineo* at the barrier's entrance, got off its course and suddenly found itself running over a hulk and entangling itself with the chains of the raft. While Captain Craven struggled to disengage his ship, Fort St. Philip delivered a severe fire on the helpless vessel. Finally getting free, Craven headed the *Brooklyn* upstream. But only moments later the Confederate ram *Manassas*, which had been prowling through the fleet, rammed the *Brooklyn*, firing its single gun from a distance of ten feet as it crashed into the enemy. The shot entered five feet above the water line and lodged itself in sandbags protecting the steam drum. Because of the *Brooklyn*'s protective chain armor, the *Manassas'* butt did no damage. As the ram slipped astern, a leadsman on the *Brooklyn* threw his lead at a couple of men standing in a scuttle just forward of the smokestack, knocking one of them overboard. At dawn, the *Brooklyn* found itself above the forts, having set on fire the *Warrior* with a broadside and having seen its grape and canister bounce harmlessly off the iron sides of the *Louisiana*.[12]

Old Melancton Smith, who would have preferred making a passage by the forts in the daylight, had turned the operation of the *Mississippi* over to twenty-four-year-old Lieutenant George Dewey. "I can't see in the night," Captain Smith declared. "I'm going to leave that to you, Dewey. You have younger eyes." So when the *Mississippi* moved into the fight, Captain Smith took charge of the battery while Lieutenant Dewey, from his post on the hurricane deck, handled the ship.

Up in the foretop, where Captain Smith had placed him so that he could better view the spectacle of battle, was William Waud, an artist for an illustrated weekly. Suddenly Waud called down to Dewey: "Here is a queer-looking customer on our port bow." Dewey looked in the direction indicated and barely made out "what appeared like the back of an enormous turtle, painted lead color." He recognized the stranger immediately as the much feared *Manassas* and realized that if the ram were able to deliver a full blow in a vital spot, she was capable of disabling any ship in the fleet.

There was no time to ask Captain Smith for advice, so Dewey on his own initiative determined to try to put the ram out of commission before it could do any damage to the fleet. "I called to starboard the helm," Dewey recounted, "and turned the *Mississippi's* bow toward the *Manassas*, with the intention of running her down, being confident that our superior tonnage must sink her if we struck her fairly."

But Dewey did not catch the *Manassas* napping. Ironically, the last service of the ram's commander, Lieutenant A. F. Warley, in the old Navy had been on the *Mississippi* on a round-the-world cruise. Warley appreciated, accordingly, the old side-wheeler's immobility in comparison with the mobility of his ram. Sheering off to avoid the *Mississippi*'s thrust, he then sheered in and struck her a glancing blow just abaft the port paddle wheel.

The severe shock gave the *Mississippi* a momentary list and partially stopped her headway. Captain Smith thought his ship had run aground. Dewey saw a big hole in the vessel's side and called out to the ship's carpenter, who was near by on the main deck: "Sound the pumps!"

"I have already, sir," replied the carpenter, "and there is no water in the wells."

Dewey knew that he had nothing to worry about if there was no water, and he rejoiced that the sturdy construction of the *Mississippi* had saved it from serious damage. "The impact of the ram . . . would have sunk any other ship in the fleet," said Dewey. It had taken out a section of solid timber seven feet long, four feet broad, and four inches deep. About fifty copper bolts had been cut "as clean as if they were hair under a razor's edge."

The *Mississippi*, being under the fire of Fort St. Philip, did not make a second run at the *Manassas*, but concentrated on shooting its way past the forts. Though it was struck a number of times, the *Mississippi*'s losses were trifling. It blazed away with grape and five-second shells, fired from alternate guns, and though the bombardment was heavy on both sides, young Lieutenant Dewey was surprised "to see how well the forts stood our pounding and also how well we stood theirs."[13]

In Fort Jackson, where Porter's mortars concentrated their fire throughout the attack, "both the officers and men stood up manfully under this galling and fearful hail," as General Duncan later reported. "The batteries of both forts were promptly opened at their longest range with shot, shell, hot shot, and a little grape, and most gallantly and rapidly fought until the enemy succeeded in getting above and beyond our range."

At Fort St. Philip, Captain M. T. Squires "fought the batteries most gallantly" and his guns fired 1591 shots of all kinds at the passing Federal vessels, the fort itself suffering but slight injury, only five of its guns being disabled, or partially so, by the broadsides from Farragut's vessels. Captain Squires gave good reason for his pride in the way his men performed: "Individual acts of heroism are numerous, but where all did so well it would appear invidious to mention names. Suffice it to say that were everything to be done again, or anything else required to be performed, one could ask no other privilege than to have the same men to do it, feeling satisfied it would be as well carried out as possible."[14]

The immobile *Louisiana*, anchored above Fort St. Philip, was the last hazard the Federal ships had to run before engaging the Confederate Navy. Only six of the *Louisiana's* sixteen guns could be employed—three in the bow and three in the starboard battery—and these went into action as the enemy gunboats came into range. As the Federal vessels passed, they returned the *Louisiana's* fire by hurling grape, canister, and shell, but without serious damage to the ironclad's hull. No one below deck on the *Louisiana* was injured, for no projectiles entered through the ports or otherwise. However, there were some casualties on deck, among them Commander Charles F. McIntosh, who was fatally wounded. These resulted from splinters from the barricade for sharpshooters, which was considerably cut up by the Yankee guns. One Federal vessel, almost in contact with the *Louisiana*, fired two 11-inch shells, which dented the iron plating and then broke into fine fragments.[15]

Meanwhile, the *Cayuga*, having run past the forts in a matter of fifteen minutes, found itself, about 4 A.M., out of range of all the Rebel land batteries. When Lieutenant Perkins looked back for the other vessels in Captain Bailey's division, his heart "jumped into [his] mouth" when he failed to see a single one. His first thought was that they had all been sunk by the forts, but he did not have time to linger over the idea, for bearing down on the *Cayuga* were eleven Rebel gunboats. Three large steamers closed on the little Yankee gunboat, apparently with the intention of boarding the *Cayuga*. One of these, on the starboard beam, was blasted at a range of thirty yards by an 11-inch Dahlgren with destructive effect. The steamer ran ashore, where it was set on fire. A second steamer was driven off by the Parrott gun on the *Cayuga's* forecastle, but the third Rebel steamer came to close quarters and Captain Bailey prepared to repel boarders.

At this moment Commander Boggs' *Varuna* roared in, both its port and starboard guns (ten in all) blazing away at everything it passed. And moments later the *Oneida* joined in the melee. "I had more rebel steamers engaging me than I could attend to without support, when Lee and Boggs came dashing up, delivering a refreshing fire," wrote Captain Bailey. "The enemy were so thick that it was like duck shooting; what missed one rebel hit another."[16]

The bulk of the Confederate gunboats—especially the River Defense Fleet, which fought ingloriously, if at all—were shot up, sunk, or run ashore and burned by their not so valiant skippers. But three Confederate vessels were fought with great skill and valor —the *Manassas*, under Lieutenant Warley; the *McRae*, first under Lieutenant Huger, and when Huger was critically wounded, under Lieutenant Charles W. "Savez" Read; and the *Governor Moore*, under Lieutenant Beverly Kennon.

No ship underwent the fire the *Manassas* experienced, and none gave Farragut's captains more concern than did the celebrated "Turtle," which had become a legend after chasing Pope's squadron from the Head of the Passes six months earlier. The *Manassas* rammed the *Brooklyn* and *Mississippi*, was seen at close quarters by the *Oneida*, *Cayuga*, *Pinola*, *Richmond*, *Iroquois*, and *Wissahickon*, and received heavy fire not only from these enemy vessels but from the two forts as well. Fort St. Philip, mistaking the *Manassas* for a disabled Federal ship, fired no less than seventy-five times at the ram, fortunately not striking her once. The lighter guns of Fort Jackson, however, scored several hits on the *Manassas*, causing Lieutenant Warley to call off a daring plan he had, to go below the forts and singlehandedly attack Porter's mortar flotilla and its supporting gunboats.

The first vessel in the stream after the alarm, the *Manassas* was the only Confederate ship that made an attempt to force the enemy warships back under the guns of the forts. In vain did Lieutenant Warley look for support from the River Defense Fleet. It was Warley's conviction that had the River Defense vessels been used as rams, as they were intended to be used, "most of the enemy's vessels would have been crippled and obliged to fall back under the guns of the fort."

The *Manassas* moved in and out of the advancing enemy vessels, seeking an opening, and received almost point-blank fire from the Federal ships as they passed. Day was beginning to break when Warley discovered the *McRae* valiantly striving against four gunboats at close range, and hurried to its assistance.

The *McRae*, like the *Manassas*, got into the fight early, and it was in the main stream firing at the *Cayuga* and other ships in Bailey's division as they crossed into the barrier and made their run by the forts. As the *McRae* turned to bring its guns to bear on a warship that had passed, it narrowly escaped being run down by two other Federal vessels, which apparently mistook the Confederate gunboat for one of their own and passed by without firing a shot.

As soon as these two ships cleared, the *McRae* sheered to port and fired its starboard broadside into one of the vessels, and then sheering quickly the other way, the *McRae* pounded the receding ship with its port guns. When the *McRae* steamed across the river, the ships opened on it with their starboard guns. One shell, striking the *McRae* forward, exploded in the sail room and set the ship on fire. Deck and engine pumps were started immediately, but the next moments were critical ones for the *McRae*. Much inflammable material was in the sail room, and only a thin bulkhead separated the flames from the shell lockers. Lieutenant Huger ordered Lieutenant Read to inform him when the fire would reach the bulkhead and then directed the *McRae* to be run close into the bank. "Savez" Read succeeded in smothering and then extinguishing the fire.

At this moment, from a distance of three hundred yards, two large ships and three gunboats began to engage the *McRae*, and when the *Manassas* rushed to its assistance, the little Confederate gunboat was answering the attack of four of them. The ram steered straight for the Federal ships, which, on spotting her, turned and made off up the river. At this stage of the fight, as the *McRae* was backing from the bank, its brave commander, Lieutenant Thomas B. Huger, was mortally wounded.

Lieutenant Read assumed command and ordered the *McRae* across the river and upstream, firing the starboard guns as rapidly as possible at moving enemy targets. He reached the bend above the forts, and perceiving eleven Federal vessels beyond the range of Confederate land batteries, he prudently avoided engaging so vastly a superior force and dropped down the river. In turning downstream, the *McRae's* tiller ropes snapped, and although the engines were stopped and immediately reversed, the ship ran ashore and stuck fast.[17]

Meanwhile, the *Manassas* pursued the retreating Yankee gunboats up the river to give the *McRae* time to retire, and it was then that Captain Melancton Smith of the *Mississippi* spotted the Rebel ram astern.

"I want permission to run down the ram," he called to a passing gunboat, under the mistaken idea that it was Captain Bailey's divisional flagship, *Cayuga*.

Fortunately for Smith, the *Hartford*, battle-scarred and smoke-blackened from the fire, steamed by, and Flag Officer Farragut, with the same idea, hailed the *Mississippi* from the rigging of his flagship and called to Smith: "Run down the ram!"

Lieutenant George Dewey, at Smith's side, remarked Farragut's "face eager with victory in the morning light and his eyes snapping." Years later he wrote: "I shall never forget that glimpse of him. He was a very urbane man. But it was plain that if we did not run the *Manassas* down, and promptly, he would not think well of us." Captain Melancton Smith, a fighting sailor, was delighted with the order.

"Can you turn the ship?" he asked Dewey.

"Yes, sir," snapped back the young executive officer.

Dewey admitted later that he did not know whether he could turn the unwieldy *Mississippi*, but "I was going to do so or run her aground." The young lieutenant succeeded in his first try, and the *Mississippi* with its 1692 tons bore down on the 384-ton *Manassas*.

Warley now knew that the jig was up for the *Manassas*. His lone gun had been dismounted and the ram had been shot through innumerable times. "I considered that I had done all that I possibly could do to resist the enemy's passage of the forts, and that it then became my duty to try and save the people under my command," he reported. Accordingly, Warley had the delivery pipes cut, ran the ram onto a steep part of the bank, and ordered the officers and men to seek safety in the swamps. The *Mississippi* sprayed the swamp with grape and poured broadsides into the *Manassas*, which eventually slid off the bank and floated downstream in a sinking condition.[18]

Meanwhile, Lieutenant Beverly Kennon of the *Governor Moore*, one of the two steamers converted by the state of Louisiana into gunboats, had a busy time of it. When the word came that the Federal fleet was in motion, Kennon tried to join the *Manassas* downstream, but his vessel was repeatedly fouled by as many as five tugs and steamers. In desperation, Kennon rammed the tug *Belle Algerine*, and probably sank her, to get clear.

By the time he got the *Governor Moore* into the stream, Farragut's lead vessels steamed by and Kennon's ship received heavy fire from the *Cayuga*, *Pensacola*, and *Oneida* at ranges of from seventy-five to two hundred yards. In addition, the *Governor Moore* was struck several times by stray shots from the forts. In the thick smoke, it was hard to distinguish friend from foe, but Kennon kept fighting his ship. When the smoke cleared, the *Governor Moore* was four hundred yards above the *Louisiana*, virtually surrounded by Federal vessels. Two hundred yards away, on the *Governor Moore's* port beam, were the *Cayuga* and *Oneida*. On the port quarter, distant two hundred to four hundred yards, were the heavy warships *Pensacola*, *Brooklyn*, and *Mississippi*, while astern a couple of hundred yards was the *Pinola*. Immediately upon recognition, the Yankee ships opened with grape and canister, to which the *Governor Moore* replied with shell from its two guns. Kennon's guns did little damage, but the concentrated fire of the Federal batteries cut up the *Governor Moore* horribly, killing and wounding many of its crew.

Ahead, and hurrying upstream, was a Yankee vessel—it was the *Varuna*, although Kennon did not know it then—and the *Governor Moore* gave chase. Its superior speed enabled it to shake the Federals with whom it had waged an unequal duel. By daybreak, the *Governor Moore* was about a hundred yards astern of the *Varuna* and about six hundred yards ahead of the pursuing ships.

When the ships passed the Quarantine Station, about seven miles above the forts, only forty yards separated the vessels and both ships delivered a raking fire. Grape, shell, and canister swept the *Governor Moore*'s spar and main decks, killing and wounding many. So many powder and shell passers had been shot down that Lieutenant Kennon himself had to assist in this important duty. Fifteen of the twenty-three men stationed on the forecastle had been killed or wounded.

So close were the vessels, Kennon found it impossible to depress his bow gun. But undaunted by this, he pointed the gun through the *Governor Moore*'s own deck and fired through it into the *Varuna*, raking it fore and aft. A second shot was fired the same way and with the same effect. Then as the *Varuna* sheered to deliver a broadside into the *Governor Moore*, Kennon quickly reacted by ordering the helm hard aport, and the Confederate vessel smashed into its adversary. "The crashing noise made by her breaking ribs told how amply we were repaid for all we had lost and suffered," reported Kennon. Because he had lost so many men and had little small-arms ammunition, Kennon discarded an early intention to board the enemy ship. Instead, he backed clear and once more drove the *Governor Moore* into the shattered *Varuna*, striking her about the same place, just abaft the mainmast on the starboard side.

The *Varuna* was sinking rapidly, and it made for the shore, reaching there just as it went down. Although Kennon had lost a third of his crew of ninety-three men, he turned away from the sinking *Varuna* to have a run at the *Cayuga*, a more equal match. But before joining the issue, Kennon saw the *Oneida, Pinola, Iroquois, Pensacola,* and *Mississippi* all hastening to the *Cayuga*'s support. None but a madman would have thought of so hopeless a fight. Moreover, the *Governor Moore*'s bow gun was now useless and its bow was riddled with balls. Kennon rounded to and started upstream, bringing his stern chaser to bear on his six pursuers.

The Federal vessels all opened with their bow guns, raking the *Governor Moore* with grape, canister, shell, and shot, which cut away the wheel ropes, greatly damaged the walking beam, and disabled the engine. For three hours the *Governor Moore* had been subjected to a terrific fire. The crew was decimated and the vessel was cut up horribly. So Kennon gave the order to fire the *Governor Moore* and carried it out himself, pouring oil on the bedding and mosquito bars and setting them afire with lamps from the engine room. At 6:30 A.M. Kennon surrendered himself and five wounded men to boats from the *Oneida*. The casualties on the *Governor Moore* were frightful. Kennon reckoned that of his crew of ninety-three, fifty-seven were killed (and were cremated with the ship), twenty-four were captured, among them seven wounded, while a dozen escaped into the swamps. None was drowned, all who had taken to the water being captured by the boats from Federal ships.

Three times during the fight the *Governor Moore*'s colors were shot away. But as it burned to the water's edge the tattered standards were still flying. "The pennant and remains of the ensign were never hauled down," proudly recounted Beverly Kennon. "The flames that lit our deck stood faithful sentinels over their halyards until they, like the ship, were entirely consumed."

Kennon surrendered himself, but not his ship or his sword. "I swore that I would never present the hilt of my sword to any man, nor haul down my colors," he reported. "My sword was demanded, but I threw it overboard."[19]

If Kennon deprived the Federals of his sword, there was some compensation. For at daylight, the *Cayuga* ran up the river to Camp Chalmette and opened fire with canister at close range on the Confederate regiment encamped there. Lieutenant Perkins shouted to the officers to come aboard and deliver their arms or else they would be blown to bits. Down came the colors and Colonel Ignace Szymanski came aboard the *Cayuga* and surrendered his sword, colors, and command of five companies. "It seemed odd for a regiment on shore to be surrendering to a ship!" Lieutenant Perkins wrote his family. But Colonel Szymanski had good reasons. "When the forts were passed, just before break of day, the fleet came upon my small camp and opened fire," he testified later. "After losing some thirty men killed and wounded, with no possibility of escape or rescue— perfectly at the mercy of the enemy, he being able to cut the levees and drown me out—I thought it my duty to surrender. A single shell could have cut the light embarkment."[20]

As the sun climbed higher in the April sky, first one then another of Farragut's ships steamed up to Quarantine and dropped anchor. The begrimed and weary gunners rested by their guns, but they were not too tired to let up a cheer whenever another vessel, its colors proudly whipping in the morning breeze, joined the group. A mighty roar went up from the fleet when the *Hartford* moved slowly "with that unspeakable calmness that only an American man-of-war can exhibit." Farragut knew that he had lost the *Varuna*, for he saw its masts sticking out of the water with its flag still flying from the masthead. He had dipped his colors and the men had given three cheers for the *Varuna* as the *Hartford* eased by the sunken craft, and other ships in the fleet had done likewise.

The flag officer counted his ships and found thirteen of them safely at anchor, albeit many of them scarred and tattered from the bitter passage of the forts. The *Varuna* was the fourteenth, but where were the other three, the *Kennebec, Itasca,* and *Winona?* Farragut feared that they were lost in passing the forts and it was not until several days later that he learned that they were safe.

Farragut's casualties, although double Signal Officer Osbon's estimate on the eve of battle, were not great considering the number of men in the fleet and the fact that for nearly four hours his vessels were under fire of the forts or the Confederate gunboats. There were thirty-seven killed and one hundred and forty-seven wounded.

Confederate casualties in the forts were astonishingly light, too, despite the almost ceaseless bombardment to which they were subjected for six days and nights by the mortar flotilla, before Farragut brought the guns of the fleet to bear. In Fort Jackson, there were nine killed and thirty-three wounded, while Fort St. Philip had two killed and four wounded. Beverly Kennon's dead on the *Governor Moore*—fifty-seven—were nine more than the combined dead in both forts and throughout Farragut's fleet. Exact figures on the Confederate naval casualties are lacking, but the records show that at least seventy-three were killed and the same number wounded.[21]

Only two of the Confederate warships, other than the *McRae* and *Louisiana*, escaped. One of these was the steamer *Jackson*, commanded by Lieutenant F. B. Renshaw, which took off for New Orleans when the Federal vessels approached the Quarantine Station. It had been placed there to guard the back door to Fort St. Philip. The other was the *Defiance*, whose commander, Captain McCoy, appears to have been drunk all day and was thereby incapable of rendering assistance. Rather, he was busy "idling away his time in running about the river in our [*Louisiana's*] vicinity, apparently without useful purpose," reported Commander Mitchell. Although the *Louisiana* had received heavy gun blasts at close range, she was practically undamaged. Her commander, one of Farragut's old Navy friends, Commander Charles F. McIntosh, was badly shot up and subsequently died of his wounds. Two other casualties were reported on the *Louisiana*, one killed, the other wounded.[22]

After checking the fleet, Farragut hurried off a message to Porter: "We had a rough time of it . . . I intend to follow up my success and push for New Orleans and then come down and attend to the forts; so you hold them *in statu quo* until I get back . . . I think if you send a flag of truce and demand their surrender, they will do it, for their intercourse with the city is cut off. We have cut the wires above the quarantine and are now going ahead . . . You supported us nobly."

General Ben Butler, impatient aboard his transport, the *Mississippi*, rushed his congratulations to Farragut. "Allow me to congratulate you and your command upon the bold, daring, brilliant and successful passage of the Forts by the fleet this morning," he wrote. "A more gallant exploit it has never fallen to the lot of man to witness." To the Secretary of War, Butler wrote in the same vein: "Of the gallantry, courage and conduct of this heroic action, unprecedented in naval warfare, considering the character of the work and the river, too much cannot be said . . ."

But Butler was not so generous to Farragut in writing to his wife:

Here I am all right and well, but now about to do the most troublesome, annoying and anxious business of the campaign—To land my troops by surf boats in the rear of St. Philip. The fleet, after bombarding the forts for six days, ran past the forts, and after taking 11 rebel gunboats and destroying a *ram*, an ironclad vessel, they ran up to New Orleans to take the city . . . Farragut has left some gunboats at the Quarantine Station in the river to protect my Army on the Gulf side. This I deem wholly an unmilitary proceeding on his part, to run off and leave forts behind him unreduced, but such is the race for the glory of capturing New Orleans between him and Commodore Foote that thus we go.

As for Commander David Dixon Porter, it would have startled him to know that, in the privacy of their thoughts, he and Ben Butler were in agreement. To his journal Porter confided:

"When Flag Officer Farragut passed the forts, I supposed that at daylight he would assemble his fleet and summon them to surrender. That was the program as I understood it . . . He did not know what force he had left behind him at the forts, nor did he stop to ascertain. To me he left the task of finishing the business at the forts and also to contend with the powerful ironclad *Louisiana* . . . Had her commander (Mitchell) possessed the soul of a flea, he could have driven us all out of the river."[23]

19

Panic in the Streets

FOR FIVE DAYS AND NIGHTS, NEW ORLEANS WAS A CITY UNNERVED BY fears and rumors and wild alarms as Porter's bombardment of the forts continued. The incessant roar of the bummers carried a great distance and, on occasions when the air was clear and the wind right, people in New Orleans distinctly heard the bursting of the bombs. On a particularly favorable night, the telegraph operators in Baton Rouge and Clinton, each more than a hundred air miles from the forts, reported that the bombardment was heard in those towns.[1]

Although rumors were still afloat in New Orleans on April 23, "some of them absurd, some plausible, all . . . unfounded," driving the too credulous to "alternations of elation and depression," many people had begun to draw hope from newspaper assurances that all was going well at the forts and confidence was gradually restored among a large part of the population. "The forts cannot be captured if our citizens move and act, nor can New Orleans be captured the present six months," declared the *Crescent*. "If the enemy does not surrender to the superiority of Southern arms, it will have to succumb to Bronze John; he will be along next month." Noting the heavy bombardment at Fort Jackson, the *Delta* promised: "Surely, by the time the Lincolnists haul off their shattered fleet, the vicinity of Fort Jackson will be a pretty good iron mine."

General Duncan's dispatch to General Lovell (". . . We can stand it, with God's blessing, as long as they can") provided an opportunity for the New Orleans press to renew its assurances. "The publication . . . had a cheering effect," observed the *Picayune*. "It gave increased confidence to those who had always been confident in our ability to repel the invader in his attempt to ascend the river, and reassured the timid and desponding, who, happily, are but few among so many." The *Commercial Bulletin* called attention to the "great cheerfulness and confidence . . . among the heroic officers and men who are there repelling the fierce assaults of the enemy," and this journal added: "This ought to be sufficient to reassure the desponding, if any there are, and strengthen the faith of all our citizens in the power of our defense, and in the fortitude, courage and ability of our defenders."

A headline in the *True Delta*—"Glorious News from the Forts"—cheered the people and they read on eagerly: "The gallant Duncan and his brave officers and men are holding the enemy at bay. The bombardment continues as ever, but without serious results."[2]

The press tried valiantly to stir adventurous Orleanians into striking a blow for the defense of the city when the Committee of Public Safety advertised rich rewards "for the destruction, through private enterprise, of the armed vessels of the enemy." For ships ranking higher than gunboats, the committee offered $50,000; for gunboats, $25,000; for mortar boats, $10,000. Said the *Commercial Bulletin*:

A splendid chance is thus afforded parties to realize something handsome by their promptitude, vigor, ingenuity and boldness. The times call for such enterprise, and we can scarcely suppose they will not produce it. Up, now, at the enemy in earnest. The motives of private interests can now be added to those of patriotism, safety and honor to induce daring, action, and ingenious methods of attacking the foe.[3]

But the inducements came too late. For early on the morning of April 24, the direst rumor of them all threw the city into a state of tremendous excitement: "Several of the enemy's gunboats had succeeded in passing the forts." The rumor spread rapidly, with confirmation following on its heels when the great bells of Christ Church on Canal Street, St. Patrick's on Camp Street, and Dr. Palmer's First Presbyterian Church were set to ringing in an unmistakable rhythm. Fearfully the people counted the methodical strokes of the clappers—one, two, three . . . ten, eleven, twelve. It was the signal of alarm, the signal for all military organizations to hasten to their armories.

Early-morning shoppers stopped in the midst of their purchasing and rushed out into the streets, which rapidly filled with excited people asking a thousand questions. Young Zoe Campbell, eating a late family breakfast, was startled when her friend Cécile Moïse, daughter of the attorney general, arrived "all trembling and of a deathly pallor," gasping that her father had just brought the news that "the Yankees had passed the forts . . . the Federals were in the river." Miss Campbell recorded in her diary: "Our hearts stood still, fright overpowering us."

In her schoolroom, Mrs. Mary Newman heard the tolling of the bells. "I . . . dropped my books, snatched my bonnet & fairly flew home," she wrote her sister. "I found everything and everybody in commotion." Annunciation Square, where the Confederate Guards were encamped, was a scene of confusion, Mrs. Newman noted; "some were packing up clothes, others tearing down tents, and still others hurrying to and fro, all eager for orders to start for the Jackson Rail Road."

The private tutor of Duncan Kenner's children, Professor Melhado, an Englishman with a son in the Confederate Army, stopped the lesson when the bells sounded. He counted them with growing dismay, which the children "shared as the fatal number rang out." Rosella Kenner Brent, many years later, recalled the incident. "As soon as he was certain that the bad news had come, Professor Melhado took up his hat, and bidding us a most informal good morning, hurried away to ascertain what was about to happen to the city and its inhabitants." Soon school children all over the city were hurriedly dismissed.

The swelling, excited crowds reached eagerly for the *Delta* extra which was soon on the streets, and "like an electric shock, the news spread all over the city." Stores began to close, business came to a standstill. Mrs. Robert Dow Urquhart, one of the city's social leaders, went to Canal Street "to see if this sad news could be true." She found it only too much so. "The alarm bells were sounding and soldiers and men rushing to and fro . . . All faces wore a look of sorrow and anxiety."

Young Clara Solomon peered through her doorway. "The excitement and commotion was an indication that something was the matter," she wrote. "Uniformed men were hurrying to and fro, and we gained from them that the whole military was ordered out."[4]

The city streetcars stopped running, their horses and mules having been commandeered by the authorities. To the already considerable noise and confusion in the streets was soon added the rattle and rumble of floats and drays, loaded with cotton bales, as they dashed over the cobblestone streets from the cotton presses and warehouses to the Levee.[5]

All the cotton in New Orleans—29,919 bales were in the city, according to the *New Orleans Price Current*—was ordered to various parts of the Levee to be destroyed to prevent its falling into the hands of the enemy. People, on every hand, it seemed, were imbued with an idea expressed the next day by the *Commercial Bulletin*: "Better sacrifice everything—presses, warehouses and foundries—than that he should seize even one bale of cotton or a single hogshead of tobacco."

In the late afternoon the torch was applied to the cotton, but the destruction did not stop there, for huge supplies of sugar, corn, and rice were likewise set ablaze. The Levee became "one general conflagration of everything that could be of use or benefit to the enemy," observed Mrs. Urquhart.

Meanwhile, the military had been caught up in the confusion. Carts and wagons of all descriptions carried military stores to the Jackson Railroad station and Confederate soldiers passed along the streets through avenues of "grief and woe indescribable." A woman novelist who viewed the evacuation said that "language can give no idea of the scene," but she made a try at it:

> Slowly they passed on through the different streets, and hushed and awful was the tread of the feet, like their now muffled hopes. Stern was their look, and they scarce dared a glance of adieu to the fair who bade them "God speed" through their tears and sobs. No drums sounded, not a note was heard, but the beating of many hearts was in unison with the dirge-like sounds of mourning.

As the troops moved along, vehicles of all descriptions laden with war materials raced by and mounted officers galloped about in an excited state, shouting orders.

At the railroad station, every available car, both freight and passenger, with engines attached and ready to depart, was on the tracks. Soldiers swarmed all over the cars—inside, on the vestibules, on top of them. The companies moved up to the cars silently, except for their measured step, the tap of the drum, or the order of command. "The coolness of the soldiers contrasted well with the confusion and mad terror around them," observed one who was there. Every moment the milling crowd grew as hacks dashed up and deposited terror-stricken women, children, and servants eager to flee the city.[6]

Meanwhile, General Lovell, who had gone down to the forts, arrived back in New Orleans. When his steamer neared Fort St. Philip, the attack had begun, and Lovell narrowly escaped capture by the *Varuna* before the latter vessel was engaged by Beverly Kennon and the *Governor Moore*. Upon his return, Lovell immediately closeted himself with Mayor Monroe and the civil authorities, pointing out the impossibility of defending New Orleans with militia armed with shotguns against warships whose heavy guns would look down into the city's streets. Against a land attack by Butler's army, Lovell had always been confident that he could defend New Orleans, even after his department had been drained of men and material for the Confederate army massed at Corinth. But gunboats were quite another thing.

Lovell, of course, in the frustration of the humiliating moment, came in for a great amount of abuse and criticism. Julia LeGrand, "never . . . so helpless and forsaken," recorded in her journal: "Lovell knew not what to do; some say he was intoxicated, some say frightened . . . The whole city was a scene of wild confusion. The *women only* did not seem afraid. They were all in favor of resistance, *no matter how hopeless* that resistance might be." And Marion Southwood, writing five years after the fall of New Orleans, bitterly assailed Lovell and Confederate authorities in the city:

> General Lovell . . . dashed around the St. Charles Hotel in grand style . . . At length the startling news was brought us that the forts were passed, and the fleet were approaching the city. Too bad, after all the *promises* to the contrary! We felt how *cruelly* we have been deceived. How had all the grand speeches, loud huzzahs, nightly drills and magnificent parades, showy flags and splendid music benefitted us? We had our own thoughts upon the subject. Some thought that if the United States had not had so much money at its disposal, the forts would not have been passed.

Mrs. Braxton Bragg wrote General Bragg in a bitter vein: "Dear Husband—we have been betrayed . . . There may be no *open* proofs—he has some shame left, & will not brand the name of Lovell with the infamy of Arnold—but there is undoubtedly some *secret* understanding with the enemy. The public have more charity than I have—they say he is incompetent; not fit for his position. No, no, we know Lovell to be able, brilliant—a man *twice* bought can be bought a *third* time."[7]

Meanwhile, wild scenes were being enacted on the Levee, where sugar, molasses, rice, bacon, hams, potatoes, corn, and other products were rolled out or carried from nearby warehouses to be destroyed. Hundreds of barrels of sugar and molasses were smashed open and the contents poured into the river or consigned to the flames. "Molasses was running in the gutters, like water," recalled Mrs. Southwood. Almost everything of a movable or destructible character was included in the frenzy of destruction. The *True Delta* painted a graphic picture of the "wicked waste," as it termed it:

Someone invited the women and children who thronged the levee to help themselves, which they did with a will. Men joined in the scramble, but they soon became disgusted with a retail operation and began to roll off sugar and molasses by the hogshead and barrel. Some men took away as many as three or four hogsheads of sugar, and molasses barrels could be seen scattered along the streets for squares from the levee. Before an order was issued to stop this wholesale destruction and plunder, hundreds of hogsheads of sugar and barrels of sugar and molasses had either been destroyed or taken away.

On every street leading to the Levee, Negroes and the poor hurried along with baskets, buckets, pans, and wheelbarrows to join in the free-for-all or return from the Levee laden with their plunder.

A schoolboy who took part in the scene later wrote a composition about his experiences: ". . . The day of the pillage . . . everybody went on the levee to seek some sugar, rice, potatoes, hams &c, because they had heard that they were giving everything . . . When we arrived there we saw several persons who were taking some sugar in hogsheads. We took a bag full of sugar each and a bag of rice, and I took five or six sweet potatoes. By 5 o'clock they began to make some arrestations. I tried to get a ham but they were fighting so much for them, that I couldn't have one."

George Devol, the gambler, having buried his arms and cut the brass buttons off his uniforms along with others in his company of cavalry, celebrated his return to civilian life by wholesale pillage. "I hired a dray (for which I had to pay $10) and loaded it down to the guards," he recalled in his memoirs. "We put on a hogshead of sugar, twenty-five hams, a sack of coffee, box of tea, firkin of

butter, barrel of potatoes, some hominy, beans, canned fruits, etc.
I would have put on more, but the dray wouldn't hold it."[8]

When the authorities finally halted the pillaging the Levee was
a desolate place, thick with the smoke of burning cotton and the
stifling odor of burning sugar and bacon which had been tossed to
the flames. This drama of devastation, starting on April 24, continued into the next day, without abatement. Mrs. Frances Hall's
cook rushed from the kitchen crying: "Oh, Miss Francie! The city
down by the river must be all on fire." Indeed, the city down by
the river was on fire. "Vast columns of flame rose in the air," recalled
an eyewitness, "and vied with the sunlight, and sublimely grand
became the scene when the torch was set to the steam-boats, ships,
and gunboats which were in the river, and they were sent floating
down the stream into the midst of the enemy's fleet . . ."[9]

Across Lake Pontchartrain, thirty miles away, the glare of the
fire "set men and women weeping and wailing." Sleepless citizens
endured a night of horror. ". . . Fear, wrath, and sense of betrayal
had run through the people as the fire had run through the cotton,"
wrote George W. Cable, who was there. "You have seen, perhaps, a
family fleeing with lamentations and wringing of hands out of a
burning house: multiply it by thousands upon thousands, that was
New Orleans, though the houses weren't burning." Crowds roamed
the streets, cursing that they had been betrayed and looking for a
victim. They found a fellow that someone said looked like a spy and
they quickly strung him up to a lamppost. Fortunately, a squad of
the European Brigade happened along and rescued the poor devil
as the mob rushed to the Levee to join "the riffraff of the wharves,
the town, the gutters . . . and the juvenile ragtag" of the city.

Young Cable, clerk in a store whose owners had fled the city,
closed up shop and joined the thick gathering on the Levee. "Are
the Yankee ships in sight?" he asked a man. The latter pointed
across the great bend in the river, and Cable discerned the naked
masts of Farragut's vessels, then engaged in silencing the Confederate batteries at Chalmette.

"Presently that was over," wrote Cable. "Ah, me! I see them now
as they come slowly round Slaughterhouse Point into full view,

silent, grim, and terrible; black with men, heavy with deadly portent; the long-banished Stars and Stripes flying against the frowning sky. Oh, for the *Mississippi!* the *Mississippi!* Just then she came down upon them. But how? Drifting helplessly, a mass of flames."[10]

The *Mississippi*, on which so much reliance had been placed by the Richmond authorities, on which the people of New Orleans had pinned high hopes for the city's safety from Farragut's fleet, floated past the crowd-jammed Levee, a burning derelict. Secretary Mallory had expected the *Mississippi* "if completed in time" to raise the blockade of every Gulf port in ten days. And Secretary Benjamin wrote A. Dudley Mann, Confederate commissioner in Brussels, on April 14 that he "will soon hear a good account" of the ironclads, "superior to the *Virginia*," which the Confederacy was about to complete. "We rely greatly on these vessels for sweeping away the wooden ships, gunboats and transports of the enemy." But, alas, the *Mississippi*, with Farragut's fleet just below the bend in the river, was burning to the water's edge, "a magnificent but awful sight," all efforts to move the powerful ironclad upstream having failed.[11]

At 5:40 A.M., on April 24, Commander Whittle received a telegram in his room at the St. Charles Hotel from the operator at the Quarantine Station stating that several Federal vessels had passed the forts and had reached Quarantine. It was probably the last word from downriver that New Orleans received, for shortly thereafter men from the *Cayuga* went ashore and cut the telegraph wires. Whittle immediately sent the telegram to Governor Moore, who also occupied a room in the St. Charles, and the latter telegraphed the bad news to President Davis.[12]

Meanwhile, Whittle, who up to now had refused to take the *Mississippi* out of the hands of Asa and Nelson Tift, because he did not feel he had the authority to do so, decided the time had come to take control of the ironclad. Accordingly, he summoned Commander Arthur Sinclair, who was to command the *Mississippi* when it was commissioned.

"The enemy has passed the forts and is coming up the river," said Whittle. "What can be done with the *Mississippi?*"

"We can try to get her up the river," replied Sinclair, "and if this is impossible, burn her."

"Well, use every exertion in your power to get her up, and failing to do so, you will destroy her," ordered Whittle.[13]

Although the Tifts thought they would have the *Mississippi* ready in two or three weeks, Commander Sinclair couldn't see how it was possible for the vessel to be ready before July 1. The *Mississippi* had no guns and no ammunition; her main propeller was in, but her other two propellers were lying on the wharf and the vessel could not move under its own power; moreover, its rudder was not on; and while some of the iron had been laid upon its shield, it had not been bolted down.

Commander Sinclair ordered the Tifts to arrange for the only available steamers, the *St. Charles* and *Peytona*, to come to the *Mississippi* and tow it upriver. For hours the steamers failed to show up, but at last they came at 8 P.M., their captains making the excuse that they were delayed because they could not round up engineers and hands. "I furnished the steamers with hands and engineers," Commander Sinclair later testified, "and after some difficulty we started. But we found it impossible to do anything with the vessel on account of the strong current. There was a freshet at the time, and this rendered the current much stronger than usual. We tugged at her the whole of the night unsuccessfully, for instead of making headway we lost ground considerably."

Shortly before 4 A.M., on April 25, a member of the Committee of Public Safety, Colonel Beggs, came on board and offered more steam power to tow the ironclad, promising to have steamers by four o'clock. But four o'clock came and went and the promised steamers did not appear. As the morning advanced, Commander Sinclair decided to go after more steamers himself. He made the *Mississippi* fast, leaving on board Lieutenant James Iredell Waddell and the naval constructor, Joseph Pearce, with instructions to the former to fire the ship if the Federal vessels arrived before he returned. Sinclair left in the *Peytona* for the city, four miles downstream, to hunt for steamers. He was not very confident, nor was

Whittle, that even with an adequate number of steamers to tow and push the *Mississippi* the vessel could be saved. Where was it to go? And would not the swift Federal vessels overtake it and capture it?

Nevertheless, Commander Sinclair pursued his mission. He found a number of steamboats, but their crews had all deserted them "to look after their own private concerns." While in New Orleans, Sinclair saw the enemy vessels coming up the river. He knew at once that the chances of saving the *Mississippi* were hopeless. So he hurried aboard the *Peytona* again to run up to Jefferson City to destroy the ironclad. "As I got around the point, I saw flames issuing from her, and was satisfied that all was right," said Sinclair.

But Asa Tift, at his side, was not. Pointing to the smoke issuing from the ports of the *Mississippi*, he asked Commander Sinclair the meaning of it. Sinclair explained that he had given orders for the match to be applied when the situation became hopeless. Tift was flabbergasted. "This spectacle was the cause of great surprise to us," he later declared.[14]

Meanwhile Lieutenant Waddell and Pearce had busied themselves preparing to destroy the ironclad. Having completed his part of the preparations, Waddell stood alone on the deck, waiting for Pearce to join him. Five men carrying a rope came aboard and the leader demanded:

"Where's Tift? Is he aboard?"

"No," replied Lieutenant Waddell.

The man uttered an oath and cried: "He is a traitor, and we brought this rope to hang him."

"I have laid a train to the magazine and the vessel will be fired in a few minutes," Waddell informed the lynching party.

Whereupon the men left quietly. "In a few minutes, I fired her through, took my man in the open boat, and regained the steamboat."[15]

The *Peytona*, with naval personnel and the Tift brothers, then started up the river to Vicksburg. As the blazing *Mississippi* broke its moorings and floated down the river, the eyes of Nelson and

Asa Tift filled and Commander Sinclair, with a heavy heart, watched the burning ironclad disappear around the bend.

"She was a formidable ship—the finest of the sort I ever saw in my life," Sinclair testified later. "She would in my opinion not only have cleared the river of the enemy's vessels, but have raised the blockade of every port in the South."[16]

20

"By the Power of Brutal Force"

AS FARRAGUT'S FLEET OF ELEVEN VESSELS—HE LEFT TWO GUNBOATS AT the Quarantine Station above the forts—proceeded up the river on the morning of April 25, the little *Cayuga* again in the lead, the flag officer had "abundant evidence of the panic which had seized the people of New Orleans." Burning ships, loaded with cotton, drifted down the river and more than a thousand cotton bales floated by the Union gunboats.

Whenever the fleet passed a sugar plantation, "people flocked down to the bank of the river, shouting and cheering and waving handkerchiefs, and those that had flags ran them up," according to Commander Alden's entry in the log of the *Richmond*. A marine aboard the *Hartford* recorded that "the negroes leave their work, run to the levee, and welcome us, waving their hats and handkerchiefs . . . A venerable old darkey gave his hat a great flourish and called for 'three cheers for Abraham,' which set the ship in a roar of laughter."[1]

At ten-thirty, without having received any opposition, the fleet reached English Turn. Shortly thereafter, when the mud fortifications at Chalmette and the Magee Line on the opposite side of the river came into view, the flag officer signaled for close order. However, Captain Bailey in the *Cayuga* was so far ahead that he didn't see the signal, and his little gunboat was alone when it came into range of the Confederate guns. From both sides of the river a heavy fire opened on the *Cayuga*. The little gunboat responded bravely, but on being struck several times, it was obliged to stop its engines and drift out of range until the rest of the fleet came up. For a while the Confederate batteries delivered a raking fire on the advancing Union vessels. The *Hartford* rushed to the *Cayuga*'s rescue, firing its two 9-inch forecastle guns until it could bring its broadsides to bear. Soon the *Pensacola* joined in, blasting away with shells, shrapnel, and grape, to be followed a few moments later by the *Brooklyn*. And as the other vessels came up, they delivered their broadsides into the Confederate works, which in less than thirty minutes were silenced. "Those who could run," reported Farragut of the passage of this last barrier to New Orleans, "were running in every direction."[2]

Actually, the Confederate batteries made a brave, if futile, effort to oppose Farragut's fleet, which numbered just three fewer ships than the total guns in the batteries, five at Chalmette and nine in the west-bank fortification. The guns were fought until every round of ammunition was expended, "through a sense of duty, but without any expectation of success," after which the gunners withdrew.

Throughout the action, which Farragut called "one of the little elegancies of the profession," he and Commander Wainwright yelled themselves hoarse to keep the gunners on the other ships from firing into the fleet in their desire to blast the Rebels. "A dash and a victory," Farragut summed it up later. It was a marked contrast to the passage of the forts, which the flag officer declared "was one of the most awful sights and events I ever saw or expect to experience."[3]

Farragut was struck with amazement at the sight that met his eye as the *Hartford* rounded Slaughterhouse Point, "The levee of New Orleans was one scene of desolation, ships, steamers, cotton, coal, etc., were all in one common blaze," Farragut wrote. ". . . The *Mississippi*, which was to be the terror of the seas, and no doubt would have been to a great extent . . . soon came floating by us all in flames, and passed down the river."

About 1 P.M., as a rainstorm broke over the city, the *Hartford* dropped anchor before New Orleans. One by one the other vessels arrived. Soon, a New Orleans youth recorded in his diary, "the dusky, long, morose demon-like Yankee steamers . . . lay like evil messengers of woe at our very front."[4]

Immediately Farragut sent Captain Bailey ashore to demand the unconditional surrender of the city. Bailey, accompanied by young Lieutenant George Perkins, took only a boat crew, and under a flag of truce they landed at the wharf, packed with a hostile crowd despite the driving rain. The throng contained many women and children, some of the former waving Confederate flags and most of them being "rude and noisy." So it seemed to Lieutenant Perkins, who later described the scene in a letter to his family: "They were all shouting and hooting as we stepped on shore but at last a man, who, I think, was a German, offered to show us the way to the council room, where we should find the mayor of the city. As we advanced, the mob followed us in a very excited state. They gave three cheers for Jeff Davis and Beauregard, and three groans for Lincoln. Then they began to throw things at us, and shout: 'Hang them! Hang them! Hang them!'"

It was indeed an ugly mob that pressed about the two Federal officers, jeering and taunting and abusing them at every step. Fully a third of the cursing, bawling rabble was armed. Ignoring the abusive language as if they were deaf, Captain Bailey and Lieutenant Perkins walked on oblivious to the shouts and threats about them:

"Hurrah for Jeff Davis!"

"Shoot them!"

"Kill them!"

"Hang them!"

Young George W. Cable, who joined the crowd and yelled "Hurrah for Jeff Davis!" as loudly as anyone, in after years recalled the conduct of the two Federal officers as "one of the bravest deeds I ever saw done." He wrote that they "walked abreast, unguarded and alone, looking not to the right or left, never frowning, never flinching, while the mob screamed in their ears, shook cocked pistols in their faces, cursed and crowded, and gnashed upon them. So through the gates of death those two men walked to the City Hall to demand the town's surrender."

Mayor John Monroe received the two officers courteously and introduced them to Provost Marshal Pierre Soulé and other gentlemen present, mostly members of the Common Council and the Committee of Public Safety. Captain Bailey stated that he brought a demand from Flag Officer Farragut for the unconditional surrender of the city, the hoisting of the United States flag over the Custom House, Mint, and Post Office, and the lowering of the state flag from the City Hall.

Mayor Monroe, supported by his advisers, declared that, since the city was under martial law, he, as the head of the civil authority, had no right to surrender the city and that General Lovell alone could receive and reply to such a demand. As for hauling down the flag of Louisiana from the City Hall, Mayor Monroe gave an unqualified refusal. The mayor sent for General Lovell, and upon his arrival Captain Bailey repeated Farragut's demands. Lovell's refusal to surrender was immediate and positive. But he added that he would retire with his troops from the city, leaving the civil authorities to act as they saw fit. Lieutenant Perkins thought Lovell was "pompous in his manner and silly and airy in his remarks." With the matter now in his hands, Mayor Monroe said that he would consult with the Common Council and would then send a formal reply to the flag officer.[5]

Meanwhile, fearful for the safety of the two Federal officers, Mayor Monroe had instructed the chief of police to call upon the European Brigade to provide troops to protect them from the crowd which, now larger than ever, had gathered in front of the City Hall, still howling abuse at Farragut's emissaries. General Paul Juge, commander of the European Brigade, immediately consulted with Count de Méjan, French consul, and George Coppell, British consul, who ordered Juge to ignore the mayor's request. "Not deeming this service required from our countrymen compatible with their positions, I in common with the Consuls of France & Spain refused to allow it," Coppell reported to the British Foreign Office.

According to Lieutenant Perkins, the mob had by now become "perfectly infuriated." They kicked at the doors of the City Hall and swore that they would have the two officers and string them up. "Of course, Captain Bailey and I *felt perfectly at our ease all this while!*" wrote Perkins. "Indeed, every person about us, who had any sense of responsibility, was frightened for our safety."

General Lovell directed Colonel W. S. Lovell and Major S. L. James of his staff to slip out the back of the City Hall with the Federal officers and escort them in a cab to the wharf while he and Pierre Soulé held the attention of the mob. Soulé, whose eloquence had won him fame in the United States Senate, spoke first, "counseling moderation, self-possession, fortitude and confidence in their cause." He praised General Lovell's answer to Farragut's demand to surrender as "worthy of the commander of a brave people."

A loud cheer went up when Lovell appeared on the steps of the City Hall. "He briefly sketched his course in the preparation of the defense of the city," reported *De Bow's Review*. "Had done all he could with the means at his disposal. That he came here six months too late, and it was beyond his resources to contend successfully against the enemy's power on water . . . The general then mounted his horse, and accompanied by his staff, rode to the Jackson railroad, when he took the last car, having already sent his army ahead of him." By this time, Captain Bailey and Lieutenant Perkins, riding in a closed carriage with their Confederate escorts, had regained the wharf. When they reached their ship safely, young Perkins drew a deep breath of relief. "Of all the blackguarding I ever heard in my life that mob gave us the worst," he said.[6]

Before dusk, the band of the *Mississippi*, which had run in close to the wharf, struck up "The Star-Spangled Banner," and some of the crowd responded with a cheer and waved hats and handkerchiefs. "At the same moment a troop of horsemen came riding up one of the streets and fired a volley into the men, women and children," states the log of the *Richmond*. "If it had not been for the innocent that would have been destroyed we would have fired a whole broadside of grape into them."

Night fell on April 25 on an abject, desolate city in which the feeling of anger, hatred, and frustration ran high. Although a 9 P.M. curfew, ordered by the provost marshals, cleared the streets of all not in the public service, an atmosphere of tenseness and fear hung over New Orleans, heavy as the lingering smell of burned cotton, sugar, and other articles which had been so wantonly sacrificed to the flames. This tense feeling extended to Farragut's fleet, anchored in the river. "We may be in a bad fix now, if the forts do not fall," observed Lieutenant Perkins in a letter home. ". . . It is not safe for anyone to leave our ships and go anywhere in a boat. We are still feeling the effects of the excitement which the attack caused. Nothing is settled, and there is danger and risk about every movement." That night Farragut ordered that revolvers and cutlasses be issued to every man against the possibility that the Rebels might attempt to board the vessels during the night.

The flag officer's concern was perhaps sharpened by advertisements in the New Orleans papers of April 25, which called for a thousand volunteers to form boarding parties "to save our homes and families from destruction and the tyrannical rule of the Northern vandals." "Major James calls for one thousand men for this heroic enterprise," stated the *Delta.* "There will be thousands to respond." Alas, the next morning at the rendezvous, only 140 volunteers showed up and the project was dropped.[7]

Meanwhile, at City Hall, Mayor Monroe had been busy preparing a message for the Common Council, which hastily arranged a meeting for 6:30 P.M. After stating what had occurred at the afternoon interviews with Farragut's officers, the mayor said:

> I am now in momentary expectation of receiving a second peremptory demand for the surrender of the city. I solicit your advice in this emergency. My own opinion is that, as a civil magistrate, possessed of no military power, I am incompetent to perform a military act such as the surrender of the city to a hostile force; that it would be proper to say, in reply to a

demand of that character, that we are without military protection; that the troops have withdrawn from the city; that we are consequently incapable of making any resistance; and that, therefore, we can offer no obstruction to the occupation of the place by the enemy; that the custom-house, post-office, and mint are the property of the Confederate Government, and that we have no control over them; and that all acts involving a transfer of authority be performed by the invading forces themselves; that we yield to physical force alone, and that we maintain our allegiance to the Government of the Confederate States.

In order not to act hastily upon Mayor Monroe's message, the Common Council adjourned until 10 A.M. on April 26. The mayor instructed his young secretary, Marion Baker, to go out to the *Hartford* early that morning and explain to Farragut that he would be unable to reply until after the Council had met. So it was that, about 6 A.M., Baker, accompanied by Chief of Police McClelland, took a boat at the foot of Lafayette Street and pulled out to the Federal flagship, having first, however, improvised a flag of truce by tying a handkerchief to a walking stick.

On making his mission known, Baker was ushered into Farragut's cabinet, where Captains Bailey and Bell were seated with Flag Officer Farragut. Farragut, who had known young Baker since the latter's boyhood, received him "with utmost kindness," and after the business had been dispatched he took "almost a boyish interest" in showing the young man about the vessel, while he described "in eloquent terms the conflict, perhaps the most terrific that had ever been withstood." Farragut told Baker: "I seemed to be breathing flame."

When Baker and the chief of police left the *Hartford* they may have brought back a brief note from Farragut to Monroe, although Baker makes no mention of it. At any rate, under the date of April 26, Farragut told the mayor "that no flag but that of the United States will be permitted to fly in the presence of this fleet so long as it has the power to prevent it; and as all displays of that kind may be the cause of bloodshed, I have to request that you will give this communication as general a circulation as possible."

The Common Council met at 10 A.M., and promptly approved the sentiments expressed in Mayor Monroe's letter and declared that "having been advised by the military authorities that this city is indefensible . . . no resistance will be made to the force of the United States."[8]

Aided by Durant da Ponte of the *Delta*, Mayor Monroe had already prepared an answer to Farragut, which Baker now read to the Common Council. This, "from expressions let fall by some of the members," appeared quite satisfactory. However, shortly thereafter, the mayor was called to the Council Chamber and asked to approve a substitute letter prepared by Pierre Soulé. The mayor, who had not been on harmonious terms with the Council, yielded to the request, wishing to conciliate them at this unhappy moment. The letter stated that General Lovell had evacuated the city, out of regard for the lives of women and children, and turned back to the mayor "the administration of its government and the custody of its honor." The mayor said that he and the city fathers had considered Farragut's demand of unconditional surrender, to hoist the United States flag and haul down the flag of the state of Louisiana from the City Hall. This answer, the mayor went on, was dictated not only by "the universal sentiment of my constituency" but by "the promptings of my own heart . . . on this sad and solemn occasion." The mayor continued:

The city is without means of defense and utterly destitute of the force and material that might enable it to resist the overpowering armament displayed in sight of it.

I am no military man and possess no authority beyond that of executing the municipal laws of the city . . . It would be presumptuous in me to attempt to lead an army to the field if I had one at my command, and I know still less how to surrender an undefended place . . .

To surrender such a place were an idle and unmeaning ceremony. The city is yours by the power of brutal force and not by any choice or consent of its inhabitants. It is for you to determine what shall be the fate that awaits her.

As to the hoisting of any flag than the flag of our adoption and allegiance, let me say to you, sir, that the man lives not in our midst whose hand and heart would not be palsied at the mere thought of such an act; nor could I find in my entire constituency so wretched and desperate a renegade as would dare to profane with his hand the sacred emblem of our aspirations.

... I beg you to understand that the people of New Orleans, while unable at this moment to prevent you from occupying this city, do not transfer their allegiance from the government of their choice to one which they have deliberately repudiated, and that they yield simply that obedience which the conqueror is enabled to extort from the conquered.

Before this letter was dispatched, Lieutenant Albert Kautz and Midshipman John H. Read arrived at City Hall with a formal written demand from Farragut for the unconditional surrender of the city. Monroe added a paragraph to his letter acknowledging the flag officer's message and promising an early answer if possible, and then sent his secretary to the *Hartford*. As Marion Baker was being conveyed to the flagship, he noticed that the United States flag was flying from the Mint, and he called to Farragut's attention the fact that the flag had been raised during negotiations. Farragut replied that, although the flag had been run up without his knowledge, he could not order it down. "Pointing to the 'tops' where a number of men were stationed with muskets, others nervously clutching the strings of the howitzers, he called my attention to their excited appearance," declared Marion Baker, "and remarked that it was as much as he could do to restrain them from firing on the crowd, and should he attempt to haul that flag down it would be impossible to keep them in bounds."[9]

Meanwhile, Lieutenant Kautz and Midshipman Read had experienced as uneasy a trip to City Hall as had Captain Bailey and Lieutenant Perkins the previous day. Kautz had come ashore with

Read and a marine guard of twenty men. Another howling and cursing mob jammed the Levee, and a tense situation developed immediately when the marines drew up in a line preparatory to escorting the two officers to City Hall. Screaming and taunting and threatening, the crowd made no effort to give space for the marines to march. Lieutenant Kautz brought the marines to an aim, thinking this would surely influence the mob. But the angry crowd pushed women and children to the front and shouted: "Shoot, you —— Yankees, shoot!" For a moment Lieutenant Kautz wavered under this great provocation. He refrained from giving the order to fire, he said, because of "the utter absence of respectability in the faces of the people."

At this moment Lieutenant Kautz saw an officer in the crowd and signified his desire to communicate with the mayor. Lieutenant Birmingham of the Crescent Reserves stepped forward and said: "Gentlemen, you must not land without a flag of truce, and must not take any men as an escort either." One of the marines cursed him and said: "If we are not allowed we shall fire." Lieutenant Birmingham offered to lead them to City Hall, but the marines must return to the fleet. There were more curses and threats of shooting. Baring his breast, Lieutenant Birmingham said: "Fire, then."

Lieutenant Kautz, conscious that his mission was to communicate with Mayor Monroe without the unnecessary shedding of blood, agreed to send all the marines back to the ship, except one noncommissioned officer, who attached a handkerchief to his musket. Then Kautz, Read, and the marine with the flag of truce moved through the cursing, jostling throng which filled the streets, and reached City Hall without incident or violence.

"I came here to reduce New Orleans to obedience to the laws of and to vindicate the offended majesty of the Government of the United States," Farragut stated in his letter. "I therefore demand of you, as its representative, the unqualified surrender of the city, and that the emblem of the sovereignty of the United States shall be hoisted over the city hall, mint and custom-house by meridian this day, and that all flags or other emblems of sovereignty other than those of the United States shall be removed from all public buildings by that hour."

The flag officer called on Mayor Monroe to exercise his authority "to quell disturbances, restore order, and to call upon all the good people of New Orleans to return at once to their vocations." He demanded that no one be molested for showing Union sentiments and promised speedy and severe punishment for such outrages as had occurred the previous day—"armed men firing upon helpless men, women and children for giving expressions to their pleasure at witnessing the old flag."

As on the previous day, the crowd that gathered in front of City Hall was in an ugly mood, and again it was deemed prudent to smuggle the Union officers out the back while the mob in front was harangued. Before this was done, however, there was considerable cheering in the crowd. Marion Baker, returning from his mission to Farragut, learned that the United States flag had been torn down from the Mint. Led by William Mumford, who had climbed to the roof of the Mint to remove the flag, the group carried it in triumph to City Hall. Lieutenant Kautz and his party were still there. "When they saw us," he stated, "they tore the flag to shreds and threw them into the open window at us. I did not comprehend the meaning of all this singular and wild demonstration at the time . . ."

Later, when Farragut reported the incident to Ben Butler, the general exclaimed: "I will make an example of that fellow by hanging him."

"You know, General, you will have to catch him before you can hang him," smiled Farragut.

"I know that," replied Butler. "But I will catch him, and then hang him." And he did.

Apparently Mayor Monroe considered his first reply an adequate answer to Farragut's formal written demand, for there is no record of another answer. Lieutenant Kautz left City Hall with the mayor's verbal reply to Farragut: "Come and take the city; we are powerless."

Slipping out through the rear, escorted by Marion Baker and two special police officers, Kautz and his party entered a carriage, which had been waiting at Carondelet and Lafayette streets, heading up-town. Just as they drove off, they were discovered, and some of the crowd started up St. Charles Street to head the vehicle off at St. Charles and Girod, the next street up, out which the route led to the landing opposite the *Hartford*. "I ordered the driver to whip up his horses and turn into Julia Street, the second street above, and drive posthaste to the river," said Marion Baker. "Many of our pursuers were armed, and I expected that we would be fired at as we crossed St. Charles Street, but we went by so rapidly that they had no opportunity to fire, even had they so intended. They kept up the chase for some distance, but we so outstripped them that the most enduring finally gave it up."[10]

In an effort to restore order to the city, Mayor Monroe called upon the European Brigade, under General Paul Juge, to serve as a police force. A 9 P.M. curfew was ordered for all who were not engaged in the public service and a countersign was given to the patrols each night, without which no citizen could pass. Negotiations were at a standstill on April 27, and the excitement which had pervaded the populace began to spend itself.[11]

However, the rumor started and circulated rapidly that in the 3d District the Negro slaves had risen up in revolt against their white owners. Beginning at 10:30 A.M., inquiries came over the Fire and Alarm Telegraph and were recorded in the message book. The first message was from the 4th District to the 3d: "What is the matter about the Negroes are they in revolt. Ans. I have heard nothing about it." Fifteen minutes later, the 2d District inquired of the 3d: "There is a Report that there is a revolt in your district among the negrows [*sic*]. Ans. Not that we have heard off [*sic*]." At 11 A.M. the 7th District asked the 3d District: "Is it true the negroes have revolted in your district against the whites. Ans: Not that we have heard off [*sic*]."

The lull of April 27 gave way to wild excitement on April 28, when Flag Officer Farragut sent Captain Henry H. Bell, accompanied by Acting Master Herbert Tyson, to City Hall with a letter threatening to bombard the city unless orders regarding the United States flags were respected.

". . . The fire of this fleet may be drawn upon the city at any moment, and in such an event the levee would . . . in all probability, be cut by the shell, and an amount of distress ensue to the innocent population which I have heretofore endeavored to assure you that I desired by all means to avoid," said Farragut. "The election . . . is with you, but it becomes my duty to notify you to remove the women and children from the city within forty-eight hours if I have rightly understood your determination."

Mayor Monroe read the letter and then asked Captain Bell:

"As I consider this a threat to bombard the city, and as it is a matter about which the notice should be clear and specific, I desire to know when the forty-eight began to run."

"It begins from the time you receive this notice," replied Captain Bell.

"Then," said Mayor Monroe, taking out his watch and showing it to Bell, "you see it is fifteen minutes past 12 o'clock."

Captain Bell and his companion followed the pattern of departure of their predecessors, and while the angry crowd in front of City Hall was engaged, they made their exit by the rear and into a cab that took them to the wharf without incident.[12]

Mayor Monroe immediately addressed a letter to the Common Council pointing out that Farragut seemed to have misunderstood the position of the city. "He has been distinctly informed that at this moment the city has no power to impede the exercise of such acts of forcible authority as the commander of the United States Naval force may choose to exercise; and that, therefore, no resistance would be offered to the occupation of the city by the United States forces."

The mayor said that if Farragut deemed it necessary to remove the flag of Louisiana from City Hall or to raise the United States flag, "the power which threatens the destruction of our city is certainly capable of performing those acts." Without a military force or commander, New Orleans was, continued the mayor, "like an unoccupied fortress of which an assailant may at any moment take possession." In all New Orleans, said Monroe, there was not "one loyal citizen who would be willing to incur the odium of tearing down the symbol representing the State authority to which New Orleans owes its municipal existence," and in conclusion, the mayor declared:

> I am deeply sensible of the distress which would be brought upon our community by a consummation of the inhuman threat of the United States commander; but I can not conceive that those who so recently declared themselves to be animated by a Christian spirit and by a regard for the rights of private property would venture to incur for themselves and the Government they represent, the universal execration of the civilized world by attempting to achieve, through a wanton destruction of life and property, that which they can accomplish without bloodshed and without a resort to those hostile measures which the law of nations condemns and execrates, when employed upon the defenseless women and children of an unresisting city.

The Common Council approved Mayor Monroe's stand without delay, and once again Pierre Soulé was entrusted with drafting the letter to Farragut for the mayor's signature. The communication opened by challenging Farragut's right to raise the United States flag at the Mint while negotiations were pending and then launched into the subject of the threatened bombardment and the forty-eight-hour time limit in which to remove women and children from the city.

"Sir, you can not but know that there is no possible exit from this city for a population which still exceeds 140,000 and you must therefore be aware of the utter inanity of such a notification," declared Mayor Monroe. "Our women and children can not escape your shells if it be your pleasure to murder them on a question of mere etiquette; but if they could, there are but few among them that would consent to desert their families and their homes and the graves of their relations in so awful a moment . . . You are not satisfied with the peaceable possession of an undefended city, opposing no resistance to your guns, because of its bearing its doom with something of manliness and dignity; and you wish to humble and disgrace us by an act against which our nature rebels. This satisfaction you can not expect to obtain at our hands.

"We will stand your bombardment, unarmed and undefended as we are. The civilized world will consign to indelible infamy the heart that will conceive the deed and the hand that will dare to consummate it."[13]

Pierre Soulé accompanied Marion Baker to the *Hartford* early on the morning of April 29 to deliver this reply to Farragut. Soulé, once in the flag officer's cabin, entered on a discussion of international law while Farragut, Captain Bell, and Captain Bailey listened patiently. Farragut replied that he was not familiar with the niceties of international law and that he was a plain sailor, aiming only to do his duty as commander of a fleet. Stating that he had an appointment at nine o'clock, Soulé asked to be put ashore and the interview ended.

Farragut found himself more deeply involved in international law than he had contemplated. At the same time that he had threatened Mayor Monroe with a bombardment of the city, he dispatched a letter to the foreign consuls in New Orleans, citing the deadlock between him and the city authorities over the flags and the repeated insults to his officers. "I am unable to say how soon I may be compelled to fire upon the city," wrote the flag officer, "and it therefore becomes my duty to notify you . . . of the fact, in order that you may remove your families into a place of great security."

There was immediate reaction from the foreign representatives, who demanded an interview with the flag officer "before you proceed from the threat of a bombardment to the realization of such an unheard of act against a town of open commerce without military defenses of any kind and virtually surrendered by the municipal authorities." And Captain Georges Charles Cloué, commander of the French warship *Milan*, which had just reached New Orleans, sent a sharp protest to Farragut, opposing, in the name of his government, as "ridiculous" the delay of forty-eight hours to evacuate women and children. "If it is your resolution to bombard the city, do it," he wrote, "but I wish to state that you will have to account for this barbarous act to the Power which I represent."[14]

To strengthen the resolution of the mayor and Common Council, the women of New Orleans addressed a petition to Monroe "begging him to be firm & hold his position and they will stand by him, though the enemy's shell should fire their homes." Mrs. Robert Dow Urquhart wrote in her journal that if Farragut went through with his threat, it would be "an act of barbarity and inhumanity . . . unparalleled in history . . . Still rather than our hands should remove that cherished flag from its place, a thousand times better to have the city burned to the ground, better lose all than honor."

A member of the Common Council, meeting Ida Slocomb, whose home was next door to City Hall, jokingly said to her: "Will you not relieve us of our difficulty by going up and taking down the flag?" "Yes," replied Miss Slocomb, "I will go up, but I will take a hammer with me and nail the flag to the staff." Recording this incident in her journal, Mrs. Urquhart said: "This noble and determined spirit actuated every woman of this unfortunate city."[15]

Meanwhile, the *McRae*, now commanded by Lieutenant Charles W. "Savez" Read, arrived in New Orleans under a flag of truce with the sick and wounded from the Confederate fleet and forts, including the ship's gallant commander, the mortally wounded Lieutenant Huger. Read had obtained permission from Captain Melancton Smith of the *Mississippi* to proceed up the river until he found the main portion of the Federal fleet, when he could arrange with Flag Officer Farragut to land his sick and wounded.

The *McRae* reached New Orleans at 11:20 A.M. on April 27, anchoring off Julia Street, whereupon Read called immediately upon Farragut. The flag officer gave permission for the wounded to be landed, provided that by 10 A.M. on April 28 the *McRae* would return to the forts "in the same condition in every respect in which she came up." Read pledged that it would.

However, during the night the *McRae* began to drag anchor, and having no other anchor to let go, Lieutenant Read started the engines and headed across the river where the water was more shallow. While crossing, the *McRae* struck an underwater obstacle and soon began to leak badly. Pumps were started and kept going, nevertheless by 11:20 P.M. the water had reached high enough to put the fire out in the furnaces. Read sent ashore for help from the police, and a lieutenant of police and ten men came on board to work the pumps. By dawn the hold had six feet of water and it was gaining steadily. "My men were exhausted, and I felt confident that further exertions were useless," reported Read. "I directed her injection pipes to be cut, so that she might sink as soon as possible, and got all hands ashore without delay."

The *McRae* went down at 7 A.M., and Lieutenant Read immediately went on board the *Hartford* to explain his inability to return to the forts. Farragut was not there, but Read spoke to Captain Craven, who told him that the only way to return to the forts was in a small boat, but that he could use his own option on returning to the forts or not. In any event, he told Read to return the next morning to see the flag officer.[16]

The forts now were very much in the minds of the people of New Orleans. In their present dark hour, they still hopefully looked to the defenses down the river to save them from the Federal fleet. For as long as Fort Jackson and Fort St. Philip held out, Farragut's position at New Orleans was far from secure. Reinforcements, supplies of ammunition and foodstuffs, and General Butler's occupation troops could not come up to New Orleans as long as the Confederate flag flew over the forts. So while the guns of Farragut's warships looked menacingly into the city's streets, New Orleans' sole hope lay in the defense of the forts by General Duncan, seventy-five miles down the river.

21

The End of Confederate New Orleans

WHILE NEW ORLEANS WAS ENDURING ITS TIME OF TROUBLE, DOWN AT Fort Jackson and Fort St. Philip another scene in the drama was being played. It opened several hours after Farragut had run past the forts—at 9:30 A.M. on April 24 to be precise—when Commander Porter dispatched Lieutenant Guest in the *Owasco* under a flag of truce to Fort Jackson to demand the surrender. The gunboat had barely steamed into range when Fort Jackson fired two shots ahead of her. Lieutenant Guest immediately ordered the engine stopped and sheered his vessel across the stream. At this moment, a gun from Fort St. Philip roared and a shell whistled over the *Owasco*. Lieutenant Guest did not return the fire, but headed back to Porter and reported that the Rebels seemed disinclined to receive a flag of truce.

About an hour later a boat from Fort Jackson, flying a flag of truce, put out into the river, and the *Owasco* steamed up to meet it. Lieutenant Guest asked to be taken into the boat so that he could deliver Commander Porter's surrender demand to the commanding officer. He was refused by the Confederate officer, who apologized for firing on the flag of truce, blaming it on a misunderstanding at

Fort St. Philip. Guest then gave the demand to the officer, who returned to the fort. Almost immediately he returned with General Duncan's reply that Porter's demand was "inadmissible."[1]

The demand carried with it the threat of a resumption of the mortar bombardment, which had stopped shortly after Farragut had passed the forts. About noon, the bummers opened up again and fired until nearly sundown. Despite this show of confidence, Commander Porter was quite concerned over the welfare of his mortar flotilla. He was worried about the *Louisiana*. "If the enemy counted so surely on destroying our whole fleet with her, it behooved me to be prudent and not let the mortar vessels be sacrificed . . ." he wrote. "I commenced, then, a bombardment on the iron-clad battery, supposing it laid close under Fort Jackson, and also set the vessels to work throwing bomb-shells into Fort Jackson again to let them know that we were still taking care of them." When the forts did not respond, Porter assumed that "the fight had all been taken out of them," but he nonetheless permitted prudence to determine his decision to move the mortar flotilla down the river.[2]

Porter's assumption that the *Louisiana* was under the guns of Fort Jackson was wrong. General Duncan had at last gotten Commander Mitchell's agreement to move the ironclad below Fort St. Philip and thus be able to enfilade the mortar flotilla if it resumed the bombardment. But when Porter opened up again, the *Louisiana* was still at its old moorings above St. Philip. Mitchell sent Duncan word that he had no steam tender upon which he could rely, that many of the volunteer troops were drunk, and that his own crew were exhausted. Accordingly "these circumstances . . . and excessive difficulty in handling the vessel, will prevent our taking the position, at least today, that I proposed and was arranged between us this afternoon."

After the mortar fleet retired, Duncan asked Mitchell to place the *Louisiana* above Fort Jackson in a position to repel an attack from Farragut's vessels up the river. This was the essential place now for the *Louisiana*, because all the heavy guns at both forts had been mounted to bear upon the lower approaches. So, with the mortar vessels no longer a factor, the forts really needed the ironclad in a position, said Duncan, "where her guns could protect our rear and sweep the long reach of river above toward the Quarantine." Mitchell reluctantly agreed to take up such a position, but later in the evening he sent another message to Duncan, canceling this arrangement, again complaining of a want of tugboats and anchor trouble. "The *W. Burton* is crippled, and the *Landis* also, and the gunboat *Defiance* will not do anything for us," wrote Mitchell. "If she comes within my reach I will deprive her captain of his command by force, if necessary . . . We shall probably remain where we are, and do all we can to defeat the enemy should he attack us again."

General Duncan's disgust at Commander Mitchell's repeated excuses for not taking positive action may well be imagined. In a letter to his wife that same day, he wrote: "The *McRae* behaved admirably and fought gallantly. For the rest done by the Navy and river fleet, the less said the better . . . Let everyone know this: Our flag still flies on both forts, and we are nearly as strong as when the fight commenced."[3]

With the communications to New Orleans cut, General Duncan, of course, was completely in the dark as to what was happening there. On April 25, he wrote his wife again that everyone at the forts was "extremely anxious to know what has been done and is going on in the city . . . We are just about as strong as we were the first day, and can hold out for some two months (until our provisions are exhausted), if the city has not fallen. If it has, the mission of the forts is about over, unless it be to prevent commerce from again resuming its sway on the river . . . What has happened in the city, and how many boats have succeeded in getting by, we really don't know at present. We are now like rats in a hole, perfectly surrounded, and cut off from all sources of supply or information." General Duncan sent these letters, along with dispatches, to New Orleans by couriers, whose return to the forts, he hoped, would bring assurance that New Orleans still held out.

All day on April 25, the men at the forts labored with the heaviest guns that would admit of modification, preparing them to traverse in a full circle and thus bear up or down the river as required.

There was no molestation by the enemy, although gunboats from Quarantine and below the point of woods steamed into view for purposes of observation only.[4]

On April 26, there was no firing during the entire day, as the Federal gunboats again devoted themselves to reconnaissance. From Fort Jackson, steamers could be discerned, across the river and beyond to the bay, working their way up the coast. General Duncan knew what this meant: General Butler's troops were about to begin landing at Quarantine, above the forts. During the day came the first information that New Orleans had fallen. Commander Mitchell, communicating with the Federals under a flag of truce, was told that the city had surrendered.

About noon on April 27, a Federal gunboat from below came up with a flag of truce, bearing a written demand for the surrender of the forts, signed by Commander David D. Porter and dated April 26. Addressed to Lieutenant Colonel Higgins, as commander of the forts, the letter asserted that Farragut was now in possession of New Orleans, troops were in possession of important points on the river, and that the forts were now cut off from all communications and supplies. "No man could consider it dishonorable to surrender under these circumstances, especially when no advantage can arise by longer holding out, and by yielding gracefully he can save the further effusion of blood," declared Porter. "You have defended the forts gallantly, and no more can be asked of you." Porter then offered generous terms, "sufficiently honorable to relieve you from any feeling of humiliation." These included the parole of officers and men, the former to retain their side arms, and neither officers nor men to serve again until exchanged.

Once again Porter was met with a refusal, but this demand was not as "inadmissible" as the last. ". . . No official information has been received by me from our authorities that the City of New Orleans has surrendered to the forces of Flag Officer Farragut," replied Higgins, "and until such information is received no proposition for a surrender can be for a moment entertained here."[5]

Duncan and Higgins sensed a change in the morale of the men at Fort Jackson. Throughout the tremendous bombardment by the mortar boats and the blistering fire during Farragut's passage, the men, despite fatigue and discomfort, had remained "cheerful, confident and courageous." The troops were mostly foreigners "without any great interest at stake in the ultimate success of the revolution," Duncan later reported. "A reaction set in among them during the lull of the 25th, 26th, and 27th, when there was no other excitement to arouse them than the fatigue duty of repairing our damages and when the rumor was current that the city had surrendered and was then in the hands of the enemy."

Duncan waited in vain for the return of his couriers, hoping to have some word from New Orleans with which to reassure the men, who were "still obedient but not buoyant and cheerful." In the hopes of reviving the courage and patriotism of the men, General Duncan issued, on April 27, an order to both garrisons:

> You have nobly, gallantly, and heroically sustained with courage and fortitude terrible ordeals of fire, water, and a hail of shot and shell wholly unsurpassed during the present war. But more remains to be done. The safety of New Orleans and the cause of the Southern Confederacy, our homes, families, and everything dear to man yet depend upon our exertions. We are just as capable of repelling the enemy today as we were before the bombardment. Twice has the enemy demanded your surrender and twice has he been refused. Your officers have every confidence in your courage and patriotism, and feel every assurance that you will cheerfully and with alacrity obey all orders and do your whole duty as men and as becomes the well-tried garrisons of Forts Jackson and St. Philip. Be vigilant, therefore, and stand by your guns, and all will yet be well.[6]

Duncan's order failed of the desired effect. Suddenly at midnight the garrison at Fort Jackson revolted in mass. The men seized the guards and posterns and reversed the fieldpieces which commanded the gates and started spiking the guns. While many men left the fort under arms, others, drawn up in ranks with their arms, positively refused to fight any more. Still others tried by force to persuade Captain F. O. Cornay's St. Mary's Cannoneers to join the mutiny, but without success. These sons of planters from St. Mary's Parish remained loyal.

The mutiny was as unexpected as it was sudden. Duncan, while realizing that morale was low, did not know that for two days the revolt had been discussed among the men. In vain did the officers attempt to bring the troops to reason and order; in vain did the post chaplain, Father Nachon, try to quell the mutineers. The latter were determined not to fight any longer. They asserted that the officers intended to hold out as long as possible, or while the provisions lasted, and then blow up the forts and the garrisons with them. They argued that New Orleans had fallen and further resistance was useless. They claimed that the Federals were about to launch a land-and-water attack on three sides and that a continued defense of the forts would result only in butchery.

So widespread was the revolt that the officers were powerless. When the officers on the ramparts attempted to halt the spiking of the guns they were fired on by the mutineers. General Duncan came to the inescapable conclusion that it was best to let the men who wanted to leave the fort go and then determine what reliance could be reposed in those who remained. Half of the garrison left immediately. These included regulars as well as volunteers, noncoms as well as privates, and among them, reported Duncan, "many of the very men who had stood last and best to their guns throughout the protracted bombardment and the final action when the enemy passed."

It did not take long for General Duncan to see that "there was no further fight in the men remaining behind . . . they were completely demoralized." Although Duncan did not know the status of Fort St. Philip, signals had been exchanged between the forts at the height of the mutiny, and the assumption among the officers at Fort Jackson was that the garrison across the river was involved. Later this proved erroneous, for there had been no revolt at Fort St. Philip, nor had any men left the fort. Duncan, accordingly, sadly concluded that the end had come. He decided that the next morning, April 28, he would send a flag of truce to Commander Porter to negotiate for surrender under the terms that the latter had offered on April 26.[7]

Early the next morning, Commander Mitchell and his aide, Lieutenant Shryock, came to Fort Jackson to confer with General Duncan, who explained to them the situation. Imagine Duncan's surprise when Mitchell said that he would return to the *Louisiana* and attempt to attack the enemy at Quarantine. This, commented Duncan, "notwithstanding that reasons had been given from time to time for not moving this vessel into her proper position, only a few hundred yards distant."

From General Duncan's report, it appears that he conferred with Mitchell, and shortly afterward with Captain Squires, who commanded at Fort St. Philip. Then, deeming the situation hopeless, he went through with his decision arrived at during the night—to send a flag of truce to Porter with a written offer of surrender.

Commander Mitchell's report gives a different version. He says that "during the night . . . of the 27th, we had so far succeeded in operating the propellers that we expected early the next day to make a fair trial of them in connection with the paddle wheels." When an officer from Fort Jackson came aboard at daylight to tell him what had happened, and of Duncan's decision to surrender, Mitchell hurried ashore. He said, "General Duncan . . . informed me that in his offer to surrender the forts he had disclaimed all control over the forces afloat. This unexpected surrender of these important land defenses seriously compromising the position and safety of my own command, I expressed to General Duncan my deep regret that a previous knowledge of his intentions to surrender had not been communicated to me, particularly as I expected in the day to test the full power of the *Louisiana* under her propellers and wheels, and if successful I might be able to achieve something against the enemy. It was, however, too late, the flag of truce had been dispatched and could not be recalled; but I informed General Duncan that in no event would the enemy be allowed to obtain possession of the *Louisiana*."

Commander Mitchell returned to the *Louisiana* and called a council of officers composed of Lieutenants John Wilkinson, W. H. Ward,

A. F. Warley, W. C. Whittle, Jr., R. J. Bowen, Thomas Arnold, F. H. Harris, and George S. Shryock. It was unanimously decided to destroy the *Louisiana* to prevent her from falling into the hands of the enemy. The Federals had an overwhelming naval force above and below, these officers reasoned, and soon would be in possession of the forts, with their defenses largely intact. Moreover, the *Louisiana* had provisions for only ten days and her surrender would be inevitable by the simple process of a blockade. And then there was the still dubious status of the ironclad's motive power.

Commander Mitchell "with most painful regret" gave the order to fire the vessel, and as the preparations commenced, Federal gunboats, flying flags of truce, came around the bend and anchored off Fort Jackson.

When Commander Porter received Duncan's acceptance of surrender—the letter was signed by Colonel Higgins—he immediately put the *Harriet Lane* under way, accompanied by three gunboats. Higgins' letter was short: "Upon mature deliberation it has been decided to accept the terms of surrender of these forts under the conditions offered by you in your letter of the 26th instant, viz., that the officers and men shall be paroled, officers retiring with their side arms. We have no control over the vessels afloat."

The last sentence in Colonel Higgins' letter is important in the light of subsequent events. Years later Porter claimed "the surrender was to include all the naval officers and whatever vessels were afloat," because this had been stipulated in his original verbal demand. But it was on the basis of Porter's written demand of April 26 that the forts offered to surrender and with an unqualified statement regarding the Navy: "We have no control over the vessels afloat."[8]

When Duncan and Higgins came aboard the *Harriet Lane*, Porter lost no time in laying the papers of capitulation before them.

"General Duncan," he said, "read them carefully."

"I will," replied Duncan. "But I am confident you would offer us no terms that it would be dishonorable to accept; one brave man would not wish to humiliate another."

Porter, who tells the story of the surrender, says that he acknowledged "the compliment so delicately expressed."

"I am satisfied with the terms," said Duncan, "and I speak for the rest of the officers."

"Where is the commanding naval officer and his staff?" inquired Porter. "I shall include the vessels in the surrender; are they not under your command?"

"Yes," replied the general, "at least they are supposed to be, but I know nothing about them. The naval officers were duly notified what was to take place. They failed in their support; otherwise matters might have turned out differently."

Porter, whose remarkable knack for distorting facts, usually to his advantage, has been remarked before, quotes General Duncan in a way directly opposite to what the record shows. "We have no control over the vessels afloat," Colonel Higgins had written. And yet Porter, in his dramatization of the surrender, would have one believe Duncan said he had control of the Navy.

At this point, Lieutenant Wainwright, captain of the *Harriet Lane*, stepped into the cabin to report that the *Louisiana* was on fire and adrift.

"This is sharp practice, gentlemen," said Porter. "And some of us will perhaps be blown up . . . If you can stand what is coming, we can, but I will make it lively for those people if anyone in the flotilla is injured."

"We do not consider ourselves responsible for anything the naval officers do," replied Duncan. "Their course has been a remarkable one throughout the bombardment. They have acknowledged no authority except their own, and although I am commanding officer here I have no power to coerce them."

Porter issued orders to his vessels to guard against the drifting *Louisiana* and then returned to the table.

"Gentlemen, we will proceed to sign the capitulation," he said, handing the paper to General Duncan and watching carefully to see how the Confederate officers would behave with the knowledge that a flaming ironclad with 20,000 pounds of powder in the magazine was descending upon them.

Duncan and Higgins were imperturbable, sitting, Porter wrote, "as coolly as if at a tea-table among their friends." There was a stir on deck, the *Harriet Lane* swayed to and fro, and then came a terrific explosion, throwing the vessels two streaks over, jostling everything in the cabin from side to side. But no one moved from the table or showed the slightest intention of doing so. Lieutenant Wainwright returned to the cabin and said that the *Louisiana* had blown up, just a hundred yards above the advance vessel, the *Owasco*, and that nobody in the fleet was hurt nor a vessel damaged.

Porter, who was keenly set on acquiring the *Louisiana* for the Federal service, was furious:

"I have no doubt the ironclad was prepared to blow up right in our midst, for the purpose of destroying us all," he declared.

"We are not responsible," replied General Duncan.

General Duncan and Colonel Higgins signed the surrender for the Confederacy; Porter, Wainwright, and Commander W. B. Renshaw signed for the Federals. Porter took care that the surrender was "to the mortar flotilla," for which Farragut was to reprove him, gently, later.[9]

At 4 P.M. on April 28, the officers of Fort Jackson and the men and officers of the loyal St. Mary's Cannoneers left for the city aboard the gunboat *Kennebec*. The Confederate flag was still flying over Fort Jackson as they steamed up the river, for Porter had graciously agreed verbally not to haul it down or hoist the Federal flag until the officers had left. The officers and men of Fort St. Philip were sent up to the city the next day.

Arriving in New Orleans on the morning of April 29, General Duncan quickly learned of Farragut's threat to bomb the city and the forty-eight-hour time limit to evacuate the women and children. He hastened to City Hall to inform Mayor Monroe of the fate of the forts. Word of the forts' surrender, meanwhile, was immediately signaled to the fleet, and wild cheering broke out on every vessel and flags were raised at every masthead.[10]

Flag Officer Farragut without delay sent a message to Mayor Monroe stating that now that the forts had fallen the mayor was the "sole representative of any supposed authority in the city" and that "you are required . . . to haul down and suppress every ensign and symbol of government, whether State or Confederate, except that of the United States." He declared that he was about to raise the United States flag over the Custom House, "and you will see that it is respected with all the civil power in the city."

After dispatching the message to the mayor, Farragut still insisted in a conversation with the mayor's secretary, Marion Baker, that the lowering of the flag of Louisiana over City Hall should be the work of those who raised it. But before young Baker left the *Hartford*, Farragut yielded on this point. "I reported to my chief that there would be no bombardment," said Baker, "and that the ungrateful task of lowering our flag would be performed by those who demanded its removal."[11]

At 11 A.M. on April 29, Captain Henry Bell went ashore with all the marines of the fleet and two pieces of artillery and proceeded to the Custom House, where the United States flag was hoisted over the Canal Street face of the building. Leaving a marine guard at the Custom House, Captain Bell proceeded with his force through "streets densely crowded, but orderly and quiet, though full of rage," to City Hall. The marines formed in two lines in front of Lafayette Square, facing City Hall, and two brass howitzers were placed to command up and down St. Charles Street. Thousands of persons filled every open space. To one observer, they were "sullen and angry"; to Marion Baker, the crowd was "silent and angry and threatening." It was a tense moment as Captain Bell, Lieutenant Kautz, and several men entered City Hall. "That immense assemblage had the will to annihilate the small force of sailors and marines," observed Lieutenant Albert Kautz. ". . . No one knew but that one or two desperate men were ready to fire the train that would lead to the magazine."

Approaching Mayor Monroe in the mayor's parlor, Captain Bell said: "I have come in obedience to orders to haul down the state flag from this building." Captain Bell later said that he stated his "proud mission very meekly."

"Very well, sir, you can do it," replied the mayor, his voice trembling with restrained emotion. "But I wish to say that there is not in my entire constituency so wretched a renegade as would be willing to exchange places with you."

Marion Baker, who was at the interview, says that Captain Bell "visibly restrained himself from reply." Bell himself recorded that he remarked that he should do nothing to hurt their sensibilities more than necessary but that he meant to haul down their flag. Lieutenant Kautz's version of the interview said Mayor Monroe "indignantly declined" the privilege of hauling down the flag which Captain Bell extended to him.

In response to an anxious inquiry as to whether he intended to run up the United States flag, Captain Bell answered in the negative. Mayor Monroe, the Council, and Pierre Soulé all seemed greatly relieved. Bell then asked the way to the roof. No one made a move to show him. Mayor Monroe referred him to the janitor, whom he would find outside. As Captain Bell turned to leave the room Mayor Monroe told him that the man who tried to take down the Louisiana flag took the risk of being shot by some indignant citizen on a nearby rooftop, and he expressed the hope that should that happen he be not held responsible for the act.

"An excited red-bearded individual" led the Federals up two flights of stairs and pointing, said: "There, sir, up through those narrow stairs. It is more than a man's life is worth to go to the top or to haul down the flag."

Lieutenant Kautz asked Captain Bell for permission to haul down the flag, but Bell had already promised the honor to Boatswain's Mate George Russell. "I replied . . . that if he desired it particularly I would alter it," said Bell, "but that officer, waiving his claim of rank, generously yielded the honor to Russell."

Meanwhile Mayor Monroe had left City Hall and placed himself directly in front of the howitzer that was pointing down St. Charles Street toward Canal Street. "There," said Marion Baker, "folding his arms, he fixed his eyes upon the gunner who stood lanyard in hand ready for action. Here he remained until Lieutenant Kautz and Captain Bell had reappeared."

A ladder led to the City Hall roof from the top floor, through a covered hatch. The boatswain's mate was first up the ladder, and he pushed the hatch cover to one side and stepped out upon the roof and Lieutenant Kautz followed. Below in the street, the huge crowd, sullen, angry, silent, overflowed into Lafayette Square, completely surrounding the marines, "pressing up even against their bayonets." It was a tense, painful, dramatic moment; it was the deathwatch of the people at the bedside of Confederate New Orleans. All eyes were on the two Yankees on the roof as they descended the slope to the flagstaff.

Finding the halyards knotted, Lieutenant Kautz drew his sword and cut them. Boatswain's Mate Russell then pulled on the ropes and the flag of Louisiana came slowly down. It was exactly 12:45 P.M., as an eloquently ungrammatical entry in the message book of the city's Fire and Alarm Telegraph System attests: "April 29 . . . 12¾. The Federal has just hawl down our Flag."[12]

Some moments later, amid profound silence, Bell, Kautz, and Russell emerged from City Hall carrying the flag. The marine guard fell into line, the two guns following, and the Federals marched to their boats and returned to the fleet. As they moved along cries now came from the crowd on the streets:

"Hurrah for Beauregard!"

"Hurrah for Jeff Davis!"

Someone threw a small stone at Captain Bell as they marched, but this was the only indignity offered the Federal force. Behind them they heard cheer upon cheer for Mayor Monroe ringing out from the crowd at City Hall.[13]

The next day's *Picayune* made no attempt to describe the excitement but confined itself to relating "what did not occur," on New Orleans' last day in the Confederacy. "Briefly," it said, ". . . we say that New Orleans did not surrender, our authorities did not take the flag of Louisiana from the City Hall, the Federal fleet did not coerce us into the commission of an act of humiliation, and the searchers for Union men in New Orleans found none."

On this latter theme, the *Commercial Bulletin* bitterly rejected the idea of reunion expressed by some of the Federal officers: "Why, there is not a man, woman or child in our community who would not prefer a reunion with either Spain, France or Great Britain, under any terms, than one with the Federal Government, even at our own dictation."[14]

Three short entries in the diary of nineteen-year-old Oscar Smith, a marine stationed on the *Hartford*, tell with graphic simplicity the end of Confederate New Orleans:

"April 30—The city seems very quiet."

"May 1—General Butler landed his troops in New Orleans this evening and marched up the streets to the tune of 'Yankee Doodle.'"

"May 2—About midnight I heard the regimental bands playing 'Dixie.'"[15]

22

Aftermath

A SHOCK RAN THROUGH THE ENTIRE CONFEDERACY WHEN THE NEWS
spread that the South's greatest city had fallen.

With prophetic brevity, Mary Boykin Chestnut recorded the bitter fact in her diary: "New Orleans is gone, and with it the Confederacy! Are we not cut in two? The Mississippi ruins us if it is
lost."[1]

In the Army of Tennessee, which had retired again to Corinth,
Mississippi, after the bloody battle of Shiloh, doubts began to permeate all ranks and grades when the word reached the camps that
the Yankees had captured New Orleans. "The effect was disheartening to everyone," wrote General St. John Liddell in his war memoirs.
"A growing impression of doubt as to our final success seemed to
enter the mind of every reflecting man. It was perceptible that nothing short of superhuman efforts could save us the Mississippi
River."[2]

But far above the jolt to southern morale and southern pride
were the far-reaching consequences produced by the loss of New
Orleans, not the least being a shattering blow to Confederate diplomatic efforts to gain from England and France recognition of the
independence of the South.

It is readily evident to anyone who studies the statistics that the South, unaided, simply did not have the physical and material capacity to win the war, provided the North retained its determination to fight. Outside help, in the form of recognition, raising of the blockade, and material assistance, was absolutely necessary for the Confederacy to establish its independence of the Federal Union.

The news of New Orleans, although fragmentary, reached London on May 10, 1862. Young Henry Adams, returning from a Sunday-afternoon stroll, was astonished to see his father, the United States minister to Great Britain, dance excitedly across the room to greet him, exclaiming: "We've got New Orleans!"

For months, Mr. Adams had labored to prevent British recognition of southern independence. He had mollified much of the indignation and overcome most of the hostility resulting from the foolish seizure of Mason and Slidell in the *Trent* Affair. Nevertheless, in the early spring of 1862 the tide of British public opinion was still running in favor of the Confederacy. Charles Francis Adams needed nothing so much as a great Federal success to help him to stem it. Here, for the first time, was a major northern victory.

Henry Adams read the dispatch his father handed him and hurried back into the streets, where the London newsboys were already shouting an evening extra: "Rumored capture of New Orleans!" The young American quickly perceived that "the whole town was in immense excitement as though it were an English defeat" and that the fall of New Orleans acted on many Britons "like a violent blow in the face on a drunken man." The American minister, writing to a son in the United States, said that the English people were "quite struck aback" by the surrender of New Orleans. "It took them three days to make up their minds to believe it," he said.[3]

At the American legation, one of Mr. Adams' secretaries, Benjamin Moran, noted in his diary that it was "one of the heaviest blows the rebellion has received," and added: "The fact is very unpalatable to the English, and many refuse to believe it, simply no doubt because they don't want it should be so." Some English sympathizers with the Confederacy had ridiculous and laughable explanations for the capture of New Orleans, Moran recorded, "excusing it on the ground of its being a masterful piece of military strategy to catch the Federals, who are to be entrapped and captured somewhere up the Mississippi."[4]

Richard Cobden, writing from England to Charles Sumner three months before New Orleans fell, provides a distinguished Briton's estimate of the sentiment of his countrymen: "The cry of arbitration had been raised and responded to . . . The only question was whether we ought to be the first to offer arbitration. I mean this was the only doubt in the popular mind. As regards our Government, they were, of course, feeling the tendency of public opinion . . . A friend of mine in London, a little behind the scenes, wrote to me, 'They are busy at the Foreign Office hunting up precedents for arbitration very much against their will.' "[5]

A week before the news of the capture of New Orleans reached England, the *Illustrated London News* editorialized: "The position of the Southern Confederacy has been much improved by the events of the last month, and it would seem that it will not be very long before there is an attempt made to terminate this fratricidal war by a mediation that will imply recognition."[6]

Across the Channel, in France, the news was a severe blow to Confederate Commissioner John Slidell. He had been sending alternatingly optimistic and pessimistic dispatches to Richmond about French recognition of the South. Late in February he reported: "France is prepared . . . to recognize our government provided that Great Britain will consent to act simultaneously with her." Two weeks later, Slidell warned that unless the debacles at Roanoke and Fort Donelson were "not soon counterbalanced by some decisive success of our arms, we may . . . bid adieu to all hopes of seasonable recognition." In April, just a few days before Porter's mortar vessels began blasting the forts below New Orleans, Slidell wrote that "much if not everything will depend upon the character of the intelligence we may receive within the next three or four weeks . . . Decided success of our arms would insure early recognition. . . ."

And now, in mid-May 1862, the worst news had come: New Orleans had fallen to Farragut's fleet. Slidell called on M. Thouvenal, French Minister of Foreign Affairs, prepared to admit quite frankly the severity of the loss of New Orleans to the South. However, Thouvenal anticipated Slidell by entering at once upon the affairs of the Confederacy. What effect, posed the minister, would the capture of New Orleans produce? Reporting the conversation to Secretary Benjamin, Slidell wrote: "I replied to him very frankly that it was a heavy blow for us and would give the enemy the command of the Mississippi and its tributaries . . . but that the occupation of New Orleans and all our other seaports would not in any degree change or even modify the fixed determination of our people to carry on the war until our independence was acknowledged by the North."

Slidell found Thouvenal's frankness and cordiality very different from a previous interview, and he got the profound impression that the French minister regretted the fall of New Orleans. "Although he did not directly say so," reported the Confederate commissioner, "it left me fairly to infer, that if New Orleans had not been taken and we suffered no very serious reverses in Virginia and Tennessee, our recognition would very soon have been declared."[7]

A month after the fall of New Orleans, Stonewall Jackson threw Washington into a panic with his Shenandoah Valley campaign, and two months after General Butler began his occupation of the Crescent City, the Union Army under General George B. McClellan was turned back by General Robert E. Lee from the gates of Richmond and forced out of Virginia. Linking the Virginia campaign with Farragut's operation below New Orleans, Admiral Alfred Thayer Mahan, America's most distinguished naval theorist and student of the influence of sea power on history, asked: ". . . Who can estimate the effect, when the scales were thus balancing, if the Navy had been driven out of the Mississippi as the Army was from Virginia?"

A recent student of naval warfare did estimate the effect of such an eventuality. Charles Lee Lewis, biographer of Farragut, declared that ". . . in the South . . . the success of Farragut's campaign meant not only the loss of a great city but even the loss of the war. There is good evidence that the failure of Napoleon III to recognize the

Confederacy and take some positive step towards bringing the war to a close even without English cooperation was due to Farragut's capture of New Orleans. If Farragut had failed, it is not unlikely that, a few months later after McClellan's army suffered such a crushing defeat in Virginia, England, too, would have taken steps towards bringing about peace with the establishment of the Confederate States of America as an independent nation. If this be true, then Farragut's capture of the Queen of the Gulf becomes an important turning point in the course of the Civil War."

James Morton Callahan, a pioneer scholar on Confederate diplomacy, held a similar view. Writing in 1901, Callahan declared: "Napoleon was held back by England and the people. He held many conversations with Slidell and was eagerly planning in the Tuileries to recognize the South and break the blockade, but the capture of New Orleans prevented any step he may have contemplated without the cooperation of England."[8]

Two Union officers, both close to the scene, grasped the significance of the fall of New Orleans. Writing a week before Farragut passed the forts, General Thomas Williams of Butler's occupation forces said:

"New Orleans *must* belong to the Union. The capture of New Orleans would tend, so much, and perhaps more than any other success, to the restoration of Union and peace. This is a commercial and political necessity to the United States. . . ."

David Dixon Porter wrote his friend Fox: "New Orleans' falling seems to have made a stampede in 'secessia.' You may put the rebellion down as 'spavined,' 'broken-backed' and 'wind-galled.'"[9]

What specifically did the loss of New Orleans mean to the South? What did its possession mean to the North? Some of the consequences of the fall of New Orleans were:

1. It meant the eventual control of the Mississippi River by the Union, for it provided the Federals with a naval base for waging war on the river from the south. This enabled the Federal Navy to flank the Confederate forces in the west.

2. It severed the Confederacy, cutting off Texas, Arkansas, and most of Louisiana from the other southern states.

3. It meant the loss to the South of Texas beef[10] and Louisiana salt, which had recently been discovered in solid form at Avery Island, about 150 miles west of New Orleans. Both were vital factors in the Confederacy's capacity to exist during the war.[11]

4. It meant the loss to the Confederacy of the two greatest warships in the world, the *Mississippi* and the *Louisiana*, both designed to raise the blockade of southern ports. Either, working upriver with the Confederate Army of Tennessee, was capable of shattering the Union river fleet. Either could have destroyed or driven off the wooden blockading vessels from southern ports. Commander Porter said that the *Louisiana* was "impervious to any shot we had . . . her iron sides had not even been indented by the shots poured into her as the vessels of the squadron passed by." Porter thanked his stars "she had not been used as she might have been and driven us all out of the river . . . It was only owing to the circumstances that the *Louisiana* . . . could only move about in tow of another vessel, that a disaster did not befall the Union fleet . . . It can be easily imagined what terrible havoc such a vessel would have made among a lot of wooden vessels had her motive power been in order." Shortly after the capture of New Orleans, Porter wrote Fox: "I shake a little now when I think how near we came to being defeated. *One* day's more delay and the game would have been blocked on us. They would have put the *Louisiana* in the only narrow channel where the ships had to pass, and she would have sunk everything that came up unless we could have put some bombs through her. She was a most formidable vessel of over 4,000 tons, and in every respect superior to the *Merrimac*. Her battery was fearful."

Upon the *Mississippi*, more powerful than the *Louisiana*, Secretary Mallory depended to raise the blockade of every southern port within ten days after her completion. That the *Mississippi* may have done so, there is ample evidence from competent witnesses. "Had she been completed in time," wrote a Confederate naval officer, "she would have been a bull in a china shop among Admiral Farragut's light wooden sloops-of-war." And Farragut himself in his report said that "the *Mississippi* . . . was to be the terror of the Seas, and no doubt would have been . . ."

Two Union naval historians, Charles B. Boynton, who wrote in 1868, and James Russell Soley, who wrote in 1903, do not minimize the possible disaster to Farragut's fleet had either the *Mississippi* or the *Louisiana* been ready for action. "Had the *Louisiana*, with her armament and armor, been properly manned, equipped, and propelled so as to equal or exceed in speed Farragut's ships, nothing but a miracle would have saved him from serious loss," declared Soley. And Boynton, discussing the *Mississippi*, said: "The rebels fully believed, and apparently with reason, that this iron-clad would not only destroy, or drive out of the river, Farragut's fleet, but that she was able to paralyze our whole wooden Navy, and lay our Atlantic cities under contribution. She was nearly ready for her work. . . ."[12]

The implication is clear in all the testimony concerning the Confederate ironclads that, had either been finished, not only would New Orleans have been saved but Farragut's wooden fleet would have been shattered. Had both been finished, this would have been doubly true. The great tragedy of the Confederacy was the failure to have the *Louisiana* and *Mississippi* completed by the time Farragut launched his attack.

Jefferson Davis realized this after the war. In prison conversations with Dr. John J. Craven shortly after the collapse of the Confederacy, Davis conceded that "the capture of New Orleans was a great calamity to his cause, but mainly injurious from its sacrifice of the . . . iron-clads . . ."[13]

5. It meant the loss to the South of the Leeds Foundry and other New Orleans machine shops which had been converted to war work. J. W. Mallett, Confederate ordnance expert, later declared that losing the Leeds Foundry, which with the Tredegar Works in Richmond constituted the Confederacy's only first-class foundries, "was one of the sorest consequences of the fall of that city."[14]

6. It meant the loss for the rest of the war of New Orleans as a port of entry for war material and supplies from Europe. While it is true that New Orleans had been closed by the blockade for almost a year before its fall, had the *Mississippi* and *Louisiana* been completed and raised the blockade, New Orleans would have boomed

again commercially and the Confederacy would have been able to convert its cotton into war materials from abroad, either directly or by way of Havana.

7. It was a severe blow to southern morale and it weakened confidence in the southern leadership.

8. It meant a great boost in Union morale and weakened the peace party in the North.

One may well ask, on adding up these consequences, some immediate, some eventual, whether the night that Flag Officer Farragut passed Forts Jackson and St. Philip was not, indeed, "the night the war was lost" by the Confederacy.

The implications of a defeat of Farragut at Forts Jackson and St. Philip would have been far-reaching. Starting from that premise, it is logical to assume that the Confederate armies in the West, supported by the ironclads on the Mississippi, would have swung from the defensive to the offensive and swept up the Mississippi Valley even as Grant swept down.

Suppose, then, in the early summer of 1862, a Confederacy with its ports reopened and commerce restored and material and supplies from abroad flowing in.

Suppose, then, a South assured of an endless supply of Texas beef to feed the armies in the field and the people on the home front and an inexhaustible supply of Louisiana salt.

Suppose, then, New Orleans as a great arsenal, with its powder mills turning out huge quantities of powder, its ammunition factories producing ammunition, its foundries and machine shops casting cannon and shells and manufacturing small arms.

Suppose, then, New Orleans as a vast shipyard, which it was about to become when it fell, building ironclad warships for operations on the inland waters as well as on the sea.

Suppose all this, then, in the light of subsequent events in Virginia —McClellan's failure before Richmond—and it is not illogical to assume that the Confederacy would have seized the psychological initiative, as well as the tactical one, and probably would have gained recognition of its independence by England or France or by both.

Why did New Orleans fall? And who was to blame?

General Lovell gave three reasons in his official report:

"1st. The want of sufficient number of guns of heavy caliber which every exertion was made to procure without success;

"2d. The unprecedented high water, which swept away the obstructions upon which I mainly relied, in connection with the forts, to prevent the passage of a steam fleet up the river; and

"3d. The failure, through inefficiency, and want of energy of those who had charge of the construction of the iron-clad steamers *Louisiana* and *Mississippi* to have them completed in the time specified so as to supply the place of obstruction; and finally the declension of the officers in charge of the *Louisiana* to allow her, though not entirely ready, to be placed as a battery in the position indicated by General Duncan and myself."

General Duncan blamed the loss of New Orleans on "the sheer result of that lack of cheerful and hearty cooperation from the defense afloat . . . and to the criminal negligence of not lighting up the river at night when the danger was imminent . . ."

Colonel Higgins was no less critical of the Navy, "whose neglect of our urgent entreaties to light up the river during this sad night contributed so much to the success of our enemies."[15]

It may be argued that Lovell, Duncan, and Higgins, being principals in the case, were naturally prejudiced witnesses in their own behalf. The same cannot be said, however, of General Viscount Wolseley, who was adjutant general of the British Army in the 1880s and a student of the Civil War. His evaluation of the New Orleans campaign will, of course, be free from bias. Writing in the *North American Review*, upon the occasion of the publication of the second volume of *Battles and Leaders*, Lord Wolseley said:

> . . . As always in war, Farragut's success was almost purely the result of the moral effect which his movement produced, and of defects other than material in the force opposed to him. It is clear that there was a complete want of unity of command over the combined naval and military defences for the protection of New Orleans . . . I do not think . . . it is

possible to read the correspondence which passed between Captain Mitchell and General Duncan without feeling that Captain Mitchell was one of those men, common enough in every service, who cannot bring themselves to imagine that anyone outside their own particular calling is other than a stupid fool. Such men usually conceive it to be their first duty to ignore, as an impertinent interference, any suggestion which comes from outside their own charmed circle . . . General Duncan saw through the intentions of Admiral Farragut, but his correct anticipation that the attempt would be made the night it was actually made was [in Mitchell's mind] an absurd landman's guess about matters he was not calculated to express any useful opinion upon. His views were, therefore, contemptuously ignored.

Had Captain Mitchell been a man large-minded enough to rise above paltry professional prejudices, he would not have continued to expend all his energies on preparing the *Louisiana* for a service she was never called upon to perform. But he would, on the other hand, have kept "the river well lit up with fire rafts," as he was again and again urged to do.

. . . It seems clear that Admiral Farragut's splendid achievement was made possible, first, by the inadequate previous preparation of the naval part of the New Orleans defences; secondly, by the want of harmonious working between the Confederate naval and military forces; and, lastly, by his own clear appreciation of the moral effect he would produce by forcing his way past the defences of Fort Jackson and Fort St. Philip and by his appearance before New Orleans.

The historian of the Confederate Navy, J. Thomas Scharf, himself a young officer during the war, basically agrees with Lord Wolseley that the "divided command at New Orleans . . . hindered and embarrassed the fighting capacity of both arms when the hour came which needed all the efforts of each."[16]

These professional opinions clearly indicate that the divided command at New Orleans was a vital factor in its fall. But just how divided the command really was is perhaps not generally appreciated.

Lovell asked for and was refused full command at New Orleans at the time of his assignment in October 1861, and several times made reference to it in his correspondence with the War Department. He closed his official report on the fall of the city on this same note: "I had frequent occasions to regret that it was found impossible to give me control of the defences afloat as well as ashore. A single controlling head might have made all the resources more available and efficient in working out the desired results."

While Lovell was responsible for the defense of Department No. 1, he could not control one of the principal means of defense, the Navy. But the diversity of command did not stop there. Commander Whittle, as commander of the naval station at New Orleans, had no command over the Navy afloat. And that "anomalous inefficient and useless" River Defense Fleet, organized by the War Department, refused to take orders from the Navy, under whom Lovell placed it. Then there was the case of the Tift brothers, builders of the *Mississippi*, who were responsible only to Secretary of Navy Mallory. Accordingly, General Lovell had no control over the progress of the ironclads, nor did Commander Whittle.[17]

It was one of the strangest defense organizations ever conceived, an incredible hodgepodge set up to defend the South's greatest city. Against it was sent a unified, determined, well-trained, and well-disciplined naval force under an indomitable fighting man whose infectious confidence was matched by a scrupulous attention to every detail upon which success or failure hinged.

Richmond's astonishing lack of comprehension of the situation at New Orleans was influenced no doubt by Mallory's obsession, which President Davis seemed to share, that the Federal fleet up the river—although hundreds of miles away—posed a greater threat to the city than Farragut's vessels less than eighty miles downstream. But how can one explain Mallory's assignment to New Orleans of three top-rank naval officers—Whittle, Mitchell, and Sinclair—who had never been to New Orleans before and knew absolutely nothing about the Mississippi River?[18] And how, with Farragut about to strike, the Navy Department could order out of New Orleans such a fighter as Flag Officer Hollins, who had asked authority to bring his vessels down the river to attack the Federal fleet, is inconceivable. Hollins was old, but he was full of energy. Yet when he telegraphed Mallory to let him strike a blow below the forts, his reply was an order to come immediately to Richmond to sit on a board to process midshipmen!

Next to the divided command as a primary cause of the fall of the city comes the Richmond government's utter lack of appreciation of the realities of the situation at New Orleans. But these were not the only reasons. Others that come to mind are: not disputing Farragut's crossing the bar at the mouth of the river; the slow work on the *Louisiana* and *Mississippi*, both of which had been promised for January; failure to defend the barrier with gunboats; failure of vessels to attack the mortar flotilla, which pounded Fort Jackson almost without opposition; Louisiana's failure to vote funds for state-constructed ironclads; the stripping of the city to reinforce Albert Sidney Johnston; apathy in New Orleans; and the already mentioned failure of the Navy to co-operate at the forts with the *Louisiana* and with fire rafts.

One is compelled to place the major blame for the fall of New Orleans squarely upon the Richmond government. It wasn't until four months after secession that a general officer was assigned to New Orleans, and then it was gouty old General Twiggs, in his seventy-second year. Twiggs, overwhelmed by infirmity and the multiplicity of things to be done, did nothing. When General Lovell arrived in New Orleans in October, he took over a desperate situation, so chaotic that he was reluctant to commit it to paper to President Davis or Secretary of War Benjamin. By working day and night, Lovell managed to create order out of confusion. What he did, he recalled in a letter to the *Delta*, written in New Orleans on April 29, after the paper had blamed the fall of the city on "the lack of energy and earnestness on the part of the agents of the Confederate Government."

This includes me in its sweep, and I think unjustly [Lovell wrote]. When I came here a few shorts months since, I found the State completely defenseless; its ports blockaded, and its young men gone to other parts of the Confederacy in the army. Without anything but what was created, every inlet was put in position to offer a protracted and gallant defense. Forts were armed, powder and munitions of every description were made, and a gallant body of troops organized and drilled. Guns were cast and materials of all kinds extemporized by incessant labor and activity. The river at the forts was twice bridged by obstructions which would have resisted anything but the formidable rush of the great Mississippi in its swollen wrath.

My troops, at the call of their country, rushed to Corinth, and the deeds of Louisiana regiments on the 6th and 7th of April, indicated their courage and their training. Our foundries were beginning to turn out heavy guns of the best quality, and a newly erected arsenal furnished us with various implements of war. All this has been done since October, besides preparing sixteen vessels for river defense, eight of which are now defending the upper river, and eight have been destroyed in the vain attempt to keep back the enemy's fleet of war vessels below . . . With no host of generals and staff officers of experience . . . almost alone, with but few exceptions, I have worked day and night, for more than five months, to defend this great city. The responsibility of its fall is not due to any want of "energy or earnestness" on my part . . .

An examination of my letter and order books and telegraphic dispatches will show that no stone has been left unturned by me to save New Orleans from this humiliation. . . . All I ask is simple justice and nothing more . . .[19]

Naturally, General Lovell could not expect justice from the people of New Orleans, certainly not immediately, while emotions were high and the feeling of betrayal was shared by so many persons. "We have been betrayed," Mrs. Bragg wrote General Bragg. "We have been sold, treacherously sold, by those whom we always thought staunch friends of the Confederacy," wrote Mrs. Mary Newman to her sister. "A pitiful affair it has been," recorded Julia LeGrand in her diary. "In the first place, Lovell, a most worthless creature, was sent here by Davis to superintend the defense of the city. He did little or nothing and the little he did was wrong . . ."[20]

These quotations suffice to show the temper of the people, who understandably, in their bitter state of frustration, looked for a scapegoat. And Lovell, as the commanding general at New Orleans, was the logical person against whom the unknowing or the unthinking directed their anger.

Yet things should have been different in Richmond, where President Davis and his War Department had been kept informed of the situation in New Orleans, but they apparently chose not to believe things were as bad as General Lovell and Governor Moore painted them. Davis' most recent biographer, Hudson Strode, states that the President "on Lovell's conduct . . . reserved his opinion."[21] The record is clear that Mr. Davis did no such thing. He deliberately permitted Lovell to be crucified during the rest of the war. And in his writings, after the war, Mr. Davis resorted to an unbecoming distortion of facts to detach himself and his Cabinet from any culpability in the fall of New Orleans.

On May 2, 1862, General Lovell asked for a court of inquiry into his conduct at New Orleans "as an act of justice to myself and officers, as well as to vindicate the truth of history." President Davis did absolutely nothing about it for months, although common courtesy, independent of justice, demanded that a general officer's request for an inquiry into his professional capabilities receive immediate action.[22] In mid-June General Lovell learned from William McKendree Gwin, former senator from California, that President Davis had told him in the presence of others that Lovell had not kept the government at Richmond informed of the danger to New Orleans—and that had Lovell done so, he, President Davis, would have taken prompt measures to prevent the catastrophe. Lovell made sure that Senator Gwin was not mistaken as to what President Davis had said, and then he showed him the official correspondence.

"The latter was amazed, by this direct proof, that Mr. Davis had perverted the facts," wrote Lovell's friend, West Point classmate, and engineering colleague Gustavus Smith.

The next day, Lovell wrote Davis that "the War Department could not certainly have communicated to you the information contained in my letters." He said that he was willing to "bide the storm of popular clamor" rather than make public "the weakness and straitened means of the Government," but confident that he could vindicate himself, he had asked for an investigation "that I might stand in the right light before the country and to prevent my usefulness from being impaired by a want of popular confidence. This request has never elicited a reply."[23]

J. B. Jones, clerk in the War Department, recorded in his diary shortly after this a particularly significant entry which appears to reflect the official thinking in Richmond. Under date of June 25, 1862, he wrote: "The people of Louisiana are protesting strongly against permitting Gen. Lovell to remain in command in that state since the fall of New Orleans . . . and they attribute that disgraceful event, some to his incompetency, and others to treason. These remonstrances come from such influential parties, I think the President must listen to them. Yes, a Massachusetts man (they say Gen. L. came from Boston) was in command of the troops of New Orleans when that great city surrendered without firing a gun. And this is one of the Northern generals who came over to our side after the battle of Manassas."[24]

Lovell was removed from his command shortly after this and not reassigned by Richmond. And still the court of inquiry which he sought was not empaneled. On January 27, Lovell, then in Richmond, wrote to President Davis: "I have the honor to request that the consideration of my case be not permitted to escape your mind. It is now two months since I was relieved from my duty in Mississippi to await the action of a court of inquiry, and it would be a source of great satisfaction to me to have this matter (so long held in suspense) finally settled." Almost nine months had elapsed since Lovell requested the court of inquiry, and still President Davis had not made a move to do the general justice.

Finally, Lovell applied to a friend in the Confederate Congress to have the official correspondence between himself and the government called for. On February 8, 1863, such a resolution was passed in the House of Representatives. This had the desired effect, for ten days later the court of inquiry was ordered.

On April 4, 1863, eleven months and two days after Lovell had requested it, the court of inquiry was sworn in at Jackson, Mississippi, consisting of Major General T. C. Hindman, Brigadier General T. F. Drayton, and Brigadier General W. M. Gardner, with Major L. R. Page as judge advocate. It sat until July 9, 1863, when it handed down an opinion, which but for two minor criticisms— Lovell's failure to inform the War Department of the insecurity of the raft and of its subsequent breaking and his failure to give proper orders for the evacuation of troops from Chalmette—gave General Lovell a clean bill of health. "General Lovell," the opinion concluded, "displayed great energy and an untiring industry in performing his duties. His conduct was marked by all the coolness and self-possession due to the circumstances and his position, and he evinced a high capacity for command and the clearest foresight in many of his measures for the defense of New Orleans."

To anyone in Richmond who had read Lovell's correspondence with the War Department with an unprejudiced eye, the court of inquiry's findings should have come as no surprise. Robert G. H. Kean, head of the Bureau of War, wrote in his diary on August 23, 1863: "Major Barton tells me that Lovell's vindication before the New Orleans court of inquiry was complete; that he comes off with flying colors. Barton made an abstract of the record for the President recently. The finding has not yet been promulgated. Lovell shows well in the correspondence with the War Department, which I had made up . . ."

But there were some in Richmond to whom the court's finding meant nothing. General Josiah Gorgas, Confederate chief of ordnance, in advance refused vindication to Lovell. In his diary for June 16, 1863, Gorgas wrote: "A dozen courts of inquiry could not reinstate him in popular estimation, or my own. He was unfit for his position." One may wonder if General Gorgas had forgotten his reply to Lovell's urgent call, on November 25, 1861, for mortars and columbiads: "No mortars or columbiads to spare at present." Or his telegrams to Lovell on December 17, 1861, and January 1, 1862, urging that a total of twenty-two 32-pounder guns be sent by Lovell to General Albert Sidney Johnston.[25]

Although the court of inquiry's report was filed with the War Department on July 13, 1863, neither the Secretary of War nor President Davis felt any obligation to promulgate its findings that vindicated Lovell. On October 3, 1863, General Lovell himself was in the dark, at least officially, for he wrote Adjutant General Samuel Cooper on that day:

"As it is now nearly three months since the court of inquiry in my case terminated its proceedings, I trust that I shall not be considered impatient in asking you to inform us of the findings and opinion of the court. I am very desirous of being assigned to duty."

It was not until a month later, in November, that the court of inquiry's findings were published, and they omitted to state that the court had been asked for by General Lovell. "Such omission is understood to imply that the subordinate had not asked for investigation," commented Gustavus Smith, "and that the proceedings in the case had been initiated by the Government."[26]

In the meantime, although General Joseph E. Johnston had asked repeatedly that Lovell be assigned to him, he was still without assignment on May 5, 1864, more than two years after he had asked for an investigation of his conduct. On that day, Lovell wrote the Secretary of War, reviewing his case:

> . . . After the publication of the opinion of that Court exonerating me from blame for the loss of New Orleans, I was entitled not only by the custom of miltary service but as an act of justice, to be restored to the command from which I had been relieved. Nearly six months, however, have elapsed since that time; but, notwithstanding my personal application for duty, and the request of the distinguished commander of one of our armies to have my services with him in the field, I still remain without a command, although during that time

twelve assignments of major-generals have been made, four of them by promotion. By this declension to restore me to duty I am virtually tried, condemned, and punished by a suspension of command, after a court of inquiry composed of three general officers detailed by the Department, has pronounced an opinion under which, according to military usage, I should at once have been placed again in position. The effect of this course of action is to impair my reputation in the eyes of the country at large, and under the circumstances there is no redress other than an appeal to the usages of military service and the sense of justice of the administration. This appeal I now make, and ask your action thereon at the earliest moment that your official convenience will allow.

Gustavus Smith, who defended Lovell ably and vigorously was bitter, and justifiably so, at President Davis' treatment of Lovell. He wrote:

"His appeal availed nothing with a Government which was fully cognizant of all the important facts at the time they occurred . . . the Government that had knowingly permitted the unjust hue and cry to prevail against him unchecked for nearly a year before granting his application for an investigation—then unnecessarily delayed the promulgation of the opinion of the court for four or five months —and withheld the evidence and proceedings in the case until the 8th of June, 1864—and, at that late date, made the facts public only in response to a resolution in the House of Representatives."

Lovell, meantime, had served as a volunteer aide to General Joe Johnston and later offered his services to the governor of South Carolina. Finally, in February 1865, Lovell got an assignment. General Johnston, in a letter after the war, reminded Lovell why he got it:

I regret very much that you have mislaid my letter to which you refer. It was written soon after the middle of summer of 1862, when I had had abundant opportunity to learn the circumstances of the fall of New Orleans. I expressed in it, as distinctly as I could, the opinion that you had made the best arrangements and preparations practicable, for the defense of the place. And that but for the removal by higher authority, of the means of defenses prepared by you, the chances of success would have been on our side.

The letter in question is not the strongest evidence I have given, of confidence in your military qualities. In Dec. 17, 1862, I applied to the President personally for your restoration to your grade in the Army of Miss.—claiming that you had been regarded in that army, in which you had recently held an important command, as the best of its several officers. When assigned to the command of the Army of Tennessee, a year later, I urged your assignment to that army—to command a corps. And when called again into service at the end of February, 1865, I again asked your restoration to command to serve with me. Only the last of these applications was successful. It was so, I suppose, because referred to Genl. Lee—who, as general-in-chief, then had power to decide it.[27]

It is significant that as soon as Robert E. Lee had anything to do with Lovell's assignment, it went through. For General Lee, at the time of the fall of New Orleans, had written Lovell twice, commending his conduct in defense of the city. On May 8, 1862, General Lee wrote: "The loss of the city is a very severe blow to us, and one that we cannot fail to feel most sensibly, but it is believed that with the means of defense at your disposal you have done all in your power." And on May 24, 1862, Lee wrote Lovell: "My reply to your former communication will have made known to you the opinion I entertain of your course in evacuating New Orleans. That opinion is confirmed by the additional particulars contained in your letter just received. After the enemy succeeded in passing the forts it seemed there was nothing left for you to do but to withdraw the troops. I think you may confidently rely upon the judgment of intelligent and reflecting men for this justification of your course as soon as the facts, as they actually existed, shall be known."[28]

But General Lee reckoned without the vindictiveness of Jefferson Davis, who took good care that "the facts, as they actually existed," were not known until almost the end of the war. And, in his postwar writing, President Davis brushed hastily past the facts, putting into print what the generous would call half-truths, and the more precise, deliberate distortions. A few examples will suffice to demonstrate this:

Davis: "New Orleans was the most important commercial port in the Confederacy . . . Its defense attracted the early attention of the Confederate Government."

Fact: The war began with the firing on Fort Sumter on April 12, 1861. On September 20, 1861, Governor Thomas O. Moore of Louisiana wrote President Davis "asking only that this city, the most important to be preserved of any in the Confederacy, and our coast, the most exposed of all the States, be no longer neglected." Again, on September 29, 1861, Governor Moore wrote Davis: "The defense of this state [requires] immediate attention, and . . . energetic measures should be taken to protect New Orleans from an attack from the enemy, and . . . the General Government should extend to us protection at this particular crisis . . ."[29]

Davis: "In the early part of 1862, so general an opinion prevailed that the greatest danger to New Orleans was by an attack from above, that General Lovell sent to General Beauregard a large part of the troops then in that city."

Fact: Mr. Davis did not say that General Lovell sent his troops to Beauregard only after receiving official orders from Richmond and against his protestation, to wit:

[Feb. 27] People are beginning to complain that I have stripped the department . . .

[March 6] This department is being completely drained . . . We have filled requisitions for arms, men, and munitions until New Orleans is about defenseless . . .

[March 9] This department has been completely stripped of every organized body of troops . . . Persons are found here

who assert that I am sending away all troops so that the city may fall an easy prey to the enemy.[30]

Davis: ". . . An inferior fleet might have engaged them [Farragut's fleet at the mouth of the Mississippi] with a prospect of success. Captain Hollins, who was in command of the squadron at New Orleans, and who had on a former occasion shown his fitness for such service, had been sent with the greater part of his fleet up the river to join the defense there being made . . . A volunteer fleet of transport-vessels had been fitted up by some river-men, but it was in the unfortunate condition of not being placed under the orders of the naval commander."

Fact: Mr. Davis did not explain that there was no "inferior fleet" to challenge Farragut because both he and Mallory considered the Union fleet up the river more dangerous than the one in the Gulf. Nor does he state that General Lovell protested this, as he did on March 6, 1862: "I hope the Secretary of the Navy will keep at least one vessel here to prevent the enemy from making reconnaissance under our very guns." Or as he did on March 10, 1862: "The enemy's fleet [is] collecting and beginning to enter the mouths of the river with boldness . . . The fleet threatening us below is much more formidable than that above, and I object strongly to sending every armed vessel away from New Orleans at this time. This city has been already too much weakened." Hollins, in his testimony before the Lovell court of inquiry, said: "I left no naval force at New Orleans. General Lovell urged me to leave some of the vessels there, but this I could not do, as my orders from the Navy Department were to take them all above." And as to the River Defense Fleet being "in the unfortunate condition of not being placed under the orders of the naval commander," why did not Mr. Davis frankly state that Congress put $1,000,000 at his disposal for defense of the western rivers, to be allotted by him to either the War or Navy Department at his discretion, and that he chose the War Department and that the fleet was outfitted with the complete understanding it would not take orders from the Navy?[31]

Davis: "On the 23rd of April, 1862, General Lovell . . . had gone down to Fort Jackson . . . The presence of the department commander did not avail to secure the full cooperation between the defenses afloat and the land-defenses, which was then of most pressing and immediate necessity."

Fact: Mr. Davis did not state that General Lovell, on his appointment to the New Orleans command, had asked for command of the forces afloat and that he had been refused it by the President.[32]

Davis: "The fall of New Orleans was a great disaster, over which there was general lamentation, mingled with no little indignation. The excited feeling demanded a victim, and conflicting testimony of many witnesses most nearly concerned made it convenient to select for censure those most removed and least active in their justification. Thus the naval constructors of the *Mississippi* and the Secretary of the Navy became the special objects of attack. The selection of these had little of justice in it, and could not serve to relieve others of their responsibility, as did the old-time doom of the scapegoat."[33]

Fact: A court of inquiry, selected by, or with the consent of, President Davis, fully exonerated General Lovell of blame for the fall of New Orleans. Yet Davis patently attempts to screen himself by stating that criticism of his administration could not "relieve others of their responsibility." What others? The implication unquestionably is that he means General Lovell. And nowhere in Mr. Davis' Rise and Fall of the Confederate Government is there any hint that a court of inquiry investigating the fall of New Orleans found Lovell blameless.

One may wonder whether Davis' utterly unjust treatment of General Lovell did not stem from the consciousness that the responsibility for the fall of New Orleans rested squarely at the door of the President of the Confederacy and his Cabinet.

After the war, General Lovell tried his hand as a planter in South Carolina, but a crop failure wiped him out and he returned to New York, where he practiced civil engineering. He died on June 1,

1884, after a short but painful illness. The *Picayune*, editorializing on his death, called General Lovell a "gallant soldier and popular gentleman" and declared that the fall of New Orleans "unjustly clouded Lovell's fame, and indeed he seems to have been made the scapegoat for the sins of others on that memorable occasion."[34]

General Duncan, after his exchange in August 1862, was assigned to Withers' division in General Leonidas Polk's corps and two months later he relieved Withers. In November 1862, he served with General Joe Johnston and then joined General Braxton Bragg as his chief of staff. Shortly thereafter, on December 18, 1862, General Duncan died of typhoid fever at Knoxville. A general order proclaimed him "among the brightest and bravest spirits of the many who have given their lives to the holy cause of Freedom." And a resolution passed by the Louisiana Regular Artillery called Duncan one of the Confederacy's "most able, gallant and efficient generals."[35]

The Tift brothers, after a threat of lynching at Vicksburg, returned to Georgia, where they continued building ships for the Confederacy. The chief criticism that may be directed at the Tifts is their misplaced confidence that they had plenty of time to complete the *Mississippi*. At the moment when time was all important, they dawdled.

Flag Officer Farragut went on to other great exploits, at Vicksburg, Port Hudson, and Mobile Bay, and Commander Porter played an important part throughout the rest of the war on the western waters.

As for General Ben Butler, he ruled New Orleans with a ruthlessness that won for him unendearing names. Archibald Mitchell, who started a diary on July 4, 1862, summed up the first two months of the Federal occupation of New Orleans:

"To no mind at a distance from this scene can be conveyed an adequate conception of the degradation, & humiliations to which we have been exposed. The tyrannies of Nero pale before the brutal murderous, & insignificant acts of . . . the unprincipled political hack and pettyfogger who now reigns uncontrolled over us."[36]

These comments, typical of people of New Orleans and the Confederacy, do little justice to Ben Butler. But for that matter, they are no harsher words than those used by David Dixon Porter, who considered Butler a "spoon lifter and a plate stealer," and who said: "Had the General lived in the time of Napoleon 1st, Fouché would not have been the chief of police."[37]

☆ ☆ ☆ ☆ ☆

Sources and Bibliography

IN PREPARING THIS BOOK, MANY THOUSANDS OF MANUSCRIPT PAGES WERE examined, some in the original, some in photostat, some on microfilm, and hundreds of books, pamphlets, and periodicals were perused. Files of the New Orleans newspapers, and others, were read, page by page, with considerable profit.

The following list of sources and bibliography includes only those items which were specifically drawn upon or which supplied useful background information:

I MANUSCRIPTS

LIBRARY OF CONGRESS:

Benjamin F. Butler Papers
Blair Papers (Mrs. Virginia Woodbury Fox Diary)
David Dixon Porter Papers
Gideon Welles Papers
Diary of Oscar Smith
James M. Mason Papers
Pickett Papers (Confederate Diplomatic Correspondence)
Mansfield Lovell Papers (scattered postwar letters received)
George B. McClellan Papers
Confederate Naval Collection

NATIONAL ARCHIVES:
Naval Records Collection of the Office of Naval Records and Library, specifically: Record Group 45; Record Group 74
Confederate Naval Records
Confederate Army Records, specifically: Record Group 109

LOUISIANA STATE UNIVERSITY ARCHIVES:
Clara E. Solomon Diary
Grace King Notebook
Zoe Campbell Diary
Thomas O. Moore Papers
Lewis Guion Diary
James Durnin Papers
Thomas Butler Papers
Alonzo Snyder Papers
Rosella Kenner Brent, Recollections (typescript)

TULANE UNIVERSITY ARCHIVES:
Jefferson Davis Papers, in Louisiana Historical Association Collection
Fisk-Urquhart Papers
Col. George Soulé Scrapbook
War Record of Gen'l St. John R. Liddell (manuscript and typescript), in Louisiana Historical Association Collection
Archibald Mitchell Journal

NEW ORLEANS PUBLIC LIBRARY:
Fire and Alarm Telegraph of the City of New Orleans, Record of Messages Received and Sent, 1860–1863

VIRGINIA STATE HISTORICAL SOCIETY (RICHMOND):
John Kirkwood Mitchell Papers

NEW YORK PUBLIC LIBRARY:
Thomas Kelah Wharton Diary
Bartholomew Diggins: Recollections of the Cruise of the U.S.S. Hartford, Admiral Farragut's Flagship in Operations on the Mississippi River, etc.

COOPER UNION (NEW YORK CITY):
Cooper, Hewitt & Co. Correspondence, Book 20

HENRY E. HUNTINGTON LIBRARY AND ART GALLERY:
Miscellaneous letters to, or from, Gideon Welles, Gustavus V. Fox, David G. Farragut, and Mansfield Lovell

Sources and Bibliography

UNIVERSITY OF TEXAS ARCHIVES:
  Bragg Papers

WESTERN RESERVE HISTORICAL SOCIETY (CLEVELAND):
  Bragg Papers, in William P. Palmer Collection

SOUTHERN HISTORICAL COLLECTION, UNIVERSITY OF NORTH CAROLINA, CHAPEL HILL:
  Stephen R. Mallory Journal
  H. W. Wilson Diary: Cruise of the Oneida

PUBLIC RECORD OFFICE, LONDON, ENGLAND:
  Consular reports from New Orleans (1860–62), in *Foreign Office 5.* Microfilm in author's possession. Photostats of some of these reports are available in the Manuscript Division of the Library of Congress.

MISCELLANEOUS:
  Letters of General Johnson K. Duncan and other Duncan papers, in possession of Mrs. Mildred Parham of New Orleans
  Diary of Captain Benjamin Warren, 26th Massachusetts Volunteers, in possession of Richard T. Colquette of Houston, Texas
  Memorandum Book of John Roy, microfilm copies in Howard-Tilton Library, Tulane University Archives, and Department of Archives, Louisiana State University
  English Composition Book, Institut Catholique, in Archives of the Archdiocese of New Orleans

II OFFICIAL RECORDS (Published)

War of the Rebellion: A Compilation of the Official Records of the Union and Confederate Armies. 130 vols. Washington, 1880–1901.

Official Records of the Union and Confederate Navies in the War of the Rebellion. 30 vols. Washington, 1894–1922.

Report of Evidence Taken before a Joint Special Committee of Both Houses of the Confederate Congress to Investigate the Affairs of the Navy Department. P. Kean, reporter. Richmond [1863].

Proceedings of the Common Council of the City of New Orleans, 1861–1862 (compilation of newspaper clippings from official journal). New Orleans Public Library.

Official Journal of the Proceedings of the Convention of the State of Louisiana. New Orleans, 1861.

Eighth Census, 1860.

Report on the Internal Commerce of the United States, by William P. Switzler, Chief of the Bureau of Statistics, Treasury Department. House Exec. Doc. No. 6, Part II, 50th Congress, 1st Session. Washington, 1888.

Executive Documents Printed by Order of the 36th Congress, 1859–1860, Series 49. Washington, 1860.

III   UNPUBLISHED THESES

Unpublished theses and dissertations provided excellent background information on economic, social, political, and military conditions in New Orleans during the period covered in this book. The following, all Master's theses unless otherwise indicated, proved particularly useful:

Barker, Dorothy Many. *An Economic Survey of New Orleans during the Civil War and Reconstruction.* Tulane University, 1942.

Bush, Toxie L. *The Federal Occupation of New Orleans.* Louisiana State University, 1934.

Dubroca, Isabelle C. *A Study of Negro Emancipation in Louisiana.* Tulane University, 1924.

Duchein, Annette O. *The Anglo-Saxon Press of New Orleans, 1835–1861.* Louisiana State University, 1933.

Elliott, Adelaide Francis. *Feeding New Orleans during the Civil War.* Tulane University, 1937.

Everett, Donald Edward. *Free Persons of Color in New Orleans, 1803–1865.* Tulane University, 1952. (Doctoral dissertation.)

Fontenot, Elfa Lavonia. *Social and Economic Life in Louisiana, 1860–1865, as Recorded by Contemporaries.* Louisiana State University, 1933.

Hébert, Mary Alice. *Louisiana Newspapers during the Civil War.* Louisiana State University, 1937.

Herron, Stella. *The Secession Movement in Louisiana, 1850–1861.* Tulane University, 1913.

Highsmith, William Edward. *Louisiana during Reconstruction.* Louisiana State University, 1953. (Doctoral dissertation.)

Sources and Bibliography

Landry, Ernest Adams. *The History of Forts Jackson and St. Philip with Special Emphasis on the Civil War Period*. Louisiana State University, 1938.

Leland, Edward A. *Organization and Administration of the Louisiana Army during the Civil War*. Louisiana State University, 1938.

Lightfoot, Marjorie Joffron. *Social Life in New Orleans during the Civil War*. Louisiana State University, 1939.

Lowery, Walter McGehee. *Navigational Problems at the Mouth of the Mississippi River, 1698–1880*. Vanderbilt University, 1956. (Doctoral dissertation.)

Marks, Janey. *The Industrial Development of New Orleans since 1865*. Tulane University, 1924.

Merrill, John Calhoun. *Louisiana Public Opinion on Secession, 1859–1860*. Louisiana State University, 1950.

Neill, John Hamilton, Jr. *Shipbuilding in Confederate New Orleans*. Tulane University, 1940.

Porter, Alice Theresa. *An Economic View of Ante-Bellum New Orleans, 1845–1860*. Tulane University, 1942.

Taylor, Ethel Harris. *Discontent in Confederate Louisiana: A Study of Attitudes*. Northwestern State College of Louisiana, 1958.

White, J. Arthur. *The Port of New Orleans since 1850*. Tulane University, 1924.

Winter, John David. *Confederate New Orleans, 1860–1861*. Louisiana State University, 1947.

IV NEWSPAPERS

Public opinion in New Orleans and the course of events there, and elsewhere, were followed in these newspapers:

NEW ORLEANS:
New Orleans Bee
Daily Crescent
Commercial Bulletin
Daily Delta
True Delta
Daily Picayune

New Orleans Price Current, Commercial Intelligencer and Merchants'
Transcript

NEW YORK:
Tribune

WASHINGTON:
National Intelligencer

LONDON:
The Times
Illustrated London News

V   PERIODICALS

Articles in the following periodicals proved valuable:
Civil War History
Confederate Veteran
Continental Magazine
De Bow's Review
Edinburgh Review
Fred Leslie's Illustrated Weekly Newspaper
Galaxy, An Illustrated Magazine of Interesting Reading
Harper's New Monthly Magazine
Journal of the Royal Service Institution
Louisiana Historical Quarterly
Magazine of American History
North American Review
Southern Historical Society Papers
Southwest Review
United Service: A Monthly Review of Military and Naval Affairs
United States Naval Institute Proceedings

VI   BOOKS AND ARTICLES

Aldis, Owen, P. "Louis Napoleon and the Southern Confederacy," *North American Review*, Vol. CXXIX (Oct. 1879).

"The American Navy in the Late War," unsigned article in *Edinburgh Review*, No. 124 (July 1866).

Anderson, John Q. (ed.). *Brokenburn, The Journal of Kate Stone, 1861–1868.* Baton Rouge, 1955.

Bacon, George B. "One Night's Work, April 20, 1862; Breaking the Chain for Farragut's Fleet at the Forts Below New Orleans," *Magazine of American History*, Vol. XV (1886).

Belknap, George E. (ed.). *Letters of Captain George Hamilton Perkins, USN*. Concord, N.H., 1901.

Biographical and Historical Memoirs of Louisiana. 2 vols. Chicago, 1892.

Blair, Montgomery. "Opening the Mississippi," *United Service*, Vol. IV (Jan. 1881).

Bonham, Milledge L., Jr. "The British Consuls in the Confederacy," in *Columbia University Studies in History, Economics and Public Law*, Vol. XLIII, No. 3 (Whole No. 111). New York, 1911.

——. "Louisiana's Seizure of the Federal Arsenal at Baton Rouge, January, 1861," *The Historical Society of East and West Baton Rouge Proceedings*, Vol. II (1917–18), 47–55.

Boynton, Charles B. *The History of the Navy during the Rebellion*. 2 vols. New York, 1867.

Bragg, Jefferson Davis. *Louisiana in the Confederacy*. Baton Rouge, 1941.

Brown, George W. "The Mortar Flotilla," in *Personal Recollections of the War of the Rebellion* (New York Commandery, Military Order of the Loyal Legion). New York, 1891.

Bruce, Robert V. *Lincoln and the Tools of War*. Indianapolis and New York, 1956.

Bulloch, James D. *The Secret Service of the Confederate States in Europe, or How the Confederate Cruisers Were Equipped*. 2 vols. 1884.

Butler, Benjamin Franklin. *Butler's Book: Autobiography and Personal Reminiscences* . . . Boston, 1892.

——. *Private and Official Correspondence of General Benjamin F. Butler during the Period of the Civil War*. 5 vols. Privately issued, 1917.

Cable, G. W. (ed.). "War Diary of a Union Woman in the South," in *Famous Adventures and Prison Escapes of the Civil War*. New York, 1893.

——. "New Orleans Before the Capture," in *Battles and Leaders of the Civil War*, Vol. II. 4 vols. New York, 1887.

Callahan, James Morton. *The Diplomatic History of the Southern Confederacy.* Baltimore, 1901.

Caskey, Willie Marvin. *Secession and Restoration of Louisiana.* Baton Rouge, 1938.

Chestnut, Mary Boykin. *A Diary from Dixie* (edited by Ben Ames Williams). Boston, 1949.

Childs, Arney Robinson (ed.). *The Private Journal of Henry William Ravenal, 1859–1887.* Columbia, S.C., 1947.

Clark, H. C. (compiler). *The Confederate Almanac, and Repository of Useful Knowledge for 1862.* Vicksburg, 1861.

Clary, Francis A. *The Color Bearer.* New York, 1863.

Craven, John J. *Prison Life of Jefferson Davis.* New York, 1866.

Dale, Edward Everett. *The Range Cattle Industry.* Norman, Okla., 1930.

Davis, Jefferson. *The Rise and Fall of the Confederate Government.* 2 vols. New York, 1881.

——. *A Short History of the Confederate States of America.* New York, 1890.

Dawson, Sarah Morgan. *A Confederate Girl's Diary.* Boston and New York, 1913.

De Forest, John William. *A Volunteer's Adventure, A Union Captain's Record of the Civil War* (edited by James H. Croushore). New Haven, 1946.

Devol, George H. *Forty Years a Gambler on the Mississippi.* Cincinnati, 1887.

Dewey, George. *Autobiography of George Dewey, Admiral of the Navy.* New York, 1913.

Dorsey, Sarah A. *Recollections of Henry Watkins Allen, etc.* New York, 1866.

Dufour, Charles L. *Gentle Tiger, The Gallant Life of Roberdeau Wheat.* Baton Rouge, 1957.

Durkin, Joseph T., S.J. *Stephen R. Mallory: Confederate Navy Chief.* Chapel Hill, N.C., 1954.

Eisenschiml, Otto. *Why the Civil War?* Indianapolis and New York, 1958.

Eliot, Ellsworth, Jr. *West Point in the Confederacy.* New York, 1941.

Farragut, Loyall. *The Life of David Glasgow Farragut. First Admiral of the U. S. Navy.* New York, 1879.

Foltz, Charles S. *Surgeon of the Seas. The Adventurous Life of Surgeon General Jonathan M. Foltz in the Days of Wooden Ships.* Indianapolis, 1931.

Ford, Worthington Chauncey (ed.). *A Cycle of Adams Letters, 1861–1865.* 2 vols. Boston and New York, 1920.

Fuller, Claude E., and Richard D. Steuart. *Firearms of the Confederacy.* Huntington, W. Va., 1944.

Geer, James K. *Louisiana Politics, 1845–1861.* Baton Rouge, 1930.

Gerdes, F. H. "The Surrender of Forts Jackson and St. Philip on the Lower Mississippi," *Continental Magazine,* Vol. III, No. 5 (May 1863).

Gluckman, Col. Arcadi, and L. D. Satterlee. *American Gunmakers.* Harrisburg, Pa., 1953.

Gorgas, Josiah. "Notes on the Ordnance Department of the Confederate Government," in *Southern Historical Society Papers,* Vol. XII, Nos. 1–2 (Jan.–Feb. 1884).

Gosnell, H. Allen. *Guns on the Western Waters. The Story of River Gunboats in the Civil War.* Baton Rouge, 1949.

——. *Rebel Raider, Raphael Semmes's Cruise in the C.S.S. Sumter.* Chapel Hill, N.C., 1948.

Greeley, Horace. *The American Conflict.* 2 vols. Hartford, 1866.

Hall, Mrs. Frances. *Major Hall's Wife.* Syracuse, 1884.

Hall, Winchester. *The Story of the 26th Louisiana Infantry in the Service of the Confederate States.* No date.

Hamilton, Admiral E. V. "Facts Connected with the Naval Operations during the Civil War in the United States," *Journal of the Royal Service Institution,* Vol. XXII (1879).

Harris, T. L. *The Trent Affair.* Indianapolis, 1896.

Hill, Frederic S. *Twenty Years at Sea, or Leaves from My Old Logbooks.* Boston and New York, 1893.

Hill, Jim Dan. *Sea Dogs of the Sixties.* Minneapolis, 1935.

Howard, Perry H. *Political Tendencies in Louisiana, 1812–1952.* Baton Rouge, 1957.

Johnson, Robert Underwood, and Clarence Clough Buel. *Battles and Leaders of the Civil War.* 4 vols. New York, 1887.

Johnson, Thomas Cary. *The Life and Letters of Benjamin Morgan Palmer.* Richmond, 1906.

Jones, J. B. *A Rebel War Clerk's Diary.* 2 vols. Philadelphia, 1866.

Kendall, Lane Carter. "The Interregnum in Louisiana in 1861," *Louisiana Historical Quarterly,* Vol. XVI, Nos. 2, 3, 4; Vol. XVII, Nos. 1, 2, 3 (1933–34).

Lewis, Charles Lee. *David Glasgow Farragut, Our First Admiral.* Annapolis, 1943. (This is Vol. II in a two-volume biography.)

Lonn, Ella. *Salt as a Factor in the Confederacy.* New York, 1933.

Macartney, Clarence Edward. *Mr. Lincoln's Admirals.* New York, 1956.

McBlair, Captain C. H. "Historical Sketch of the Confederate Navy," *United Service,* Vol. III (Nov. 1880).

Maffitt, John N. "Reminiscences of the Confederate Navy," *United Service,* Vol. III (Oct. 1880).

Mahan, Alfred Thayer. *The Gulf and Inland Waters.* New York, 1883.

——. *Admiral Farragut.* New York and London, 1892.

Mallet, J. W. "Work of the Ordnance Bureau of the War Department of the Confederate States, 1861–1865," *Southern Historical Society Papers,* Vol. XXXVII (1909).

Massey, Mary Elizabeth. *Ersatz in the Confederacy.* Columbia, S.C., 1952.

Mearns, David C. (ed.). *The Lincoln Papers.* 2 vols. New York, 1948.

Merrick, Caroline E. *Old Times in Dixie Land, A Southern Matron's Memories.* New York, 1901.

Merrill, James M. *The Rebel Shore, The Story of Union Sea Power in the Civil War.* Boston and Toronto, 1957.

Moore, Frank. *Rebellion Record: A Diary of American Events, etc.* 12 vols. New York, 1864–71.

Morgan, James Morris. *Recollections of a Rebel Reefer*. New York and Boston, 1917.

Nichols, James L. *Confederate Engineers*. Tuscaloosa, Ala., 1957.

Nicolay, John G., and John Hay. *Abraham Lincoln, A History*. 10 vols. New York, 1890.

Nevins, Allan. *Abram S. Hewitt, with Some Account of Peter Cooper*. New York, 1935.

O'Connor, Florence J. *The Heroine of the Confederacy, or Truth and Justice*. London, 1866.

O'Connor, Thomas (ed.). *History of the Fire Department of New Orleans*. New Orleans, c. 1900.

Osbon, B. S. (ed.). *The Cruise of the U.S. Flagship Hartford, 1862–1863 . . . From the Private Journal of William C. Holton*. New York, 1863. Reprinted in *Magazine of American History*, Vol. XXIII, No. 3 (1922), Extra No. 87.

———. *Handbook of the United States Navy, Being a Compilation of All Principal Events in the History of Every Vessel of the United States Navy from April, 1861, to May, 1864*. New York, 1864.

Owen, William Miller. *In Camp and Battle with the Washington Artillery of New Orleans*. Boston, 1885.

Owsley, Frank L. *King Cotton Diplomacy; Foreign Relations of the C.S.A.* Chicago, 1931.

Paine, Albert Bigelow (ed.). *A Sailor of Fortune: Personal Memories of Captain B. S. Osbon*. New York, 1906.

Parks, Rear Admiral (Ret.) W. M. "Building a Warship in the Southern Confederacy," *United States Naval Institute Proceedings*, Vol. LXIX, No. 8 (Aug. 1923).

Parton, James. *General Butler in New Orleans: Being a History of the Department of the Gulf in the Year 1862 . . .* New York, 1863.

Porter, David Dixon. *Incidents and Anecdotes of the Civil War*. New York, 1885.

———. *The Naval History of the Civil War*. New York, 1886.

———. "The Opening of the Lower Mississippi," *Battles and Leaders of the Civil War*, Vol. II. 4 vols. New York, 1887.

Pratt, Fletcher. *Civil War on Western Waters.* New York, 1956.

Preble, G. H. *History of the Flag of the United States.* 3d ed. Boston, 1882.

Rains, George W. *History of the Confederate Powder Works.* Augusta, Ga., 1882.

Randall, James G. *Lincoln the President.* 2 vols. New York, 1945.

Ransom, Commodore George M. "Some Incidents of the Passing of the Forts Jackson and St. Philip," *United Service,* Vol. II (May 1880).

"Reminiscent of War Times, Eventful Days in New Orleans in the Year 1862," *Southern Historical Society Papers,* Vol. XXIII (1895). Reprinted from New Orleans *Picayune,* Dec. 1, 1895.

Report of the Naval Engagements on the Mississippi River Resulting in the Capture of Forts Jackson and St. Philip and the City of New Orleans, and the Destruction of the Rebel Naval Flotilla. Washington, 1862.

Richardson, Albert D. *The Secret Service, The Field, The Dungeon, and the Escape.* Hartford, 1865.

Robinson, William Morrison, Jr. *The Confederate Privateers.* New Haven, 1928.

Roland, Charles P. *Louisiana Sugar Plantations during the American Civil War.* Leiden, Netherlands, 1957.

Rooney, William H. "The First 'Incident' of Secession: Seizure of the New Orleans Marine Hospital," *Louisiana Historical Quarterly,* Vol. XXXIV (April 1951).

Roman, Alfred. *The Military Operations of General Beauregard.* New York, 1884.

Rowland, Dunbar. *Jefferson Davis, Constitutionalist, etc.* 10 vols. Jackson, Miss., 1923.

Rowland, Kate Mason, and Mrs. Morris L. Croxall (eds.). *The Journal of Julia LeGrand—New Orleans, 1862–1863.* Richmond, 1911.

Russell, William Howard. *My Diary North and South.* Boston, 1863.

Scharf, J. Thomas. *History of the Confederate States Navy.* New York, 1887.

Semmes, Raphael. *Memoirs of Service Afloat during the War between the States.* Baltimore, 1869.

Sherman, W. T. *Memoirs of General W. T. Sherman Written by Himself.* 2 vols. New York, 1891.

Shugg, Roger Wallace. *Origins of Class Struggle in Louisiana.* Baton Rouge, 1939.

———. "A Suppressed Cooperationist Protest against Secession," *Louisiana Historical Quarterly,* Vol. XIX (1936).

Smith, Gustavus W. "Mansfield Lovell," *Fifteenth Annual Reunion of the Association of the Graduates of the U. S. Military Academy, 1884.* E. Saginaw, Mich., 1884.

———. *Confederate War Papers.* New York, 1884.

Soley, James Russell. *The Blockade and the Cruisers.* New York, 1883.

———. *Admiral Porter.* New York, 1903.

———. *The Sailor Boys of '61.* Boston, 1888.

Southwood, Marion (A Lady of New Orleans). *"Beauty and Booty": The Watchword of New Orleans.* New York, 1867.

Steuart, Richard D. "How Johnny Got His Gun," *Confederate Veteran,* Vol. XXXII (1924).

Strode, Hudson. *Jefferson Davis, Confederate President.* New York, 1959.

Thompson, Robert Means, and Richard Wainwright (eds.). *Confidential Correspondence of Gustavus Vasa Fox, Assistant Secretary of the Navy, 1861–1865.* 2 vols. New York, 1920.

Trexler, H. A. "The Confederate Navy Department and the Fall of New Orleans," *Southwest Review,* Vol. XIX, No. 1.

Vandiver, Frank E. (ed.). *The Civil War Diary of General Josiah Gorgas.* Tuscaloosa, Ala., 1947.

Villiers, Brougham, and W. H. Cheasson. *Anglo-American Relations, 1861–1865.* London, 1919.

Walker, Jennie Mort. *Life of Captain Joseph Fry, the Cuban Martyr.* Hartford, 1875.

Wallace, Sarah Agnes, and Frances Elma Gillespie (eds.). *The Journal of Benjamin Moran.* 2 vols. Chicago, 1949

Walpole, Spencer. *The Life of Lord John Russell.* 2 vols. London, 1889.

Warner, Ezra J. *Generals in Gray. Lives of the Confederate Commanders.* Baton Rouge, 1959.

Watson, William. *Life in the Confederate Army: Being the Observations and Experiences of an Alien in the South during the American Civil War.* London, 1887.

Welles, Gideon. *Diary of Gideon Welles, Secretary of the Navy under Lincoln and Johnson.* 3 vols. Boston and New York, 1911.

——. "Admiral Farragut and New Orleans," *Galaxy*, Nov. and Dec. 1871.

West, Richard S., Jr. *The Second Admiral: A Life of David Dixon Porter, 1813–1891.* New York, 1937.

——. *Mr. Lincoln's Navy.* New York, London, and Toronto, 1957.

——. *Gideon Welles, Lincoln's Navy Department.* Indianapolis and New York, 1943.

——. "Lincoln's Hand in Naval Matters," *Civil War History*, Vol. IV, No. 2 (June 1958).

——. "The Relations between Farragut and Porter," *United States Naval Institute Proceedings*, Vol. LXI, No. 7 (July 1935).

——. "(Private and Confidential) My Dear Fox—," *United States Naval Institute Proceedings*, Vol. LXIII, No. 5 (May 1937).

——. "Admiral Farragut and General Butler," *United States Naval Institute Proceedings*, Vol. LXXXII, No. 6 (June 1956).

Wilkinson, John. *The Narrative of a Blockade Runner.* New York, 1877.

Williams, T. Harry. *P. G. T. Beauregard, Napoleon in Gray.* Baton Rouge, 1955.

Wolseley, Lord. "An English View of the Civil War," *North American Review*, Vol. CXLIX (July 1889).

Younger, Edward (ed.). *Inside the Confederate Government: The Diary of Robert Garlick Hill Kean.* New York, 1957.

Notes

CHAPTER 1

1. Official election returns. Quoted in Jefferson Davis Bragg, *Louisiana in the Confederacy* (Baton Rouge, 1941), 19. Hereafter cited as Bragg, *Louisiana in the Confederacy*.
2. *Crescent*, Dec. 11, 1860; *True Delta*, Nov. 15, 1860.
3. *Bee*, Dec. 10, 1860, and dates listed in text; Diary of John Purcell. Quoted by J. R. Ficklen in *History of Reconstruction in Louisiana through 1868*, 23; William Mure to Lord John Russell, Dec. 13, 1860, No. 21 from New Orleans, in *Foreign Office 5, Vol. 744*, Public Record Office, London. Reprinted in *Louisiana Historical Quarterly*, Vol. XIII (Jan. 1930), 32.
4. Thomas Carey Johnson, *The Life and Letters of Benjamin Morgan Palmer* (Richmond, 1906), 213–19 passim. Dr. Palmer's sermon was printed three times in the *Delta*, which asserted that 30,000 copies of it were circulated. The discourse "was more than eloquent; it was sacramental in its fervor," said the *Delta* on Dec. 2, 1860.
5. Roger Wallace Shugg, *Origins of Class Struggle in Louisiana* (Baton Rouge, 1939), 162. Hereafter cited as Shugg, *Origins of Class Struggle*.
6. For excellent accounts of the Louisiana Secession Convention, see Shugg, *Origins of Class Struggle*, 157–70; Bragg, *Louisiana in the*

Confederacy, 1–33; Lane Carter Kendall, "The Interregnum in Louisiana in 1861," *Louisiana Historical Quarterly*, Vols. XVI, XVII (1933, 1934). Hereafter cited as Kendall, "The Interregnum."

7. Shugg, *Origins of Class Struggle*, 163–64; *Picayune*, Jan. 9, 1861. The paper further stated: "The vote in this city prefigures the result in the State. The chief hope of the favorers of united Southern action, as opposed to immediate secession, was in carrying the city for the Cooperationists."

8. *War of the Rebellion: A Compilation of Official Records of the Union and Confederate Armies*, Series I, Vol. I, 495–96. Hereafter cited as *O.R.*, and all references will be to Series I, unless otherwise indicated.

9. *O.R.*, I, 491. Gov. Moore to Maj. Paul E. Théard, Jan. 10, 1861; *Picayune*, Jan. 11, 1861. A week after the "capture" of the forts, the *Picayune* reported that the men were enjoying the excursion and that friends in a chartered boat had brought down fine dinners, wines, etc. "Don't believe that these rejoicings . . . were anything like a 'spree.' The rules are very strict, and I have not yet seen a man in the fort excited with liquor," wrote the correspondent.

10. Milledge L. Bonham, Jr., "Louisiana's Seizure of the Federal Arsenal at Baton Rouge, January, 1861," *The Historical Society of East and West Baton Rouge Proceedings*, Vol. II (1917–18), 47–55; *O.R.*, I, 489–91; William Miller Owen, *In Camp and Battle with the Washington Artillery of New Orleans* (Boston, 1885), 5. The Washington Artillery, organized in New Orleans before the Mexican War, was one of the most famous Confederate units in the Civil War, fighting in all the campaigns in the eastern theater from Manassas to Appomattox. An Englishman who fought for the Confederacy wrote: ". . . A finer body of men than the Washington Artillery I have never seen, and for discipline and efficiency I have yet to see them surpassed even in the armies of Europe." William Watson, *Life in the Confederate Army, etc.* (London, 1887), 158.

11. *Commercial Bulletin*, Jan. 12, 1861; William H. Rooney, "The First 'Incident' of Secession: Seizure of the New Orleans Marine Hospital," *Louisiana Historical Quarterly*, Vol. XXXIV, No. 2 (April 1951), 135–42; *O.R.*, Series III, Vol. I, 302. Cameron to Lincoln, July 1, 1861.

12. *Official Journal of the Proceedings of the Convention of the State of Louisiana* (New Orleans, 1861). The most courageously outspoken

defender of the Union was James G. Taliaferro, of Catahoula Parish, whose address from the floor was not printed in the official journal. The *Crescent* printed it as "an act of justice to a very worthy member of the convention." Taliaferro said, in part: "I oppose the Act of Secession, because in my deliberate judgment the wrongs alleged might be redressed under the Constitution . . . Because I believe that peaceful secession is a right unknown to the Constitution . . . Because secession may bring anarchy and war . . . withering blight upon the prosperity of the State, and a fatal prostration of all its great interest. . . ." The complete text will be found in *O.R.*, LIII, 614–15. See also Roger Shugg, "A Suppressed Cooperationist Protest against Secession," *Louisiana Historical Quarterly*, Vol. XIX, No. 1 (Jan. 1936), 199.

13. *Official Journal . . . of the Convention; Crescent*, Jan. 28, 1861; *Thomas Kelah Wharton Diary*, Jan. 26, 1861. Manuscript in New York Public Library. Hereafter cited as Wharton, *Diary*.

14. *Crescent*, Jan. 28, 1861; *Picayune*, Jan. 27, 1861.

CHAPTER 2

1. *Eighth Census, 1860, Population*, 195–96.

2. *Report on the Internal Commerce of the United States by William P. Switzler, Chief of the Bureau of Statistics, Treasury Department.* House Exec. Doc., No. 6, Part II, 50th Congress, 1st Session (Washington, 1888), 225; 209.

3. Alice Theresa Porter, *An Economic View of Ante-Bellum New Orleans, 1845–1860* (Master's thesis, Tulane University, 1942), 2, 26.

4. *Executive Documents Printed by Order of the 36th Congress, 1859–1860*, Series 49 (Washington, 1860), 163–68, 278. Quoted in Bragg, *Louisiana in the Confederacy*, 37.

5. John S. Foster to Alonzo Snyder, Dec. 13, 1860, in *Alonzo Snyder Papers*, Department of Archives, Louisiana State University.

6. *Biographical and Historical Memoirs of Louisiana* (2 vols.; Chicago, 1892), Vol. II, 82.

7. *Bee*, Jan. 30, 1861; *Official Journal of . . . the Convention*, Jan. 29, 1861.

8. Ibid., Jan. 30, 1861; *True Delta*, Jan. 30, 1861; Kendall, "The Interregnum," *Louisiana Historical Quarterly*, Vol. XVI, 644–47; *Picayune*, Feb. 1, 1861.

9. *Official Journal of . . . the Convention*, Feb. 5, 1861; ibid., Feb. 2, 5, 1861.

10. Ibid., Feb. 4, 11, 12, 1861.

11. *Picayune*, Feb. 19, 1861; Alfred Roman, *The Military Operations of General Beauregard* (2 vols.; New York, 1884), Vol. I, 421. Beauregard wrote Richard Taylor on Feb. 12, 1861, as follows: "Upon reflection and consultation with my friends, I have come to the conclusion that I ought not and cannot accept that Colonelcy of Engineers and Artillery in the State army—but my professional knowledge, experience, and service, *without military rank*, are at the command of the State, even unto death." On Feb. 19, Beauregard assured Governor Moore of his willingness to serve "without military rank; not, however, through any jealousy of General Bragg's appointment, for I am happy to state that it is a most excellent choice; and I should have been very happy to serve with him or under his orders, in the defence of our rights and firesides, if I could have accepted the Colonel and Chief of Engineers and Artillery position tendered me." Ibid., 423.

12. Ibid., 316n. Beauregard's name was preserved on the rolls of the Creole Guards even after he had become a Confederate general officer. Whenever his name was called, the color sergeant stepped forward and said: "Absent on duty."

13. *O.R.*, I, 500–1; Roman, *Beauregard*, 422; John Roy, *Memorandum Book* (manuscript), Feb. 11, 14, 15, 16, 19, 1861. Microfilm in Howard-Tilton Library, Tulane University.

14. Albert D. Richardson, *The Secret Service, the Field, the Dungeon, and the Escape* (Hartford, 1865), 59.

15. *Official Journal of . . . the Convention*, March 16, 1861; *True Delta*, March 19, 1861; *Picayune*, March 19, 1861.

16. *Official Journal of . . . the Convention*, March 21, 25, 26, 1861. The *True Delta*, March 28, 1861, called the convention a "revolutionary farce" of anti-popular "composition" which practiced "factions, stupidity and malignity against popular government." It "arrogated to itself powers utterly unknown to this or any other people," and it proved "a body which generations yet unborn, as those now existing, will long curse as the heaviest and most disastrous affliction that poor Louisiana . . . has ever had to support."

CHAPTER 3

1. *Picayune*, April 10, 1861; ibid., April 7, 1861.
2. Ibid., April 12, 1861; ibid., April 13, 1861.
3. Ibid., April 14, 20, 25, 1861; John Q. Anderson (ed.), *Brokenburn, The Journal of Kate Stone, 1861–1868* (Baton Rouge, 1955), 16–17; Charles L. Dufour, *Gentle Tiger, The Gallant Life of Roberdeau Wheat* (Baton Rouge, 1957), 6.
4. George H. Devol, *Forty Years a Gambler on the Mississippi* (Cincinnati, 1887), 116–17.
5. G. W. Cable, "War Diary of a Union Woman in the South," in *Famous Adventures and Prison Escapes of the Civil War* (New York, 1893), April 20, 1861; ibid., April 25, May 10, 1861.
6. Rotchford, Brown and Co. to Alonzo Snyder, April 17, 1861; Buckner, Stanton and Newman to Alonzo Snyder, April 19, 1861; Richard Nugent and Co. to Alonzo Snyder, May 14, 1861. All in *Alonzo Snyder Papers*, Department of Archives, Louisiana State University. Snyder was a prominent lawyer, judge, and cotton planter in northern Louisiana.
7. *Picayune*, April 16, 20, 1861.
8. James D. Bulloch, *The Secret Service of the Confederate States in Europe, or How the Confederate Cruisers Were Equipped* (2 vols.; New York, 1884), 31–35.
9. *Picayune*, July 2, 1861; William Mure to Lord John Russell, May 3, 1861 (with enclosures), in *Foreign Office 5, Vol. 788*, Public Record Office, London; *Picayune*, July 6, 1862. William Mure was a forceful personality who worked tirelessly for his British compatriots in New Orleans at this time. His assistant, George Coppell, acting consul in Mure's absence, was also prompt in looking out for the interests of his countrymen.
10. *Picayune*, May 12, 15, 1861.
11. Ibid., April 24, 26, May 10, 11, 28, 1861.
12. Ibid., May 12, 24, 1861.
13. Ibid., May 18, 22, 25, 27, 1861; Frank Moore, *Rebellion Record: A Diary of American Events, etc.* (12 vols.; New York, 1864–71), May 30, 31, 1861; Wharton, *Diary*, May 27, 1861. Although the correct name for the pass in French is *Passe à la Loutre*, the form used here, *Pass a Loutre*, appears on U. S. Coast and Geodetic Sur-

vey maps, pilot charts, etc. There is no justification for *Pass à l'Outre.*

14. *Picayune*, May 31, 1861; *O.R.*, LIII, 744; Ezra J. Warner, *Generals in Gray. Lives of the Confederate Commanders* (Baton Rouge, 1959), 312.

15. Sarah A. Dorsey, *Recollections of Henry Watkins Allen, etc.* (New York, 1866), 69; Bragg to Gov. Moore, Oct. 31, 1861, in *Thomas O. Moore Papers*, Department of Archives, Louisiana State University.

CHAPTER 4

1. *O.R.*, LIII, 668. Judah P. Benjamin to William E. Starke, April 9, 1861. Benjamin wrote: "Maj. M. L. Smith, an engineer officer of high character, has been sent to the forts to perfect the defenses . . ."

2. Ibid., 669. Gov. Moore to Sec. of War Walker, April 10, 1861. Gov. Moore to Benjamin, April 11, 1861. Benjamin to Gov. Moore, April 11, 1861.

3. Ibid., 668. Benjamin to Starke, April 9, 1861; ibid., 696. Twiggs to Walker, June 10, 1861; ibid., 699. Twiggs to Walker, June 18, 1861. Twiggs was particularly concerned with the threat to New Orleans from upriver. "If the Valley of the Mississippi falls into the hands of the Black Republicans this city will be in a very critical condition," he wrote Walker on June 25, 1861; ibid., 703. This may have been the basis for the obsession in Richmond that the greater danger to New Orleans was from above.

4. *Picayune*, May 29, June 11, 1861; Dufour, *Gentle Tiger*, 125; *Picayune*, June 7, 8, 1861. A Martello tower is a small round fort located on a coast to prevent enemy landings. It is named for Cape Martello, Corsica, where the British in 1794 captured such a tower.

5. *Proceedings of Common Council (Board of Aldermen and Board of Asst. Aldermen) of City of New Orleans*, June 11, 1861, in New Orleans Public Library; *O.R.*, LIII, 707. Twiggs to Walker, July 9, 1861.

6. This ridiculous situation can be followed, step by step, in the correspondence found in *O.R.*, LIII, 681–89.

7. *Picayune*, June 25, 26, 1861.

8. Ibid., June 27, 29, 1861.

9. Ibid., July 1, 1861. In his *Memoirs of Service Afloat*, Semmes expressed surprise that during the nine days he was at the Head of the Passes the Federals did not attack him: "The enemy watched

me closely, day by day, and bent all his energies toward preventing my escape, but did not seem to think of the simple expedient of endeavoring to capture me, with a superior force."

10. *O.R.*, LIII, 706. Twiggs to Walker, July 7, 1861; ibid., 712. Twiggs to Walker, July 15, 1861.

11. *Picayune*, July 19, 21, 24, 25, 26, 29, 1861; *Delta*, July 28, 1861.

12. "Report of Joint Committee on City Defences, Aug. 2, 1861," in *Proceedings of Common Council*, in New Orleans Public Library.

13. *O.R.*, LIII, 715–16. P. O. Hébert and M. L. Smith to Twiggs, July 27, 1861 (two communications).

14. "Report of Joint Committee on City Defences," op. cit.

15. *Proceedings of Common Council*, Aug. 9, 27, 1861.

CHAPTER 5

1. Quoted in H. Allen Gosnell, *Rebel Raider, Raphael Semmes's Cruise in the C.S.S. Sumter* (Chapel Hill, N.C., 1948), 16; William Mure to Lord John Russell, June 6, July 30, 1861, in *Foreign Office 5, Vol. 788*, Public Record Office, London. Mure reported on the latter date that "no public or official notice touching the blockade, has been made in this City. . . ."

2. *Picayune*, July 17, Aug. 1, 1861.

3. *Report of Evidence Taken before a Joint Special Committee of Both Houses of the Confederate Congress to Investigate the Affairs of the Navy Department*. P. Kean, reporter (Richmond [1863]), 45–46. Hereafter cited as *Investigation of Confederate Navy Department*.

4. *Dictionary of American Biography*, Vol. IX, 152.

5. *Investigation of Confederate Navy Department*, 46; miscellaneous papers in *Area 5, 1861–1865 File*, in *Record Group 45*, National Archives.

6. *O.R.*, LIII, 722. Twiggs to Walker, Aug. 9, 1861; ibid., 731–32. Walker to Twiggs, Aug. 24, 1861.

7. William Morrison Robinson, Jr., *The Confederate Privateers* (New Haven, 1928), 165–68; *Picayune*, Aug. 7, 1861; ibid., Sept. 10, 1861.

8. Ibid., Aug. 21, 28, 1861; *Bee*, Aug. 8, 1861; *Crescent*, Oct. 2, 1861; *Delta*, Nov. 1, 1861.

9. *Picayune*, Aug. 20, Oct. 24, 26, 1861. The *Picayune*'s enthusiasm over New Orleans' new-found economic freedom from the North would have amused Richardson, the New York *Tribune* correspond-

ent, who earlier in the year visited the Southern Shoe Factory in
New Orleans and wrote: "It was admirably calculated to appeal to
local patriotism, and demonstrate the feasibility of Southern manufacturing. Its northern machinery, run by northern workmen, under
a northern superintendent, turned out brogans of northern leather,
fastened with northern pegs, and packed in cases of northern pine,
at an advance of only about one hundred percent upon northern
prices!" Richardson, *The Secret Service, etc.,* 64.

10. *Proceedings of Common Council,* Oct. 9, 1861; P. O. Hébert to
T. K. Wharton, Feb. 22, 1861, in *Confederate Records, Chapter
III, Vol. 19½, Letters Sent, Artillery and Engineering Department,
New Orleans, La., Feb. 1861,* in National Archives; Wharton, *Diary,*
July 18, 1861. Of John Roy, the Algiers *News Boy* said that he "is
the master mind by which all the vast preparations of cannon in
and around the city have been superintended ever since the war
broke out." Quoted in *Picayune,* Oct. 10, 1861. Capt. Raphael
Semmes of the *Sumter* wrote that Roy "contrived most ingeniously,
and constructed out of railroad iron, one of the best carriages (or
rather, slide and circle) for a pivot gun which I have ever seen."
Quoted in Gosnell, *Rebel Raider,* 13.

11. J. W. Mallet, "Work of the Ordnance Bureau of the War Department of the Confederate States, 1861–1865," *Southern Historical
Society Papers,* Vol. XXXVII (1909), 6–7; Roy, *Memorandum Book,*
various dates; Wharton, *Diary,* May 11, 1861.

12. *Bee,* Aug. 5, 1861; Col. Arcadi Gluckman and L. D. Satterlee,
American Gunmakers (Harrisburg, Pa., 1953), 40; Claude E. Fuller
and Richard D. Steuart, *Firearms of the Confederacy* (Huntington,
W. Va., 1944), 146.

13. *Picayune,* July 18, Oct. 18, Sept. 11, 1861; *Crescent,* Dec. 27, 1861.
In connection with the manufacture of pikes, not only in New
Orleans but throughout the Confederacy, the comment of the Confederate Chief of Ordnance, Brig. Gen. Josiah Gorgas, after the war
is self-explanatory: ". . . We resorted to the making of *pikes* for the
infantry and lances for the cavalry; many thousands of the former
were made at the various arsenals, but were little used. No access
of enthusiasm could induce our people to rush to the field armed
with *pikes.*" *Southern Historical Society Papers,* Vol. XII, 74.

14. *Crescent,* Oct. 7, 1861; *Picayune,* Aug. 1, 1861; *Commercial Bulletin,* Nov. 27, 1861; *Crescent,* Oct. 7, 1861; *Proceedings of Common*

Council, Dec. 3, 1861. The appropriation of $550 was to supplement $950 Wingard had raised privately. The city fathers stipulated that Wingard's gun must be retained in New Orleans for use there "until such time as the city is reimbursed in said amount by the afore-named inventor."

15. *Bee*, Aug. 16, 1861.

16. *Picayune*, Sept. 15, 1861. Describing the fortifications above the city, the *Picayune* said: "The moat, or ditch, in front of the works averages 30 feet in width, but in many places is much wider, and about six feet in depth. The parapets are 9 feet in height, and are constructed for batteries at the angles"; *O.R.*, LIII, 742. Twiggs to Benjamin, Sept. 19, 1861; Wharton, *Diary*, July 17, Sept. 30.

17. *O.R.*, LIII, 740. Duncan's report, Sept. 17, 1861. The evacuation was begun on Sept. 14 and completed by sundown of Sept. 16, with "all the guns, carriages, equipments, implements, &c., ammunition, commissary and quartermaster's stores, engineer's tools, and all other public and private property . . . saved"; Wharton, *Diary*, July 7, 1861; *O.R.*, LIII, 699. Twiggs to Walker, June 18, 1861; ibid., 708. Walker to Twiggs, July 10, 1861.

18. *Stephen R. Mallory Journal*, Sept. 16, 1861, in Southern Historical Collection, University of North Carolina, Chapel Hill; *O.R.*, LIII, 739. Roman to Davis, Sept. 15, 1861; *Investigation of Confederate Navy Department*, 303–4. Moore to Davis, Sept. 20, 1861; ibid., 304. Moore to Benjamin, Sept. 22, 1861; ibid., 306. Davis to Moore, Sept. 26, 1861.

19. *O.R.*, LIII, 743. Special Orders, No. 162, Richmond, Sept. 25, 1861; ibid., 747. Special Orders, No. 168, Oct. 1, 1861; ibid., 748. Twiggs to Benjamin, Oct. 5, 1861; Warner, *Generals in Gray*, 194; *O.R.*, LIII, 748–49. Benjamin to Twiggs, Oct. 9, 1861; *Crescent*, Oct. 11, 1861; *Picayune*, Oct. 17, 1861.

20. *Bee*, Oct. 1, 1861; *Picayune*, Sept. 29, 1861; *Crescent*, Oct. 1, 1861; the *True Delta*'s report (Oct. 1, 1861) said that "a few unruly boys and some children of an older growth indulged . . . in a few hisses and other unseemly indications of popular indignation" as the prisoners moved by.

21. Accounts of various benefits and charities appear frequently in the New Orleans newspapers throughout 1861. For Free Market, see *Picayune*, Aug. 17, 21, Oct. 15, 1861; Marion Southwood (A Lady of New Orleans), *"Beauty and Booty": The Watchword of New*

Orleans (New York, 1867), 77–78. Hereafter cited as Southwood, *"Beauty and Booty"*; Kate Mason Rowland and Mrs. Morris L. Croxall, *The Journal of Julia LeGrand—New Orleans, 1862–1863* (Richmond, 1911), 37. Hereafter cited as *Journal of Julia LeGrand*; *Crescent*, Nov. 18, 1861; *Picayune*, Nov. 17, 1861.

22. *Picayune*, Aug. 13, 20, Sept. 15, 1861. Wharton recorded in his diary for July 28, 1861: ". . . The impudent 'Lincoln Blockade' is acting in our favor by keeping out yellow fever. . . ."

CHAPTER 6

1. *Picayune*, May 12, 1861; Robinson, *The Confederate Privateers* (New Haven, 1928), 154–57.

2. *National Intelligencer*, July 11, 1861. Quoted in Moore, *Rebellion Record*; *Official Records of the Union and Confederate Navies in the War of the Rebellion*, XVI, 602. Porter to Mervine, July 19, 1861. Hereafter cited as *O.R.N.*; Anderson, *Brokenburn*, 43.

3. *National Intelligencer*, Aug. 17, 1861; *O.R.N.*, XVI, 746–47. Anderson to Seward, Sept. 11, 1861; Wharton, *Diary*, Aug. 15, 1861; *True Delta*, Sept. 11, 1861.

4. *Picayune*, Oct. 4, 1861; *Crescent*, Oct. 4, 1861; *True Delta*, Oct. 4, 1861; *Commercial Bulletin*, Oct. 4, 1861; Wharton, *Diary*, Oct. 8, 1861.

5. *True Delta*, Oct. 13, 1861; James Morris Morgan, *Recollections of a Rebel Reefer* (New York and Boston, 1917), 55. Hereafter cited as Morgan, *Rebel Reefer*.

6. Ibid., 55–56; *True Delta*, Oct. 15, 1861.

7. Roy, *Memorandum Book*, Oct. 4, 8, 9, 1861; Wharton, *Diary*, Oct. 10, 1861. Roy wrote that the *Manassas* was delayed by "a leak in her condenser or in the valves."

8. *O.R.N.*, XVI, 699–700. Pope to McKean, Oct. 9, 1861; ibid., 711. Pope to McKean, Oct. 17, 1861.

9. H. Allen Gosnell, *Guns on the Western Waters*, 37–38. Hereafter cited as Gosnell, *Guns on the Western Waters*; *True Delta*, Oct. 15, 1861.

10. *O.R.N.*, XVI, 714. Lieutenant Francis Winslow to McKean, Oct. 24, 1861; ibid., 703. Pope to McKean, Oct. 13, 1861.

11. *True Delta*, Oct. 15, 1861; *O.R.N.*, XVI, 712. Commander H. French to McKean, Oct. 22, 1861; ibid., 730a. Warley to Hollins,

undated; ibid., 704. Pope to McKean, Oct. 13, 1861; Gosnell, *Guns on the Western Waters*, 40.

12. Jennie Mort Walker, *Life of Captain Joseph Fry, the Cuban Martyr* (Hartford, 1875), 146–47. Hereafter cited as Walker, *Life of Captain Joseph Fry*. The direct quotations are from a rough draft of Fry's report to Hollins, dated Oct. 14, 1861, found among Fry's papers after his death.

13. *O.R.N.*, XVI, 704. Pope to McKean, Oct. 13, 1861; ibid., 711–12. Handy to Pope [Oct. 12, 1861]; ibid., 712. Pope to Handy, Oct. 12, 1861.

14. Walker, *Life of Captain Joseph Fry*, 147; *O.R.N.*, XVI, 704. Pope to McKean, Oct. 13, 1861. Pope reported: ". . . The enemy . . . commenced firing at us, while we returned the fire, . . . our shot, however, falling short of the enemy, while their shell burst on all sides of us . . ." Fry reported, on the other hand, that the Federal shots "reached us, passed over and by us."

15. Walker, *Life of Captain Joseph Fry*, 147–48, 150.

16. *O.R.N.*, XVI, 709. Handy to McKean, Oct. 14, 1861; ibid., 720. Sworn statement of Seaman Nathaniel P. Allen, Oct. 28, 18⸍ ibid., 719–20. Sworn statement of Signal Quartermaster William Burrows, Oct. 28, 1861; ibid., 710. Pope to McKean, Oct. 17, 1861. In an earlier report, Pope set the time of Handy's leaving the *Vincennes* at about 9:30 A.M.

17. Walker, *Life of Captain Joseph Fry*, 148; *Picayune*, Oct. 13, 1861.

18. *O.R.N.*, XVI, 709. Handy to McKean, Oct. 14, 1861; Gosnell, *Guns on the Western Waters*, 43.

19. *O.R.N.*, XVI, 710–11. Pope to McKean, Oct. 17, 1861; ibid., 748. McKean to Welles, Oct. 24, 1861; Adm. David D. Porter, in his *Naval History of the Civil War* (New York, 1886), 91, wrote of "Pope's Run" as follows: "Put this matter in any light you may, it is the most ridiculous affair that ever took place in the American Navy." Adm. Alfred Thayer Mahan, in *The Gulf and Inland Waters* (New York, 1883), 7, characterized Pope's retreat from the Head of the Passes as "a move which brought intense mortification to himself and in a measure to the service."

20. *Picayune*, Oct. 13, 1861; Clara Solomon, *Diary of a New Orleans Girl*, Oct. 13, 1861, typescript p. 101. Manuscript and typescript in Department of Archives, Louisiana State University. Hereafter referred to as Solomon, *Diary*; Wharton, *Diary*, Oct. 12, 1861.

21. *Delta*, Oct. 15, 22, 1861; *Crescent*, Oct. 15, 22, 1861; *Picayune*, Oct. 15, 22, 31, 1861.

22. Walker, *Life of Captain Joseph Fry*, 146; *Picayune*, Oct. 16, 1861.

23. There were some, such as Elise Ellis Bragg, who took a realistic view of the situation. Mrs. Bragg wrote General Bragg: "The papers have informed you . . . that our *Turtle*, alias *Manassas*, made a grand charge & would have done wonders if it had not been disabled. All these things made a sensation, but I fear they help our cause but little, & a dark & gloomy winter seems closing around us. Our resources are all being expended, while the enemy will open another year with everything in new and fine order." Mrs. Bragg to Bragg, Oct. 18, 1861, in *Bragg Papers*, University of Texas Archives.

CHAPTER 7

1. Mrs. Bragg to Bragg, Oct. 13, 1861, in *Bragg Papers*, University of Texas Archives.

2. Ibid. Mrs. Bragg to Bragg, Oct. 18, 1861.

3. *True Delta*, Oct. 17, 1861; *Delta*, Oct. 18, 1861; *Picayune*, Oct. 17, 1861.

4. Gustavus W. Smith, "Mansfield Lovell," in *Fifteenth Annual Reunion of the Association of the Graduates of the U. S. Military Academy, 1884* (E. Saginaw, Mich., 1884), 113–26. Hereafter cited as Smith, *15th Annual Reunion*.

5. Roman, *Beauregard*, Vol. I, 15; Davis to Semmes, Feb. 21, 1861, in Dunbar Rowland, *Jefferson Davis, Constitutionalist, etc.* (Jackson, Miss., 1923), Vol. V, 55.

6. *O.R.*, LIII, 126–27. Beauregard to Smith, Feb. 27, 1861; ibid., 129. Smith to Beauregard, Mar. 5, 1861.

7. Smith, *15th Annual Reunion*, 117; *O.R.*, LIII, 743. Special Orders, No. 162, Richmond, Sept. 25, 1861; *Picayune*, Oct. 12, 1861.

8. Dorsey, *Recollections of Henry Watkins Allen*, 68–69; *Investigation of Confederate Navy Department*, 238–39. Davis to Lovell, Oct. 17, 1861.

9. *O.R.*, VI, 558. Lovell's testimony; Lovell to Davis, Oct. 18, 1861, in Emory University Library.

10. *Investigation of Confederate Navy Department*, 239. Lovell to Benjamin, Oct. 18, 1861. Also in *O.R.*, VI, 753.

11. *O.R.*, VI, 754. Benjamin to Lovell, Oct. 23, 1861; ibid., 754–55. Lovell to Benjamin, Oct. 25, 1861.
12. Ibid., 558–59. Lovell's testimony; Wharton, *Diary*, Oct. 7, 1861.
13. *Delta*, Nov. 3, 1861; *Picayune*, Oct. 31, 1861.
14. J. B. Jones, *A Rebel War Clerk's Diary* (2 vols.; Philadelphia, 1866), Vol. I, 89; *True Delta*, Nov. 2, 1861; *Delta*, Nov. 3, 1861.
15. Bragg to Benjamin, Oct. 30, 1861. Copy in *Thomas O. Moore Papers*, Department of Archives, Louisiana State University; Bragg to Moore, Oct. 31, 1861.
16. *O.R.*, VI, 560–61. Lovell's testimony; *Picayune*, Oct. 19, 25, 1861; *O.R.*, VI, 760. Lovell to Davis, Oct. 31, 1861. Col. Duncan was born in York, Pennsylvania, March 19, 1827. He served in the Third Artillery after graduating No. 5 in the West Point class of 1849. In 1855, he resigned his commission, becoming superintendent of government construction in New Orleans. At the outbreak of the war, Duncan was chief engineer of the Board of Public Works in Louisiana. He was commissioned major in the Confederacy in March 1861, and colonel in September of the same year. Warner, *Generals in Gray*, 77–78; Ellsworth Eliot, Jr., *West Point in the Confederacy* (New York, 1941), 329.

CHAPTER 8

1. Roy, *Memorandum Book*, Sept. 20, 1861; *Investigation of Confederate Navy Department*, 123–24; Joseph T. Durkin, S.J., *Stephen R. Mallory: Confederate Navy Chief* (Chapel Hill, N.C., 1954), 34.
2. Rear Admiral W. M. Parks, "Building a Warship in the Southern Confederacy," *United States Naval Institute Proceedings*, Vol. XLIX, No. 8 (Aug. 1923), 1300–1.
3. *Investigation of Confederate Navy Department*, 153–54. Nelson and Asa Tift to Mallory, Aug. 26, 1861; Mallory, *Journal*, Sept. 1, 1861; Roy, *Memorandum Book*, Sept. 2, 1861.
4. *Investigation of Confederate Navy Department*, 196–97. Mallory to N. and A. Tift, Sept. 5, 1862; ibid., 415.
5. Roy, *Memorandum Book*, Sept. 20, 1861; *Investigation of Confederate Navy Department*, 415; ibid., 159. N. and A. Tift to Mallory, Oct. 9, 1861.
6. Ibid., 156–58. N. and A. Tift to Mallory, Sept. 28, 1861.
7. *Investigation of Confederate Navy Department*, 117–18. Pearce's

testimony; ibid., 109. Nelson Tift's testimony; ibid., 162–64. N. and A. Tift to Mallory, Oct. 29, 1861.

8. *Investigation of Confederate Navy Department*, 437. Contract of E. C. Murray with Navy Department, Sept. 18, 1861; ibid., 372. Murray's testimony.

9. Ibid., 374. Murray's testimony; ibid., 130–31. Nelson Tift's testimony; *True Delta*, Nov. 10, 1861.

10. *Investigation of Confederate Navy Department*, 391. The conversation has been slightly paraphrased from Asa Tift's testimony and placed in direct quotation. In a letter to Mallory on Nov. 12, 1861 (ibid., 166), the Tift brothers wrote: "All of our carpenters left us . . . We waited three or four days on the assurance that the proprietors of yards and docks, the people or the authorities, would speedily adjust the difficulty; but believing the strike was for an indefinite time, and fearing serious, and perhaps fatal delay, we determined to advance the wages of the best ship carpenters to four (4) dollars per day, and the others to rates corresponding to their skill. We now have a large and superior gang of men, and our work is progressing satisfactorily."

11. *True Delta*, Oct. 26, 1861; *O.R.*, LIII, 722. Twiggs to Walker, Aug. 9, 1861; Wharton, *Diary*, Oct. 24, Nov. 9, 1861; *True Delta*, Oct. 19, 1861; *Picayune*, Nov. 16, 18, 19, 1861; Lieutenant John J. Guthrie's *Notebook*, in *Confederate Navy Records, Record Group 45*, National Archives; Commander W. C. Whittle to Lieutenant W. Gwathmey, Dec. 10, 1861, in *Area 5, 1861–1865 File*, in *Record Group 45*, National Archives.

12. *Investigation of Confederate Navy Department*, 52. Hollins' testimony; Bill of steamer *Landis* and owners, Dec. [?], 1861, for transporting floating battery from Algiers to City, in *Area 5, 1861–1865 File*, in *Record Group 45*, National Archives.

13. *Picayune*, Oct. 20, 1861; *Commercial Bulletin*, Dec. 11, 1861; *Bee*, Dec. 12, 1861.

14. *Delta*, Oct. 27, 1861; *Crescent*, Nov. 8, 1861; *Proceedings of Common Council*, Nov. 7, 1861; *Commercial Bulletin*, Nov. 9, 1861; *Picayune*, Nov. 13, 1861; *Commercial Bulletin*, Dec. 24, 1861.

15. *Investigation of Confederate Navy Department*, 98–100. Kennon's testimony; *True Delta*, Nov. 1, 1861; *Investigation of Confederate Navy Department*, 398. Minor to Mallory, Dec. 2, 1861.

16. Ibid., 119. Pearce's testimony; ibid., 167. N. and A. Tift to Mallory,

Nov. 21, 1861; ibid., 169. N. and A. Tift to Mallory, Dec. 6, 1861; ibid., 172. N. and A. Tift to Mallory, Dec. 26, 1861.

17. Ibid., 374. Murray's testimony; *Delta*, Nov. 29, 1861; *Crescent*, Nov. 29, 1861.

CHAPTER 9

1. *Delta*, Nov. 1, 1861; *Commercial Bulletin*, Oct. 28, 1861; Algiers *News Boy*, quoted in *Commercial Bulletin*, Nov. 2, 1861.

2. *English Composition Book, Institut Catholique*, 109, in Archives of Archdiocese of New Orleans; Mary Elizabeth Massey, *Ersatz in the Confederacy* (Columbia, S.C., 1952), 166; *Picayune*, Oct. 18, Nov. 16, 27, Dec. 6, 1861.

3. Algiers *News Boy*, quoted in *Picayune*, Dec. 13, 1861; *O.R.*, VI, 761. Lovell to Davis, Oct. 31, 1861.

4. J. C. Kline to Alonzo Snyder, Dec. 5, 1861, in *Alonzo Snyder Papers*, Department of Archives, Louisiana State University; George W. Cable, "New Orleans Before the Capture," in *Battles and Leaders of the Civil War*, Vol. II, 17. Hereafter cited as *Battles and Leaders*; *True Delta*, Nov. 17, 1861.

5. *Picayune*, Sept. 19, 1861; *True Delta*, Oct. 16, Nov. 13, 1861; *Delta*, Oct. 12, 1861; *Crescent*, Oct. 15, 1861.

6. *Delta*, Oct. 13, 1861; *Picayune*, Dec. 12, 1861. It is interesting to note that during World War I spy hunters in New Orleans were as active as in 1861, although their activities did not get into print.

7. *Picayune*, Oct. 25, 1861; *True Delta*, Nov. 13, 1861; *Picayune*, Nov. 22, 1861; ibid., Oct. 10, 1861.

8. Ibid., Nov. 18, 1861; *Delta*, Nov. 19, 1861; *Crescent*, Nov. 18, 1861. For a full account of the incident, see T. L. Harris, *The Trent Affair* (Indianapolis, 1896).

9. *Picayune*, Nov. 12, 1861.

10. *Delta*, Oct. 11, 1861; *Crescent*, Oct. 17, 1861.

11. *Picayune*, Nov. 9, 1861; *Fire and Alarm Telegraph of the City of New Orleans, Record of Messages Received and Sent, 1860–1863*, June 3, 4, 8, Oct. 30, 1861, in New Orleans Public Library; *Picayune*, Dec. 4, 1861; ibid., Dec. 29, 1861; *True Delta*, Nov. 17, 1861; Caroline E. Merrick, *Old Times in Dixie Land, A Southern Matron's Memories* (New York, 1901), 30.

12. *Delta*, Nov. 24, 1861; *True Delta*, Nov. 24, 1861; *Crescent*, Nov.

25, 1861; *Picayune*, Nov. 24, 1861; *Commercial Bulletin*, Nov. 25, 1861.

13. *Delta*, Nov. 19, 1861; *O.R.*, VI, 770. Lovell to Benjamin, Nov. 19, 1861; ibid., 787. Lovell to Benjamin, Dec. 24, 1861; ibid., 774–76. Lovell to Benjamin, Dec. 5, 1861.

14. George W. Rains, *History of the Confederate Powder Works* (Augusta, Ga., 1882), 6–7; *Delta*, Dec. 11, 1861.

15. *Picayune*, Dec. 15, 1861; *O.R.*, VI, 788. Lovell to Benjamin, Dec. 27, 1861.

16. *Picayune*, Dec. 29, 1861; *True Delta*, Dec. 29, 1861; *Delta*, Dec. 31, 1861; *Crescent*, Dec. 30, 1861; Wharton, *Diary*, Dec. 29, 1861; *O.R.*, VI, 790. Lovell to Benjamin, Dec. 29, 1861; *True Delta*, Dec. 29, 1861.

17. *Diary of Captain Benjamin Warren, 26th Mass. Volunteers*, Dec. 3, 1861. Manuscript in possession of Richard T. Colquette, Houston, Texas; *Crescent*, Dec. 18, 1861.

18. *Picayune*, Dec. 12, 1861; *Delta*, Dec. 15, 1861; *Crescent*, Dec. 18, 1861; *O.R.*, VI, 790. Lovell to Benjamin, Dec. 29, 1861.

CHAPTER 10

1. David C. Mearns (ed.), *The Lincoln Papers* (2 vols.; New York, 1948), Vol. II, 556–58.

2. For Scott's Anaconda Plan in detail, consult John G. Nicolay and John Hay, *Abraham Lincoln, A History* (10 vols.; New York, 1890), Vol. IV, 298–303.

3. Scott told Lincoln that he, Scott, was "the greatest coward in America," because he had permitted the attack on Beauregard at Bull Run against his better judgment. Lincoln's reported reply was: "Your conversation seems to imply that I forced you to fight this battle." See James G. Randall, *Lincoln the President* (2 vols.; New York, 1945), Vol. I, 391.

4. *O.R.N.*, XVI, 627. The full report takes twelve printed pages.

5. *O.R.N.*, XVI, 572. Porter to Mervine, July 4, 1861; James Russell Soley, *Admiral Porter* (New York, 1903), 135–36. Hereafter cited as Soley, *Porter*.

6. Porter to Fox, July 5, 1861, in Robert Means Thompson and Richard Wainwright, *Confidential Correspondence of Gustavus Vasa Fox*,

etc. (2 vols.; New York, 1920), Vol. II, 73. Hereafter cited as *Confidential Correspondence of Fox.*

7. Gideon Welles, *Diary of Gideon Welles, Secretary of the Navy under Lincoln and Johnson* (Boston and New York, 1911), Vol. I, 157. Hereafter cited as Welles, *Diary*; ibid., Vol. I, 88.

8. Soley, *Porter*, 80; Clarence E. Macartney, *Mr. Lincoln's Admirals* (New York, 1956), 258–59. Hereafter cited as Macartney, *Mr. Lincoln's Admirals.*

9. Porter to Welles, March 12, 1861, and Porter to Welles, March 14, 1861, in *Record Group 45, Officers Letters, Navy Department,* National Archives.

10. Gideon Welles, "Admiral Farragut and New Orleans," *Galaxy*, Nov. and Dec. 1871, 677. Hereafter cited as Welles, *Galaxy*. Good accounts of the *Powhatan* affair will be found in Soley, *Porter*, 96–124; Richard S. West, Jr., *Mr. Lincoln's Navy* (New York, 1957), 19–28; and Macartney, *Mr. Lincoln's Admirals*, 263–68. Otto Eisenschiml's *Why the Civil War?* (Indianapolis and New York, 1958) is an interesting and provocative book which also discusses the *Powhatan* incident.

11. Soley, *Porter*, 124–26; Porter to Welles, June 1, 1861, in *Record Group 45, Officers Letters, Navy Department,* National Archives.

12. *O.R.N.*, XVI, 571–72. Porter to Mervine, July 4, 1861.

13. Porter to Welles, Aug. 13, 1861, in *Record Group 45, Officers Letters, Navy Department,* National Archives; *O.R.N.*, XVI, 638. Mervine to Welles, Aug. 17, 1861.

14. *Crescent*, Sept. 11, 1861; Algiers *News Boy*, Sept. 14, 1861, quoted in *Picayune*, Sept. 15, 1861.

15. Soley, *Porter*, 126–31, gives a good account of Porter's vain pursuit of the *Sumter*; *O.R.N.*, XVI, 750–51. Porter to McKean, Oct. 25, 1861. Porter's report on the *Powhatan's* condition is interesting: "Before leaving the United States her boilers were considered unfit for use; they have been patched and repatched since that time . . . they may give out at any moment . . . she is rotten throughout . . . Her standing rigging is rotten . . . 500 sheets of copper are off the bottom and what is left is loose. The bottom is covered with barnacles where the wood is exposed . . . Her planking won't bear caulking, and above the water you can run a knife through the seams. She leaks badly . . . In fact, it is a case of complete wear out . . ."

CHAPTER 11

1. David D. Porter, *Incidents and Anecdotes of the Civil War* (New York, 1885), 64. Hereafter cited as Porter, *Incidents and Anecdotes*; Horace Greeley, *The American Conflict* (2 vols.; Hartford, 1866), Vol. II, ch. 5; James Parton, *General Butler in New Orleans* (New York, 1863), 191. Hereafter cited as Parton, *Butler*.

2. Welles, *Galaxy*, 819, 821, 676; Welles to Fox, June 10, 1871, quoted in Fox to Welles, June 17, 1871, in Huntington Library; Montgomery Blair, "Opening the Mississippi," *United Service*, Vol. IV (Jan. 1881), 34. Hereafter cited as Blair, "Opening the Mississippi"; George Dewey, *Autobiography of George Dewey, Admiral of the Navy* (New York, 1913), 41. Hereafter cited as Dewey, *Autobiography*.

3. Welles to Fox, July 8, 1871, in Huntington Library; Welles, *Galaxy*, 673, 676.

4. Ibid., 676–77. In his letter to Fox of July 8, 1871, he was even more specific about Porter: "On his return in November we were glad to obtain from him direct information in regard to the hydrography, topography, the channels, depth of water, and all information to the Mississippi—the forts, etc."

5. Welles, *Galaxy*, 677. On July 8, 1871, Welles wrote Fox: "This meeting took place, I think on the 16th or 17th of November, I cannot determine which. *Can you inform me?* On the 18th of November Porter had orders to go and get mortar vessels . . ." Fox wasn't very helpful in clarifying the date for Welles, for he had previously written that Porter proposed the mortar flotilla in a conversation with him on Nov. 30. Mrs. Fox's diary, in the *Blair Papers* in the Library of Congress, sets the correct date. Her entry for Nov. 14, 1861, reads: "Gus consulting President and McClellan about another 'big expedition,' 12 o'clock before he returned."

6. Welles, *Galaxy*, 677; Porter's two versions will be found in Porter, *Incidents and Anecdotes*, 63–66, and *Battles and Leaders*, Vol. II, 23–28.

7. Porter, *Incidents and Anecdotes*, 65.

8. Fox to Welles, June 19, 1871, in Huntington Library; Welles to Fox, July 8, 1871, in Huntington Library; Porter, *Incidents and Anecdotes*, 66; *Battles and Leaders*, Vol. II, 26; Blair, "Opening the Mississippi," 38.

9. Welles, *Galaxy*, 681.

10. *Battles and Leaders*, 27; Alfred Thayer Mahan, *Admiral Farragut*, 33–50.

11. Ibid., 51–68, 94–95, 99, 112; Welles, *Galaxy*, 680–82.

12. *O.R.N.*, XVIII, 3. Welles to Porter, Nov. 18, 1861.

13. Charles Lee Lewis, *David Glasgow Farragut, Our First Admiral* (Annapolis, 1943), 10–11. Hereafter cited as Lewis, *Farragut*. The description here follows Lewis, who based his account on Porter's manuscript *Journal of Occurrences during the War of the Rebellion, 1860–1865*, Library of Congress, Manuscript Division, I, 181. The present author agrees with Lewis' evaluation: "Porter's story is probably inaccurate and, at best, highly exaggerated."

14. *Battles and Leaders*, Vol. II, 28; Farragut to Welles, Dec. 7, 1869, in Huntington Library.

15. Welles to Farragut, Dec. 15, 1861, in *Record Group 45, Letters Received by D. G. Farragut*, National Archives; Welles, *Galaxy*, 682–83; Blair, "Opening the Mississippi," 39. Fox wrote Welles that his conversation with Farragut came after dinner at Blair's on the twenty-first. Mrs. Fox's diary bears out her husband's recollection, for she recorded for Dec. 21, 1861: "Had Judge Meigs & Com. Farragut, who is to command at New Orleans, to dine, he is very pleasant and gay." The probability is that Fox and Farragut met both times, for Farragut wrote his wife that day that he had seen both Fox and Welles and that he had been given "a flag in the Gulf." Since Welles did not want to talk to Farragut until Fox had made a preliminary evaluation of him, it seems certain that Farragut and Fox met that morning and that Farragut left the breakfast conversation to go directly to Welles' office.

16. Welles, *Galaxy*, 683; Farragut to Welles, Dec. 7, 1869, in Huntington Library; Farragut to Mrs. Farragut, Dec. 21, 1861, quoted in Lewis, *Farragut*, 419. Loyall Farragut, *The Life of David Glasgow Farragut, etc.* (New York, 1879), 208, edits the message to read "Keep your lips closed," in place of "Now to begin, you must keep your mouth shut."

CHAPTER 12

1. Soley, *Porter*, 140. Soley states in his preface that his life of Admiral Porter "was undertaken in fulfillment of his wish." It is, accordingly, an "official," not a critical, biography; Richard S. West, Jr., *The*

Second Admiral: A Life of David Dixon Porter, 1813–1891 (New York, 1937), 118. Hereafter cited as West, *The Second Admiral.*

2. *Statement of Vessels Purchased at New York for United States Government now undergoing alterations and repairs to fit them for gun boats,* in *Record Group 45, Miscellaneous Letters, Navy Department,* National Archives. Hereafter cited as *Statement of Vessels Purchased at New York.* This statement, signed by Albert H. Pook for L. M. Pook, N.C. [Naval Constructor], is dated Nov. 4, 1861, five days before Porter arrived in New York on the *Powhatan.* The list included all but two of the vessels later used as mortar boats, and these two the Navy had already purchased at Philadelphia.

3. *O.R.N.,* XVIII, 3. Welles to Porter, Nov. 18, 1861; Wise to Porter, Nov. 21, 1861, in *Record Group 74, Letters and Telegrams Sent, Navy Ordnance,* National Archives; Welles to Porter, Jan. 8, 1862, in *Record Group 45, Officers, Ships of War, Vol. 65, Navy Department,* National Archives.

4. Wise to Porter, Nov. 22, 1861, in *Record Group 74, Letters to Officers, Navy Ordnance,* National Archives; Wise to Knap, Nov. 23, 1861, ibid.; Hewitt to Knap, Rudd & Co., Dec. 4, 1861, in *Cooper, Hewitt & Co. Correspondence, Book 20,* 156, Cooper Union Library; Porter to McClellan, Nov. 24, 1861, *McClellan Papers,* Library of Congress.

5. Welles to Bell, Nov. 25, 1861, in *Record Group 45, Officers, Ships of War, Vol. 65, Navy Department,* National Archives; *Statement of Vessels Purchased at New York*; *O.R.N.,* XVIII, 6.

6. New York *Tribune,* Nov. 29, 1861. In an exchange of telegrams between Gustavus Fox and George Morgan, Nov. 23–25, 1861, during Porter's absence from Washington, it was agreed that white pine would be substituted for the scarce and expensive white oak in building the blocking between the keel and the deck in the mortar schooners so that they could stand the shock of the firing of the mortars. This cut the cost in half and speeded up preparations. *Record Group 45, Miscellaneous Letters, Navy Department,* National Archives.

7. *O.R.N.,* XVIII, 3. Welles to Porter, Dec. 2, 1861.

8. Wise to Knap, Rudd & Co., Dec. 3, 1861, in *Record Group 74, Letters and Telegrams Sent, Navy Ordnance,* National Archives; Bell to Captain Andrew A. Harwood, Dec. 5, 1861, ibid.; Wise to

Knap, Rudd & Co., Dec. 8, 1861, ibid.; Welles to Fox, July 8, 1871, Huntington Library.

9. Hewitt to Captain W. B. Renshaw, Dec. 19, 1861, in *Cooper, Hewitt & Co. Correspondence, Book 20,* 280; Hewitt to Wise, Jan. 6, 1861, ibid., 403–4.

10. Welles to Porter, Dec. 21, 1861, in *Record Group 45, Officers, Ships of War, Vol. 65, Navy Department,* National Archives; New York *Tribune,* Jan. 4, 17, 21, 1862.

11. Harwood to Knap, Rudd & Co., Dec. 12, 1861, in *Record Group 74, Letters and Telegrams Sent, Navy Ordnance,* National Archives; Harwood to Knap, Rudd & Co., Dec. 21, 1861, ibid.; Wise to Porter, Jan. 30, 1862, ibid.; Porter to Wise, Jan. 30, 1862, ibid.; Wise to Porter, Jan. 31, 1862, ibid.

12. Alfred Thayer Mahan, *The Gulf and Inland Waters* (New York, 1883), 55–56. Hereafter cited as Mahan, *The Gulf and Inland Waters;* O.R.N., XVIII, 5. Welles to Farragut, Jan. 9, 1862; Lewis, *Farragut,* 16.

13. *O.R.N.,* XVIII, 5. Welles to Farragut, Jan. 13, 1862; Log of *Hartford,* cited in Lewis, *Farragut,* 17; Farragut to Mrs. Farragut, quoted in ibid., 17.

14. *O.R.N.,* XVIII, 7–8. Welles to Farragut, Jan. 20, 1862.

15. Ibid., 9. Welles to Farragut, Jan. 25, 1862; ibid., 11. Farragut to Welles, Jan. 30, 1862; ibid., 11. Welles to Farragut, Jan. 30, 1862; ibid., 13. Farragut to Welles, Feb. 5, 1862; ibid., 27. Farragut to Welles, Feb. 12, 1862; ibid., 33. Farragut to Welles, Feb. 21, 1862; West, *The Second Admiral,* 119.

16. Welles, *Galaxy,* 674–75; *O.R.,* VI, 465.

17. Parton, *Butler,* 191–92; Welles, *Galaxy,* 818; ibid., 820–21.

18. *O.R.,* VI, 694–95. McClellan to Butler, Feb. 23, 1862; ibid., 695–96. General Order No. 20, Feb. 23, 1862.

19. Benjamin Franklin Butler, *Butler's Book, etc.* (Boston, 1892), 336. Hereafter cited as Butler, *Butler's Book.*

CHAPTER 13

1. *Crescent,* Jan. 1, 7, 1862; Post Returns, Fort Jackson and Fort St. Philip, in *Confederate Army Records, Record Group 109,* National Archives.

2. *Picayune,* Jan. 3, 1862; *Commercial Bulletin,* Jan. 7, 1862; *Delta,* Jan. 10, 1862; *True Delta,* Jan. 10, 1862; *Crescent,* Jan. 11, 1862.

3. *O.R.*, VI, 795. Benjamin to Lovell, Jan. 5, 1862; ibid., 798–99. Lovell to Benjamin, Jan. 7, 1862.

4. *Crescent*, Jan. 3, 1862; *Picayune*, Jan. 12, 1862; *Commercial Bulletin*, Jan. 13, 1862; *Crescent*, Jan. 13, 1862.

5. *Delta*, Jan. 28, 1862; New York *Tribune*, Feb. 1, 1862; *O.R.*, VI, 808. Lovell to Benjamin, Jan. 15, 1862; ibid., 815. Benjamin to Lovell, Jan. 27, 1862; *Picayune*, Feb. 4, 1862.

6. *O.R.*, VI, 799. Lovell to Benjamin, Jan. 8, 1862; ibid., 808. Benjamin to Lovell, Jan. 15, 1862; ibid., 796. Benjamin to Lovell, Jan. 7, 1862. "I have to announce to you that the President has authorized the appointment of Colonel Duncan as brigadier-general," wrote Benjamin, "and his nomination will be sent to Congress tomorrow." Ellsworth Eliot, Jr., *West Point in the Confederacy* (New York, 1941), 329, states incorrectly that Duncan was made a brigadier general in April 1862. Duncan's promotion was popular. "Brigadier General Duncan is no holiday officer . . ." commented the *True Delta* (Jan. 16, 1862).

7. *Investigation of Confederate Navy Department*, 260–61. Benjamin to Lovell, Jan. 14, 1862; ibid., 261. Lovell to Benjamin, Jan. 15, 1862; *O.R.*, VI, 809. Lovell to Benjamin, Jan. 16, 1862.

8. *True Delta*, Jan. 16, 1862; *Delta*, Jan. 17, 1862; *O.R.*, VI, 811–12. Benjamin to Lovell, Jan. 19, 1862; ibid., 816–17. Lovell to Benjamin, Jan. 28, 1862.

9. St. John R. Liddell, *War Record of Gen'l St. John R. Liddell*, 35. Manuscript and typescript in Louisiana Historical Association Collection, Tulane University Archives. (Page numbers refer to typescript.)

10. Ibid., 43. The conversation presented here has been put into direct quotation.

11. Ibid., 46–47. The conversation has been put into direct quotation.

12. *True Delta*, Jan. 26, 1862; *Propagateur Catholique*, Jan. 25, 1862, quoted in *Picayune*, Jan. 26, 1862; *Commercial Bulletin*, Jan. 28, 1862; *Crescent*, Jan. 28, 1862; *Delta*, Jan. 28, 1862.

13. *Picayune*, Jan. 29, 1862; *Delta*, Jan. 31, 1862; *Crescent*, Feb. 1, 1862.

14. *Picayune*, Jan. 19, 1862; *Crescent*, Jan. 27, 1862; *Commercial Bulletin*, Jan. 20, 1862; *Picayune*, Feb. 7, 1862; *True Delta*, Feb. 7, 1862; *Investigation of Confederate Navy Department*, 119. Testimony of Joseph Pearce.

15. The *True Delta* noted on Feb. 12, 1862, "a foolish and mischievous rumor" that Beauregard had been captured on his way from Bowling Green, Ky., to Columbus, Ky. "The author or authors of these and similar false statements should have their ears nailed to the most conspicuous telegraph post until they were made to repent the falsehood they, with cruel indifference to the feeling of families, put into general circulation."

16. *Crescent*, Feb. 8, 1862; *O.R.*, VI, 823–24. Benjamin to Lovell, Feb. 8, 1862; ibid., 825. Lovell to Benjamin, Feb. 12, 1862.

17. *True Delta*, Feb. 18, 1862; *Delta*, Feb. 19, 1862; *True Delta*, Feb. 19, 1862.

18. *Proceedings of Common Council*, Feb. 18, 1862; *True Delta*, Feb. 18, 1862; Mrs. Bragg to Bragg, Mar. 12, 1862, in *Bragg Papers*, University of Texas Archives. Mrs. Bragg's comments nine days later reflect her contempt for Lovell: "Our City papers are nobly striving to allay the panic—& urgent calls are made to all to show themselves equal to the great emergency. It is impossible to read them unmoved. Lovell has not their confidence, & he knows it. At a party not long since, someone asked him a question about Manassas. *Mary Linton* with a sweeping curtsy replied for him, 'You should not ask Gen. Lovell, he was at *that time sweeping the streets of N. York.*' Such taunts are not calculated to improve his temper or his efficiency." Mrs. Bragg to Bragg, March 21, 1862, in *Bragg Papers*, William P. Palmer Collection, Western Reserve Historical Society, Cleveland.

19. *O.R.*, VI, 573. Lovell testified before the court of inquiry that his last request for funds from the Committee of Public Safety was met by a subcommittee's request for information on how the money would be spent before the request would be granted. "This I declined to do," said Lovell, "as I did not wish to make public the weak points of my department."

20. *Crescent*, Feb. 17, 1862; *Commercial Bulletin*, Feb. 18, 1862; *Delta*, Feb. 18, 1862; *Crescent*, Feb. 19, 24, 1862; *True Delta*, Feb. 21, 1862; *Picayune*, Feb. 18, 1862.

21. Coppell to Lord Russell, Jan. 3, 1862, in *Foreign Office 5, Vol. 848*, Public Record Office, London; Coppell to Lord Russell, Feb. 13, 1862, ibid.; Coppell to Lord Russell, Feb. 19, 1862, ibid.; Gov. Moore to Foreign Consuls, Feb. 18, 1862, ibid.

22. *True Delta*, Feb. 27, 1862; *Delta*, Feb. 28, Mar. 1, 1862.

23. *Delta*, Feb. 25, 28, 1862; *O.R.*, VI, 832-33. Lovell to Benjamin, Feb. 27, 1862.

CHAPTER 14

1. *O.R.N.*, XVIII, 33–34. Farragut to Welles, Feb. 21, 1862; ibid., 35. Farragut to Bailey, Feb. 22, 1862; ibid., 49–50, Farragut to Welles, Mar. 6, 1862.
2. Ibid., 43–44. Farragut to Welles, Mar. 3, 1862.
3. Ibid., 42. Porter to Welles, Feb. 28, 1862.
4. Ibid., 46. Farragut to Porter, March 4, 1862; ibid., 47. Farragut to Fox, March 5, 1862. Farragut reported to Fox that "I know all the forces of the Confederates from two deserters who came off from Fort Pike. They have seven companies at Forts Jackson and St. Philip. The deserters tell me they are sending every man they can to the northern army."
5. Ibid., 48–49. Farragut's General Order (no date, but presumably March 5, 1862).
6. Ibid., 47. Farragut to Fox, March 5, 1862; Welles to Farragut, Feb. 10, 1862, quoted in Lewis, *Farragut*, 23.
7. Fox to Porter, Feb. 24, 1862, in *David D. Porter Papers*, Library of Congress; *Confidential Correspondence of Fox*, Vol. II, 89–91. Porter to Fox, March 28, 1862; ibid., 98. Porter to Fox, April 8, 1862.
8. *O.R.N.*, XVIII, 64. Farragut to Welles, March 14, 1862; ibid., 67–68. Farragut to Fox, March 16, 1862; ibid., 62–63. Bell to Farragut, March 13, 1862; Loyall Farragut, *Farragut*, 217.
9. *O.R.N.*, XVIII, 68. Farragut to Fox, March 16, 1862; ibid., 71. Farragut to Welles, March 18, 1862; ibid., 68. Porter to Welles, March 16, 1862; ibid., 71. Porter to Welles, March 18, 1862.
10. *Delta*, March 6, 1862. The *Delta* berated those who are "seeking by various means to depreciate the securities or paper issues of our Government . . . Those who seek to discredit the Government directly or indirectly are as dangerous and disloyal citizens as those who are ready to extend a welcome to the invader"; ibid., March 16, 1862; the *Picayune*, March 26, 1862; commented: "It is said in town that a few farsighted speculators attempted lately to buy all the black dry goods they could find in every store in town, for the purpose of carrying on a double speculation. Should the militia be

uniformed with black cloth, as it was proposed in some quarters, those speculators would have been able to dictate their own prices, for all the black cloth in New Orleans would have been in their hands. On the other hand, should any murderous battle take place near our city, as it was expected some days ago, all the unfortunate widows and orphans of the New Orleans heroes fallen on the battlefield would be compelled to resort to the stores of these speculators to buy their mourning weeds, and then again these shameless sharks could reap a handsome benefit. Happily for the honor of our population, a number of merchants, suspecting there was a nefarious plan on the *tapis*, refused to sell their black goods on any terms, and the speculation was abandoned."

11. *O.R.*, VI, 842. Lovell to Benjamin, March 6, 1862; ibid., 847. Lovell to Benjamin, March 9, 1862; ibid., 850. Lovell to Benjamin, March 10, 1862; ibid., 562. Lovell's testimony before court of inquiry.

12. *Delta*, March 11, 1862; *Picayune*, March 12, 1862; Moore, Moise, and Lovell to Davis, March 12, 1862, in *Jefferson Davis Papers*, Louisiana Historical Association Collection, Tulane University Archives; *O.R.*, VI, 856. Davis to Moore, March 13, 1862; ibid., 857–58. General Orders No. 10, Department No. 1, March 15, 1862; *True Delta*, March 16, 19, 1862; *Crescent*, March 17, 18, 19, 20, 1862.

13. *O.R.*, VI, 860–61. General Orders No. 11, Department No. 1, March 18, 1862; ibid., 864–65. Lovell to Benjamin, March 22, 1862.

14. The correspondence between the Tifts and Mallory will be found in *Investigation of Confederate Navy Department*, 153–204.

15. Loyall Farragut, *Farragut*, 217; *Confidential Correspondence of Fox*, Vol. II, 92. Porter to Fox, March 28, 1862; Lewis, *Farragut*, 30; Butler, *Butler's Book*, 355.

16. *O.R.N.*, XVIII, 732. Log of *Richmond*; *Confidential Correspondence of Fox*, Vol. I, 307. Farragut to Fox, March 21, 1862; *O.R.N.*, XVIII, 88. Farragut to Bailey, March 28, 1862; *Confidential Correspondence of Fox*, Vol. I, 310. Farragut to Fox, April 8, 1862; ibid., Vol. II, 96–97. Porter to Fox, April 8, 1862; Porter, *Journal*, Library of Congress.

17. *Confidential Correspondence of Fox*, Vol. I, 310. Farragut to Fox, April 8, 1862.

18. *O.R.*, VI, 521–23. Duncan's report, April 30, 1862.

19. *O.R.*, VI, 535. Duncan to Stevenson, April 6, 1862; ibid., 535–36. Duncan to Stevenson, April 9, 1862; ibid., 522–23. Duncan's report, April 30, 1862.

CHAPTER 15

1. These "broadcasts" are practically verbatim comments from the various sources listed below, with several additions and slight changes in tense and sentence structure.
2. *Diary of Captain Warren.* Entries quoted: Dec. 3, 1861; March 23, 26, 31, April 1, 3, 1862.
3. The New Orleans papers quoted in the narrative were as follows:
   Picayune, Feb. 21, March 5, 30, April 8, 9, 1862.
   Crescent, March 14, 15, 31, April 15, 19, 1862.
   Delta, March 2, 11, 14, 15, 22, April 1, 4, 5, 1862.
   True Delta, March 2, 16, 22, 1862.
   Bee, March 25, 1862.
4. The lengthy account of Fort Jackson's first fight was printed in the *Picayune*, April 15, 1862.
5. Dewey, *Autobiography*, 57; *Battles and Leaders*, Vol. II, 56–58; Jim Dan Hill, *Sea Dogs of the Sixties* (Minneapolis, 1935), 15. Hereafter cited as Hill, *Sea Dogs*; Mahan, *The Gulf and Inland Waters*, 54; Lewis, *Farragut*, 33; *O.R.N.*, XVIII, 155; ibid., 734–36; ibid., 199; Charles S. Foltz, *Surgeon of the Seas, etc.* (Indianapolis, 1931), 213. Hereafter cited as Foltz, *Surgeon of the Seas*.

CHAPTER 16

1. Hill, *Sea Dogs*, 17.
2. *O.R.N.*, XVIII, 14–15. Welles to Farragut, Feb. 10, 1862; ibid., 15–23. Barnard's memorandum, Jan. 28, 1862. Barnard was long familiar with the Mississippi and the forts, having been associated for a number of years with Beauregard in that area. In 1853, Barnard and Beauregard served on a board of engineers considering the feasibility of deepening the passes of the river. See *House Document 16*, 33d Congress, 1st Session.
3. *O.R.N.*, XVIII, 684–86. Private diary of H. H. Bell; ibid., 89. Bell to Farragut, March 28, 1862.
4. Ibid., 799. Log of *Iroquois*, April 5, 1862; Albert Bigelow Paine (ed.), *A Sailor of Fortune: Personal Memoirs of Captain B. S. Osbon*

(New York, 1906), 178. Hereafter cited as Paine, *A Sailor of Fortune.* Osbon erroneously gives the date as March 29, 1862; Asher Taylor, *Notes of Conversations with a Volunteer Officer in the United States Navy on the Passage of the Forts Below New Orleans* (privately printed, New York, 1868), 8. Hereafter cited as Taylor, *Notes of Conversations.* The officer was Captain Gorham Coffin Taylor of New York, who died in 1868, and the author was his father. One hundred copies were printed, but a penciled note in the Library of Congress copy states: "but only 40 issued"; *O.R.N.,* XVIII, 734. Journal of *Richmond,* April 13, 1862.

5. F. H. Gerdes, "The Surrender of Forts Jackson and St. Philip on the Lower Mississippi," *Continental Magazine,* Vol. III, No. 5 (May 1863), 558; *O.R.N.,* XVIII, 424. Gerdes' report to Bache; ibid., 362. Porter to Welles, April 30, 1862.

6. Ibid.; Porter's *Journal,* Library of Congress.

7. *Ordnance Instructions for the United States Navy* (4th ed.; Washington, 1866), 115, 118; George W. Brown, "The Mortar Flotilla," in *Personal Recollections of the War of Rebellion* (New York Commandery, Military Order of Loyal Legion, New York, 1891), 175–76. Hereafter cited as Brown, "The Mortar Flotilla."

8. *Confidential Correspondence of Fox,* Vol. II, 93; *O.R.N.,* XVIII, 362–63. Porter to Welles, April 30, 1862.

9. *O.R.,* VI, 878. Moore to Davis, April 17, 1862; ibid., 650. Whittle to Lovell, April 11, 1862. Whittle to Lovell: "May it not be that the city is in as much danger from above as from below? This opinion, it would seem, is entertained in a high quarter in Richmond; I mean at the Navy Department"; ibid., 878. Davis to Moore, April 17, 1862.

10. Ibid., 646. Lovell to Randolph, April 11, 1862; ibid., 877. Lovell to Randolph, April 15, 1862; ibid., 650. Lovell to Randolph, April 17, 1862.

11. *Investigation of Confederate Navy Department,* 48; ibid., 95. Hollins to Mallory, April 9, 1862; ibid., 95. Mallory to Hollins, April 10, 1862; ibid., 96. Hollins to Mallory, April 11, 1862; ibid., 48–50.

12. *O.R.N.,* XVIII, 363. Porter to Welles, April 30, 1862; B. S. Osbon (ed.), *Cruise of the U.S. Flagship Hartford, 1862 . . . From the Journal of William C. Holton* (New York, 1863). Reprinted in *Magazine of History,* Vol. XXII, No. 3, Extra Number No. 87 (1922), 19.

13. *O.R.N.,* XVIII, 693. Private diary of H. H. Bell, April 18, 1862;

ibid., 402. Log of *C. P. Williams*; ibid., 421. Log of *Sea Foam*; *O.R.*, VI, 525. Duncan's report, April 30, 1862.

14. *O.R.N.*, XVIII, 364. Porter to Welles, April 30, 1862; ibid., 693. Private diary of H. H. Bell; Brown, "The Mortar Flotilla," 178–79.

15. Manuscript, *Journal of Carpenter's Mate William M. Philbrick, Aboard Portsmouth*, April 19, 1862, in *Naval Records Collections, Record Group 45*, National Archives; Manuscript, *Diary of 2nd Assistant Engineer Isaac De Graff, Aboard Hartford*, April 18, 1862, ibid.; *O.R.*, XVIII, 693. Private diary of H. H. Bell; *O.R.*, VI, 525. Duncan's report, April 30, 1862.

16. *O.R.N.*, XVIII, 364. Porter to Welles, April 30, 1862; *O.R.*, VI, 550. Report of Captain M. T. Squires, April 27, 1862; *O.R.N.*, XVIII, 736. Journal of *Richmond*.

17. Ibid., 364. Porter to Welles, April 30, 1862; *O.R.*, VI, 525. Duncan's report, April 30, 1862; *Philbrick Journal*, in National Archives.

18. *O.R.*, VI, 525. Duncan's report, April 30, 1862; *O.R.N.*, XVIII, 364. Porter to Welles, April 30, 1862.

19. *Bee*, April 19, 1862; *Delta*, April 19, 1862.

20. *O.R.N.*, XVIII, 428. Report of Julius Kroehl, June 2, 1862. Kroehl stated that on April 15, accompanied by Porter, he had blown up a raft, lodged on the bank, with a 50-pounder charge exploded by a galvanic battery.

21. *O.R.N.*, XVIII, 694. Private diary of H. H. Bell; ibid., 365. Porter to Welles, April 30, 1862; *O.R.*, VI, 525. Duncan's report, April 30, 1862; *O.R.N.*, XVIII, 776. Log of *Oneida*.

22. Mrs. Butler to Blanche Butler, April 19, 1862, in *Private and Official Correspondence of General Benjamin F. Butler during the Period of the Civil War* (privately issued, 1917), Vol. I, 416; *Delta*, April 19, 1862; *True Delta*, April 20, 1862.

23. Dewey, *Autobiography*, 55; Foltz, *Surgeon of the Seas*, 216; *O.R.*, VI, 525. Duncan's report, April 30, 1862.

24. This account of the deserter from Fort Jackson is based upon the following: *Diary of Oscar Smith, U. S. Marine Corps, Aboard Flagship Hartford, 1861–1862, etc.*, April 20, 1862, Library of Congress; *O.R.N.*, XVIII, 367, 399; Osbon, *Journal of William Holton*, 20; *Diary of Isaac De Graff*, April 20, 1862, National Archives.

25. *O.R.N.*, XVIII, 695. Private diary of H. H. Bell; Loyall Farragut, *Farragut*, 218–19.

CHAPTER 17

1. *Bee*, April 21, 22, 23, 1862; *True Delta*, April 22, 1862; *Delta*, April 22, 1862; *Picayune*, April 23, 1862.
2. *Delta*, April 23, 1862; *Crescent*, April 23, 1862; *Commercial Bulletin*, April 21, 1862.
3. *O.R.N.*, XVIII, 324. Whittle to Mitchell, April 19, 1862; ibid., 290. Mitchell to Mallory, Aug. 19, 1862; *Investigation of Confederate Navy Department*, 30. Mitchell's testimony.
4. Ibid., 187–88. Tifts to Mallory, April 5, 1862; ibid., 187. Pearce to Tifts, March 27, 1862; *O.R.*, VI, 578; *Investigation of Confederate Navy Department*, 191, 194.
5. *O.R.N.*, XVIII, 695. Private diary of H. H. Bell, April 20, 1862; *Confidential Correspondence of Fox*, Vol. II, 100. Porter to Fox, May 10, 1862; *O.R.N.*, XVIII, 145–46. Proposition of Commander D. D. Porter.
6. Ibid., 160. Farragut's general order, April 20, 1862.
7. Lewis, *Farragut*, 49; *O.R.N.*, XVIII, 136. Farragut to Welles, April 20, 1862. This appears to be the rough draft of a letter dated April 21, 1862, with the flag officer's complaint toned down somewhat. See ibid., 134–35.
8. Ibid., 695. Private diary of H. H. Bell, April 20, 1862; Porter's *Journal*, Library of Congress.
9. *O.R.N.*, XVIII, 696. Private diary of H. H. Bell; Lewis, *Farragut*, 49, errs when he places Bell on the *Itasca*; Hill, *Twenty Years at Sea*, 168; *O.R.N.*, XVIII, 429. Kroehl's report, June 2, 1862; J. F. Cooke to A. T. Mahan, Feb. 1883, in *Naval Records Collections, Area 5 File, 1861–1865*, National Archives. Cooke was an officer on the *Pinola* and corresponded with Captain Mahan when the latter was writing *The Gulf and Inland Waters*; ibid. Cooke to wife, April 22, 1862; *O.R.N.*, XVIII, 696. Private diary of H. H. Bell. The conversation has been put into direct quotation.
10. Ibid.; Cooke to Mahan, op. cit.; *O.R.N.*, XVIII, 813. Log of *Itasca*, April 21, 1862.
11. Hill, *Twenty Years at Sea*, 169; *O.R.N.*, XVIII, 720. Log of *Hartford*, April 21, 1862; Farragut to Mrs. Farragut, April 21, 1862, in Loyall Farragut, *Farragut*, 226–27.
12. *O.R.N.*, XVIII, 720. Log of *Hartford*, April 21, 1862; ibid., 738. Journal of *Richmond*, April 21, 1862; ibid., 756. Log of *Sciota*, April 21, 1862; ibid., 800. Log of *Iroquois*, April 21, 1862.

13. *O.R.*, VI, 525–26. Duncan's report, April 30, 1862; ibid., 535. Duncan to Stevenson, April 6, 1862.

14. Hill, *Twenty Years at Sea*, 166–67; Dewey, *Autobiography*, 55; *O.R.N.*, XVIII, 366. Porter to Welles, April 30, 1862; Brown, "The Mortar Flotilla," 179; Francis A. Clary, *The Color Bearer* (New York, 1863), 41; *Diary of Captain Warren*, April 20, 1862.

15. *O.R.*, VI, 526. Duncan's report, April 30, 1862; *O.R.N.*, XVIII, 366. Porter to Welles, April 30, 1862; ibid., 324. Mitchell to Duncan, April 22, 1862; ibid., 370. Duncan to Mitchell, April 22, 1862; ibid., 325. Mitchell to Duncan, April 23, 1862.

16. Dewey, *Autobiography*, 58; Butler, *Butler's Book*, 364; *O.R.*, VI, 527. Duncan's report, April 30, 1862.

17. *O.R.N.*, XVIII, 328. Stevenson to Mitchell, April 21, 1862; ibid. Mitchell to Duncan, April 23, 1862.

18. *O.R.*, VI, 569. The conversation is reconstructed and placed into direct quotations from the testimony of S. L. James before the court of inquiry; *O.R.N.*, XVIII, 329. Whittle to Mitchell, April 23, 1862; ibid. Duncan to Mitchell, April 23, 1862; ibid. Mitchell to Whittle, April 23, 1862; *O.R.*, VI, 590. Higgins' testimony before the court of inquiry.

19. Farragut to Porter, April 22, 1862, in *Porter Papers*, Library of Congress; Foltz, *Surgeon of the Seas*, 213–14.

20. Porter, *Journal*.

21. Paine, *A Sailor of Fortune*, 182–84. Porter's comments on Osbon in his manuscript journal are interesting: "This fellow came to me, while I was fitting out the mortar fleet in New York and asked me to give him a situation on board, but not liking his looks I declined doing so . . . He asked me if I would give him a letter to Farragut . . . He caught the *Hartford* before she left New Castle . . . and . . . Farragut accepted his service . . . When I arrived at the squadron I found Osbon to be the most important personage on board the flagship. He was signal officer, secretary, aid, 'chief cook and bottle washer' . . . If a vessel was seen coming up the river, Farragut would call Osbon to see which one it was, if a gun was heard, Osbon was enquired of to learn who fired, and in fact, he kept Farragut posted in all that was going on. Had Osbon been a decent fellow this would have been very well, on the contrary, however, he was despised by everyone on board the *Hartford*, yet he is the only one who ever wrote a history of the operation below

New Orleans. Whence Osbon got his data, no one knows, for it is well known fact that he stowed himself away in a state room when the first shot struck the *Hartford* and was not seen again, until all was over!"

22. *O.R.N.*, XVIII, 367. Porter to Welles, April 30, 1862; *Confidential Correspondence of Fox*, Vol. II, 100. Porter to Fox, May 10, 1862; Welles, *Galaxy*, 827–28.

23. *O.R.N.*, XVIII, 156. Farragut to Welles, May 6, 1862; ibid., 141. Farragut to De Camp, April 23, 1862; ibid., 141. Farragut's general order, April 23, 1862; ibid., 754. Log of *Cayuga*; Harrison to J. T. Headley, Aug. 24, 1866, typescript, in *Record Group 45, Area 5 File, Naval Records*, National Archives.

24. *O.R.N.*, XVIII, 813. Log of *Itasca*; Paine, *A Sailor of Fortune*, 185–86.

25. Hill, *Twenty Years at Sea*, 173–74; H. H. Wilson, *Diary, Cruise of the Oneida*, April 23, 1862. Manuscript in Southern Historical Collection, University of North Carolina; *O.R.N.*, XVIII, 768. Francis A. Roe, *Diary*.

26. *Picayune*, April 24, 1862; *O.R.*, VI, 541. Duncan to Mitchell, April 24, 1862.

CHAPTER 18

1. Bartholomew Diggins, *Recollections of the Cruise of the U.S.S. Hartford, etc.*, 78. Manuscript in New York Public Library. Hereafter cited as Diggins, *Recollections*.

2. Hill, *Twenty Years at Sea*, 174–75.

3. Paine, *A Sailor of Fortune*, 188; *O.R.N.*, XVIII, 768.

4. Paine, *A Soldier of Fortune*, 190–91; *O.R.*, VI, 528. Duncan's report, April 30, 1862; *O.R.N.*, XVIII, 754. Log of *Cayuga*, April 24, 1862; *Battles and Leaders*, Vol. II, 100; *O.R.*, VI, 540–41. Duncan to Mitchell, April 24, 1862.

5. George E. Belknap (ed.), *Letters of Captain George Hamilton Perkins, USN* (2d ed.; Concord, N.H., 1901; originally published 1886), 73. Hereafter cited as Belknap, *Perkins Letters; O.R.N.*, XVIII, 754. Log of *Cayuga; Army and Navy Journal*, July 17, 1869.

6. Paine, *A Sailor of Fortune*, 191; Osbon, *Holton Diary*, 22; *O.R.N.*, XVIII, 792. Log of *Kineo*, April 24, 1862; ibid., 739. Journal of *Richmond*, April 24, 1862; Hill, *Twenty Years at Sea*, 176; *O.R.N.*, XVIII, 769. Roe, *Diary*.

7. Newspaper clippings of letter from Union officer to his mother, in scrapbook of Col. George Soulé, Tulane University Archives; Paine, *A Sailor of Fortune*, 193; *O.R.N.*, XVIII, 157. Farragut to Welles, May 6, 1862.

8. Paine, *A Sailor of Fortune*, 192, 193–95.

9. *O.R.N.*, XVIII, 154. Farragut to Fox, April 25, 1862; ibid., 142. Farragut to Porter, April 24, 1862; *Battles and Leaders*, Vol. II, 64; ibid., 45; Diggins, *Recollections*, 88–90; Foltz, *Surgeon of the Seas*, 222.

10. Paine, *A Sailor of Fortune*, 196–97; Diggins, *Recollections*, 94–96. Diggins wrote that it was his belief that "this incident . . . passed intirely [*sic*] without record of farther notice. Yet it was one of the most daring . . . acts of Bravery that I knew of through out the war, it was a choice between giving up the Ship, or blowing up the Ship and Capt. Wainwright chose the later [*sic*] . . . Some of the firemen told me afterwards that they expected every moment to be their last, and the danger was increasing every moment untill [*sic*] She came off . . ."; *Journal of Second Assistant Engineer Edward B. Latch, Aboard Hartford, etc.*, April 24, 1862, in *Record Group 45, Naval Records*, National Archives.

11. *O.R.N.*, XVIII, 224–25. John H. Russell to Farragut, April 29, 1862; ibid., 225–26. Caldwell to Farragut, April 24, 1862; ibid., 226–27. Ed. T. Nichols to Farragut, April 30, 1862.

12. Ibid., 182. Craven to Farragut, April 26, 1862; ibid., 197–98. Craven to Mrs. Craven, May 16, 1862.

13. Dewey, *Autobiography*, 61, 63–65, 67.

14. *O.R.*, VI, 528. Duncan's report; ibid., 548. Higgins' report; ibid., 552. Squires' report.

15. *O.R.N.*, XVIII, 294–95. Mitchell to Mallory, Aug. 19, 1862.

16. Ibid., 754. Log of *Cayuga*, April 24, 1862; Belknap, *Perkins Letters*, 73; *O.R.N.*, XVIII, 171. Bailey to Farragut, April 25, 1861; ibid., 210. Boggs to Farragut, April 29, 1862; ibid., 150. Bailey to Montgomery Blair, May 8, 1862.

17. A. F. Warley, "The Ram *Manassas* at the Passage of the New Orleans Forts," in *Battles and Leaders*, Vol. II, 90–91; *O.R.N.*, XVIII, 332–33. Read to Whittle, May 1, 1862.

18. Dewey, *Autobiography*, 68–70; *O.R.N.*, XVIII, 303. Warley to Mitchell, June 8, 1862.

19. Ibid., 304–9. Kennon to Mitchell, May 4, 1862; Writing to Alfred

T. Mahan, on March 12, 1883, Kennon, in a very long letter, said, "Had I had one thousand men, I would have lost nine hundred, for the heaviest shot and shell were thrown at very close range—in some instances but ten feet distance. My vessel was honeycombed above and toward the end of the fight below water. I had 61 killed & 13 wounded out of a complement of ninety-three persons. [In his report Kennon gave fifty-seven dead and seven wounded.] The preponderance of killed over wounded was caused by the projectiles killing men long wounded, and let me add that the dead were struck so often that they were unrecognizable." Letter is in *Record Group 45, Naval Records, Area 5 File*, National Archives.

20. *O.R.N.*, XVIII, 171. Bailey to Farragut, April 25, 1862; Belknap, *Perkins Letters*, 74; *O.R.*, VI, 580. Szymanski's testimony before court of inquiry.

21. *O.R.N.*, XVIII, 769–70. Roe, *Diary*; ibid., 152. Farragut to Welles, April 25, 1862; ibid., 180. Foltz to Farragut, May 18, 1862; ibid., 283–84. Fort St. Philip and Fort Jackson casualty lists; Lewis, *Farragut*, 63.

22. *O.R.N.*, XVIII, 309. Kennon to Mitchell, May 4, 1862. Kennon said: "The gunboat *Jackson*, Lieutenant Commanding F. B. Renshaw, C.S., Navy, when last seen was going with all haste toward the source of the Mississippi"; ibid., 297. Mitchell to Mallory, Aug. 19, 1862; ibid., 302. Jos. D. Grafton to Mitchell, April 24, 1862; Soley, *Porter*, 196.

23. *O.R.N.*, XVIII, 142. Farragut to Porter, April 24, 1862. Commander Boggs used a bayou at Quarantine to reach the Gulf and thence upriver to deliver the message to Porter; Butler's *Correspondence*, Vol. I, 420. Butler to Farragut, April 24, 1862; ibid., 426. Butler to Stanton, April 29, 1862; ibid., 422. Butler to Mrs. Butler, April 26, 1862; Porter, *Journal*, Library of Congress. Porter's biographer, James Russell Soley, agreed with Porter: "Had the *Louisiana*, with her armament and armor, been properly manned, equipped, and propelled so as to equal or exceed in speed Farragut's ships, nothing but a miracle would have saved him from serious loss." Soley, *Porter*, 196.

CHAPTER 19

1. *Delta*, April 24, 1862; *Picayune*, April 24, 1862.
2. *Picayune*, April 24, 1862; *Crescent*, April 24, 1862; *Delta*, April 24,

1862; *Commercial Bulletin*, April 24, 1862; *True Delta*, April 24, 1862.

3. *Picayune*, April 24, 1862; *Commercial Bulletin*, April 24, 1862.

4. *True Delta*, April 25, 1862; Zoe Campbell, *Diary*, Department of Archives, Louisiana State University; Mrs. Mary Newman to sister, May 28, 1862, in *Benjamin F. Butler Papers*, Library of Congress; Rosella Kenner Brent, *Recollections*, typescript in Department of Archives, Louisiana State University; *English Composition Book, Institut Catholique*, 208; *Southern Historical Society Papers*, Vol. XXIII (1895), 182; Mrs. Robert Dow Urquhart, *New Orleans Confederate Journal*, in Urquhart, papers of Urquhart collection, Tulane University Archives; Clara Solomon, *Diary*, Department of Archives, Louisiana State University.

5. A. Mazureau to Ben Bland, Esq., and Col. James M. Putnam, April 24, 1862, in *Benjamin F. Butler Papers*, Library of Congress. The letter, in part, reads: "You are hereby commanded to have all the cotton stored up in this City removed immediately to such place as you may select and to have it piled up there that it may be turned to such purposes as the defense of the city may require—and you are empowered and commanded to require such draymen as may be pressed into immediate service to transport said cotton to the place or places thus selected . . ." Approved by Provost Marshal Pierre Soulé, this order bears an endorsement authorizing Putnam to take the horses and mules of the Railroad Company or any other horses or mules.

6. *New Orleans Price Current, Commercial Intelligencer and Merchants' Transcript*, April 26, 1862. The *Delta*, May 2, 1862, said 15,000 bales of cotton were destroyed; *Commercial Bulletin*, April 25, 1862; Mrs. Robert Dow Urquhart, *Journal*; Florence J. O'Connor, *The Heroine of the Confederacy* (London, 1866), 248–49; Mrs. Frances Hall, *Major Hall's Wife* (Syracuse, 1884), 10.

7. *O.R.*, VI, 565. Lovell's testimony; *Journal of Julia LeGrand*, 40; Southwood, *"Beauty and Booty,"* 19; Mrs. Bragg to Bragg, April 29, 1862, in *Bragg Papers*, Palmer Collection, Western Reserve Historical Society.

8. Southwood, *"Beauty and Booty,"* 21; *True Delta*, April 26, 1862; *English Composition Book, Institut Catholique*, 210; George H. Devol, *Forty Years a Gambler on the Mississippi*, 118–19.

9. O'Connor, *The Heroine of the Confederacy*, 250; Hall, *Major Hall's Wife*, 9.

10. George W. Cable, "New Orleans Before the Capture," in *Battles and Leaders*, Vol. II, 19–20.

11. *O.R.N.*, Series II, I, 466. Mallory to Mitchell, March 15, 1862; Benjamin to Mann, April 14, 1862, in *Confederate Naval Collection*, Library of Congress.

12. *Investigation of Confederate Navy Department*, 11–12. Whittle's testimony; *O.R.N.*, XVIII, 330. Moore to Davis, April 24, 1862.

13. *Investigation of Confederate Navy Department*, 11, 63. Conversation reconstructed from testimony.

14. Ibid., 62–63, 390. Writing to Mallory on Aug. 26, 1862, the Tifts said of the destruction of the *Mississippi*: ". . . We knew nothing of the order to burn her until we saw her on fire. It is impossible to describe our feelings."

15. James Iredell Waddell, *Autobiography*, typescript in Division of Naval History, National Archives.

16. *Investigation of Confederate Navy Department*, 63. Sinclair's testimony. Feeling ran high against the Tifts after the *Mississippi* was fired, doubtless stemming from their opposition to what they considered a premature launching of the vessel. When the *Peytona* reached Vicksburg they were arrested on telegraphic orders from Pierre Soulé, charging them with setting the *Mississippi* on fire. Despite the testimony to the contrary from Whittle, Sinclair, and Paymaster Felix Senac, the military governor of the district did not release the Tifts, but sent them to Governor Pettus of Mississippi at Jackson, who examined the testimony and released the brothers. At the time of their arrest in Vicksburg, the Tifts were threatened with mob violence. The Tifts credited the moral courage of Senac with helping to save them. "He met the excitement of the crowd, and the insolence of the officer who arrested us, with the spirit of a brave man and a true friend." *Investigation of Confederate Navy Department*, 194–95.

CHAPTER 20

1. *O.R.N.*, XVIII, 158. Farragut to Welles, May 6, 1862; ibid., 741. Journal of *Richmond*; ibid., 740; Oscar Smith, *Diary*, April 25, 1862, Library of Congress.

2. *O.R.N.*, XVIII, 755. Log of *Cayuga*, April 25, 1862; ibid., 158. Farragut to Welles, May 6, 1862; ibid., 770. Roe, *Diary.*

3. *O.R.*, VI, 553. Report of Gen. M. L. Smith; *O.R.N.*, XVIII, 154. Farragut to Fox, April 25, 1862.

4. Ibid., 158. Farragut to Welles, May 6, 1862; ibid., 722. Log of *Hartford*, April 25, 1862; *Southern Historical Society Papers*, Vol. XXIII (1895), 183.

5. Belknap, *Perkins Letters*, 76; *Battles and Leaders*, Vol. II, 21; Marion A. Baker, "Farragut's Demand for the Surrender of New Orleans," in *Battles and Leaders*, Vol. II, 95.

6. Coppell to Lord Russell, May 9, 1862, *Foreign Office 5, Vol. 848*, Public Record Office, London; Belknap, *Perkins Letters*, 76–77; *De Bow's Review*, New Series, VIII (1862), 89.

7. *O.R.N.*, XVIII, 741. Log of *Richmond*, April 25, 1862; *Crescent*, April 25, 1862; Belknap, *Perkins Letters*, 78; *Crescent*, April 25, 1862; *Delta*, April 25, 1862; *O.R.*, VI, 568. Major James' testimony.

8. *O.R.N.*, XVIII, 229. Mayor Monroe to Common Council, April 25, 1862; *Battles and Leaders*, Vol. II, 95; *O.R.N.*, XVIII, 231. Farragut to Monroe, April 26, 1862; ibid., 230. Resolution of Common Council, April 26, 1862.

9. *Battles and Leaders*, Vol. II, 96; *O.R.N.*, XVIII, 231–32. Monroe to Farragut, April 26, 1862.

10. Albert Kautz, "Incidents of the Occupation of New Orleans," in *Battles and Leaders*, Vol. II, 91–92; *Southern Historical Society Papers*, Vol. XXIII (1895), 184; *O.R.N.*, XVIII, 230–31. Farragut to Monroe, April 26, 1862; *Battles and Leaders*, Vol. II, 92–93, 97.

11. *Battles and Leaders*, Vol. II, 98; *The Fire and Alarm Telegraph. Records of Messages Received and Sent, 1860–1863*, New Orleans Public Library, listed the countersign for April 26 as "Beauregard," with those of subsequent nights being "Providence and Patience," "Order and Orleans," "Courage and Confidence," "Public Safety," "Washington and Wisdom."

12. *The Fire and Alarm Telegraph. Records of Messages, etc.*, April 27, 1862; *O.R.N.*, XVIII, 232–33. Farragut to Monroe, April 28, 1862; ibid., 697. Private diary of H. H. Bell, April 28, 1862; *Battles and Leaders*, Vol. II, 98.

13. *O.R.N.*, XVIII, 233–34. Monroe to Common Council, April 28, 1862; *Battles and Leaders*, Vol. II, 98; *O.R.N.*, XVIII, 234–35. Monroe to Farragut, April 28, 1862.

14. *Battles and Leaders*, Vol. II, 98; ibid., 238. Farragut to British consul, April 28, 1862; ibid., 239. Foreign consuls to Farragut, April 28, 1862; *Delta*, May 1, 1862. Captain Cloué's letter is reprinted in *O.R.N.*, XVIII, 239.

15. Mrs. Robert Dow Urquhart, *Journal*. Other testimony bears out Mrs. Urquhart's statement. The unidentified diarist whose account appears in the *Southern Historical Society Papers*, Vol. XXIII (1895), p. 186, wrote: "The ladies of New Orleans signed a petition and handed it to the mayor, requesting him not to give up to the demands of the Yankees."

16. *O.R.N.*, XVIII, 331. Memorandum of agreement signed by C. W. Read, April 27, 1862; ibid., 333–34. Read to Whittle, May 1, 1862. Farragut and other Federal officers accused Read of bad faith in the matter of the *McRae*, but that he tried to save the vessel and did send ashore for police help is proved in an entry in the *Fire and Alarm Telegraph Message Book*, April 27, 1862: "11¼ p.m. The Gun Boat *McRae* has broke from her moorings and drifting down the river leaking badly. Lieut. Brooks has sent 10 Workmen to render assistance."

CHAPTER 21

1. *O.R.N.*, XVIII, 379. Guest to Porter, April 28, 1862.

2. *O.R.*, VI, 529. Duncan's report, April 30, 1862; *O.R.N.*, XVIII, 368–69. Porter to Welles, April 30, 1862.

3. *O.R.*, VI, 541. Mitchell to Duncan, April 24, 1862; ibid., 529–30. Duncan's report, April 30, 1862; ibid., 541. Mitchell to Duncan, April 24, 1862 (second letter); Duncan to Mrs. Duncan, April 24, 1862, in *Duncan Papers*, in possession of Mrs. Mildred Parham of New Orleans.

4. Ibid. Duncan to Mrs. Duncan, April 25, 1862, in *Duncan Papers*; *O.R.*, VI, 531. Duncan's report, April 30, 1862.

5. Ibid., 530; ibid., 543. Porter to Higgins, April 26, 1862; ibid., 543–44. Higgins to Porter, April 27, 1862.

6. Ibid., 531. Duncan's report, April 30, 1862; ibid., 544.

7. Ibid., 531–32. Duncan's report, April 30, 1862.

8. Ibid., 532. Duncan's report, April 30, 1862; *O.R.N.*, XVIII, 298–99. Mitchell's report; Porter, *Incidents and Anecdotes*, 49.

9. Ibid., 52–54.

10. *O.R.*, VI, 533. Duncan's report, April 30, 1862; Oscar Smith, *Diary*, April 29, 1862, Library of Congress.

11. *O.R.N.*, XVIII, 235. Farragut to Monroe, April 29, 1862; *Battles and Leaders*, Vol. II, 98.

12. *O.R.N.*, XVIII, 698. Private diary of H. H. Bell, April 29, 1862; Mrs. Robert Dow Urquhart, *Journal*; *Battles and Leaders*, Vol. II, 99; ibid., 93; *Fire and Alarm Telegraph Message Book*, April 29, 1862.

13. *O.R.N.*, XVIII, 698. Private diary of H. H. Bell, April 29, 1862; *Battles and Leaders*, Vol. II, 21.

14. *Picayune*, April 30, 1862; *Commercial Bulletin*, April 29, 1862.

15. Oscar Smith, *Diary*, dates listed. Library of Congress.

CHAPTER 22

1. Mary Boykin Chestnut, *A Diary from Dixie*, edited by Ben Ames Williams (Boston, 1949), 215. Two days later, Mrs. Chestnut entered in her diary: "The news from New Orleans is fatal to us."

2. Liddell, *War Record*, 67.

3. Worthington Chauncey Ford (ed.), *A Cycle of Adams Letters, 1861–1865* (2 vols.; Boston and New York, 1920), 143–46.

4. Sarah Agnes Wallace and Frances Elma Gillespie (eds.), *The Journal of Benjamin Moran* (2 vols.; Chicago, 1949), Vol. II, 1003, 1005.

5. Cobden to Sumner, Jan. 23, 1862. Quoted in Brougham Villiers and W. H. Cheasson, *Anglo-American Relations, 1861–1865* (London, 1919), 66.

6. *Illustrated London News*, Vol. XL, No. 1142 (May 3, 1862).

7. Slidell to Sec. of State Hunter, Feb. 26, 1862; Slidell to Hunter, March 10, 1862; Slidell to Benjamin, April 14, 1862; Slidell to Benjamin, May 15, 1862. All in *Confederate State Department Correspondence*, in *Pickett Papers*, Library of Congress.

8. Mahan, *Farragut*, 176; Lewis, *Farragut*, 77; James Morton Callahan, *The Diplomatic History of the Southern Confederacy* (Baltimore, 1901), 101. Earlier (p. 25) Callahan declared: "The Confederacy had a *de facto* Government, though it was not formally recognized by any power. For over three years it made its home in Richmond, and the vast armies of the United States unsuccessfully beat against its stronghold. It adopted a flag and a seal of its own. More important than flag or seal, it had an army whose achievements won

the admiration of the world; but it had no navy with which to open the blockade and give the Government that probability of permanence which was necessary to secure European recognition."

9. "Letters of General Thomas Williams, 1862," *American Historical Review*, Vol. XIV (1908–9), 311; Porter to Fox, no date, in *Porter Papers*, Library of Congress. This is a rough draft of part of letter to Fox, May 24, 1862, in *Confidential Correspondence of Fox*, Vol. II, 107.

10. See Edward Everett Dale, *The Range Cattle Industry* (Norman, Okla., 1930), 24, 26, 28, 54. According to Dale, there were 4½ million cattle in Texas in 1860. He stated: ". . . After the Mississippi River had fallen into the hands of the North through the capture of New Orleans and Vicksburg the provision storehouse of Texas was virtually closed to the South. . . ."

11. See Ella Lonn, *Salt as a Factor in the Confederacy* (New York, 1933), 32–35. "As early as the fall of 1861, when the half-million sacks [of salt] which had entered New Orleans in 1860–61 had shrunk to almost nothing, stringency in the supply of salt was beginning to be felt and anxiety for the future supply manifested," states Miss Lonn. Had New Orleans not fallen, Avery Island could have provided "salt for all the Confederacy," as Governor Pettus of Mississippi wrote President Davis.

12. Porter, *Incidents and Anecdotes*, 50, 55; Porter to Fox, May 24, 1862, in *Confidential Correspondence of Fox*, Vol. II, 106; *O.R.N.*, Series II, I, 466. Mallory to Mitchell, March 15, 1862; Morgan, *Recollections of a Rebel Reefer*, 72; *O.R.N.*, XVIII, 158. Farragut's report, May 6, 1862; Soley, *Porter*, 196; Charles B. Boynton, *The History of the Navy during the Rebellion* (2 vols.; New York, 1867), Vol. II, 213. Boynton wrote (pp. 211–13): ". . . A failure at New Orleans would have been a disaster whose consequences no one can now measure. It seems, as we look back upon it, that it would have greatly prolonged the rebellion. The control of the lower Mississippi would have enabled the rebel Government to draw almost unlimited supplies from the country west of the river . . . But one of the most important effects of the capture of New Orleans has not been duly considered. Had the city remained in possession of the rebels a short time longer, they would have completed some very powerful ships that would have driven our squadron out of the river or destroyed it, and they might have completed a navy

which would have been a very formidable antagonist of our own . . . It is readily seen, then, that had the attack on the forts failed, or even had it been delayed for a few weeks, or perhaps days, the aspect of the war might have been changed."

13. John J. Craven, *Prison Life of Jefferson Davis* (New York, 1866), 209. Craven further quoted Davis, indirectly: "With the mouth and headquarters of this vital river [Mississippi] in our [Union] possession, no energy could have warded off the result beyond a certain time, if the North with its superior resources of manufacture and preponderance of population, should see fit to persist."

14. J. W. Mallett, "Work of the Ordnance Bureau of the War Department of the Confederate States, 1861–65," in *Southern Historical Society Papers*, Vol. XXXVIII (1909), 6–7.

15. *O.R.*, VI, 517. Lovell to Cooper, May 22, 1862; ibid., 534. Duncan's report, April 30, 1862; ibid., 548. Higgins' report, April 27, 1862.

16. *North American Review*, Vol. CXLIX (July 1889), 32–34; J. Thomas Scharf, *History of the Confederate States Navy* (New York, 1887), 301. Hereafter cited as Scharf, *History of the Confederate . . . Navy*.

17. *O.R.*, VI, 518. Lovell to Cooper, May 22, 1862; Scharf, *History of the Confederate . . . Navy*, 251.

18. H. A. Trexler, "The Confederate Navy Department and the Fall of New Orleans," *Southwest Review*, Vol. XIX, No. 1, 88.

19. *Delta*, April 29, 1862. The *Crescent* of May 1, 1862, reprinted Lovell's letter.

20. Mrs. Bragg to Bragg, April 29, 1862, in *Bragg Papers*, Western Reserve Historical Society; Mrs. Mary Newman to sister, May 28, 1862, in *Benjamin F. Butler Papers*, Library of Congress; *Journal of Julia LeGrand*, 39–40.

21. Hudson Strode, *Jefferson Davis, Confederate President* (New York, 1959), 240.

22. *O.R.*, VI, 570. Lovell to Cooper, May 2, 1862. Lovell testified that no official notice was taken of his application for a court of inquiry.

23. Gustavus W. Smith, *Confederate War Papers* (New York, 1884), 96. Hereafter cited as Smith, *Confederate War Papers*.

24. J. B. Jones, *A Rebel War Clerk's Diary* (2 vols.; Philadelphia, 1866), Vol. I, 135.

25. Smith, *Confederate War Papers*, 98, 99; *O.R.*, VI, 555–56; ibid., 642; Edward Younger (ed.), *Inside the Confederate Government: The Diary of Robert Garlick Hill Kean* (New York, 1957), 101. Hereafter cited as Younger, *Kean Diary*; Frank E. Vandiver (ed.), *The Civil War Diary of General Josiah Gorgas* (Tuscaloosa, Ala., 1947), 44; *O.R.*, VI, 560; ibid., 646.

26. Lovell to Cooper, Oct. 3, 1863, in Lovell file in *Confederate Records*, National Archives; Smith, *Confederate War Papers*, 137.

27. Ibid., 114–15; Smith, *15th Reunion*, 126; Johnston to Lovell, March 29, 1869, in *Lovell Papers (Letters Received)*, Library of Congress; Younger, *Kean Diary*, 135. On Jan. 31, 1864, Kean entered in his diary: "Hood has been made (or rather nominated) a lieutenant general and will be ordered, I expect, to Johnston. The latter has asked for Lovell but did not get him. The Secretary referred the application to the President with the remark that the assignment of General Lovell would not, he feared, tend to reassure that army."

28. *O.R.*, VI, 652–53. Lee to Lovell, May 8, 24, 1862.

29. Jefferson Davis, *The Rise and Fall of the Confederate Government* (2 vols.; New York, 1881), Vol. II, 210. Hereafter cited as Davis, *Rise and Fall; O.R.*, VI, 740. Moore to Davis, Sept. 20, 1861; Moore to Davis, Sept. 29, 1861, in *Jefferson Davis Papers*, Tulane University Archives.

30. Davis, *Rise and Fall*, Vol. II, 210; *O.R.*, VI, 832, 841, 847.

31. Davis, *Rise and Fall*, Vol. II, 211; *O.R.*, VI, 843, 850; ibid., 610; ibid., 811–12.

32. Davis, *Rise and Fall*, Vol. II, 221–22, *Investigation of Confederate Navy Department*, 238–39.

33. Ibid., 225.

34. Smith, *15th Reunion*, 123; *Picayune*, June 5, 1884.

35. Eliot, *West Point in the Confederacy*, 329; Headquarters, Dept. No. 2, Gen. Order No. 157, Dec. 20, 1862, in *Duncan Papers*, in possession of Mrs. Mildred Parham of New Orleans; Resolution of Louisiana Regular Artillery, Dec. 30, 1862, in *Duncan Papers*, in possession of Mrs. Parham.

36. *Mitchell Journal*, in Tulane University Archives.

37. Porter, *Journal*, Library of Congress.

☆ ☆ ☆ ☆ ☆

Index

Abby Bradford (Confederate ship), 132

Abolitionists, 30, 40, 41

Adams, Charles Francis, 332

Adams, Daniel W., 19

Adams, Henry, 332

Adolph Hugel (Federal ship), 150, 152, 231

Alabama:
  convention at, 27
  secession of, 18

Alden, James, 244–45, 268, 299

Algiers, La., shipyard at, 105, 106

Algiers *News Boy*, 110, 112, 133

Allen, Nathaniel P., 82–83

Anaconda Plan, 126

Anderson, James H., describes *Manassas*, 73

Andrew, John Albion, 158

Anglo-Norman (Confederate ship), 169

Anglo-Saxon (Confederate ship), 169

Annunciation Square, 289

Appropriations for New Orleans defense, 57, 65, 170–72

for ironclads, 107
to repair obstruction, 194

Arizona (Confederate ship), 169

Arletta (Federal ship), 152, 231, 237

Armory, military school at, 117

Arms and ammunition, 119–20
  manufacture of, 64–66, 108–9
  on ships, *see* Confederate Navy;
    Union Navy
  shortages, 46, 52, 91–94, 120–21, 211

Arnold, Thomas, 324

Atlantic (Confederate ship), 169

Austin, Charles, and "Pope's Run," 77ff.

Austin (Confederate ship), 169

Bache, A. D., 126, 223

Bailey (*Cayuga* captain), 261, 266, 268, 276–77, 300
  and New Orleans surrender, 301–3

Baker, Marion:
  quoted, 310, 327, 328
  and surrender negotiations, 305, 307, 309, 313

Barataria Bay, 48, 118
Barbarin, Arthur, 65
Barnard, J. G.:
  memo on forts, 220–22
  and New Orleans plan, 126, 136, 159, 394
Barrow, Robert J., 51, 52
Bartlett, John R., and David Porter, 128
Barton (Confederate major), 346
Bates, Edward, and blockade, 125
Baton Rouge, La.:
  militia (Pelicans), 21
  seizure of arsenal in, 19, 20–22
Batteries, floating, 62, 105
Battery Bienvenu, 120
Battery Dupré, 48
Bayou Bienvenu, 46, 48, 120
Bayou Lafourche, 28, 87
Bayou Mazant, 120
Beauregard, P. G. T., 43, 177, 209
  at Bull Run, 54
  calls for volunteers, 184–85
  at Charleston, 33, 34
  and Louisiana army, 28–29, 372
  and Lovell, 89–90, 350
Beggs, Colonel, and the *Mississippi*, 296
Bell, Henry H., 151, 153, 155
  fires first shots, 192
  at forts, 222, 261, 268
  on Porter, 233, 236, 245
  and river obstruction, 247–50
  and surrender, 310–11, 327–29
Bell, John, 15
Belle Algerine (Confederate ship), 254, 280
Benit, Jules, 55, 56
Benjamin, Judah P.:
  and Bragg, 95–96
  and Bulloch, 37
  defeated as delegate, 27
  and Lovell, 90–93, 120, 165–66, 168–72, 177–78
  and Mann, 295
  and Moore, 45, 67
  as senator, 19

and Slidell, 334
and Twiggs, 42, 46, 68
Benton (Federal ship), 122
Berwick Bay, 48, 60, 118, 163
Beuter, Franz, 65
Bienville (commercial ship), 37–38
Bienville (Confederate gunboat), 105, 176
Biloxi, Miss., 48, 188
Birmingham (Crescent Reserves officer), 308
Bivouac Plantation, 87
Blair, Montgomery, and New Orleans plan, 135, 142, 146–47
Blockade:
  begun by *Brooklyn*, 41–42
  effects of, 59–70, 111ff., 163ff., 332
  and gunpowder shortage, 120–21
  measures to raise, 71–85, 336
  and recognition, 332, 335
  Sumter escapes, 53
Board of Aldermen, 54, 57, 107
Board of Assistant Aldermen, 107
Boggs (*Varuna* commander), 277
Bonus system for enlistments, 38
Bowen, R. J., 324
Bowie, T. C., 223
Bowling Green, Ky., Conferedate defeat in, 180
Boynton, Charles B., 337
Bradford, Charles M., 22
Bragg, Braxton, 59
  and arsenal seizure, 20
  and Louisiana army, 28, 29, 33, 43, 46
  and Lovell, 87, 95–96, 97, 179, 292
Bragg, Mrs. Braxton, quoted on Lovell, 87, 179, 292
Break of Day (Confederate schooner), 164
Breckinridge, John C., Louisiana votes for, 15
Breese, K. R., 227, 231
Brent, Rosella Kenner, recollections of, 289–90
British Fusiliers, 184

British Guards, 184
British Neutrality Association, 184
British subjects, *see* Great Britain
"Bronze John," *see* Yellow fever
Brooklyn, N.Y.:
　Farragut-Porter meeting, 145
　Navy Yard, 134, 143, 151, 154
Brooklyn (Federal man-of-war):
　and blockade, 41–42, 53, 59, 72
　dragged across bar, 191–92
　passing forts, 268, 273–74, 277, 300
　seizure of telegraph station, 187
　tonnage and armament, 216
Brokenburn Planation, 72
Brown, George W., 226, 232–33
Buisson, Benjamin, 55
Bull Run, battle of, 54
Bullet-making machine, 65
Bulloch, James D., 37–38
Burrows, William, 83
Butler, Benjamin F.:
　Lovell on, 186
　in New Orleans, 207ff., 284–85
　　and coal ballast, 199–200
　　rule over, 353–54
　　and surrender, 309
　ordered to New Orleans, 158–61
Butler, Mrs. Benjamin F., 237, 284–85

C. P. Williams (Federal Ship), 152,
　231
Cable, George W., recollections, 113–
　14, 294–95, 301–2
Caddo Parish, 27
Calcasieu Bay, 118
Caldwell, Charles H. B., 249–50, 261
Calhoun:
　as Confederate ship, 77ff.
　as Federal ship, 164
　as privateer, 41
Callahan, James Morton, 335
Cameron, Simon, 22
Camp Benjamin, 117
Camp Chalmette, 116, 299–300
　surrender of, 282–83
Camp Lewis, 117

Camp Moore, 40
Camp Roman, 117
Camp Walker, 40, 49
Campbell, Zoe, diary quoted, 289
Carondelet (Confederate ship), 105
Carrollton, La., 117
Cayuga (Federal gunboat), 295, 299,
　300
　at the forts, 231, 261, 266–67, 276
　and surrender of Camp Chalmette,
　　282–83
　tonnage and armament, 216
Centreville, Miss., 54
Chalmette, La., 346
　regiment from, 204
　see also Camp Chalmette
Charity Hospital, 22
Charles Morgan (Confederate ship),
　169
Charleston, S.C., 33, 34
Charleston (S.C.) *Courier,* 167–68
Chef Menteur pass, 48, 119
Cherub (British ship), 143
Chestnut, Mary Boykin, diary quoted,
　331
Christ Church, 289
Clifton (Federal ship), 155, 193, 231
Cloué, Georges Charles, protest to
　Farragut, 313
Coal shortage in Farragut's fleet, 187–
　88, 198–200
Coast survey and passage of forts,
　223–24
Cobden, Richard, quoted, 333
Coffee shortage, 63
Colorado (Federal ship), 192
Columbus, Ky., 106, 177
Commercial Bulletin, see New Orleans
　Commercial Bulletin
Commission of military and civil en-
　gineers, 55–57
Committee on defense (New Or-
　leans), 54–57
Committee of Public Safety (New Or-
　leans), 243–44, 288, 302
　and Lovell, 178, 179–80

Common Council of New Orleans, 26, 63, 302, 304ff.
  appropriations by, 47, 57, 65, 107, 194
  and morale, 54–55, 178–79
Condon, David, 39
Confederate Army, 33–36, 39–40ff., 87–97, 116–22
  Department No. 1, 42, 46, 47, 341
  forced enlistments, 38–39, 116
  Lovell and, *see* Lovell, Mansfield
  and panic, 290–92ff.
  preparation of New Orleans defense, 46–58, 65–67
  Twiggs and, *see* Twiggs, David E.
  see also Appropriations; Arms and ammunition; Militia; specific regiments; various forts
Confederate Guards, 289
Confederate Navy, 60–63, 71–85, 99–110, 164–66, 175–76
  and Farragut expedition, 196ff., 227–30ff., 351
  escaping blockade, 53, 164
  Higgins criticizes, 339
  Hollins' mosquito fleet, *see* Hollins, George N.
  seizure of steamboats, 169–72
  see also Appropriations; Arms and ammunition; River Defense Fleet; Shipbuilding; specific ships
Confederate States of America, 27, 45ff.
  Congress of, 42
  Constitution of, 30–31
  and European intervention, 111, 164, 210, 331ff., 407
  War Department, Lovell controversy with, *see* Lovell, Mansfield
  see also Confederate Army; Confederate Navy
Conrad, Charles M., 27
Constitution, Confederate, 30–31
Conventions:
  Louisiana, 22–23, 26–28, 372
  and Constitution, 30–31
  delegates elected, 18–19
  of southern states, 27
Cook, Ferdinand W. C., 64
Cook, Francis, 64
Cooper, Samuel, 49, 52, 347
Cooper, Hewitt and Co., 150, 151
Co-operationists, 18–19, 23, 370
Copland (inventor), 65
Coppell, George, and British subjects, 181–84, 302–3, 373
Coppens, Gaston, 33
Corinth, Miss., 209, 292
Cornay, F. O., 322
Cotton:
  burning of, 290
  and European recognition, 111
Court of inquiry and Lovell, 344–48
Craven (*Brooklyn* captain), 187, 273, 315
Craven, John J., talks with Jefferson Davis, 337
Creole Guards, 21, 372
Cresent, see New Orleans *Daily Crescent*
Crescent Reserves, 308
Custom House (New Orleans):
  ordnance workshops in, 64, 94
  seizure of, 27
  U.S. flag atop, 327

Dan Smith (Federal ship), 152, 231, 232
Da Ponte, Durant, 306
Dart, Henry, 20
Davis, C. H., 126
Davis, Jefferson:
  assures New Orleans of arms, 56
  and *Bienville*, 38
  on ironclads, 337
  and Johnston's reinforcements, 172
  and *Louisiana*, 227, 228
  and Lovell, 90–92, 344ff.
  and Martial law for New Orleans, 194
  orders Hollins to Richmond, 230
  as Secretary of War, 28
  sends to New York for arms, 89

and Ship Island troops, 50, 51
on Twiggs, 67
Deas, George, 28
De Bow's Review, 303
De Camp, John, 260–61
De Clouet, Alexandre, 27
Defiance (Confederate ship), 204, 284, 319
Delta, see New Orleans *Daily Delta*
De Méjan, Count, 302
Department of the Gulf, 160
De Soto Parish, 27
Devol, George, recollections of, 35, 293–94
Dewey, George, 238, 251, 274–75, 279
and Gustavus Fox, 135
Diggins, Bartholomew, recollections of, 271, 400
Dix, John, quoted, 22
Docks, floating, 62, 105
Douglas, Stephen A., 15
Drayton, T. F., 346
Dreux, Charles D., 34
Dry Tortugas, Fla., 130
Duels, 117
Du Pont, Samuel F., 126, 134, 139
Ducros, Adolphe, 46
Dufour, Cyprien, 195, 210
Duncan, Johnson K., 41, 94, 97, 339
background, 381
and battle with fleet, 213, 232ff., 263, 275–76
death, 353
and mutiny at fort, 321–22
preparation of forts, 202–5
promotion of, 169
and requests for *Louisiana*, 228, 252–54, 255–56, 263, 318–19, 340
and River Defense Fleet, 251, 254–55
surrenders, 317–18, 320, 323–26

Eighth Louisiana Regiment, 46
Ellis, Charles, 114

Engineers, commission of military and civil, 55–57
England, *see* Great Britain
English Turn, 299
Enoch Train, conversion of, 71
Essex, U.S.S., 143
Europe and Europeans:
in Confederate Army, 181–84
see also European Brigade; Great Britain
and fall of New Orleans, 331–35
and intervention, 111, 164, 210
and recognition of Confederacy, 111, 331ff., 407
European Brigade, 210, 294, 302, 310
Explosion of powder mill, 121–22

Farragut, David Glasgow, 142–48, 353
on New Orleans expedition, 187–93, 198–202ff., 219–24ff., 244–47, 257–85
confers on plan of operation, 244–45
Lewis comments on, 334–35
opinion of *Mississippi*, 336
opinion of mortar fleet, 147–48, 239
and surrender, 299–301ff., 326
ordered to New Orleans, 155–57
Farragut, Mrs. David Glasgow, 145, 148
Federal forces, *see* Union Army; etc.
Fire rafts, 205, 250–51, 266, 271–72
at "Pope's Run," 75, 80
First Presbyterian Church (New Orleans), 17, 289
Flags:
Louisiana adopts, 28
lowered in New Orleans surrender, 302–14
Floating docks converted to batteries, 62, 105
Florida:
Porter's expedition to, 130–31
secession of, 18
Florida (Confederate ship), 62, 169

Foltz, Jonathan, recollections of, 238, 257–58, 272
Foote, Andrew Hull, 285
Fort Berwick, 118
Fort Chêne, 118
Fort Donelson, 180
Fort Henry, 177, 180
Fort Jackson, 41, 47, 83, 90, 94
  awaits attack, 202–5
  Barnard memo on, 220–21
  battle with fleet, 212–15, 222–39, 248–63, 266–76, 318–20
  casualties in, 283
  deserter from, 238–39
  firepower, 119, 203
  importance of capturing, 136, 160
  mutiny at, 321–22
  Porter's memo on, 244–45
  preparedness of, 28, 30, 48, 66, 97
  seizure of, 19–20
  surrender of, 317–18, 322–26
Fort Jefferson, 130
Fort Livingston, 48, 118–19
  condition of, 94
  occupied, 27
Fort Macomb, 27, 48, 94, 119
Fort Pickens, 33, 131
Fort Pike, 48, 119
  condition of, 94
  seizure of, 19, 20
Fort Pillow, Tenn., 229
Fort Pitt Foundry, 150
Fort St. Philip, 47, 90, 94
  awaiting attack, 202–5
  Barnard memo on, 220–21
  battle with fleet, 213–15, 222–39, 248–63, 266–76, 318–20
  casualties in, 283
  firepower, 119, 203
  importance of capturing, 136, 160
  Porter's memo on, 244–45
  preparedness, 30, 48, 66, 97
  seizure of, 19–20
  surrender of, 317–18, 322–26
Fort Sumter, 33, 34, 36
Fort Taylor, 130
Fort Warren, 116

Foster, Lieutenant (reported spy), 168
Fourth Louisiana Regiment, 51
Fox, Gustavus V.:
  correspondence with Porter, 128–29, 201–2, 336
    on Farragut, 190–91, 198–99, 244, 260
  and mortar flotilla, 150, 227
  and New Orleans plan, 135–37, 138, 141–48, 159–60
France, and fall of New Orleans, 331, 333–35
Free Market, 69, 106
French (*Preble* commander), 78
Frolic (Confederate schooner), 80
Freret, William, 195
Fry, Joseph, and "Pope's Run," 80–81, 82, 83, 85
Funds, *see* Appropriations; Money

Gainesville, Miss., shipbuilding facilities, 60
Galaxy (magazine), on Farragut at New Orleans, 136, 137, 138, 141, 159
Galveston (Confederate ship), 169
Gardner, W. M., 346
Gayarré, Charles, 27
General Quitman (Confederate ship), 204
Gilmore (inventor), 64
Gorgas, Josiah, 96, 346–47, 376
Governor Moore (Confederate ship), 204, 277, 280–82
Grand Terre Island, 48
George Mangham (Federal ship), 150, 152, 231
  hit in action, 234
Georgia (merchant ship), 129
Gerdes, F. H., and coast survey, 223–24
Grant, A. (*General Quitman* commander), 204
Great Britain:
  and fall of New Orleans, 331–33, 335

subjects of, and militia, 38–39,
181–84
and *Trent* Affair, 116
Greeley, Horace, 135, 152, 153
Greenville, La., 117
Gretna, La., powder mill at, 120
Grimes, James W., and Porter-Welles
meeting, 139
Grosse Tête (Confederate ship), 105
Guest, Lieutenant, 317–18
Gulf Blockading Squadron, 77ff., 134
West, 148, 155, 156
see also Farragut, David Glasgow
see also Blockade
Gulf of Mexico, 48, 61, 156
Gunpowder shortage, 46, 120–21
Guns, *see* Arms and ammunition
Guthrie, John J., and defense of upper
Mississippi, 106
Guthrie, Sheldon, and abolitionism,
40–41
Gwin, William McKendree, 344–45

H. E. Spearing (bark), 42
Habana (Confederate ship; later *Sumter*), 61
Hale, John P., and Porter-Welles
meeting, 139
Halter, R. E., and coast survey, 223
Hampton Roads, Va., Farragut assigned to, 156
Hand, Daniel, and spy activities, 114–15
Handsboro, Miss., removal of powder
mill, 121
Handy, Robert, and "Pope's Run," 81–84
Hardee, William Joseph, 117
Hardy, William, and "Pope's Run," 78, 79, 80
Harney, William S., 42
Harriet Lane (Federal ship), 155, 157, 188, 193
in attack on forts, 223
and surrender, 324ff.
Harris, F. H., 324

Harris, Joseph, 223
Harrison, Lieutenant, 261
Hartford (Federal ship), 155–56, 157,
191, 192
attack on forts, 219, 250, 259, 260
passage of forts, 261, 265–73, 283,
300
at New Orleans surrender, 301, 305,
307, 313, 315
tonnage and armament, 155, 216
Haskins, Joseph A., and Baton Rouge
arsenal, 20–22
Hastings-on-Hudson, N.Y., 143
Hatch, Frank M., 22
Hatteras Inlet, N.C., Union successes
at, 133, 137
Hays, Harry, gallantry at Manassas,
54
Head of the Passes, 53, 74, 187, 192,
215
"Pope's Run" at, 76–85
Hébert, P. O., 30, 55
replaces Beauregard, 29
replaces Bragg, 36–37
Henry Janes (Federal ship), 152, 231
Hewitt, Abram, and mortar flotilla,
151, 154
Higgins, Edward, 169, 203, 266
criticism of Navy, 339
need for *Louisiana*, 228, 257
surrender of forts, 320, 324–26
Hill, James, 41
Hindman, T. C., 346
Hodge, B. L., 27
Hollins, George N., 70, 105, 106, 109
background, 61–62
and Mallory, 229–30, 342, 351
and *Mississippi*, 100
at "Pope's Run," 73–85, 163
and powder shortage, 93, 121
Hollins Guards, 85
Hooper, Captain, 204
Horace Beals (Federal ship), 152, 231
Hubert, Father, 23
Huger, Thomas B., 253
wounded, 277, 278, 314

Hughes, John, and Confederate ship-building, 61, 104

Illustrated London News, 333
Independence Day, Louisiana's, 174–75
Ingomar (Confederate steamer), 103
Irish in New Orleans, 26
Ironclads, 62, 71–72
see also Louisiana; Manassas; etc.
Iroquois (Federal ship):
in collision, 250
at forts, 222, 231, 234
tonnage, 216
Itasca (Federal gunboat), 216, 268
clears obstruction, 248-50
crippled, 273
Ivy (Confederate ship), 41, 62
attempted capture of, 131–32
at "Pope's Run," 74, 76ff.

Joseph H. Toone (Federal coaler), 78
Juge, Paul, 302, 310
Jackson (Confederate ship), 62, 74, 204, 284
at "Pope's Run," 76ff.
Jackson (Federal ship), 155
Jackson and Co., 101
Jackson Railroad, 40, 303
James, S. L., 303
calls for volunteers, 304
Jefferson City, La., *Mississippi* built in, 101, 297
Jefferson Parish, martial law in, 194
John Griffith (Federal ship), 152, 231
Johnston, Albert Sidney:
death, 209
defeat in Bowling Green, 180, 181
needs troops, 172–73
Johnston, Joseph E., 90, 347
letter to Lovell, 348–49
Jones (Federal sailor), 261
Jones, J. B., diary quoted, 345

Katahdin (Federal gunboat), 216
Kautz, Albert, 271
and surrender, 307–10, 327, 328, 329

Kean, Robert G. H., diary, 346
Kennebec (Federal gunboat), 192, 216, 222
at forts, 232, 268, 273, 326
Kenner, Duncan F., 27, 289
Kennon, Beverly C., 204, 277
gallant action, 280–82
and ordnance, 108–10
recollections of, 401
Key West, Fla., 157
Porter's mission to, 130
Kineo (Federal gunboat), 192, 216, 250
in collision, 268
Knap, Charles, and mortar flotilla, 151
Knap, Rudd and Co., 150, 151, 153, 154
Kroehl, Julius H., 236, 247, 248, 249

Lake Borgne, 48, 119, 120, 166
Federal ships in, 46
Lake Pontchartrain, 19, 20, 48, 119
Landis (Confederate ship), 319
Lee, Robert E., letter to Lovell, 349–50
Lee, Thomas B., 115
Leeds and Co., 64, 97, 337
LeGrand, Julia, diary quoted, 292, 344
Levee, New Orleans, 26
burning and looting of, 292–94, 300
Lewis, Charles Lee, 199
and European recognition, 334–35
Liddell, St. John, 172–74
war memoirs, 331
Lincoln, Abraham, 58, 126, 131
Cameron letter to, 22
election, 15
and General Scott, 384
and New Orleans plan, 136, 138, 140, 159–61
proclaims blockade, 59
Linfield, Reverend, 23
Livingston (Confederate ship), 105
Lizzie Simmons (Confederate ship), 105
Louisiana:
army created, 27–30

convention, 22–23, 26–28, 372
  and constitution, 30–31
  delegates elected, 18–19
  flag created, 28
  joins Confederacy, 31
  legislature, 18, 108
  secession and independence, 15–24
  war preparations, 25–31
  see also New Orleans
Louisiana (Confederate ship), 336, 337, 339
  construction and delays, 103–5, 110, 176, 197, 242–43
  destruction of, 323–26
  Duncan and, 203, 227–28, 252–57, 263, 318–19
  and Federal fleet, 274, 276, 284
  Hollins and, 229, 230
Louisiana Brigade, 95
Louisiana Legion, 49
Louisiana Tigers, 35
  gallantry at Manassas, 54
Louisiana Zouaves, 33
Lovell, Joseph, 88
Lovell, Mansfield:
  background, 88–89
  and Benjamin, 165–72, 177–78, 186, 193, 195–97
  and Committee of Public Safety, 179–80, 244, 391
  court of inquiry on, 344–48, 391
  and Davis, 67–68, 89-92, 113, 348, 350–52
  death, 352–53
  declares martial law, 194–95
  and defense preparations, 90–97, 116, 118–23, 172–73, 202, 291–92
  Delta on, 185
  and fall of New Orleans, 339, 341, 342–45, 348–49
  and *Louisiana*, 255–56
  Mrs. Bragg on, 179, 292, 343, 391
  and Randolph, 228–29
  refuses to surrender, 302, 303, 306
  True Delta on, 178–79

Lovell, Mrs. Mansfield, 89
Lovell, W. S., 303

McClellan, George B., and New Orleans expedition, 136, 138–41, 151, 153, 160
McClelland (New Orleans police chief), 210, 305
McClintock, James R.:
  and ordnance, 65
  and submarine, 62–63
McCoy (*Defiance* commander), 204, 284
McDowell, Irvin, 126, 384
McIntosh, Charles F., 253, 276, 284
McKean, William W., 134, 156, 187
  and "Pope's Run," 77, 84
McRae (Confederate ship), 61, 108, 253, 266
  gallant action, 277, 278–79, 319
  at "Pope's Run," 74ff.
  sinking of, 314–15
Madison Parish, 27
Magee Line, 299–300
Maginnis, John, 15–16, 165
Magnolia (Confederate ship), 169
Mahan, Alfred Thayer, on naval campaign in New Orleans, 334
Mallett, J. W., 337
Mallory, Stephen R., 106–7, 202, 229–30, 336, 341
  appoints Hollins, 61–62
  Crescent blasts, 180–81
  and Lieutenant Kennon, 108
  and *Mississippi* construction, 99ff., 197–98, 243–44
Manassas (formerly *Enoch Train*), 71–80ff., 266, 273–75, 277–80
  conversion of, 71–72
  joins River Defense fleet, 204
Manassas Junction, 43, 54, 68
Mandeville, La., 120
Mann, A. Dudley, 295
Marcy, R. B., 161
Mare Island Navy Yard, 143
Maria J. Carlton (Federal ship), 152, 231, 236

Marques de la Habana, conversion of, 61

Marshall, Henry, 27

Martello tower, 46, 48, 374

Martial law declared, 193ff., 210

Mary Clinton (Confederate ship), 42

Mason, James M., and *Trent* Affair, 115–16

Mason, John Y., 143

Massachusetts (Federal ship), 66

Matagorda (Confederate ship), 169

Matthew Vassar (Federal ship), 152, 231

Maurepas (Confederate ship), 106

Meigs, Montgomery C., 131

Melhado, Professor, 289

Memphis (Confederate ship), 105, 106

Mercer, Samuel, 131

Merchants' Exchange, 71

Merrick, David, 117

Merrick, Edwin T., 117

Merrimac, 234

Mervine, William, 72, 127, 133

Metairie Race Course, 40

Metcalf, Dr., 40

Mexican Gulf Railroad, 48

Mexico (Confederate ship), 169

Miami (Federal ship), 155, 231

Milan (French warship), 313

Military and Naval Affairs Committee, Louisiana, 27

Militia, 20–22, 116, 178
  Europeans in, 181–84

Millaudon, Laurent, 101

Miller, Buck, 22

Minor, R. D., on Kennon, 109

"Minute Men," 30

Mississippi, State of:
  Biloxi, 48, 188
  and gunboat construction, 60
  secession, 18

Mississippi (Confederate ship), 229, 257, 336–37, 339
  burning of, 295–98
  construction, 99–105, 110, 176, 197–98, 243–44

Mississippi (Federal ship), 161, 192, 200-1, 303
  in action, 274–75, 277, 279–80
  and fire raft, 250
  tonnage, guns, 216

Mississippi River, 23, 111
  blockade of, *see* Blockade
  defense of, 29, 37, 119, 331
  as invasion route, 47, 160
  results of loss of, 335, 407, 408

Mississippi Sound, 49, 53, 61

Mitchell (*Louisiana* commander), 252ff., 323–24
  Duncan and, 252ff., 263, 266, 318, 340

Mitchell, Archibald, diary quoted, 353

Mobile, Ala., 59, 165

Moïse, Cécile, 289

Moïse, E. W., 173–74

Money:
  shortage of, 113–14
  subscriptions for shipbuilding, 41, 71, 107
  see also Appropriations

Monroe, John T., 63, 291, 302
  and abolitionists, 40–41
  and spies, 114–15
  and surrender, 304–14, 326–29

Montgomery, Ala., 27

Moore (*Richmond* engineer), 216

Moore, Thomas O., 18, 64, 67, 295
  and army, 28–29, 34, 116
  and *Bienville,* 37–38
  and British subjects, 182–83
  and defense, 45, 55-57, 59, 67, 350
  Liddell and, 173–74
  and *Louisiana,* 227–28
  Lovell and, 95–96, 186
  and seizure of forts, etc., 19–22
  and Ship Island confusion, 49–51
  and spies, 115

Moran, Benjamin, diary quoted, 332–33

Morgan, George D., 149

Morgan, James Morris, and *Manassas,* 75

Morgan (Confederate ship), 105

Morris (*Pensacola* captain), 266, 269
Mortar fleet, Federal, 122
  Farragut's opinion of, 147–48, 239
  on New Orleans expedition, 188,
    193, 216, 225–27ff., 248ff., 318
    and surrender, 326
  outfitting and dispatching, 149–56
Mosher (Confederate tug), 254, 271
Mosquito fleets:
  Confederate, 106
  at "Pope's Run," 74–85
  see also Hollins, George N.
  Union, 46
Mouton, Alexandre, 22, 23
Mullen, W. G., 204, 214
Mumford, William, 309
Murdock, Samuel, 40
Mure, William A., 16, 41
  and seizure of British subjects, 38–
    39, 373
Murray, E. C., 103–5
Music (Confederate ship), 41, 254
Mutiny at Fort Jackson, 321–22
Myers, A. C., 28
Mystic, Conn., 144, 151

Nachon, Father, 322
Napoleon III, and recognition of Con-
    federacy, 334–35
National Intelligencer, 72
Negro revolt, rumors of, 310
New Orleans:
  awaits invasion, 111–23, 168–86,
    209–12, 287–94
  blockade of, 41–42, 59–70, 71–85,
    163–65
  defense preparations, 27–43, 45–58,
    87–97, 116–23, 165–86
  invasion of, 135–61, 187–203, 207–
    9, 212–39, 244–85, 287–330
  martial law declared, 194–95
  reasons for fall of, 339–43, 350–52
  significance of loss of, 331–38
New Orleans (Confederate ship), 105,
    106
New Orleans *Bee*, 16, 63, 64, 65

New Orleans *Commercial Bulletin:*
  on blockade, 111–12, 164
  on destruction of cotton, 290
  on Federal fleet, 242, 288
  on reunion, 329–30
  on Secession Day, 174
  on ship construction, 107
  on spies, 166
New Orleans *Daily Crescent:*
  on blockade, 163
  on defense, 165
  on Federal prisoners, 69
  on Fort Henry, 177
  on forts, 287
  on Johnston, 180
  on militia, 116
  on *Mississippi*, 110
  on national election, 15
  on recognition, 116
  on rumors, 166–67
  on secession, 24
  on shipbuilding, 107
  on Twiggs, 68
New Orleans *Daily Delta:*
  on blockade, 111
  on Federal fleet, 122, 236, 237, 241,
    288
  on Lovell, 95, 342–43
  on military service, 184
  on naval weakness, 175
  on powder-mill explosion, 121
  on shipbuilding, 107
  on speculators, 193
  on *True Delta*, 170
  on volunteers, 185, 304
New Orleans *Daily Picayune:*
  on abolitionists, 41
  on convention, 31
  on Federal fleet, 63, 175
  on fortifications, 66
  on forts, 288
  on Hand, 115
  on intervention, 164
  on Johnston, 181
  on Lovell, 353
  on Manassas, 54

New Orleans *Daily Picayune—Cont'd.*
  on military appointments, 29
  on rumors, 166
  on secession, 19, 24
  on Shiloh, 209
  on Ship Island, 52–53
  on shipbuilding, 60, 107
  on shortages, 112
  on surrender, 329
  on Twiggs, 68
  on yellow fever, 69
New Orleans, Opelousas and Western
    Railroad, 48
New Orleans *Price Current*, 290
New Orleans *True Delta:*
  on floating batteries, 106
  on forts, 238, 241
  on Johnston, 181
  on Kennon, 109
  on Lincoln, 15–16
  on Lovell, 95
  on *Manassas*, 75
  on neutrality, 184
  on pillage, 293
  on powder-mill explosion, 121–22
  on Secession Day, 174
  on separation, 165
  on steamship seizure, 169–70
  on shipyard strike, 104
New York, N.Y.:
  mortar fleet preparation, 122, 149–
    54
  Porter and Farragut in, 145
New York *Commercial Advertiser*, 72
New York *Herald*, 22
New York *Times*, 22
New York *Tribune*, 152–53, 167
Newman, Mary, recollections, 289, 344
9th Connecticut Regiment, 122
9th Louisiana Regiment, 95
Nixon, J. O., 55, 57
Norfolk, Va., 143, 145, 234
Norfolk Packet (Federal ship), 231,
    238, 252
  tonnage, 152
North American Review, 339–40

North Carolina:
  secession, 41
  Union victory, 133

Obstructions, river:
  attempts to explode, 236, 245, 247–
    50
  chain barrier completed, 66, 205
  damage to, 205, 248–50
  description, 119
  Lovell and, 94
  see also Fire rafts
Ogden, H. D., 195
Old Dominion Guards, 34–35, 38
Oliver H. Lee (Federal ship), 152,
    231
Oltmanns, J. G., and coast survey, 223
Oneida (Federal ship), 216, 277
  Kennon surrenders to, 282
  shelled, 237
Orizaba (Confederate ship), 169
Orleans Cadets, 34
Orleans Guards, 29, 174
Orvetta (Federal ship), 152, 231
Osbon, B. S., 222, 261–62, 265–66,
    268
  describes shelling, 259–60, 270–71
  explodes fire raft, 272
  Porter on, 398–99
Overall, J. W., 69
Owasco (Federal ship), 155, 188, 193
  and shelling of forts, 231
  and surrender of forts, 317–18

Page, L. R., 346
Palmer, Benjamin M., 16–18, 27, 369
Pamlico (Confederate ship), 62
Panama (merchant ship), 129
Para (Federal ship), 152, 231, 252
Parish Prison, 68
Parton, James, 135, 158–59
Pascagoula, Miss., 42
Pass a Loutre, 41, 164, 373–74
  Federal ships in, 41, 59
Pass Christian, 118
Patrick Henry (Confederate ship),
    109

Index

Patterson Iron Works, 101

Pearce, Joseph:
and *Mississippi* construction, 102, 110, 243
destroys *Mississippi*, 296–97

Pearl River, Miss., 60, 94

Pearlington, Miss., 60

Pensacola, Fla., 33, 34, 43, 45
Porter's expedition to, 131

Pensacola (Federal ship), 187, 188, 192, 262
passing the bar, 200–2
passing the forts, 266, 269, 300
tonnage, guns, 216

Perché, Abbé Napoléon, 174

Perkins, George H., 267, 276
and Camp Chalmette surrender, 282–83
and New Orleans surrender, 301–3, 304

Perkins, John, 27

Perrit Guards, 34

Peytona (Confederate ship), 296–97

Phelps, John W., 122, 158

Philadelphia Navy Yard:
Hartford at, 155
and ordnance, 144, 150–51, 154

Philips (*Stonewall Jackson* captain), 204

Phoebe (British ship), 143

Picayune, see New Orleans *Daily Picayune*

Pickens (Confederate ship), 74, 105

Pierpont House, 145

Pinckney (Confederate Commander), 229

Pinola (Federal gunboat), 216, 248–50, 268

Plaquemines Bend, 119

Plaquemines Parish, 194

Platosz, Oscar, 117

Plympton, Emily M., 89

Plympton, Joseph, 89

Polk, Leonidas, 62, 106, 168–69

Pontchartrain (Confederate ship), 106

Pope, John, and "Pope's Run," 76–85, 379

"Pope's Run," 76–85, 379

Port Royal:
Farragut at, 157
Union victory at, 134, 136, 137, 138

Porter, David D., 127–34ff.
comments on Butler, 354
comments on ironclad, 72
correspondence with Fox, 128–29, 201–2, 336
on Farragut, 190–91, 198–99, 244, 260
on New Orleans expedition, 188ff., 223–25ff., 285
accounts of conversation with Farragut, 258–60
and surrender, 317–18ff., 324–26
see also Mortar fleet
plans for mortar fleet, 137, 138, 140, 149ff.

Powder-mill explosion, 121–22

Powhatan (Federal ship):
on blockade duty, 42, 72, 127, 132
pursuing *Sumter*, 133–34, 385

Preble (Federal ship), 74
at "Pope's Run," 76–85

Prisoners arrive in New Orleans, 68–69

Proctorsville, La., 48, 120

Propagateur Catholique, 174

Provost marshals, 195, 304

Public Safety Committee, *see* Committee of Public Safety

Puerto Cabello, Venezuela, 132

Purcell, John, diary quoted, 16

Purdy (*Hartford* engineer), 272–73

Quarantine Station, 245
Farragut at, 283, 285, 295, 299
troops at, 246, 320

Queen, W. W., 227, 231

Quitman, John, Lovell with, 88–89

Racer (Federal ship), 152, 231

Rafts, fire, 205, 250–51, 266, 271–72
at "Pope's Run," 75, 80

Rains, George W., 120

Randolph, George Wyth, 228

Read, Charles W., 277, 278–79, 314–15
Read, John H., 307–10
Relief activities, 69, 106
Renshaw, F. B., 204, 284
Renshaw, W. B., 326
Resolute (Confederate ship), 204
Richmond (Federal ship), 74, 200, 250, 303–4
  passing the forts, 262, 268–69
  at "Pope's Run," 76–85
  rammed by *Manassas*, 78–79
  tonnage, guns, 216
Rigolets, 48, 65, 119
Rise and Fall of the Confederate Government (Davis), 352
River Defense Fleet, 196, 204–5, 251, 277
  independence from Navy, 254–55, 341, 351
Robertson, William B., 266–67
Roe, Francis A., 269
  diary quoted, 262
Roman, A. B., 67
Rousseau, Laurence, 66
  Hollins replaces, 69
  and Twiggs, 66
Roy, John:
  and *Mississippi*, 100, 101
  and ordnance, 64, 94, 105, 376
  and river obstructions, 29–30
Rozier, Joseph A., 31
Ruggles, Daniel, 96, 118, 177
  illness, 97
  ordered to Pensacola, 68
Russell, George, 328–29
Russell, John, 16
  and British subjects, 39, 182

Sachem (coast survey steamer), 223
St. Andrew Bay, Fla., 157
St. Bernard Parish, 194
St. Charles (Confederate ship), 296
St. Charles Hotel, 25, 85
St. Charles Parish, 27
St. Louis, Mo., 47
St. Louis Hotel, 25

St. Martin Parish, 27
St. Mary's Cannoneers, 322, 326
St. Mary's Parish, 322
St. Patrick's Church, 289
Saltpeter, shortage of, 92, 120–21
San Jacinto (Federal ship), 115
San Juan d'Ulloa, 143
Santa Rosa Island, 33
Sarah Bruen (Federal ship), 152, 231
Scharf, J. Thomas, 340
Sciota (Federal gunboat), 250, 268
  shelled by forts, 232
  tonnage, guns, 216
Scott, Winfield, 42, 384
  and Anaconda Plan, 126
Sea Foam (Federal ship), 152, 231
Secession, 15–24, 371
  anniversary of, 174–75
Semmes, Raphael, 89
  and blockade, 53, 59, 374–75
  pursuit by Porter, 133
Senac, Felix, 403
7th Louisiana Regiment, 46, 54
Seward, William:
  and Florida expedition, 130–31
  and New Orleans plan, 140
"Shinplasters," 113–14
Ship Island:
  Confederates evacuate, 66–67
  Confederates occupy, 48–54
  Farragut at, 157, 186, 187–88, 192, 199–200
  Federals occupy, 122–23, 158–61, 207–9
Shipbuilding, 59ff., 99–110, 176, 197–98
Ships, *see* Confederate Navy; Union Navy; Shipbuilding; specific ships
Shyrock, George S., 253, 323
  and *Louisiana* destruction, 324
Sidney C. Jones (Federal ship), 152, 231
Sinclair, Arthur, 295–98
6th Louisiana Regiment, 46
Slaughterhouse Point, 294, 300
Slidell, John, 19
  defeated as delegate, 27

and French recognition, 333–34
and *Trent* Affair, 115–16
Slocomb, Ida, 314
Smith, Gustavus W., 89, 95
on Lovell, 88, 345, 347, 348
Smith, H., and seizure of Ft. Jackson, 20
Smith, M. L., 91
and fortifications, 45, 46, 52, 57, 65
Smith, Melancton, 257, 314
and *Manassas* sinking, 274–75, 279–80
Smith, Oscar, diary quoted, 330
Smith, Watson, 227, 231
and *Ivy*, 132
Soley, James R.:
on *Louisiana*, 337
on Porter, 149
Soloman, Clara, 290
Sophronia (Federal ship), 152, 231
Soulé, Pierre, 195
and surrender, 302, 303, 312, 313
South Carolina, secession of, 18
South Pass, 81
Southwest Pass:
action at, 78–85
ordered closed, 37
Southwood, Marion, 292, 294
Sparrow, Edward, 27
Speculators, 112–13, 193, 195, 392–93
Spies, 30, 53, 114–15, 166–68, 212
Squires, M. T., 275–76
Stanton, Edward, and New Orleans plan, 135, 158, 160–61
Star of the West (Confederate ship), 132
Stevenson, John A., 62
and fire rafts, 205, 251
and *Manassas*, 71, 76
and River Defense Fleet, 204, 254–55
Stone, Kate, diary quoted, 72
Stonewall Jackson (Confederate ship), 204
Strike in Confederate ship construction, 103–5
Submarines, 63, 65

Subscription funds for shipbuilding, 41, 71, 107
Sumner, Charles, 333
Sumter (Confederate ship), 59
escapes blockade, 53, 61
Porter tries capture, 131–33
Surrender negotiations, 301–15ff., 326–29
Szymanski, Ignace, 204
surrenders regiment, 282–83

T. A. Ward (Federal ship), 152, 231, 234
Taliaferro, James G., on secession, 371
Tangipahoa, La., 40
Taylor, J. W., 20
Taylor, Richard, 95
defeated as delegate, 27
military proposal, 27–28
Tennessee (Confederate ship), 120
Texas (Confederate ship), 169
Théard, Paul E., 19–20
3rd Mississippi Regiment, 168–69
13th Louisiana Regiment, 168–69
Thornton, Lieutenant, and *Hartford* fire, 272
Thouvenal (French Foreign Minister), and recognition of Confederacy, 333–34
Tift, Asa and Nelson, and *Mississippi*, 353, 403
construction, 99–105, 110, 176, 197–98, 382
destruction, 296–98
launching, 243–44
Tiger Rifles, 34, 35, 38
Todd, J. W., 20
Tower Dupré defenses, 120
Tredegar Works, 64, 102, 197
Trent (Confederate ship), 176
Trent (English ship), 115–16
Trudeau, James, and Ship Island confusion, 49–52
True Delta, see New Orleans *True Delta*
"Turtle," *see Manassas*

Tuscarora (Confederate ship), 62
  armament, 74
  and "Pope's Run," 77–85
26th Massachusetts Regiment, 122
Twiggs, David E.:
  age and incapacity, 42, 65, 342
  background, 42–43
  and defense, 46–58, 62, 65, 66–67
  evacuation of Ship Island, 67
  letter to Walker, 374
Tyson, Herbert, and surrender nego-
    tiations, 310–11

Union Army, 136ff., 157
  Butler's expedition, 158–61, 186,
    199–200
    lands on Ship Island, 122–23,
      284–85, 330
    occupation of New Orleans, 353–
      54
Union Navy, 126–34ff., 335
  blockade by, *see* Blockade
  Farragut's expedition, 187–93, 198–
    202ff., 219–24ff.
    see also Farragut, David Glasgow
  mortar fleet, *see* Mortar fleet
  mosquito fleet, 46
  at "Pope's Run," 76–85
  see also specific ships
United States Army, etc., in Civil War,
    see Union Army; Union Navy
United States Mint, seizure of, 27
United States Marine Hospital (New
    Orleans), 22
  powder mill at, 120
Urquhart, Mrs. Robert Dow, diary
    quoted, 290, 314

Vanderbilt (Confederate ship), 164
Van Dorn, Earl, 67
Varieties Theatre (New Orleans),
    military school at, 117
Varuna (Federal ship), 277, 283
  Governor Moore sinks, 280–81
  tonnage and armament, 216
Vicksburg, Miss., 297

Vicksburg and Shreveport Railroad,
    103
Vincennes (Federal ship), 74
  at "Pope's Run," 78–85
Virginia, State of:
  Farragut and, 143, 145
  Federal troops in, 41
  Louisiana troops in, 46
  Norfolk falls, 234
Von LaHache, Theodore, 69

W. Burton (Confederate ship), 319
Waddell, James Iredell, and burning
    of *Mississippi*, 296, 297
Waggaman Plantation, 55
Wainwright, J. M., 244
  and *Hartford* fire, 271–73, 400
  and surrender of forts, 325, 326
Walker, Leroy Pope:
  and Moore, 45
  and Ship Island confusion, 49–52
  and Twiggs, 46, 47, 62, 66
Walker, W. H. T., 95
Ward, W. H., and *Louisiana* destruc-
    tion, 323–24
Warley, A. F.:
  and *Louisiana*, 253, 324
  and *Manassas*, 75–85, 274–75, 277–
    80
Warrior (Confederate ship), 204, 274
Washington, D.C., 158–61
  Porter in, 138–41, 157
Washington Artillery, 21–22, 46, 54,
    370
Water Witch (Federal ship), 74
  at "Pope's Run," 78–85
Watson, Baxter:
  and ordnance, 65
  and submarine, 63
Waud, William, 274
Weapons, *see* Arms and ammunition
Welles, Gideon:
  and Farragut, 187–88, 190, 247
  and New Orleans plan, 126, 135–
    48, 156–59
  and Porter, 129–31, 133, 193, 260
West, Richard S., on Porter, 149

West Gulf Blockading Squadron, 148, 155, 156
  see also Farragut, David Glasgow
Westfield (Federal ship), 155, 193, 231
  in collision, 250
Wharton, T. K.:
  diary quoted, 42, 85, 105, 121
  and ordnance, 64, 66
Wheat, Roberdeau, 35, 38, 46
  gallantry at Manassas, 54
White, Alex, 34, 38
White, John, 41
Whittle, W. C., 341
  and Hollins, 229, 230, 255–56
  and *Louisiana*, 227, 228, 242
  and *Mississippi*, 295–97
Whittle, W. C., Jr., 324
Wilkes, Charles, 115–16
Wilkinson, John, 323
William Bacon (Federal ship), 152, 231

William Heines (Confederate ship), 169
William H. Webb (Confederate ship), 169
Williams, Thomas, 335
Wilson's Rangers, 35
Wiltz, P. S., 55–57
Wingard, J. C., 65, 377
Winona (Federal gunboat), 192
  passing of forts, 268, 273
  tonnage, armament, 216
Wise, Henry A., 150–51, 153, 154–55
Wissahickon (Federal gunboat), 216, 222, 231
Wolseley, Garnet, Viscount, on New Orleans campaign, 339–40
Wool, John E., 42

Yancey, William L., 210
Yankee (steamer), 20
Yellow fever, 25, 69, 116, 211–12